In Another Country

COLONIALISM, CULTURE,

AND THE ENGLISH

NOVEL IN INDIA

Priya Joshi

Columbia University Press New York

COLUMBIA UNIVERSITY PRESS

Publishers Since 1893

New York   Chichester, West Sussex

Copyright © 2002 Columbia University Press

All rights reserved

Library of Congress Cataloging-in-Publication Data

Joshi, Priya.

In another country : colonialism, culture, and the
English novel in India / Priya Joshi.

p. cm.

Revision of thesis (Ph.D)—Columbia University 1995.

Includes bibliographical references and index.

ISBN 0–231–12584–4 (cloth)

ISBN 0–231–12585–2 (paper)

1. Indic fiction (English)—History and criticism.

2. Anglo-Indian fiction—History and criticism.

3. Books and reading—India—History.

4. Fiction—Appreciation—India.

5. Language and culture—India.

6. Imperialism in literature.

7. Postcolonialism—India.

8. India—In literature.   I. Title.

PR9492.2 .J68   2002

823'.809954–dc21   2001047921

♾

Columbia University Press books are printed
on permanent and durable acid-free paper.

Printed in the United States of America

c 10 9 8 7 6 5 4 3 2 1

p 10 9 8 7 6 5 4 3 2 1

for Orfeo

WHO REASONED NOT THE NEED

CONTENTS

ILLUSTRATIONS AND TABLES

ACKNOWLEDGMENTS

Research and writing for this book have taken me into libraries, archives, and disciplines far from my own, and the intellectual and material debts I have incurred are enormous. It is my pleasure to honor them here:

to the scribes, annotators, record-keepers, list-compilers, printers, publishers, and scores of others, both Indian and British, who documented the colonial world of print in such revealing detail;

to the Indian readers and writers whose passions I have tried to reconstruct here;

to the librarians and staff at the India Office and the British Library, especially Dipali Ghosh, Elizabeth James, Graham Shaw, Ian Baxter;

to librarians and staff at the many libraries and archives I visited in India, especially the National Library, the Uttarpara Public Library, the People's Free Reading Room and Library in a city I can only know as Bombay, and the Connemara Public Library;

to those who read my work, enriched it with their critique, or shared their formidable knowledge of print and its powers with me: Elizabeth Abel, Srinivas Aravamudan, Kalpana Bardhan, Homi Bhabha, John Bishop, Jean Comaroff, Robert Darnton, Ian Duncan, Angus Fraser, John Handford, Anne Humpherys, Abdul JanMohamed, Steven Justice, Sudipta Kaviraj, Robin Lewis, Meenakshi Mukherjee, V. Narayana Rao, Veena Oldenburg, Nick Paige, Jonathan Rose, Parama Roy, Edward Said, Katie Snyder, Rajeswari Sunder Rajan, Harish Trivedi, Peter Zinoman; the intellectual community at SHARP; the 1998-99 Fellows of the Townsend Center for the Humanities at Berkeley; Mary Murrell and Ken Wissoker for their commitment and belief in this book; Susan Stanford Friedman, for her unparalleled mentorship and her example of intellectual clarity;

to Jennifer Crewe, my generous editor at Columbia, for her steadfast hospitality to this book and her always calming support; to Susan Heath, for her vigilant eye and diplomatic pen in so unobtrusively copyediting my prose; and to John F. Lynch for preparing the index;

to my gifted and cheerful research assistants, Stephan Sastrawidjaja, Susan Zieger, Hena Basu, and Jason E. Cohen;

to my students and friends at Berkeley, especially Lawrence Cohen for his matchless intellectual generosity, and Raka Ray for her innumerable gifts of friendship;

to my friends outside academia who plied me with a bed, bourbon, and laughter whenever I needed it: Rachel Porter, Manlio Narici, and Cliff Simms in New York; Christian Déséglise and Gigi Maquinay in Paris; Victor Buchli in Cambridge and London; and Linde and Michael Fioretos in Athens and Zaharo, who probably have little idea how much their hospitality has nourished me;

to my aunts, the marvelous mausis in Delhi, who fed me, housed me, argued with me over the years of this research and became in many ways the empirical tests of my claims: Kunni Mausi, Lalli Mausi, and Chingee; and to my only mama, T. K. Pande, who took me to some of the best-hidden restaurants in Calcutta;

to my grandmother, Lakshmi Pande, whose passion for Mills and Boon's romances continues to inspire the questions that sustain this project;

to my mother and sisters—Kusum Joshi, Priti Joshi, and Chaya Nanavati—for their unconditional, if often nonplussed, support of this *bal kati mem*;

to those who provided the material means to complete this book: the National Endowment for the Humanities for its two very generous awards that were crucial to my research during the summer of 1997 and my writing during the 1998–99 academic year; the American Institute for Indian Studies, which made working in India during 1997–1998 possible; the Hellman Family Faculty Fund for its immense confidence in junior faculty research; Berkeley's Humanities Research Fellowship for its flexibility and leave-time in 1997–98; the English Department and the the Graduate School of the University of Wisconsin, Madison, for providing a crucial term free from teaching in 2000; and Berkeley's forthcoming and confidence-building Committee on Research without whose continual support from 1995 to 1998 none of these other awards would have been possible.

Portions of the argument in chapters 1 and 2 appeared in *Book History* 1 (1998); my thanks to the journal's editors and the Penn State University Press.

Finally, there are some who belong in a group of their own. Franco Moretti's lengendary seminars at Columbia inspired the dissertation that became this book: many of its ideas have been worked through in conversations with him, and I hope he will forgive me if I now claim some of them as my own; his friendship and loyalty have so marked the past decade that it's impossible to think of this book without him. Ann Banfield and Michael Rogin nourished me in countless ways with their intelligence and solidarity. Both my work and I have been inspired by their example, and I remain the grateful, if tongue-tied, recipient of their immeasurable generosity. Ann will forgive me, I hope, if I am unable to say more: she more than most knows the power of unspeakable sentences.

And to my beloved Orfeo Fioretos, soulmate, inspiration, and interlocutor, without whose presence or example neither this I nor book would be here: "the best gesture of my brain is less than your eyelids' flutter which says we are for each other."

When an early reader of mine encountered this project, she remarked how viscerally it resonated with her own brief experience of India in the late 1990s. Rather than noting the dirt, the poverty, or the crowds, this reader—an anthropologist who has ways of seeing that continue to dazzle me—was forcibly struck by how much the stuff of reading and writing was evident to her everywhere in India. She noted the ubiquitous bookstalls, news-vendors, mobile book-carts, and traffic-light magazine sellers during her brief visit, to the extent that she began to wonder whether the United States in contrast was, among other things, altogether postliterate.

My reader's time was largely spent in a big city, but she is entirely right in her observation, which applies to most parts of India including those she could not have been to: print is just about everywhere in the country, but not always in the form one would expect. Print in India has many lives: it forms the material of reading and writing and in this context is purveyed, purchased, purloined, borrowed, loaned, exchanged, copied, and "zeroksed" much like it is anywhere else in the world. In both urban and less urban India, the printed word is projected from billboards and building walls, bus shelters and shanties, vehicle mudguards, and public urinals, often with hilarious and poignant injunctions such as the much-reproduced laconic ad for contraception: "*Hum do, Hamare do*" (Us Two, Our Two), or the seductive come-on printed alongside truck exhausts, "*Harn pliss. Phir milaingey*" (Blow hard. Let's meet again).

More extensively, printed paper performs the role of exchange value in ways one seldom encounters elsewhere anymore: in many parts of India, households sell old newspapers and print of all types by weight to an army of highly organized ragmen in exchange for kitchen goods such as stainless-steel pots and pans that mothers stash for their daughters' trousseaux. Eventually, this textual currency—which now includes used school notebooks full of childish scribbles in Quink and graphite, old examination copy, magazines, and textbooks—returns to the marketplace deftly folded and pasted afresh to form the disposable cups and cones in which food vendors sell their roasted nuts and street food to the illiterate and superliterate hungry. From holy cow (whose diet inevitably includes the print thrown in rubbish heaps) to humble untouchable (whose livelihood often comes from collecting it), the feast of print is simply everywhere, to be read, written, eaten, bartered, and exchanged by the literate and illiterate alike.

Of the twin impulses behind this book, the first one arose in the 1970s precisely out of this world seething in print and textuality. As a small girl growing up in a dusty backwater town in central India, my sole hope of salvation lay in the weekly visits to the dank circulating library where my sisters and I read and reread every Children's Book we could find before moving on to the Adult's Section at the ripe ages of seven, nine, and ten, respectively. The maternal eye was exceedingly firm here: we were strictly forbidden Sidney Sheldon, Harold Robbins, and Jacqueline Susann, which were characterized as "Dirty Books." We naively interpreted this to mean that these books must be full of the bad bookworms that routinely destroyed entire libraries in India. However, Marie Corelli, G. W. M. Reynolds, and F. Marion Crawford were alright for us since they were approved of as "classics."

So began my journey into books that everyone in India seemed to read but about which none of my pen friends in the West nor my flesh friends when we moved to the United States had ever heard. At the age of nine, I had wept over Miss Letty and Robert D'Arcy-Muir in Corelli's *Boy*, identified with Crawford's Paul Griggs in *Mr. Isaacs*, and taken delight in the seemingly unending stock of Reynolds's *Mysteries* novels the dour librarian always seemed to have. These were Classics indeed. Meanwhile, I found Jane Eyre a prig, *Waverley* interminably boring, and Dorothea Brooke annoying. I also won prizes in virtually every subject in school (including moral science and sports, in which I have failed abysmally ever since) and by age ten, I considered myself fully learned.

Years later, after modesty and age had set in, I started writing a dissertation on countermodernisms. By pure coincidence of the kind that Reynolds and Corelli would surely have exploited into a multivolume novel, I was asked to explain what British novels Indians read for pleas-

ure in the nineteenth century. Many years of research in national
libraries and archives in India and Britain followed, which taught me
what I had already known by the time I reached ten. My forebears too
had been reading the very same novelists I had as a girl: Reynolds,
Corelli, Crawford.

In Another Country is about two episodes in the making of the English
novel in India. The first studies the Indian consumption of fiction during the nineteenth century, and the second, the world of novelistic production in the late-nineteenth and twentieth centuries. The first
impulse behind this book arose out of biographical experience of the
kind I have sketched above: the desire to document what English books
Indians read in their leisure during the nineteenth century and to try to
explain why they chose to read the books they did. The word "choice"
is key here, for it gets to a central preoccupation of this project. In a
century during which the British consolidated their hold over virtually
every part of India, I want to investigate how literate Indians addressed,
absorbed, consumed, and otherwise responded to the world of textuality and print that originated in and arrived from Britain.

The novel came to India more than two hundred years ago in the
massive steamer trunks that accompanied the British there. By the early
years of the nineteenth century, it had become an important object of
trade and import in its own right, one that was avidly anticipated and
widely consumed by Indian readers, as well as British residents. However, while most accounts of imperialism point to the success of British
culture in India (with special acclaim reserved for tea, cricket, and the
English language), few probe what Indians did with or made of these
imports. By focusing on Indian consumption practices, *In Another
Country* explores this dimension of the colonial encounter and shows
that despite the British novel's great popularity in India, its consumption by Indian readers highlights the vast terrain ultimately uncon-
quered by Englishness and empire. Though frequently regarded as a
tool for inspiring assent and anglicization among colonial subjects in
the nineteenth century, the novel, as we will see, paradoxically emerged
in India as one of the most effective vehicles for voicing anticolonial
and nationalist claims in the late-nineteenth and early-twentieth centuries.

The second impulse behind this book, then, explores the manner in
which Indian writers claimed the English novel and produced it to their
own ends once they began writing anglophone novels in the last
decades of the nineteenth century. For some literary critics, India's

English novelists still have less in common with their Indian language counterparts than they do with British writers. For these scholars, India's indigenous narrative traditions coexist with its English novel in a parallel universe as untouchables: untouched by the West and unwilling to let the West touch them. Part 2 of this book explores the relatively late emergence of the Indian novel in English and its efforts to engage in a complex and eventually rewarding transaction between domestic and imported narrative traditions as it indigenized the novel in India.

This book as a whole, with its two distinct sections spanning two long centuries and two modes of literary circulation—consumption and production—is an attempt to uncover two linked stories. What unites them here is an overarching thesis on narrative indigenization, a process by which first Indian readers and then writers transmuted an imported and alien form into local needs that inspired and sustained them across many decades. Inevitably, as the individual chapters reveal, this process occurred very differently in the two historical moments and in the different parts of the consumption-production cycle.

During the nineteenth century, as I show in chapters 2, 3, and 4, Indian readers' affection for British popular fiction in the melodramatic mode helps illuminate the manner in which they consumed the imported novel and found unexpected points of contact between it and traditional Indian narrative forms such as the epic. In the twentieth century, Indian writers indigenized the novel in a diversity of ways that included claiming new social agency for the form (Krupa Satthianadhan, chapter 5) and reconfiguring it around or in concert with older narrative traditions such as the eighteenth-century Urdu *shehrashob* (Ahmed Ali, chapter 6) and the oral epic (Salman Rushdie, chapter 7). The muted presence of popular Victorian novelists in this section is in part because Victorian cultural influence eventually receded in the twentieth century. The politics and practices of indigenization occur differently here given the different set of preoccupations confronting Indian novelists (for whom, for instance, nationalism and social reform rather than colonialism had become the defining struggles).

In short, my aim throughout *In Another Country* is to scrutinize what Indians did with or made from the works they read. If Victorian fiction in the melodramatic mode interpellated Indian readers and enabled them to recognize unexpected affinities between India's epic tradition and narratives of modernity associated with the novel, my argument on narrative indigenization in chapters 2 and 3 allows me to show how a receding domestic literary tradition (the epic) was refashioned and made usable by the consumption of an imported form (the novel). By the time Indians started producing an English novel at the turn of the twentieth century, it was not Victorian fiction they carried with them so much as the practices of cultural translation and bricolage that they had developed from their consumption of this fiction, practices that I call "indigenization" and that remain evident in the divergent sources and multiple narrative idioms that continue to characterize the Indian novel in English.

Therefore, the methods of book history and literary criticism that I deploy in parts 1 and 2 of my book, respectively, are inherently and intimately linked with the logic of my argument: one allows me to provide empirical substance and detail to flesh out readerly practices, while the other enables me to scrutinize the textual and literary strategies that are in many ways the outcome of the process I have called indigenization. What links the two sections is a structural analogy between the processes of reading and writing the anglophone novel in India. Not only does each part of my book require a different methodology: more significantly, each also requires the other to balance and complete it. By focusing on both consumption and production and the nineteenth and the twentieth centuries, I hope to tell a more inclusive story that incorporates the big picture of empire and nation along with one that engages the details of literary form and textual production. Together, the two parts of my book help make sense of the status and cultural work performed by the English novel in Indian letters.

IN ANOTHER COUNTRY

Consuming Fiction

CHAPTER I

The Poetical Economy of Consumption

INTRODUCTION

Q. D. Leavis opens her classic account of the novel, *Fiction and the Reading Public* (1932), by documenting British readers' immense affection for the genre. She reports that although novels comprised only a third of the total holdings in British public libraries in the late-nineteenth and early-twentieth centuries, they were requested over four times more often than works of nonfiction. From this, Leavis concludes:

> Considering that the 11 percent minority which takes advantage of its right to borrow books from the public libraries is probably the more enterprising section of the poorer reading public, [this] shows convincingly enough the supremacy of fiction and the neglect of serious reading which characterise the age.[1]

"The supremacy of fiction and the neglect of serious reading"—the remainder of Leavis's magisterial study proceeds to dismantle any hint of parataxis between the two phrases. It is *precisely* the supremacy of fiction in mid- to late-nineteenth-century Britain that bred the neglect of

"serious" reading in the twentieth century concludes Leavis trenchantly, amassing a formidable body of research in what became the
first study of its kind to include—indeed, to introduce—the category of
readership into the systematic analysis of a literary genre. For Leavis,
reading bad fiction—by which she meant works that "make a brute
assault on the feelings and nerves" such as the fiction of Marie Corelli
and William Le Queux (154)—meant liking it *and* looking for more of
it, thus leading to "the disintegration of the reading public" (the title of
Leavis's longest chapter) and a decline in the British novel from the
days of Richardson and Scott, Austen and Eliot, when it had "serious
standards" (123).

   This book studies the emergence of the novel in India from its introduction under the aegis of nineteenth-century British colonial policies
through the 1980s. My research on the success of British popular fiction in India documents virtually identical readership figures as Leavis
does for Britain, yet my conclusions are markedly different. The
British novel of "serious standards" was introduced in India in the nineteenth century as a means of propagating and legitimating Englishness
in the colony. Yet the fiction consumed most voraciously—discussed,
copied, translated, and "adapted" most avidly into Indian languages
and eventually into the Indian novel—was the work of highly popular
British novelists, today considered relatively minor and far from serious, whose fortunes soared for generations among enthusiastic and
loyal Indian readers long after they had already waned in Britain.
Despite this apparent "neglect of serious reading," the Indian novel
ascended to "serious standards." In order to better understand this
process and the subsequent morphology of the Indian novel, this study
begins by documenting the culture of novels and reading in nineteenth-century India with particular attention to the pervasiveness of
British popular fiction in the colony.

   Inspired by Leavis and what she terms her "anthropological"
research, I study the actual readers of fiction in colonial India in an
attempt to understand the forces behind the genre's ascendance. My
implicit premise is that if the British novel was a success in India in certain select forms, its colonial readers made it so. Therefore, studying
readership patterns (i.e., the novel's *consumption*) from extant records
might provide the clearest key to uncovering the processes of cultural
transmission in a colonial and, later, postcolonial context. Here, recog-

nizing the disjunctions between the novel's actual readers in India versus the readers implied in the English novel (who shared its larger cultural concerns) opens up new fields of meaning from which to approach a study of the novel's development in colonial and ex-colonial India.

Rather than approaching the colonial archive from the abstraction of positions held and proposed by the colonial elite, this study excavates the practices of individuals and groups in mid- to late-nineteenth-century India. Cultural and literary historians of India have until recently tended to draw conclusions about empire and its aftermath largely by examining imperial policies and pronouncements, thus implicitly suggesting that the edicts propagated at the helm were uncontroversially and seamlessly adopted into native practice. In the case of the novel in India, using this approach yields a bland and familiar narrative of imperial zealots such as Thomas Babington Macaulay on the one end and silent and compliant natives on the other. The relationship between the two comes across as unidirectional: the colonizer issued directives and the native, it has been assumed, more or less complied. Moreover, in conflating intention with effect, this approach has immense difficulty explaining the forms in which the Indian novel emerged, forms that look very different from their initial ingredients: British texts and the colonial policies that brought them to India.

Gauri Viswanathan's pathbreaking study, *Masks of Conquest* (1989), provides a useful caveat to its own focus on the vast textual archive that preceded and accompanied the institutionalization of British literary education in nineteenth-century India.[2] Viswanathan argues that the deployment of English literary education and the ensuing desire for anglicization that it generated among Indians served to fortify colonial interests in India while camouflaging ("masking") British intentions. Acknowledging that "detailed records of self-incrimination are not routinely preserved in state archives" (2), Viswanathan provides a subtle reading of the impulses behind the vigorous and extensive debates preserved in British *Parliamentary Papers* and the East India Company's voluminous correspondence on its educational policy toward India that form the basis of her study. She rightly insists that the considerable depth and detail present in what today have in fact become self-incriminatory documents come not from British hubris emanating from a sense of stable authority and absolute power over India but from the

exact opposite. "The vulnerability of the British, the sense of belea-
guerment and paranoid dread, is reflected in defensive mechanisms of
control" that find their articulation in the extensive official records and
documents of the sort Viswanathan draws upon in her influential
monograph (10–11). "The inordinate attention paid by parliamentary
discussions and debates and correspondence between the Court of
Directors and the governor-general to *anticipated* reactions by the
native population . . . is often in excess of accounts of *actual* response,"
she further proposes in an extremely provocative reading of the colonial encounter between British literary texts and Indian readers of these
texts (11; emphases in original).

Yet, rather than pursuing the opportunities implicit in her argument
and analyzing the *actual* responses of Indians to the East India Company's efforts on their behalf, Viswanathan largely ignores them altogether. Initially conceding they are "outside the scope of this book,"
with its clearly defined emphasis on studying the psychology and ideology of a British power that has "no comprehension or even awareness" of its Others (12), she judiciously proffers that the story of Indian
response "can, and perhaps must, be told separately for its immensely
rich and complex quality to be fully revealed" (12).

To an extent, Viswanathan is right in defining her inquiry as nar-
rowly as she does. Indian responses are in fact complex and rich, requiring volumes to do them justice. Anything less would be irresponsible.
However, her insistence that the story of British power and rule, belea-
guered and paranoid though it may be, can be told on its own mono-
chromatic terms without illumination, insight, or even reflection from
the most direct source and recipient of its paranoia and rule is an awkward one. Perhaps recognizing this as she explains her refusal to
include Indian voices in her study, Viswanathan's syntax with its
repeated and contorted negatives suggests that she too is less than fully
persuaded by her logic: "to record the Indian response to ideology is no
more an act of restoring the native's voice as not recording it is to render him mute" (12).

Drawing upon many of the insights and opportunities Viswanathan's
important work has made available, this study differs from hers in both
impulse and inclination in two significant ways. First, it resists the
tempting and often easy Manicheanism that accounts for empire and its
complex, clotted history with the disarming simplicity of ruler-ruled,

colonizer-colonized. Insisting that each party inserted and imposed itself in unexpected quarters of the other's domain, I see each side of the colonial encounter illuminating the other in multiple and irrefutable ways. No account of colonial India can do it justice without taking into direct account the presence and practices of the British, much the way that a story of Britain in the nineteenth and twentieth centuries can never be complete or even fully accurate without acknowledging and addressing her colonies and their inadvertent and considerable presences within her. While this remark may appear a truism today in a world that has indigenized the dialectic of master and slave into a glib mantra, it is one worth restoring to status when reading arguments such as those Viswanathan advances in her meticulous study of British ideology that nonetheless ignores Indian responses altogether.

If the distinction I have just highlighted is one of outlook, there is a second difference in approach. Sensitive to Ashis Nandy's claim that there were at least two colonialisms if not more, I read the colonial encounter in India from the perspective that dissent and consent, cooperation and corruption characterized both sides in it. Not only were there elements on both sides that contested and corroborated with the other, there was something far more complex taking place. If the visual image of empire that Viswanathan's approach invokes is of two creatures with their backs to each other facing different directions with mutually excluding histories, my image of the British Empire in India is of two sides facing each other with their arms outstretched, each side taking, snatching, pilfering, plundering what and when it could, but also giving, exchanging, and unevenly borrowing, fitfully and sporadically, but persistently, from the other. The thesis then is less one of exclusion and a strict textual and ideological apartheid than what Harish Trivedi some years ago outlined as a transaction between two unequal, and unequally motivated, sides in an encounter that, despite its unevenness, was still characterized by exchange of some sort.[3]

In no way do I intend to invalidate or ignore the brutality of empire or the innumerable economic, psychic, and social costs it extracted from India when I propose an interpretive model based on transaction of the kind I do. However, I take seriously the urgency of examining the colonial archive from a perspective that reconfigures Viswanathan's focus on a hierarchy of elites in which the British and their concerns rank uppermost to one in which I give Indians and their practices importance. The outcome of my approach yields another and altogether less familiar narrative that is full of surprises and rich with hitherto overlooked insights into the history of the British presence in India.

Rather than focusing on the colonial policies that brought the novel to India, I examine instead the British novel's impact on Indian readers and their responses to it and ask questions such as: What did the introduction of a hitherto unknown genre do in Indian letters? What was the effect of the newly introduced British novel beyond the institutional spaces of classrooms and universities and in more informal venues such as public libraries, Indian reading groups, and the domestic press where literature was increasingly being discussed and debated in the nineteenth century? What does Indian readers' relative neglect of the "serious" novels encouraged by librarians and officials in the Department of Public Instruction tell us about the cultural landscape of nineteenth-century India? The image that emerges from this research indicates an involuted portrait of cultural influence and consumption. Despite its colonial legacy, when the Indian novel emerged, it did so in forms that successfully subverted earlier colonial policies and radically reversed the priorities of Englishness and empire within the once foreign form of the novel. It is my argument that studying consumption patterns of nineteenth-century readers helps us better understand this process.

My assumption is that studying the role of the novel in the culture of print in mid-nineteenth-century India helps uncover the entangled processes at work in the transmission of culture between Britain and India. My method has been to focus on the culture of books and the practices of reading fiction occurring *on the ground* rather than at the more abstract, propagandist plane occupied by remote policymakers. *In Another Country*, then, is an attempt to combine some of the methodological insights from history of the book with the sociology of reading in order to understand the complex and contrapuntal processes at work in the consolidation of literary culture in colonial India within wider cultural and historical fields.

"Consuming Fiction," the first part of *In Another Country*, works intensively with early trade and publishing data of the nineteenth century in order to establish how Indians consumed the British novel and to explicate how these patterns of consumption both shaped and were shaped by their social and cultural horizons. The research into the circulation, consumption, and production of print in nineteenth-century India that forms the core of this part helps identify the two different tracks on which ideas and ideologies operated in British India. The vast import of textual matter underscores the origin of the encounter with British books during the first two-thirds of the nineteenth century. Following that, with the rise and consolidation of domestic publishing in the regional languages, European books were translated into numerous Indian languages, and Indian readers and writers engaged in a long, sustained, and passionate dialogue with issues and ideas that had their source in the earlier part of the century, in the workings of the colonial state, and in social identities and perspectives introduced through readers' contact with various forms of British print. Part 2 of this book, "Producing Fiction," switches tracks to production and studies four moments marking the rise of the English novel in India from the late nineteenth century to the late twentieth. Each moment bears traces of nineteenth-century consumption practices, and this section rounds out my account of the colonial past that reaches into the present.

The following three sections of this chapter concentrically lay out and work through the main methodological and theoretical arguments of *In Another Country*. The first two elaborate on the relevance of culture generally and the novel specifically in amplifying the colonial encounter in India, while the final section maps some of the theoretical and practical insights offered by focusing on consumption within the social life of books.

COLONIALISM AND CULTURE

The larger ambitions of this project arise partly out of a curiosity to identify the limits and successes of the British Empire in India. Most imperial historians today acknowledge that both commerce and culture, gunpowder and print played a role in creating and maintaining the colonial state.[4] As Jean and John L. Comaroff have persuasively argued, modern European empires "were built not merely on the violence of extraction, not just by brute force, bureaucratic fiat, or bodily exploitation. They also relied heavily on the circulation of stylized objects, on disseminating desire, on manufacturing demand, on conjuring up dependencies. All of which conduced to a form of bondage, of conquest by consumption, that tied peripheries to centers by potent, if barely visible, threads and passions."[5]

The insertion of culture and its consumption into studies of the colonial encounter so apparent in the works of the Comaroffs and others has broadened both the scope of inquiry into colonialism's cultures and the findings to emerge from it. No longer is the historical record weighed by accounts that adumbrate the success of European cultural products in the colonies: research into their consumption is providing a valuable corrective that considerably complicates our understanding of the politics and psychology of the colonial encounter.

The following three brief examples help illuminate my point more concretely. In their ethnohistory of clothing and fashion in nineteenth-century southern Africa, the Comaroffs show that the European clothing introduced by missionaries was not simply a marker of the cultural terrain conquered by the British. They demonstrate how native use of Western clothing surprisingly and quite contrary to all expectations "opened up a host of imaginative possibilities for the Africans. *It made available . . . a language with which also to speak back to the whites*" (235; emphasis added).

In another salient example that pushes this point even further, Ashis Nandy maintains that not only did colonized Indians soon create an "alternate language of discourse" to British colonialism, which he identifies as "their anti-colonialism" (xvii). He also reflects upon the multiple colonialisms taking place in India and demonstrates the extent to which the Indian alternative, articulated in practical and cultural politics by figures such as M. K. Gandhi and Aurobindo Ghose, visibly seeped back and began to shape crucial aspects of the "internal culture of Britain."[6]

And finally, John MacKenzie's research into the propaganda of empire—imperial exhibitions and societies, radio and cinema, schoolbooks and juvenile literature—assails the view that empire was what happened in far-flung overseas territories with little visible impact upon domestic debates or popular representations. Studying what he calls the "centripetal effects of Empire," MacKenzie persuasively makes the case that the cultural and commercial propaganda intended centrifugally (i.e., to radiate British influence outward from metropolis to periphery) in fact ended up being crucial "in creating for the

British a world view which was central to their perceptions of themselves," a worldview that he suggests was perceptible well into the 1980s during the Falklands War and the ensuing British victory.[7]

Each of these examples theoretically and empirically underscores the premise that studying colonialism through mainstream cultural practices allows one access to the many languages in which empire was both "spoken" and "spoken back to." In studying institutional structures and everyday practices within areas as diverse as religion, architecture, medicine, literature and language, polity, fashion, and advertising—together broadly termed as culture—historians of the British Empire have begun to document two important correctives to the earlier centrifugal account. The first and most critical project has been to make apparent the effective, if not widespread, ripostes and resistances to colonial priorities that were almost everywhere and almost immediately taking place on the ground during the colonial encounter. The second, as evidenced by Nandy, MacKenzie, and others, has been to demonstrate the centripetal and unintended consequences of the imperial will to rule. Together these correctives help us see that the colonial "replies"—frequently couched within a variety of consumption practices of the colonizer's own language and tools—were often as important, if not more so, than the original metropolitan utterance, for they eventually came to shape and sometimes paradoxically to define the field in which they operated.

Revealingly, however, these correctives and the three examples I cite to exemplify them have largely come from disciplines in the social sciences (anthropology, social psychology, and history, respectively) and significantly not from literature where the emphasis on colonialism has historically been placed on the cultural product and not on its consumption. Literary analyses have most typically focused on interpreting imperial ideology as it is embedded within narrative and textual material, and the scrutiny of literary critics has most typically worked largely within the text (i.e., reading it as product) rather than outside it (i.e., reading its consumption).[8] Literary critics have, in other words, approached the question of colonialism through the lens of their disciplinary object, subjecting what is within it to insightful and often paradigm-shifting analysis. Not surprisingly, some of these techniques have been picked up outside the discipline: all three of the examples I cited earlier have significantly drawn upon literary texts to amplify their arguments.[9] Literary analysis, however, which initially renewed the study of empire almost a quarter century ago with the publication of Edward Said's *Orientalism* (1978), has been slow to reciprocate fully in this cross-disciplinary commerce and to include consumption more fully in its analysis of textual production.

In *Orientalism*, a groundbreaking and immensely influential study of the cultural politics of imperialism, Said has persuasively and powerfully argued that the discourses and practices of studying the non-West both legitimated Western political hegemony over lands as disparate and far-flung as India and the Levant and also provided the cultural and ideological justification for this dominance. The outcome of these Western labors was the creation of what Said identifies as "a complex Orient suitable for study in the academy, for display in the museum, for reconstruction in the colonial office, for theoretical illustration in anthropological, biological, linguistic, racial, and historical theses about mankind and the universe, for instances of economic and sociological theories of development, revolution, cultural personality, national or religious character" (7–8). Moreover, the power of Western mastery was such that the Orient neither participated in nor was permitted to challenge its fabrication in Western words and forms of knowledge. It was, quite simply, an invention of the mind with powerful and long-lasting geopolitical implications, the product, Said maintains, of Western "desires, repressions, investments, and projections" (8). In subtle readings of figures such as Flaubert, T. E. Lawrence, Kipling, Renan, and Sylvestre de Sacy among numerous others, Said demonstrates how European textual production created "not only knowledge but also the very reality they [the texts] appear to describe" (94), a reality from which the Oriental Other was almost entirely excised as agent.

Orientalism's influence in a number of disciplines that had made the non-West their area of study (such as history, anthropology, area studies, religion, and even philosophy) was transformative: whole disciplines with their objects and methodologies that often bore colonially inscribed priorities and interpretations underwent widespread intellectual scrutiny, often revealing the masks of conquest at the heart of many of them. In this regard, *Orientalism* served as a useful corrective to the ways in which imperialism and its legacies have been studied in the academy.

However, though a work on the silencing of the Other, *Orientalism* was itself curiously silent on the responses and resistances to the totalizing practices of the metropole occurring on the ground during the colonial encounter.[10] Moreover, given its widespread influence in so many other areas of scholarship, *Orientalism*'s influence upon literary studies has created a less than total transformation. A number of important and illuminating accounts published since it appeared continue to rehearse within them *Orientalism*'s narratives of the imperial will to rule and of colonial self-legitimation implicit in literary texts. These accounts, many of which are far-reaching in their own right, have further focused on literary texts as products and producers of empire, often overlooking key aspects of textual consumption and circulation among the subjects of empire. Viswanathan's *Masks of Conquests*, as I have already discussed, ignores the impact of British policies on Indian subjects as well as Indian responses to them. More recently, Anne McClintock's *Imperial Leather* (1995), a breathtaking work on metropolitan commodities and ideologies (such as soap and domesticity) that were purveyed in empire often puts off their wider transaction altogether.[11] Indeed, McClintock does not so much ignore consumption as defer it to much later. Two-thirds of *Imperial Leather* dwells upon the invention and deployment of what she calls imperial modernity in southern Africa; only the final third of the book explicitly deals with what she calls anticolonial refusal in the writings of black South Africans such as Poppie Nongena's *The Long Journey of Poppie Nongena* (1980) and Sophiatown and Soweto poetry from the 1950s and 1970s.

It is not my intention to question the richness and importance of this research, which has provided valuable insights into the persistence of imperialism and its practices, but rather to build upon it and the opportunities it has opened up. The main issue it seems to me that has been raised by Said's *Orientalism* and these more recent accounts of empire is what the colonized's response to colonial practices and commodities was at the time of their arrival. Exploring contemporaneous consumption practices alongside production, I will argue, is a way to thicken and complicate our understanding of empire that helps illuminate both sides of the colonial encounter and extends our understanding of its long and often unexpected trajectories. Now that many of its far-reaching insights have been assimilated, *Orientalism* in particular invites a scholarly response resembling what Mary Layoun in a different context so insightfully summoned as an inquiry into "the cultural and textual responses to hegemony rather than mourning its occurrence."[12]

Collaborating with many of the insights that Said's brilliant work has made available, this book is in part an attempt at expanding *Orientalism*'s important legacy in literary studies and restoring balance to the disciplinary exchange that it has spawned in the cross-disciplinary world of postcolonial studies. It looks both within and without literature's traditional disciplinary object, complementing close literary and textual analysis—the look within—with material and historical research into how the textual object itself was produced, circulated, and consumed—i.e., the look without. In doing so, I draw upon the multidisciplinary tools of historian and ethnographer using them to understand better literature's particular role in the technologies of colonialism. Thus the presentation of quantitative data on the circulation and consumption of the British novel in chapters 2 and 3 is an attempt to use empirical findings to address a literary puzzle: What novels did Indians read in the nineteenth century and, if possible, how did they read them? The literary chapters in part 2 build upon the empirical and historical findings of this earlier section in order to pursue a related literary question: namely, how might we theorize the production of literary form to earlier conditions of textual and ideological consumption?

The quantitative findings that frame part 1 of this book are, therefore, not antithetical or opposed to the literary analyses that accompany them and follow in part 2. On the contrary, these empirical findings help reveal patterns within larger fields that an exclusively and more conventionally literary study of single authors and unique texts could not do on its own. In studying periods of tumult and change, as Robert Darnton and other book historians have shown, quantitative findings have frequently been able to index and illuminate shifting values more accurately than purely textual or literary analysis.[13] My own quantitative research serves as a crucial tool to bridge the domains of the literary and the historical: its findings help connect the production of texts to their social and economic contexts, a matter much analyzed by historians of the *Annales* group.[14] Through these findings, I hope to show that the British and Indian literary texts I study were not simply products of colonialism or informers of the imperial will; they were also objects of cultural consumption engaged in multiple and varied forms of transaction and exchange whose marks remain visible both within *and* without them.

THE NOVEL AND EMPIRE

Edward Said's work reminds us of the considerable extent to which literary narratives informed, directed, and themselves embodied the traffic of ideas and values between metropole, periphery, and back. "The main battle in imperialism is over land, of course," he writes, "but when it came to who owned the land, who had the right to settle and work on it, who kept it going, who won it back, and who now plans its future—these issues were reflected, contested, and even for a time decided in narrative."[15] The narratives Said most focuses on and the archive upon which the main evidence of his argument in *Culture and Imperialism* rests is that of the novel. As he maintains, "imperialism and the novel fortified each other to such a degree that it is impossible, I would argue, to read one without in some way dealing with the other" (71).[16] Said shows how the literary institution of the novel—particularly in its British manifestation—rested upon a broader world of politics and economics: through its structures, impulses, and allusions, the novel projected the world of its composition outward and in so doing gave coherence and authority to what would otherwise have been a series of discontinuous and dispersed facts of political and imperial practice.[17]

In Said's account, the novel expanded and also determined European horizons about overseas territories—about habits, habiliments, peoples, and attitudes. Moreover, it performed the cultural and ideological work of empire by reinforcing upon its readers (both European and colonial) the authority of the imperial state. The novel was, in other words, a part of what constituted the colonizing mission. However, not only did it succeed in cementing national bonds through its subtle and not so subtle accounts of the "deeds of empire" (Martin Green's phrase), it was also, as we shall see in the case of India, a widely popular literary form among colonial readers, who themselves voraciously consumed the English novel as a way of understanding and learning about British culture.

For this, the British novel has come to be considered a particular success not just because of the cultural labor it performed in Britain but also because of the labor it performed *for* Britain, most notably for its apparently successful reception among and seduction of readers in the colonies. Some critics have suggested that British influence and prestige were so marked in the nineteenth century that Indian readers "considered [British novels] to be far superior to anything which was available in their own languages";[18] or, in a related vein that "Indians took to fiction as a part of their attempt to familiarise themselves with the language, style, and manners of the ruling race."[19] Yet other critics have taken a more subtly sociological approach, maintaining that the British novel opened up "a whole new world" for nineteenth-century Indian readers, who discovered irresistible new possibilities in it.[20] Either way, the British novel was considered an immediate and immense success among readers in India, requested three to four times more frequently than any other printed form in Indian public libraries, and liberally and visibly advertised and discussed in the local press and in periodicals.[21] It is largely to understand the nature of what constitutes this success and to instantiate the role of culture broadly and the novel more specifically in the colonial encounter that this book investigates what English books Indians read and how they did so during the nineteenth century. Were literate Indians colonized by the plethora of literature arriving from Britain, or did they, through their choices and ways of reading, themselves colonize the British literary forms to their own ends, thus eluding in nimble and skillful ways the long reach of the colonizing mission?

Nineteenth-century India, it ought to be remembered, was a world increasingly under British influence and dominance. It went from being a territory tightly controlled by a group of London merchants with an exclusive trading charter in the early part of the century to a possession ruled by Crown and Parliament by the century's end. British involvement in Indian affairs during this period escalated from trade to taxation, education to administration, occupation to rule. The English language and English ways entered India in a major way during this period and penetrated more widely and deeply within the Subcontinent. Many Indians who came in contact with this anglicist and anglicizing world, however, did not regard it as altogether a bad thing, nor did they ever fully abjure it: acquiring proficiency in the language, for instance, was seen as a way of entering the well-paying and upwardly mobile ranks within the colonial administration. Moreover, nationalists, traditionalists, anticolonialists, and reformers alike used English language and learning at different times (however contradictory this may appear to have been) in order to advance causes as diverse as Hinduism, social reform, modernization, and liberation.[22]

In this mixed world where dominance and hegemony alternately and variously existed—occasionally and uncomfortably alongside each other—I am interested in probing how literate Indians exercised choice in their consumption of the world of print; what, if anything, their choices reveal about what they themselves produced; and what these choices might tell us about the colonial world and the nature of its cultural exchanges. While I will be speaking about the print world quite broadly in the pages that follow, I should say at the outset that to have made this large and diverse world in its entirety and complications the focus of my project would be an enormous undertaking, well beyond the scope of any single book.

I have focused instead on a smaller and more manageable field of textuality that Indians encountered through contact with the British. I look specifically at how readers responded to the novel, a form I selected in large part because it had never existed in India prior to its introduction under the aegis of the British commercial and colonial presence in the Subcontinent. It was a form, furthermore, that was initially outside the immediate sphere of the colonial state apparatus, whose emphasis on literature in the educational curriculum was primarily conveyed by English poetry, with essays and drama following. While the machinery of the colonial state increasingly made education one of its cornerstones by using select literary texts in the curriculum to enhance, underwrite, and otherwise underscore the superiority of the English language and the sophistication of English learning more generally, the novel as such was not at first included in this official purvey of print and ideas. Alongside the apparently marginal role it initially played in the ideology of rule (a role, incidentally, that was to increase dramatically as the nineteenth century wore on), what we see unfolding is the great and sustained enthusiasm with which Indians literate in English turned to reading British novels in their leisure.

As increasing numbers of Indians started reading English books for pleasure, the novel and Indian responses to it provide ideal variables to help track the development of a population that was not just consuming the novel as a new form of literature and entertainment but was simultaneously encountering in this form a world of new values and ideas inevitably associated with Englishness, modernity, and the colonizer. Tracking how Indians consumed the novel, then, opens up a way of examining how a colonial population responded to a world of culture and priorities inherently different from and often apparently antithetical to their own. In studying the consumption of the British novel, I submit, we begin to see most clearly how ideas and ideologies were received, transmogrified, rejected, or refashioned by that small but influential part of the Indian population who had access to this world of print. By focusing primarily on the novel, I attempt to make some sense of the vast textual apparatus that imagined, achieved, understood, retained, and reproduced empire through a large and varied array of print. By further emphasizing what literate Indians both consumed as well as produced, we begin to uncover with some specificity the details of a world in which writing served not simply as an instrument of power and expansion but also as one of seduction, explication, translation, negotiation, transaction, consolidation, and resistance.[23] In short, as the next two chapters detail, the focus on the novel helps us see that Indian readers were neither passive recipients of British print nor bit players in a story dominated by European production. Indeed, it is the very nature of print that in many ways enabled the multiple and varied transactions that this book documents. The act of reading as such leaves few textual or representational remains: its consumption, initially at least, is entirely invisible, taking place in what Benedict Anderson has elegantly called the "lair of the skull" that conceals its most extensive and revealing byproducts.[24] All readers, even those being read to, consume in the privacy of the mind, which actively enables the kinds of inventions that I propose in chapters 2 and 3.

For practical and methodological reasons, I have further focused this study upon novels in English. As I discuss in the chapters that follow, British books constituted approximately 95 percent of book imports into India between 1850 and 1900 and were present in equivalent or higher percentages among Indian library holdings (see chapter 2). Therefore, to study the circulation of the British novel over other European imports in nineteenth-century India makes considerable methodological sense. Furthermore, while I make numerous references in the chapters that follow to novels and figures who wrote in various Indian languages, my argument on Indian production in part 2 is based primarily upon Indian writing in English. Attempting to provide a pan-Indian account of the novel would require linguistic competence in at least a dozen languages and would practically lie beyond the capabilities of any single author or volume.[25]

Moreover, there is a further methodologically sound rationale for focusing on the Indian novel in English. It was the language in which Indians first encountered the form, although paradoxically it was one of the last languages in which Indians wrote their own novels. This gulf between the consumption of novels in English and their production in the language is itself provocative for it suggests that the response to colonialism was far slower in colonialism's own terrain (English) than in vernacularized and translated forms where it gained momentum rapidly, an issue that I address in chapter 4 on the Bengali novelist, Bankim Chandra Chatterjee. Indeed, colonial writing in English has carried a particular burden and relish apparent not just in the Indian context. For Stephen Dedalus in Ireland, the charge was memorably one of unrest and despair:

> The language in which we are speaking is his before it is mine. How different are the words *home*, *Christ*, *ale*, *master*, on his lips and on mine! I cannot speak or write these words without unrest of spirit. His language, so familiar and so foreign, will always be for me an acquired speech. I have not made or accepted its words. My voice holds them at bay. My soul frets in the shadow of his language.[26]

For others, the trauma came from writing not just in an acquired speech but in a borrowed form as well. Seamus Heaney writes in a powerful stanza:

> Ulster was British, but with no rights on
> The English lyric: all around us, though
> We hadn't named it, the ministry of fear.[27]

Views similar to this can be found among nineteenth- and twentieth-century Indian writers as well, some of whom, as Harish Trivedi documents, found British cultural influence initiating "a period of crisis, of bewilderment and trial by new historical forces not always fully grasped or entirely welcome" (186).[28]

However, alongside the powerlessness and despair echoed above, one also detects a celebration of the new linguistic and creative possibilities that writing a novel in English ushered in in India. Upamanyu Chatterjee's *English, August* (1988) opens with just such relish and abandon. "Amazing mix, the English we speak," chortles August in the novel's first page. "Hazaar fucked. Urdu and American . . . a thousand fucked, really fucked. I'm sure nowhere else could languages be mixed *and* spoken with such ease."[29] For Chatterjee's irreverent protagonist, the particular pleasures came not just from writing in English but also from writing the language in the amazing mix in which "we" speak it. His novel and its use of English gesture to a process of cultural indigenization that has rendered both the imported form and its language Indian. If, *pace* Said and Viswanathan, colonialism staged its presence largely through literary culture, *In Another Country* is invested in exploring the languages in which that culture was mixed and spoken, apparently with such ease. It therefore focuses on the colonial encounter as it took place in India in an entirely colonial realm—i.e., within an imported genre (the novel) as well as in an acquired language (English)—even as it shows both dimensions of this realm being indigenized within a domestic cultural sphere.

THE POETICAL ECONOMY OF CONSUMPTION

I embarked on this project increasingly convinced that political economy's traditional emphasis on production and the commodity within the trade cycle significantly obscures a fuller understanding of the social life of things. Production and circulation tell only part of the story. It is my contention, strengthened over the course of my research, that consumption crucially shapes the telling and sometimes even the tale of the cycle. The title of this chapter, "The Poetical Economy of Consumption," therefore, invokes two registers. It is in part a play on Marx's "Introduction to a Critique of Political Economy" (1857), in which he maps out a theory of production, distribution, and consumption that was to remain his view on the trade cycle under capitalism.[30] For Marx, "the process always starts afresh with production" (139), which fundamentally creates, determines, and shapes consumption through the commodities it produces. While his essay skillfully places production as an originary moment in the trade cycle—before distribution, exchange, and consumption—it ends there without substantially connecting consumption to production or ever fully closing the gap between the two. Political economy is powered by production for Marx; consumption largely marks the requisite endpoint of a chain rather than the beginning of another one. In this regard, therefore, the word "cycle," which he uses to describe trade in abstraction is something of a misnomer. Consumption for Marx remains subordinate to production: it is that which "falls properly outside the sphere of economy" (130); that "cannot be the decisive element [in political economy]" (139).[31]

Finding Marx's refusal to link consumption to production unsatisfactory and curious to investigate what would happen if the trade cycle were closed around these two points, I propose an alternative model in this chapter. While I too draw upon political economy, I focus considerably on its subjective trajectory rather than purely on its objective and abstract elements, specifically as it relates to the circulation of print in nineteenth-century India. Working within a frame that emphasizes consumption's influence upon social meanings and relations, my account here differs substantially from the Marxist one outlined above. Rather than locating political meaning solely within the product (i.e., within the various ideological utterances putatively contained in the text), I suggest instead that the political effects of a text lie outside it in its consumption by readers who are not its makers. Drawing upon Michel de Certeau's illuminating argument that consumers are "unrecognized producers, poets of their own affairs,"[32] I offer here what I somewhat playfully contrast with the political: namely, a poetical economy of the circulation of goods. The second register that my title invokes—of poetical economy and consumption—therefore inverts the first one—of political economy and production.[33]

In *The Practice of Everyday Life* (1979), de Certeau described consumption as "another production," arguing that "it insinuates itself everywhere, silently and almost invisibly, because it does not manifest itself through its own products, but rather through its *ways of using* the products imposed by a dominant economic order" (xii–xiii; emphasis in original). In their dissident ways of using goods that they neither make nor produce, consumers nonetheless manipulate, re-imagine, appropriate, and re-fashion the products at their disposal. Separated, marginalized, or alienated from the economy of production, users express themselves through their choices and forms of consumption. They skillfully and ceaselessly adapt or otherwise evade the rules and structures under which they live without overthrowing the rules and structures themselves. As de Certeau maintains, "the tactics of consumption, the ingenious ways in which the weak make use of the strong, thus lend a political dimension to everyday practices" (xvii).

De Certeau's examples of dissidence through consumption are numerous: shopping, watching television, reading, walking in the city. Although these ways of producing by consuming, multiple and minor as they are, often leave few textual traces and lie outside the historical record or the sphere of statistics, he nevertheless maintains that they are apprehensible to the researcher attentive to them. Drawing upon Spanish colonial attempts to implant European culture and religion among indigenous peoples in the New World, for instance, de Certeau vividly argues that Spanish success was only partly and superficially achieved:

> Submissive, and even consenting to their subjection, the Indians nevertheless often *made of* the rituals, representations, and laws imposed on them something quite different from what their conquerors had in mind; they subverted them not by rejecting or altering them, but by using them with respect to ends and references foreign to the system they had no choice but to accept. They were *other* within the very colonization that outwardly assimilated them; their use of the dominant social order deflected its power which they lacked the means to challenge; they escaped it without leaving it. (xiii; emphasis in original)

The example is particularly relevant to de Certeau's thesis on consumption in part because it so starkly identifies the dominant power (the Spaniards) and because this power had the strategic and military means to impose and engineer its influence upon a host of everyday indigenous practices from polity, language, and religion to architecture, jurisprudence, and trade. Yet, as de Certeau insists, users within this colonial order had ways of mutating its power through their manner of consuming its products.

Subjected to a force vastly more powerful than their own, indigenous subjects of Spanish colonialism employed the tactics of the weak. Imbuing alien regulations and representations with vernacular ones, "they metaphorized the dominant order: they made it function in another register" (32). They rescripted the colonial narrative and created a new role and new possibilities for themselves within it. Submitting to Spanish power—and language and religion—native groups nonetheless found ways of evading it by digesting (or consuming) its practices within their own social priorities. De Certeau calls this process "metaphorization," but we could as well call it an act of cultural translation, a practice through which groups make sense of differences between the worlds they encounter in ways that allow them to convert differences through consumption and to divert the apparatus of dominance by reimagination.[34] Translation in this context serves to underscore the gulf between the worlds of the colonizer and the colonized rather than to accentuate the common ground they share. Instead of discovering likeness and equivalence between the two orders, consumption-as-translation highlights the vast chasm separating them. Through acts of cultural interpretation (or, what Daniel Miller has usefully called "recontextualization"[35]), the colonized produces new and unintended meanings of the products deployed by the colonizer, meanings that only tangentially relate to their original ones and that thus mark the paucity of shared signification between the two orders.

To focus on consumption, therefore, is not to study how goods and commodities are acquired by consumers; rather, it is to study the diversity of ways in which they are recontextualized and put to use. Indeed, this is the key distinction between my use of consumption and that of its predominant theorists, Thorstein Veblen and Pierre Bourdieu. Veblen's *The Theory of the Leisure Class* (1899) defined the theoretical terrain that mapped the cultural determinants to consumption studies that his successor, Bourdieu, has today come to occupy (though, significantly, Bourdieu makes no mention of Veblen in his work on consumption). Both Veblen and Bourdieu, despite their differences, form a single axis within consumption theory: both emphasize the manner in which commodities define consumers, who seek identity and realization from the goods and services they can command and consume.[36] Veblen's account comes from a reading of late-nineteenth-century American *nouveaux riches* who sought to erase any hint of labor from the source of their wealth and, therefore, preferred to consume conspicuously those goods that themselves had no overt reference to labor (and, more specifically, to industrial labor): hence a vacation "doing nothing" or a purely decorative lapdog that had no ostensible or visible use value, not even hunting or protection.

On the other hand, Bourdieu's work in *Distinction* (1979) focused on consumers' desires to cultivate and project a particular kind of labor underpinning their consumption practices and to identify their class position through it: namely, that of higher education. Consumers select those commodities that identify their education in taste: thus the emphasis on "educated" forms of recreation (music, museum visits, art), food, reading materials. Despite differences that need not detain us here, there are two marked similarities: both Veblen and Bourdieu emphasize material culture over its users; commodities over consumers. Following de Certeau, however, the emphasis in my study is upon the consumers themselves rather than the commodity; upon sociology not materiality; upon less visible uses and ruses from those below rather than conspicuous displays from those near the top.

It ought to be clear from my account that the slippages that consumption helps make visible, especially in the context of empire, are also significantly different from those in the much used notion of mimicry. In Homi Bhabha's influential description of it, mimicry is a form of Western desire imposed upon its Others as a way of both inventing them and articulating mastery over them.[37] For Bhabha, mimicry in the case of India refers to British desires for an anglicized Other who is nevertheless not permitted to be English (or, as Macaulay had infamously put it, one who is "Indian in blood and colour but English in taste, opinions, morals, and intellect"[38]). Bhabha's concept of mimicry thus comes to represent the ambivalences and disavowals inherent in the European colonial enterprise. It is "an erratic, eccentric strategy of authority in colonial discourse" (90), originating in European power— and not the mockery or copy of that power as V. S. Naipaul maliciously portrayed it in his novel *The Mimic Men* (1967).

The differences between my argument of what consumption enables in a situation of unequal power such as colonial rule and Bhabha's of mimicry are straightforward but substantial. First, whereas the agency of consumption explicitly lies with the user (typically, the colonized), agency in mimicry is exclusively the domain of the producer (i.e., the colonizer). Mimicry is all about the European will to rule and the projection of that will upon the colonized: it is articulated and made visible in European writing, which Bhabha cites extensively and almost exclusively in his essay. The colonized are presented in this account as an undistinguished mass, deprived of any agency, whose sole historical relevance is to reveal the colonizer's will and desire for reproduction. Second, whereas mimicry is invested in explicating the colonizer's will to power, consumption on the other hand is marked by its investigation into the *effects* of that power. At best, mimicry is elusive ("erratic, eccentric"): it "conceals no presence or identity behind its masks" (88). Consumption, in marked contrast, is part of everyday practice; in many cases it is implicated in material history and culture, often leaving traces within the historical record. Finally, consumption signals the gulf between two worlds that it attempts to bridge through metaphorization; mimicry indicates a gulf that is never fully bridged because of the multiple slippages inherent in it. Mimicry is marked on both sides of the colonial encounter by ambivalences ("almost the same, but not quite"), consumption by inadvertent agency and action. Even in a later essay, where Bhabha allows the voice of anticolonial refusal to come through, the source of this refusal lies not in the colonized's particular practices of consumption (Anund Messeh's interlocutors still read the Bible *qua* Bible under the tree in Delhi) but in the hybridity and ambivalences embedded within the *colonizer's* practice of authority.[39] Consumption, therefore, details the agency and weapons of the weak, mimicry those of the strong.

Predictably and not surprisingly given mimicry's source in imperial desire, the colonial record—maintained by the rulers—is full of its presence. Mercifully, however, the colonial archive is also rife with examples of consumption as cultural translation and metaphorization. In a subtle reading of José Rizal's 1886 novel, *Noli Me Tangere* ("The Lost Eden"), Vicente Rafael describes a scene where a cleric, Father Damaso, gives a bombastic sermon to a congregation of locals, starting with a Latin quote then moving on in Spanish to end his remarks in Tagalog.[40] The gathering soon loses the point of the sermon, noting instead "the sour face of the lieutenant, the bellicose gesture of the preacher" (2) along with a few words here and there from which they make out a whole other meaning than the one Father Damaso intended (and upon which Rizal's narrative dwells at length). In annotating the scene, Rafael suggests that the priest's words rouse in the Tagalog listeners other thoughts that have only the most tenuous connections to what he is actually saying. . . . Their response, however, is not simply a matter of boredom, indifference, or rejection. In fact, they anxiously attend to Damaso's voice, hoping to catch some of the words that are thrown their way. *It is as if they saw other possibilities in those words* . . . another place from which to confront colonial authority—one that appears to be tangential to the position of subordination ascribed to them by both Father Damaso and Rizal.

(3; emphasis added)

In this case, then, the congregation evaded the entire battery of associations hurled in Father Damaso's sermon—of Christian superiority, colonial justice, Filipino underdevelopment, and so on—instead hearing within the "flood of words" a story in which, as Rizal writes, "San Francisco would destroy the *guardias civiles*" (2) and fulfill the deepest—and anticolonial—desires of the Tagalog. Unfettered by their mistranslation, the cleric's listeners "redoubled the attention with which they followed Father Damaso" (2).

As Rafael helps us see, through this example and others in his extraordinary ethnohistory of Christianity in the Philippines, not only did Tagalog consumption-translation reconfigure colonial priorities, it also actively enabled native fantasies. Even as religion, language, and new technologies of representation were produced and placed before colonial consumers, they found ways of indigenizing foreign influences by recontextualizing or translating the alien and the unknown within their own local narratives or, in some cases, using ideological imports to talk back to the colonial authorities. In each case, by producing new meanings of and uses for products they had no initial hand in making, colonial consumers found ways both of evading full submission into the dominant economy of interest and of inserting themselves within the circulation of its products. As we will shortly see in the Indian context, consumption was not (not just) a tactic of preserving the self under external ideological onslaught by preserving a rich fantasy world in the mind; it also managed to affect the pathways through which products that originated in the colonial apparatus circulated and, even possibly, were eventually produced.

Accepting the broad premise that consumption is another production, its most significant outcome is not always or only dissidence, opposition, or subversion as de Certeau maintains (although these are abundantly present and initially at least salient markers of the colonial encounter). Rather, it is something more participatory with the dominant order, something that, following Harish Trivedi, one might call transaction. Although the colonial state apparatus is initially the major point of reference and source of conflict in this project, to study opposition exclusively serves not toward uncovering another production, but rather a *reproduction*, in negative or distorted form, of the colonial priorities and ideologies that practices of consumption in fact seek to replace.[41] For me, instead, focusing materially and rigorously on broad consumption practices within the everyday that engage with and translate outer forms of power holds the promise of unearthing something more nuanced: the production of new methodological and interpretive possibilities, new meanings, different vistas, new findings within an order that has hitherto emphasized production as the main source of social and historical meaning.

Within a historical record that has emphasized the data of production, patterns of reading as consumption nonetheless make themselves visible, paradoxically within the very data and statistics that apparently eschew them. Despite the fact that Indian readers have left so few textual records of their novelistic consumption, the print archive of nineteenth-century India nonetheless offers revealing glimpses. From this archive it is possible to learn something about the novels that were available to literate Indians, where and how, and something of the conditions under which Indians availed themselves of this reading matter. It also yields information on local conditions of printing and publishing, on the role of the nascent serial press, and on the ways in which books were purveyed and discussed, translated and adapted through the nineteenth century. In short, this quantitative archive provides the social context in which the British novel was consumed in nineteenth-century India, a consumption different from that of many other commodities in that it required not just purchasing power but literacy as well.

By reading novels as well as reading how novels might historically have been read, consumption's multiply layered practices reveal themselves from within the textual analysis and statistical data of the chapters in part 1 as trends rather than individual practice, diachronically rather than synchronically. Consumption's contribution to social meaning emerges in between the domains of the literary and the historical, asserting its presence and influence upon the economics of cultural production. The poetics of consumption manifest itself through the quantitative record: therefore, rather than abrogating statistics altogether as de Certeau might have, this study uses them against the grain for their ability to lend both clarity and complexity to cultural analysis by helping reconfigure the historical, sociological, and textual in useful new ways.

In India's encounter with the British novel, what we see is neither a large-scale boycott nor a widespread opposition to British literary culture. The immediate and sustained enthusiasm for the form was contrary to what the preceding theoretical discussion might lead one immediately to predict, especially given the statistical popularity of this form in just about any register. Readers vigorously and unambiguously embraced the novel for their leisure reading, often choosing it over indigenous literary forms, discussing it in the domestic press, in literary societies, and in homes in a manner that would suggest the novel's successful conquest of the Indian literary and cultural marketplace. In examining the record more closely, however, a different pattern emerges: what we see is not consumption by opposition but consumption through selection. Individual readers in multitudes variously indicated the differences between their world and the colonial state's in two ways: first, by the specific novels they consumed (both the selections they made *for* as well as *against* certain books are revealing here); and second, by how they read, misread, translated, mistranslated the British novel. These descriptions of reading are not just writerly sleights: the historical record is full of British novels translated and adapted into Indian languages, and what got translated and how signals a form of consumption characterized not by opposition but by adaptation; it articulates a narrative of production by abduction, diversion, invention.

Consumption's use for me, therefore, lies in its ability to reveal the interstices between vernacular, everyday practices and a dominant social and political economy. In Daniel Miller's keen words, it opens new interpretive possibilities through the way it "translates the object from being a symbol of estrangement and price value to being an artefact invested with particular inseparable connotations" (190). Consumption contributes meaning and clarity to the denotative data of production and its circuits of exchange. The accounts it makes visible are not the replication of a grand historical narrative but a multiplication and correction of it.

In the particular context of this project, specifically in chapter 2, consumption focuses attention on local practices occurring on the ground: knowing what readers consumed and why they did so clarifies crucial aspects of the politics and psychology of the colonial encounter. The novel, as Meenakshi Mukherjee and others have suggested, indeed provided a host of imaginative possibilities to Indian readers: it became a new form involved in inventing and representing the self; it provided its readers in India with a new language for figuring out the calculus of emerging social relations associated with modernity; and almost simultaneously, it also became one of the most powerful vehicles, first of the anticolonial and later of the nationalist struggle. In this regard, studying the novel's consumption helps us get to what Ashis Nandy earlier identified as the alternative discourse to empire; through it, in pointed ways Indians discovered themselves and manifested their anticolonialism.

Chapter 2 studies the wider world of print and ideas from which the novel eventually emerged in India. Through an analysis of extant library circulation records, public library catalogues, and translation rosters, I document how the British novel circulated among Indian readers roughly between 1835 and 1900. These patterns of use allow me to analyze the dual structure of similarity and difference in reading tastes between colonial India and Britain during the same period. Despite the sociological, political, and cultural differences in the two contexts, the canon of popular and most-sought-after novels had both striking similarities and marked differences. As a revealing example of these, I analyze the pervasive appeal of G. W. M. Reynolds (1814–79), possibly the most popular British novelist in India. I show how Indian readers consumed and interpreted Reynolds, and I argue that Reynolds's writing, with its embrace of extravagantly antirealist modes, participated in a moral, literary, and psychic economy that resonated with Indian consumers' symbolic and subconscious needs as readers in a subordinate political context.

On the other side lies the unexpected exchange visible through consumption practices in India. What novels Indians chose to read inevitably influenced the kinds of books British publishing firms such as Macmillan began to ship to the country. The success of this Indian-selected fiction, however, soon became apparent in Paternoster Row and began to motivate the forms of the novel that were published there. Colonial literary consumption, in other words, eventually began to inspire literary production in the metropolis, thus highlighting and making explicit a colonial encounter characterized by transaction and exchange, rather than one marked exclusively by dominance and conquest.

Chapter 3 engages with a long-held critical commonplace among publishing historians that British firms dumped unsold and unsellable books into the colonies, so that studying colonial readership for insights into broader cultural or social trends can be dismissed as futile: the world of print in the colonies, this argument claims, simply documents metropolitan excess and excrescence. Intrigued by this line of reasoning, I spent several summers at the British Library working in the archives of Macmillan and Company, the most successful British publishing firm in nineteenth- and twentieth-century India, in order to understand the firm's success in the colonial world. Based on this research, I propose that the firm (as well as others including Murray, Routledge, Bentley, and Cassells) was acutely aware of the profits to be made from selling books directly to Indian readers, and it carefully cultivated this marketplace, first with textbooks and educational materials in the 1860s and then with novels through its "Colonial Library" series that was started in 1886. The success of Macmillan's fiction series lay largely with the firm's willingness to satisfy the tastes of their Indian readers, a fact well documented in the firm's private correspondence files and readers' reports. Therefore, not only is research into the colonial marketplace useful for gaining insights into the circulation of print and ideas between metropolis and periphery, but analyzing the nature of *what* Macmillan sold discloses an understudied economic aspect of the production of the British novel. The willingness of British firms such as Macmillan to please this new and palpable colonial market might also, as I show, be reflected in the kinds of novels that were eventually published in Britain, thus highlighting the contribution of the colonial marketplace to the shape of the English novel.

The outcome of this literary encounter has persisted in Indian letters well past the demise of the colonial state, most notably in the development of the Indian novel in English, which records a narrative in considerable contrast to the one on the rise of the novel in Britain. The origins of the English novel have spawned a veritable research industry devoted primarily to identifying the novel's sources in England and the reasons behind its subsequent literary hegemony.[42] The actual forms that the English novel has taken have tended to be less of an issue for researchers than its sources.[43] With the novel in India, exactly the opposite is true: understanding the origins of the novel is less of a puzzle than understanding its trajectory. Why the English novel developed in the forms that it did and when it did in India is a question that has yet to be fully addressed. Part 2 of this book is a beginning in that direction, and chapter 4 serves as both transition and bridge between the two parts of *In Another Country*.

In chapters 4 to 7, I study the attempts Indian novelists made to indigenize what was initially a foreign form and idiom. In some ways, the story told is one of failures and reroutings, in other ways, of oddly satisfying reversals and triumphs. Bankim Chandra Chatterjee (whom I discuss in chapter 4) gave up on language but not the form to become the first nationally renowned novelist in India when he abandoned an early experiment in English and started writing novels in Bengali in the last quarter of the nineteenth century. Krupa Satthianadhan (discussed in chapter 5), a woman and a convert to Christianity, abandoned form but not the language in her fin-de-siècle visions of an India freed of oppressions from without and within. As a "nobody" of the kind one critic has named certain woman writers in the British marketplace,[44] Satthianadhan's was a striking but short-lived and even more shortly remembered moment in the development of the English novel in India.

Yet her writing also illuminates an extraordinary success. If the colonizer's language proved to be an obstacle for effectively rendering an Indian subjective consciousness for Bankim and other early Indian novelists who turned instead to regional languages, Satthianadhan elicits both interiority and intimacy from the imported language and the particularly autobiographical form of the novel that she cultivates. Her success in this matter gestures to a shift between novelists in the regional languages and those in English: while novelists such as Bankim (Bengali), O. Chandu Menon (Malayalam), Naro Sadashiv

Risbud (Marathi), and Devakinandan Khatri (Hindi) reveled in the fictionality of fiction and in fabricating worlds suitable for the novel, Satthianadhan's writing begins to mark a particular turn that the English novel in India took toward embracing the biography of known subjects. Satthianadhan writes about her own and her mother's *Bildung* in different households; Ahmed Ali (discussed in chapter 6) wrote a novel in 1940 that includes the social history of a city; and Salman Rushdie in 1980 produced a novel of the nation's political history. If Indian "reality" was deemed an encumbrance in the development of the novel in regional languages, which instead crafted massively fictional worlds for it, the novel in English reflects an apparent ease with "reality," placing it at the very center of its production.

With indigenizing the English novel, then, comes a paradox: while the language alienated Indian novelists in the nineteenth century, it embraced them in the twentieth. Far from being an uncomfortable language of production, English and the English novel became vehicles of intimacy and acclaim by the end of the twentieth century. If the earlier discomforts lay with rendering an Indian "reality" in a foreign tongue, the later success lay in submitting that the only reality that mattered was the subjective one that the English novel almost single-mindedly pursued in its uneven, century-long development.

What follows in the second part of *In Another Country* is an expansion and exploration of the questions initiated in part 1. In no way are chapters 4 to 7 to be thought of as an attempt to craft a literary history of the English novel in India. Rather, these chapters with their accounts of formal experimentation, narrative indigenization, and literary production explore the extent to which literary history itself is explained and complicated by the analysis of consumption that precedes it. If, to borrow a phrase from Roger Chartier, variations in the dispositions of readers help uncover a more nuanced account of the colonial encounter (in part 1), then variations in the dispositions of writers in part 2 help clarify a number of literary and formal questions that confront the Indian novel in English. If part 1 helps explain realism's failure among Indian readers in the nineteenth century (see especially chapter 3), part 2, with its readings of specific moments of literary production, helps elaborate the kinds of struggles Indian novelists confronted in rendering Indian "reality" in a form of the novel that was rapidly being vernacularized. Together these two parts explore a process by which first readers then writers of the English novel in India indigenized the form and put it to their own uses in the nineteenth and twentieth centuries.

It is not my intention to claim a causal link between the history of consumption and the account of production I provide—such a link would likely be almost impossible to sustain. Rather, while each of the following chapters has its own internal coherence and historical specificity, the chapters together illuminate six episodes or moments in a process of narrative and cultural indigenization according to which the anglophone novel was vernacularized in Indian literary and cultural life. As such, the chapters on consumption help expand and render complexity to questions of literary history, novelistic form, and literary production that comprise part 2 of *In Another Country*. With this in mind, I have chosen literary moments and novelists that lend the greatest depth and dimension to the kinds of questions I ask, all figures crucial and celebrated in their day whose status helps explain the long journey toward self-expression undergone by the English novel in India.

Some might argue that to have Christians, women, and Muslims represent Indian novelistic production in English in the way this book does is an anomaly given the minority status increasingly enjoined upon these groups in India. To the extent that this is a valid concern, one might recall Gilles Deleuze and Felix Guattari's pioneering work on Kafka with its insistence that a literature constructed by a social or political minority often exerts a considerable critical and political force on a "great" (or established) literature as it revises and exposes the triumphalist narratives of groups in power.[45] That the minority does this in the language of the majority (German in the case of Kafka, English in the case of Satthianadhan, Ali, and Rushdie) renders the power and insights of minority literature all the more compelling. As Salman Rushdie claimed with some circumspection not too long ago: "the only people who see the whole picture . . . are the ones who step out of the frame."[46]

This book is in part that picture or, rather, two of them. Part 1, on the nineteenth century, is crowded in the way old photos are with ancestors and relatives, near and distant, whose bloodlines and genes, habits and tendencies are still visible in the generations that followed them. Part 2 is a more intimate picture—a family photo—that, in keeping with the conventions of the form, is of a much smaller group whose influence and importance is most closely felt among those who consider themselves part of the family. If this part of the book appears selective in its genealogy to some, this too is in keeping with the nature of families—and family romances.

seemingly everything that the empire of print purveyed and made available, including policy edicts, administrative records, newsprint, schoolbooks, histories, geographies, poetries, works of "useful knowledge," and, most abundantly it seems, the novel. "A majority of those who read, read fiction even if they read something else, and a majority of those who read fiction, read very few other things except it," reported Thakorelal M. Desai in a 1919 essay in the *Calcutta Review*, echoing a commonplace that is almost entirely ignored in the representations of India in British fiction, or for that matter, in the British press.[2]

It could of course be that Indians read unexpected things, that they read what nobody else did, or what nobody else thought that they did, which might help explain the British novel's blindness regarding Indian reading practices. Mulk Raj Anand describes horrifying Virginia Woolf with a confession of his literary preferences: "'I read several volumes of a long novel by George W. M. Reynolds,' I apologized. 'I am afraid his long sentences may have affected my writing.' 'Who on earth is George W. M. Reynolds?' Virginia Woolf said, sweeping me with a broad smile from her embarrassed face, in a strained voice controlling itself from becoming the measure of my vulgarity."[3] Acutely mortified by Woolf's question, Anand the aspiring novelist clumsily threw out a few more influences upon his writing: "'I find the same about Rider Haggard who wrote *She*, and Marie Corelli and Charles Garvice,' I said persisting in the folly of lowbrowness" (105), to which Leonard Woolf, the other "tropical" in the room, reassured his wife her ignorance of Reynolds with: "Hardly ever mentioned here . . . the fodder on which the subalterns chew the cud in the cantonments of the empire" (105).

At the time of this conversation in the early 1930s, Anand was at the peak of his Gandhian phase and was shortly to publish a warmly praised first novel, *Untouchable* (1935), with its now-famous introduction by E. M. Forster. The exchange he has with the Woolfs over tea is a telling one that makes explicit a number of key issues surrounding India's encounter with the British novel in the nineteenth century and the persistence of this influence well into the twentieth. It indicates the almost complete unawareness of Indian reading practices among literary-minded Britons that helps explain the representation of what amounts to Indian illiteracy in the British literary imagination. Anand's reform novel, *Untouchable*, which claims Reynolds and Corelli as influences, further gestures toward the sustained popularity of forgotten Victorian novelists who are "hardly ever mentioned here" anymore and yet who continued to provide not just entertainment but inspiration in an Indian literary universe considerably removed in time and place, theme and sensibility from metropolitan Britain. Anand, like Reynolds, was a political radical who used the novel as an expression of class outrage, at one point calling it a "weapon of humanism."[4] The gulf between his latrine cleaner, Bakha, and the sahibs is as vast and impassable as that between Reynolds's "toilers" and "harristocrats" in the *Mysteries* novels. Indeed, an unspoken dimension of Virginia Woolf's question regarding Reynolds is not just *who* he was but *why* he was so popular in India, a query that her husband's bovinely imaged response does something to address by implying that the remoteness of empire and the paucity of reading material generated the habits Anand confesses to, habits no more distinguished than the nocturnal chewing of the cud. It is a serious explanation delivered with the inadvertent arrogance of conventional wisdom about the Subcontinent: if anyone read there, they read unimaginatively whatever came their way in much the way that cows did, without exercising much discrimination of taste or distinction of choice.

This chapter is far from an effort to correct the British literary imagination for its representations of Indian textual practices. Rather, it critically examines some of the very different commonplaces thrown out in Thakorelal Desai's, Mulk Raj Anand's, and Leonard Woolf's descriptions of Indian reading preferences for the British novel. If Elleke Boehmer is indeed right in calling the British Empire "a vast communications network" that "in its heyday was conceived and maintained in an array of writings—political treatises, diaries, acts and edicts, administrative records and gazetteers, missionaries' reports, notebooks, memoirs, popular verse, government briefs, letters 'home' and letters back to settlers," then this chapter is committed to investigating what role Indians played in this teeming world of print.[5] It especially probes Desai's contention on the popularity of the novel among Indian readers and seeks to uncover the details of what they consumed with such avidity and why in the nineteenth century. What follows are a series of profiles on print, its readers and censorship in India; the culture of public libraries through which novels were most frequently made available in the nineteenth century; the proliferation of British novels in Indian translations; and an inquiry into the particular and sustained appeal that G. W. M. Reynolds enjoyed among Indian readers well into the twentieth century.

PRINT, READERS, AND CENSORSHIP

The emergence and early history of print in India from its origins in the mid-sixteenth century are dominated by European presences and distinguished by the number of languages in which print was produced. Yet what also marks this period is the very negligible role played by English until the eighteenth century. India's first printing press was set up in 1556 by Jesuits in the Portuguese colony of Goa for the express purpose of printing Christian texts for missionary activity. The languages of print were varied: in the roughly two decades following the arrival of the press in Goa, some eight books were printed in Portuguese, Latin, Ethiopian, Tamil, and Konkani.[6] By the early eighteenth century, when the first Protestant missionaries were active in India, printed works in Dutch, Danish, and German made their appearance, but it was not till 1716 that the first English work, Thomas Dyche's *A Guide to the English Tongue*, was printed.[7]

The relatively late appearance of English printing in India provides little indication of its later profusion: the end of the eighteenth century saw a burst of commercial, philological, and literary printing in the language, and the early European languages were completely superseded by the predominance of English presses as well as by increasingly vigorous printing in the languages of India. Prose fiction or the novel, however, was underrepresented in this plethora of print: the first work of fiction to be printed in India was a 1793 Tamil translation of John Bunyan's *Pilgrim's Progress* (2 parts, 1678 and 1684); other translations of mostly British novels followed in the domestic press until the latter half of the nineteenth century when the novel began to be written and published in half a dozen Indian languages—though significantly not in English.

This summary profile requires two accompanying caveats. First, while print had an unmistakable influence in shaping India's encounter with modernity, the colonial apparatus, and eventually with itself, it is absolutely crucial to recall that the culture of print coexisted with that of manuscript and orality up to and beyond the mid-nineteenth century. This fact is critical for understanding why particular forms of the novel (most notably realism) had such trouble putting down roots in Indian soil where the different and often contesting discursive fields of orality and manuscript exerted their own volatile influence and claims upon the consumers of print. Unlike Benedict Anderson's contention that the novel and the newspaper influenced the transformation of individual consciousness into some more abstract collective identity in the creation of European nationalisms, what we see in India is that notwithstanding the influence of print, preprint forms of textuality and cultural transmission persisted for a long while and consistently revealed fissures and discontinuities in print's purportedly "unifying" process.[8] Multiple preprint forms contested the supremacy of print in India in numerous ways just as we will see other literary forms contesting the emerging novel. Therefore, any discussion of print in nineteenth-century India has to acknowledge its limits and to recognize the ongoing nature of the challenges it encountered in both real and symbolic ways.

The second caveat to this story is that Indian printed matter is only a part of the world of Indian print: a substantial amount of what Indians read, particularly through the 1870s, arrived printed and shipped from Britain. Extant trade figures record the value and amount of this export but not its contents, yet even the broad statistics provide some indication of the considerable volume of print arriving in India from British presses. These figures, represented visually in figure 2.1, help put into perspective the highly contested £10,000 bursary with which English education "began" in India, following the enactment of the 1835 Education Act: what they reveal are the dramatic consequences that followed the endowment of this greatly symbolic but in the end fairly negligible sum.

Between 1850 (the first year that data are available) and 1863–64, the export of books and printed matter from Britain to India doubled in value from £148,563 in 1850 to £313,772 in 1863–64.[9] These figures amplify what we already know from other sources such as library records, memoirs, and the domestic press: that in the decades following the onset of formal English education, an increasing number of English publications (such as histories, grammars, schoolbooks, "useful books," poetry, novels, biographies) became available in the Indian market. Critics have suggested that the increase in book exports may have had something to do with expediting the policy of cultural anglicization articulated so forcefully by Thomas Macaulay in his infamous 1835 Minute on English Education, which claimed that "a single shelf of a good European library was worth the whole native literature of India and Arabia."[10] Macaulay's was certainly a position consistent with the manner in which earlier cultural Anglicists had themselves suggested "ruling" India. In 1792, almost half a century before education became one of the cornerstones of East India Company policy and expansion, Charles Grant had suggested that "multitudes, especially of the young, would flock to [the English schools], and *the easy books used in teaching, might at the same time convey obvious truths on different subjects.*"[11] Despite Grant's influence (he later became chair of the East India Company), his proposals for anglicist reform were shelved as the administrators in India House were still wary of offending their subjects by appearing to intervene too much in daily affairs. Almost half a century later, Macaulay echoed the implications of this position very specifically when he successfully argued that the goal of education was

FIGURE 2.1 Book Imports Into India, 1850–1901

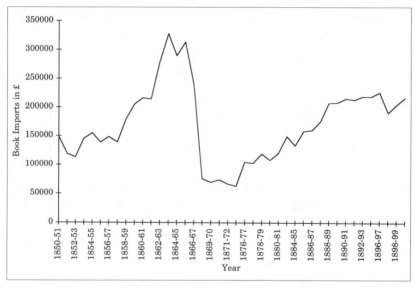

SOURCE: *Annual Statement of the Trade and Navigation of British India with Foreign Countries and of the Coasting Trade of the Several Presidencies and Provinces* (Calcutta: Government Printing Press, 1850–1901).

not simply literary but something akin to the large-scale invention of a new social identity for Indians, a culturally bichromatic Cartesian self he described as "a class of persons, Indian in blood and colour, but English in taste, in opinions, in morals, and in intellect" (249).

If the £10,000 bursary was to initiate and affect this cultural revolution, we realize how symbolic a sum it really was in contrast to the fifteen- to thirtyfold greater sums expended on exporting print to India. Trade figures of book imports underscore the fact that the print "revolution" was only partly carried out through expenditures for English learning. Other kinds of printed works from far outside the curriculum also clearly constituted the corpus of imports of which the English novel formed some portion, though we can only ascertain how much through indirect means.[12] Booksellers in the major cities routinely placed advertisements for newly acquired books and novels, listing them extensively by titles and volumes. Furthermore, printed library catalogues of the period listed book titles with places of publication, as did reviews in the domestic press. From these sources, we know that novels were imported in considerable numbers, although it remains impossible to establish what percentage of the total they made up.

The records of imports also help in establishing two salient issues regarding the print world in mid- and late-nineteenth-century India. First, print imports from Britain made up approximately 95 percent of the trade into India, with imports from Europe and the United States making up between 4 to 7 percent of annual totals. This monopoly can be attributed in part to the 3 percent "foreign" print tax the colonial authorities levied on imports from all countries other than Britain; it also helps substantiate why British books and ideas had such influence in the Subcontinent throughout the nineteenth century.

Second, the vast bulk of print, approximately 80 percent or more, arrived in the ports of Calcutta and Bombay. Not surprisingly, these presidency capitals were most visibly Europeanized in part because of their exposure to British administrative and cultural imports. Paradoxically, however, these two regions also produced India's most powerful anticolonial voices: both the 1857 Mutiny and the 1905 Swadeshi movement were inaugurated in Bengal, and the figure of Gandhi emerged most palpably from the Bombay Presidency.

If the exact content of print imports into India remains impossible to ascertain from the historical record, it is clear that a considerable

amount of what did not end up in the classroom found its way into rapidly emerging public libraries throughout the Subcontinent where
printed matter was made available to literate Indians, many of whom
did not, or could not, themselves purchase the books, magazines, and
newspapers that they so voraciously consumed. Membership in these
institutions varied considerably across classes and regions, and in many
ways a study of readership from extant library records may be the most
reliable way possible today to reconstruct how a cross-section of literate Indians approached the novel.

While it is, of course, correct to insist on the varied nature of the
"Indian reader" in the nineteenth century, it remains increasingly difficult to profile this figure with precision, and the sources that exist to
do so often seem unintentionally misleading. According to the census
of 1881, full literacy among Indian males was 6.6 percent, while at 0.3
percent it was considerably lower among females, suggesting that the
typical "reader" was male.[13] Yet James Long, an esteemed civil servant
in the Bengal Presidency commissioned to write a report on the culture
of print in India, notes: "Native females are very intelligent, many are
now learning to read from their husbands and brothers."[14] Even for
those who could not read, print was still available, according to Long
who further reports: "With Orientals, it is a common practice to be
read to, and hence numbers who cannot read themselves listen to those
who can. . . . We know a native who was for years employed by a rich
Babu to read 2 hours daily to 40 to 50 females in his house . . . women
sometimes sit in a circle round a woman who reads a book to them"
(xv). Long's testimony alerts one to the fact that despite the low female
literacy rate, women nonetheless had access to the world of print and
seemed to avail themselves of it in considerable numbers. Yet despite
his assertion, little "hard" data corroborate or amplify this in public
library circulation records of reading, and scholars have had to back-
track from the extremely few memoirs and biographies available to fill
in the many silences within the archive.[15]

Even when extant nineteenth-century circulation data from public
libraries begins to provide some sense of what Indian readers selected
for their leisure reading, it has remained difficult to retrieve a complete
picture of who these readers were. In this regard, I have envied Janice
Radway's access to her readers in *Reading the Romance* (1984), where a
number of enthusiasts from a midwestern town in the United States

provided her with detailed responses about why they read romance novels and what this reading did for them.[16] Meanwhile, Cathy Davidson whose readers in the early American republic, like mine, have long passed on, has shown with great subtlety and diligence the ways in which traces of their consumption survive in inscriptions and marginalia left over in the extant copies of early American fiction that form the core of her influential and inspiring study of the novel in an emerging nation.[17] Traces such as those Davidson has located have long vanished with the deterioration of paper that occurs in India's climate and the accompanying rapidity with which old books find a new market with the itinerant *raddiwalla*, or rag man, who has learned that libraries, rather than being just good customers are often reliable sellers as well. However, if Davidson's readers to a large extent have been anonymous, Carlo Ginzburg's have not: not only does *The Cheese and the Worms* (1976) name its reader, Menocchio, a sixteenth-century Italian miller, it also names the specific books Menocchio read during his lifetime, as well as his extensive and detailed responses to them as preserved in trial records from the Inquisition.[18]

To these accounts of researching a single genre (Radway), a small corpus (Davidson's one hundred titles), and a single individual's reading (Ginzburg), another should be added: Michael Denning's *Mechanic Accents* (1987) that, like this study, profiles long-deceased readers, this time of a prolific body of nineteenth-century American dime novels.[19] Denning's critical strategies and his theoretical insights illuminate many of the pages that follow—with one enviable difference, however. His task of portraying the reader was to some extent made easier by the novels themselves, which directly invoked and addressed their specific audience—a crucial detail entirely absent from the British novels circulating in India. Denning reveals how the dime novel of his study both shaped and was shaped by the working-class reading public toward whose concerns it addressed itself as it sought both to contain and give expression to its readers' social horizons. This kind of symbolic affiliation came to constitute the identity of dime novels, Denning demonstrates, recalling to mind Fredric Jameson's claim that literary genres are "a social contract between a writer and a *specific* public, whose function it is to specify the proper use of a particular cultural artifact."[20] Freed by distance and trade from any such contractual obligations, the British novel circulated in India among readers with substantially divergent dispositions and expectations than the British public for whom it was at least initially intended, thus rendering Denning's influential findings only partially applicable in my own research on the novel in empire. Having said that, each of these very different approaches to the consumption and the uses of fiction has nonetheless been enormously educative in helping me address a very real historical conundrum: how to sketch readers' identities from the details of their consumption of products that were never really intended for them in the first place.

The alternating silences and effusions in the British colonial archive in all its official and less official forms nevertheless underscore one significant point over and over again: namely, the unimaginable popularity of the British novel among Indian readers who actively chose this reading—and certain very specific forms within it—over any other kind available to them during the nineteenth century. Despite all that the colonial archive recalcitrantly withholds or ignores, it is this fact that powers my inquiry and that generates its questions. In other words, if the Indian readers' profile is hazy, their preferences are not, and it is to addressing the legacy of these absent and anonymous readers that this study is devoted.

Reading backward from census figures and sideways from membership rosters in public libraries, it is clear that through most of the nineteenth century Indian readership of the British novel was extremely wide-ranging, including civil servants of all ranks, university and school teachers, students of all sorts, householders and their women, minor ranks of the aristocracy, employees in the print and text industries, members of mercantile groups, and, toward the end of the nineteenth century, newly literate English readers from first- and second-generation rural backgrounds who had moved to cities, often for jobs in the colonial apparatus. These readers included Hindus, Muslims, Parsis, Sikhs, Jains, Buddhists, and Christians; they were obviously not of a single class or distinguished by a similar set of interests, yet what marks them, as we shall shortly see, was a shared preference for certain forms of the British novel. In this regard, the distinct identity that the British middle class bore in the nineteenth century and the sorts of cleavages that historians of the book have noted in reading tastes among "middle-class" readers in Britain (i.e., between lower- and middle-class and between lower-middle and working-class) do not really exist among readers in nineteenth-century India. A varied and often indistinct group ill-served by a purely class-derived label forms the reading public of nineteenth- and early-twentieth-century colonial India. It is predominantly but not exclusively male and largely but not entirely connected with urban centers.

Into a population, then, of which thirty-five individuals out of a thousand were literate, and some further fraction literate in English, insisting on any class-based identity such as "middle-class" for these readers further becomes deeply problematic because it is so imprecise and uneven, often with little correlation between economic and social markers. Moneylenders, merchants, farmers, and freeholders (just to name a few groups) do not comfortably fit into any conventional definition of this reading audience, either because their literacy did not extend into English or because they were only functionally literate. While in purely economic terms they may have been solidly bourgeois, they did not correspond to this aggregate community of readers of the English novel. The "reading public" is, therefore, not in any reasonable way "middle-class," nor collectively even of a single class.

While "westernized" might appear to be a more valid label for these readers, here again the variances are substantial: many Indian readers consumed the English novel but rejected westernization altogether, a theme revealingly played out in numerous Indian novels, most notably in Tagore's *The Home and the World* (1916) where Bimala and Sandeep show distinct preferences for novels but eschew most other forms of anglicist culture. Many others read the British novel only in the translations or adaptations into regional languages that began as early as 1835. The point that emerges and that the following pages corroborate, therefore, is that despite the internal cleavages between the groups that made up the reading public of the British novel in India, we do not note a corollary range or diversity in the preferences of Indian readers. There was a remarkable consistency in Indian readers' preference for the most popular forms as they circulated through libraries and reading rooms, and it is this popularity and consistency that I want to probe.

The emergence of Indian public libraries followed close upon the heels of English education. Libraries in this period went from being private collections, which housed mostly manuscripts for the sole provenance and purview of feudal rulers and aristocrats, to public and civic institutions that boasted community pride and interest in their mostly print collections. Public circulating libraries came to reflect a complex set of mutually dependent relationships within the communities of which they were part, functioning at times as extensions for schools and at other times as their substitute. They became almost immediately visible within the colonial landscape, with more established libraries often helping to start newer institutions in their cities. Some, such as the Calcutta Public Library (CPL), (established 1836) and the Madras Literary Society (established 1818) had both paying members as well as a policy of permitting entry gratis to students and "respectable strangers visiting the City."[21] Others were absolutely free. Some included both British and Indian users, most only Indians. A small village library in Bengal assesses the particular importance of public libraries to the development of the rural community in its annual report thus:

> Immediately after the establishment of schools in the villages, the reading public felt the necessity of circulating libraries to supplement the schools, and to supply them with sufficient food for the intellect. It was to meet this crying demand of the public that Babu Akshay Coomar Das . . . by dint of unflagging zeal and disinterested co-operation got up a collection of books hardly sufficient to fill an almirah and put up with the name, "Maju Public Library" in 1902. From a very small and modest beginning the library, nursed by the liberality and active sympathy of persons who have identified their cause with education has now developed into a very promising institution pretty well-equipped to cater for the reading public of Maju and its adjoining villages.[22]

These activities were not lost upon the colonial government who seemed to receive numerous requests for support in starting libraries or in funding them, as the following typical letter makes clear:

> In the month of March 1838, we received a letter from the Acting Judge at Ahmednuggur, stating that the Native community of that town had formed a Society for the Establishment of a "General Library"; but that the people being poor, would require some

assistance at the outset. He therefore solicited a pecuniary donation from Government, in aid of the institution and a few copies
of any works in the Native Languages which Government had at
its disposal; considering the object an excellent one, we requested
the sanction of the Government of India to grant a donation of
100 Rs. which that Government was pleased to sanction.[23]

The immediate—albeit often paternalist—assistance that the Company provided in order to support Indian library initiatives in the form
of grants, books, and later in the century, book subventions, gestures in
part to the openness and freedom with which books circulated and
were made available. The *Annual Reports of the Administration of the
Madras Presidency* include an index of "Scientific and Literary Societies" listed for the entire presidency. While this index also includes a
number of professional associations toward the end of the century, it is
for the most part a list of libraries and reading rooms present in the
region. Between 1887 and 1900, the number of scientific and literary
societies in the Madras Presidency increased almost threefold, from
146 institutions in 1887 to 401 in 1900. Annual membership figures
varied greatly in these institutions, from 5 members or visitors to
14,532 (a considerable range of readers that nonetheless remained relatively consistent across time). *Thacker's India Directory* indicates pro-
portionate increases in the number of libraries and reading rooms for
other regions as well: Calcutta went from having 49 libraries and reading rooms in 1886 to 137 in 1901, an almost threefold increase; while
the number of such institutions in Bombay increased more than five-
fold, from 13 in 1886 to 70 in 1901.[24]

The presence of these figures on institutions and their membership
makes it tempting to surmise that public institutions such as libraries
were closely monitored by the colonial authorities, possibly as venues
of sedition and anticolonial agitation. There is some speculation by
library historians in India that in the 1920s public libraries encountered
surveillance, but during the period of this study this was not the case.
Indeed, given the role that print eventually played in the anticolonial
struggle, it is remarkable that the British authorities were as sanguine
toward it as they appeared to be through much of the nineteenth century. Even after the 1857 Mutiny, no special procedures were instituted
to monitor print establishments and libraries, and what censure was

exercised was used in a few sporadic and celebrated cases against the newspapers only.[25]

Following the 1857 Mutiny, Reverend James Long was commissioned to assemble a *Report on the Native Press in Bengal*, and the document, written as it is by a highly respected educator and influential civil servant, is a striking indictment against any movement toward censorship. I cite from it at length, for it reveals both the conditions behind its composition (namely, concerns regarding the Mutiny) as well as the view of an informed and particularly scrupulous class of civil servants toward the robust world of print in India:

> The preparing of this Report on the Native Press, a work which involved far more laborious research than the author originally expected, was suggested by the mutiny of 1857. Much at that period was written and spoken on the subject of the Native Press, and many hasty remarks were made respecting it, while some said it was so radically corrupt that it ought to be abolished. It was found that on this ground as well as for statistical purposes, it was most desirable to test the question, as far as related to the Bengali Press, by an accurate investigation of the *facts* of the case. . . . Of late, some officials have proposed cutting the knot, and either suppressing the Native Press or establishing a rigorous censorship. We trust that the perusal of this report will show how suicidal any measure of the kind would be to the interests of good Government and sound education.[26]

Notwithstanding the "immense amount of irritation" that censorship "confined [only] to *natives*" would generate among their subjects, Long mildly inquired, "Who would be the Censor? . . . Few Europeans would have leisure or ability to act as censors, besides if a man held principles of some Europeans, he would condemn native sentiments as treasonable, even though in accordance with the Queen's Proclamation" (iii).

Given the obvious bias of those Europeans calling for censorship, Long viewed it a failed enterprise even before entertaining it as a possible policy choice. On the contrary, he argued that a free Native Press was more useful for colonial authorities, for it provided the astute administrator with a window into the soul of India from which he could freely gather public sentiment about the government. "The opinion of the Native Press may often be regarded as the safety valve which gives warning of danger," he concluded. Instead of an official censor, Long's report advocated the "patronising and encouragement of useful Vernacular Periodicals and Newspapers" (iv). Rather than restraining the print industry, Long used his considerable influence to promote a loosening of control and surveillance, a policy that was implemented and that officially continued more or less throughout the nineteenth century.[27]

Even when the 1867 Press and Registration of Books Act was initiated, it came about not through fears of another mutiny (it was enacted too many years after 1857 for there to be any suggestion that the revolt inspired this piece of legislation) but, rather, by the combined efforts of librarians at the British Museum and the India Office in London. These bibliographers asked for the legislation and its deposit mandate in order to assist them in acquiring books for their own collections. One of the consequences of this act has, however, been a boon to book historians: each presidency was required to print a list of every title published during the year, along with a general description of its contents, in order to assist library accessions in Britain. The result is the multivolume *Catalogue of Books Printed* (sometimes called the *Appendices to the Gazettes*) published quarterly in each presidency. Here again, the temptation to cry censorship is strong, except that the job of summarizing was often left to Indian scribes, who either through blindness or insight provided notably bland abstracts for volumes that were in fact marked by their anticolonial sentiments. Bankim Chandra Chatterjee's highly nationalist novel, *Anandamath* (1882), is summarized rather innocuously with the conclusion that the anticolonial rebels in the work, "perceive the necessity and wholesomeness of the English regime in India, and in the spirit of true patriots, break up their armed league," almost as if the reviewer were intentionally protecting the novelist from the authorities' attention.[28] This description of the work is only partly true, and Bankim's novel seemed to suffer no great restriction perhaps because of it. Indeed, during the nineteenth and twentieth centuries *Anandamath* was widely translated into virtually every major Indian language.[29]

A more striking intervention appears in the column summarizing one of the numerous translations of Lieutenant Colonel James Tod's *Annals and Antiquities of Rajasthan* (2 volumes, 1829–32), a work that had a dramatic and sustained effect on Indian readers. A scrupulous but fairly unassuming history of the warlike Rajputs of western India by a British civil servant, *Annals and Antiquities* inspired innumerable fables and romances of Indian glory in at least half a dozen languages, as well as an interest in history more generally among nineteenth-century Indian writers and novelists. The scribe who noted Gopal Chandra Mukharji's 1884 Bengali translation reported: "it is published in the hope that its perusal will rouse the historical sense of the Hindus, and enable them to understand their position as descendants of the brave, warlike, chivalrous and patriotic people whose achievement it records."[30] Rather than defusing or restraining nationalist sentiment, remarks such as these by Indian civil servants in official publications seem pointedly to fan it. The eye of the censor, it appears clear from these records, was either blind or indifferent to the print world of books in the nineteenth century, and at most only sporadically interested in that of newspapers.[31]

LIBRARIES AND THEIR USERS

While the statistics on the number of libraries and their members give us an idea of some of the venues through which books circulated in nineteenth-century India, library catalogues and extant circulation data provide a fuller sense of what was actually available (in the case of catalogues) and what actually circulated (in the case of loan data). It has remained every book historian's dream, both in India and elsewhere, to locate circulation records from a nineteenth-century public library in order to conduct a sustained intellectual history of reading alongside broader social and political trends. To the best of my knowledge, however, these data have proven extremely elusive. Among the closest anyone has come to them has been Paul Kaufman in his report on the lending records of the Bristol Library Society (a subscription library) between 1773 and 1784. As Kaufman recounts it, these records were discovered "from the upper storey of the Museum and Library" in 1889 and have been known to scholars ever since because they included a record of Southey's and Coleridge's borrowings between 1793 and 1798.[32] Frank Robinson and P. J. Wallace of Newcastle-upon-Tyne have indexed records of books published by subscription from 1617 to

1973.[33] Given the publishing trend toward a rapid decline in print by subscription, however, the index is of little use to those surveying the entire circulation and production of print in the nineteenth century. Meanwhile, in his work on publishing in prerevolutionary France, Robert Darnton rues the absence of individual book purchase or circulation records but presses on anyway to make a case, based on the Société-typographique de Neuchâtel's (STN) sales records to French booksellers, for the influence of "forbidden best-sellers" upon the revolution. The STN archives, Darnton argues, "provide an exceptional opportunity to follow the flow of literary demand, title by title, and to trace the supply of books to local markets everywhere in France . . . [by which] one can discover which books sold best" and thus, presumably, arrive at some reliable sense of readership.[34] In this regard, Darnton is following Kaufman's lead of some quarter-century earlier: sales records and library catalogues provide a rough index of what was considered "vendible" (Kaufman's term) and are, therefore, of great interest to book historians—although as Kaufman cautions, "they are no sure index of what actually were borrowed [or read]."[35] Acknowledging the paucity of hard data in his work on forbidden best-sellers, Darnton nevertheless counters with the proposition that "our knowledge of production and distribution can compensate to a certain extent for the limitations of our knowledge of reception" (184).

In an attempt to arrive at a more substantial sense of reception, a number of book historians have tried to do just as Darnton suggests: to extrapolate from data on production and circulation in order to come closer to knowing how books might have been received and read. Some historians have researched entire fields of textual production in nineteenth-century Britain from print sources such as the London *Publisher's Circular* in order to isolate microtrends such as the rise of juvenile fiction alongside the decline of travel writing in the latter half of the nineteenth century.[36] Others have focused exclusively on fiction and the "fiction industry," using data on publishing and distribution to arrive at some broader understanding of the role of readers in the production and consumption of fiction in Victorian England.[37] One could multiply these examples and their research strategies many times, but the point remains that circulation data from public libraries have proven extremely difficult to come by; Bristol, after all, was a private subscription library, which skews the data toward a narrow class of readers, thus rendering it difficult to apply more broadly.

One wonders now whether a full set of nineteenth-century lending records would prove that useful after all: the conclusions one could draw from a single library's circulation would need to rest closest to the regional, class, and social history of that library only and could probably not be applied too widely before becoming irrelevant. For instance, the conclusions drawn from a public library in London might be irrelevant to Salisbury or Bath readers with their very different intellectual and social profiles, while those drawn from a Calcutta library would likewise be too narrow to be broadly applied to colonial India as a whole. The diachronic presentation that follows in this study is in part an attempt to avoid these kinds of ahistorical pitfalls where, forced by the paucity of hard data, one particular decade is made to stand in for the entire nineteenth century, or one particular region made to represent all of colonial India. In fact, one has to ask whether the lack of the golden fleece has not made book history a richer field after all, as book historians have found creative and robust ways of boring in on the history of print in order to isolate information on readership. Lacking the direct route, book historians have had to take unexpected detours through distribution (Sutherland, Darnton) and production (Eliot, among numerous others), thereby illuminating the entire sociology of print more clearly than if they had simply studied library circulation records.[38]

For my own study, I did not find loan records of the kind Kaufman reports for Bristol in the eighteenth century. I found, however, general statistics on borrowing made by two Indian libraries in the nineteenth century. These statistics were compiled by the individual libraries themselves and were included in the library's annual and biannual reports. The Bagbazar Library in Calcutta (established 1883) seems to have divined the task of later historians, for it further tabulates the various classes of books in stock (history, geography, science, fiction, drama, etc.) as well as books issued by category and language during the year. Meanwhile, the Calcutta Public Library compiled continuous statistics on circulation between 1847 and 1893 under two categories only— "general literature" and "prose works of imagination"—already indicating the attention that fiction was attracting among nineteenth-century readers in Indian public libraries.[39] Along with subscription figures, acquisition records, and published catalogues, we can thus begin to make an educated assessment of what circulated in colonial India and, perhaps even, to whom. Public libraries in Bombay and Madras provided variations on this data, and along with their catalogues and Kaufman's injunction that public libraries mostly carried only "vendible" material, we can begin to make a reasoned estimate of what books were available in nineteenth-century India for leisure reading.

The Calcutta Public Library. Momentarily bracketing my earlier reservations about letting the Bengal Presidency stand in for the rest of India, it makes sense to begin my story with the Calcutta Public Library, established in 1836 as the result of a heroic collaboration between Indians and Britons. The institution was founded in part to commemorate Acting Governor General Charles Metcalfe's Act XI of 1835, which abolished press restrictions and granted freedom of expression to all in British India. The Metcalfe Press Law as it came to be called was in fact drafted by none other than Thomas Babington Macaulay. In promoting its legislation, Metcalfe (called a "Romantic," by Eric Stokes) justified his action with the view that "I look to the increase of knowledge with a hope that it may strengthen our empire; that it may remove prejudices, soften asperities, and substitute rational conviction of the benefits of our Government; that it may unite the people and their rulers in sympathy, and that the differences that separate them may be gradually lessened, and ultimately annihilated."[40] In gratitude, a number of Calcutta residents, both British and Indian, raised the capital to build a library and persuaded the governor of Bengal to donate a substantial plot of land for the purpose. From the "Resolutions passed at a Meeting of the Inhabitants of Calcutta . . . on Thursday, the 20th August 1835," we learn that "the Building which shall be ornamental and Commodious be offered free of rent and in trust for the reception of a public subscription Library to be formed on a scale and conducted in a liberal manner worthy of this metropolis."[41]

The Calcutta Public Library is historically important in part because of these origins: it was a public subscription library insistent on the liberality of its provisions, as well as being expressly set up with the fiscal, political, and ideological collaboration between Indians and the British. The Bombay General Library preceded it by half a decade, and the Madras Literary Society by almost two, yet the latter was almost exclusively intended for British users and the former almost exclusively for Indians. We will turn to the Bombay Library later, in chapter 3, but for the moment the Calcutta Public Library testifies to the importance placed on institutions of its kind by both groups of colonial society. The largest contributions to endow the CPL came from Indians, including Dwarkanath Tagore, Rabindranath's grandfather, whom Dickens commemorated after his death as "the Oriental Croesus."[42] The library eventually absorbed into it several smaller libraries for government officials and became the Imperial Library in 1903; following Independence, it became the National Library of India in 1948. With the formation of the Imperial Library, the CPL ceased to be a public circulation library and became instead a reference and deposit library for research material on India. Despite this eventual shift in the early twentieth century, the Calcutta Public Library began as and remained throughout the nineteenth century a public circulating library, and its holdings and policies during this period document a civic and institutional ideology beginning to be practiced throughout India in which all readers had and could exercise freedom of access to and choice in their reading.

Inspired by the success of this institution, a number of wealthy *zamindars* started libraries modeled on it on their rural estates around Bengal, and substantial public libraries, patronized exclusively by Indian users, soon appeared in Midnapore (established 1851), Jessore, Rangpur, Bogra, Barishal and Hooghly (all established 1854), Krishnanagar (established 1856), Konnagar (established 1858) and Uttarpara (established 1859). The *Report of the Calcutta Public Library* for 1851 indicates the active role the library often played in supporting these institutions: "The committee feels much interested in the establishment and well-working of libraries in the Mofussil. A few duplicates [of books and periodicals] were presented during the last year to the Howrah Institute and it would no doubt further the objects of this Institution to render similar aid to other mofussil libraries from time to time."[43] In 1854, the report indicates a further offspring, this time in Calcutta itself:

A Resolution was passed at the last annual meeting, appointing the Rajah Pertaup Chunder Singh, Baboo Ramanauth Tagore, and Mr. P. S. D'Rozario, as a consequence to act with the Curators for the purpose of establishing a Branch Library in the Native part of the Town, experimentally, for one year, if they were of opinion that it would likely be attended with success. The curators agreed to make over to the Branch Library such old furniture and duplicates of periodicals and books as might not be required.

(10–11)

In the first half of the nineteenth century, the Calcutta Public Library became exemplary not only for promulgating Metcalfe's views on the value of increasing knowledge and "uniting the people and their rulers in sympathy," but also for the openness with which it responded to its reading public, both Indian and European. Its annual reports reflect the kind of liberal thinking on library access and collection development that eventually marked the growth of public libraries in Britain following the 1850 Ewart Act, as well as in the United States during the same period.[44] These reports further testify to the importance placed upon readers' requests in developing the collection, and they provide a useful index when the library's catalogue is analyzed. For example, in the CPL's 1850 report, the Committee on Selection documented a complaint from the membership regarding the "paucity of fiction" in the library's holdings, to which the committee responded by reminding members that the library was intended to be a "general library combining the advantages of a library of reference and resort with those of a circulating library." The complaint was noted, however, and the committee revised its instructions to local booksellers, indicating that "it has since been deemed necessary to increase the number of copies of the works of some of the novelists and authors of established reputation . . . with a view of meeting the increased demand for works of the most popular novelists" (9–10).

More interestingly, the topic of readerly taste in popular fiction persisted in 1854, for the report for that year indicates that it continued to receive the selection committee's "anxious consideration." However, rather than capitulating to readerly requests for more fiction this time, as it appeared to have done in the 1850 report cited above, the selection committee in 1854 asserted its indignation at the pervasive interest in popular fiction, and it retrenched with the following statement:

> The nature of reform [the selection committee] purpose[s] is to exclude as much as possible works of questionable reputation, and secure the early addition of only such publications as are useful and interesting. It was thought necessary to destroy the copies of the "Mysteries of London" which the Library possessed, in consequence of the very objectionable nature of its contents.　　(6)

If the story had ended here, we might have concluded with a fairly good instance of mild censorship and of institutional will asserting itself over public demand, Lord Charles Metcalfe's earlier ideals be damned. We could have used this report and the library's published catalogues to draw all sorts of conclusions about how ideological and institutional wills drove public library collections in India, and we could have tried to use these collections in turn to document the manner in which libraries and books were harnessed by the imperial project of creating perfect colonial subjects through the almost exclusive selection of "useful and interesting" books. We could, in other words, have exposed the masks of conquest behind British rule in India.

Fortunately, the archive provides for a corrective salvo that unmakes this possibility. First, the reports provide us with the total number of subscribers to the library each year, an important fact to record because despite its middle name, the Calcutta Public Library was after all both

FIGURE 2.2　Indian Subscribers to the Calcutta Public Library, 1861–1892

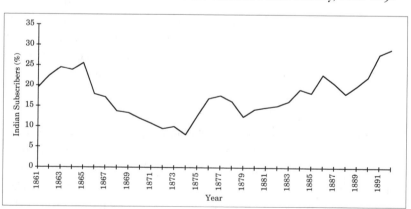

SOURCE: *Report of the Calcutta Public Library for 1847–93* (Calcutta: Sanders, Cones, 1847–1893).

public and subscription, with four classes of paying members contributing from Rs. 6 to Rs. 1 per month. Using these statistics on membership, we can assess the library's relative health within the community. In the years following the 1854 report declaring the selection committee's high-handed purchase of "useful and interesting publications" rather than the fiction requested by members, things did not seem to be going so well. Subscription numbers decreased dramatically from 4,703 total subscribers to the library in 1856 to 2,128 in 1872, a decline of 55 percent. Figure 2.2 charts, in part, the decline in Indian members especially evident between 1864 and 1874.

In an entirely separate document entitled, *Finances of the Calcutta Public Library, Report of the Subcommittee Appointed on the 10th February 1873*, we learn what might have caused this precipitous decline in membership at an institution that began in such solid fiscal health with such robust public support. The subcommittee's report not only outlines the cause for the decline in membership but also provides a solution to it, and it is worth citing in full for its significance:

> A mere increase of funds for buying books will, however, be of little avail in making the library popular, *unless the tastes of the subscribers, who in fact support the Library are consulted* by allowing the subscribers to be fully represented in the governing body, as regards the selection and purchase of books. To illustrate this, we append a statement compiled from the various annual reports of the number of sets of books purchased in each year from 1858 [to 1872]. . . . It has been shown in a previous paragraph that *three-fourths of the circulation consists of novels and periodicals, while it appears here that nearly two-thirds of the books purchased in 1870 and 1872 consisted of graver reading, so that the purchases did not harmonise with the prevailing taste.* (20–21; emphases added)

The subcommittee's report identifies the major problem confronting the library—namely, the drastic fall in membership—as well as its solution—"to harmonise purchases with prevailing tastes." Later reports do not mention whether this proposal was actually carried out, and a look at the 1894 *Catalogue of the Calcutta Public Library* would appear to suggest that it was in fact largely ignored. Yet, when I examined the library's more recently compiled card catalogue of actual holdings, I discovered over fifty titles in mid- and late-nineteenth-century imprints of the very same G. W. M. Reynolds whose *Mysteries of London* the librarians had reportedly purged in 1854 due to "the very objectionable nature of [their] contents."

It seems, then, that in the end, readerly preferences prevailed robustly over the selection committee's objections and that holdings in public libraries inevitably reflected public taste, with little lasting interference or impact from the pieties of the higher-ups. I by no means intend to suggest that the libraries ever fully gave up their attempts to improve or educate public taste. Rather, the record seems to adumbrate the futility of these efforts in the long run, as readers began to vote with their feet and their subscription fees, leaving libraries in hordes when their tastes were ignored or rejected. Indian readers exercised their preferences particularly pointedly as figure 2.2 demonstrates: after the stark decline in subscriptions to the Calcutta Public Library by the early 1870s that followed the earlier antifiction policies, the percentage of Indian members increased threefold from a low of 10 percent of total subscribers in 1873 to almost 30 percent in 1893 when purchasing trends converged with readerly demands for fiction.

Part of the reason behind the overall decline in membership to the

FIGURE 2.3 Circulation of Books (Calcutta Public Library, 1847–1892)

SOURCE: *Report of the Calcutta Public Library for 1847–93* (Calcutta: Sanders, Cones, 1847–1893).

Calcutta Public Library seems to have been a fallout in the shared civic sympathy between Indians and the British as the century wore on. One library historian declared that this occurred, "due to the mistrust between [the groups]," and while that is certainly part of the reason, a fuller explanation derives from the fact that the total number of public libraries was also increasing all over Calcutta and that many of these were "public" in the real sense, with no membership fees at all.[45] Rather than being the only institution of its kind, the Calcutta Public Library now had competitors, many of whom it had earlier encouraged, and these competitors had learned to satisfy readerly taste without raising the objections enumerated by their more aristocratic colleague. Institutions such as the Burra Bazar Family Literary Club (established 1857), the Chaitanya Library & Beadon Square Literary Club, the Hindu Literary Society (established 1876), the Mahomedan Literature Society (established 1863), and the Bagbazar Reading Library (established 1883), were some of the many new libraries and reading rooms serving Indian users exclusively that had begun to flourish.

From extant annual reports, we can gather something of the culture of libraries in the latter half of the nineteenth century in order to complement what we have already learned of the first half from the Calcutta Public Library. Fiction, or "Prose Works of Imagination" as it was called by the CPL, made up approximately one third of the CPL's total holdings, yet it circulated more than two-and-a-half times more often than "General Literature," which constituted everything else (i.e., history, biography, voyages, philosophy, science, theology, medicine, fine arts and poetry, East Indies, law, miscellaneous). Figure 2.3 schematically represents the circulation of fiction from the Calcutta Public Library in relation to other categories of holdings, and it clarifies several matters. Although fiction dominated the circulation rosters throughout, in the period up till 1863, when membership was at its height, the circulation of "general literature" managed to parallel that of fiction almost exactly. However, following the decline of membership in the late 1860s, this pattern was broken: fiction continued to forge ahead in circulation, while general literature inversely reflected the circulation of fiction. This was a period, as we have already noted, when Indian membership at the CPL was proportionally gaining ground, and the continued robustness in the circulation of fiction over that of general literature may in part be due to the loyalty of this segment of the library's users.

Bagbazar Public Library. The Bagbazar Reading Library in Calcutta, a small neighborhood library established entirely by and for "middle-class native gentlemen," reported similar figures for its holdings in 1902: fiction in both Bengali and English (in roughly equal numbers) together made up a third of the library's holdings, although it circulated almost three times as often as everything else. Unlike the CPL, the Bagbazar Reading Library seems much more sanguine about this tendency in reading tastes:

> The enormous preponderance of fiction and the comparatively small attention paid to more serious literature are no doubt to be regretted, but they indicate the tendency of the age from which Bengali society is by no means free. It is hoped that the progress of education and a due appreciation of the requirements of practical life will lead to a more reasonable distribution of the readers' patronage.[46]

Table 2.1 lists these data on library holdings and circulation, and figures 2.4 and 2.5 graphically make visible these stunning proportions, as

TABLE 2.1 Circulation of Books by Category
(Bagbazar Reading Library, 1902)

	In Stock		Issued	
	ENGLISH	BENGALI	ENGLISH	BENGALI
Fiction	802	903	524	5,306
Poetry/Drama	109	964	13	897
History	279	61	47	53
Biography	178	162	19	152
Science/philosophy	133	123	28	32
Travels	86	37	10	51
Literature and essays	126	134	39	63
Religion	42	241	3	119
Miscellaneous	535	488	65	445
TOTAL:	2,290	3,113	748	7,118

SOURCE: *Report of the Bagbazar Reading Library for the 19th Year Ending on June 1902* (Calcutta: K. P. Mookerjee, 1903).

well as the extent to which the circulation of all other categories of holdings was dwarfed by that of fiction at the Bagbazar Library.

Specifically, in the Bagbazar's distribution, the circulation of fiction made up 74 percent of the total circulation of books, followed by poetry and drama at almost 12 percent of the borrowing requests, then miscellaneous (6.5 percent), biography (2.1 percent), religion (1.6 percent), and history (1.3 percent). Unusually then, we see that the taste for fiction (over 90 percent of which circulated in Bengali) did not spill over to requesting other imaginative or narrative genres, such as travel,

FIGURE 2.4 Proportion of Fiction Holdings to Circulation
(Bagbazar Reading Library, 1902)

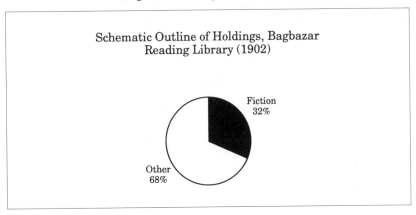

Schematic Outline of Holdings, Bagbazar
Reading Library (1902)

Fiction
32%

Other
68%

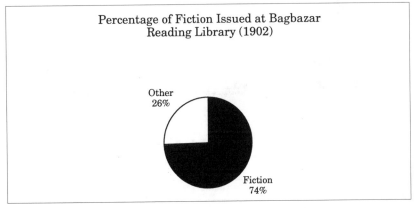

Percentage of Fiction Issued at Bagbazar
Reading Library (1902)

Other
26%

Fiction
74%

SOURCE: *Report of the Bagbazar Reading Library for the 19th Year Ending on June 1902* (Calcutta: K. P. Mookerjee, 1903).

biography, or even history, a pattern that was often visible in British public libraries of the same period.

The circulation profile from these two libraries in Calcutta makes the following general patterns visible: first, that while fiction constituted approximately a third of the total holdings in each library, it was requested two-and-a-half to three times more often than other forms. In the Calcutta Public Library, fiction circulated almost entirely in English, while in the Bagbazar Library, it did so in Bengali. Second, we learn that both libraries noted this readerly tendency toward fiction, the CPL with alarm and the Bagbazar with relative equanimity. Yet the persistence of the fiction holdings in both libraries as evidenced in their reports and catalogues makes clear that neither institution was in much of a position to change matters: readers, it seemed, exercised a considerable voice over what they wanted to read, and the libraries were more or less forced either to oblige or to risk losing members. From this we can begin, at least preliminarily, to corroborate Paul Kaufman's point

FIGURE 2.5 Book Circulation (Bagbazar Reading Library, 1902)

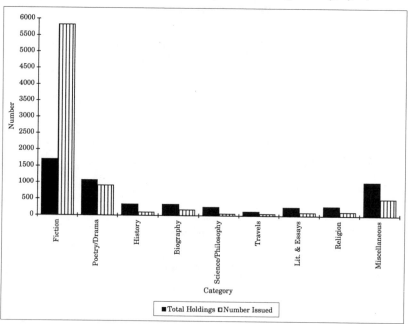

SOURCE: *Report of the Bagbazar Reading Library for the 19th Year Ending on June 1902* (Calcutta: K. P. Mookerjee, 1903).

on catalogues: that they are a single, albeit invaluable, index to readerly taste in the sense that they signify what was considered acquisition-worthy at the time, although not, of course, what actually circulated. Finally, G. W. M. Reynolds's fate at the CPL alerts us to one crucial axis of readerly taste in India, which veered toward books considered to be "objectionable" or of "demoralizing tendency" that nonetheless circulated and found a home in public library holdings at least in Calcutta.

Before drawing wider conclusions from these three preliminary observations, it is worth establishing whether they remain valid for public libraries in other regions of India as well. The Calcutta Public Library and Bagbazar Library are the only institutions I found that reported borrowing statistics for the nineteenth century. The Connemara Public Library in Madras (established 1896 and public in the true sense with no admission or membership charge) provides useful data on book circulation within general categories for approximately twenty years, from 1910 to 1932, but in order to know what books were available for circulation in the nineteenth century, we will have to rely on published catalogues, of which a small number are extant.

One other possible source, largely though not exclusively for Bombay, is the daily *Times of India*, regarded as the government newspaper, which nonetheless ran front-page advertisements several times a week for books "just arrived by steamer," available in various libraries patronized by Indians and British, some jointly and some separately. To the extent that these advertisements provide us with an index of what was deemed popular by the booksellers, we can begin to assemble a list of approximately twenty of the most popular titles among Indian readers in the nineteenth century.[47] By using sources as widely as possible in concert with each other (i.e., advertisements next to catalogues next to circulation statistics next to translation records), we can generate a picture that despite its discontinuities provides a rough outline of what was considered "popular," "vendible," and of interest to Indian readers after the novel was introduced into the cultural and literary landscape.

Examining extant catalogues from fourteen public libraries catering almost exclusively to Indians spread out in Bombay (3), Calcutta (4) and its environs (1), Madras (3), Delhi (1), Allahabad (1), and Patna (1), I generated a master list of all the European authors available to Indian readers in the nineteenth century. Working from this list, I compiled further a shortlist of notably "vendible" authors who were present in multiple copies or in multiple titles at any of the libraries. Two hundred and seven writers, the vast majority British, fall within this shortlist. Finally, I isolated authors who were available in all, or virtually all, the libraries in order to factor in (or out) any regional variances or collection eccentricities. The twenty-two authors in this final list form the corpus of those most consistently available to Indian readers in public

TABLE 2.2 Novelists in Indian Library Catalogues, I

AUTHOR	NUMBER OF LIBRARIES	BRITISH BEST SELLER
Bulwer-Lytton, Edward	14	√
Scott, Sir Walter	14	√
Dickens, Charles	13	√
Disraeli, Benjamin	13	√
Thackeray, William	13	—
Corelli, Marie	12	—
Crawford, F. Marion	12	√
Dumas, Alexandre	12	—
Eliot, George	12	√
Kingsley, Charles	12	√
Marryat, Captain Frederick	12	—
Reynolds, G. W. M.	12	√
Taylor, Philip Meadows	12	—
Ainsworth, William	11	√
Braddon, Mary Elizabeth	11	√
Collins, Wilkie	11	√
Doyle, Sir Arthur Conan	11	—
Harte, Bret	11	—
James, G. P. R.	11	—
Lever, Charles	11	—
Reade, Charles	11	√
Stevenson, R. L.	11	√

(TABLE 2.2 *continued on next page*)

libraries during the period between roughly 1850 to 1901. The first two columns of table 2.2 list these authors as well as indicate in how many of the fourteen library catalogues they appeared.

Two novelists, Bulwer-Lytton and Scott, appeared in all fourteen library catalogues; a further three—Dickens, Disraeli, and Thackeray—in thirteen out of fourteen; another eight—Corelli, Crawford, Dumas, Eliot, Kingsley, Marryat, Reynolds, and Taylor—in twelve out

TABLE 2.2 *continued*

SOURCES: *Alphabetical Catalogue of the Punjab Public Library* Rev. ed. (Lahore: Victoria Press, 1897); *Catalogue of the Printed Books of European Languages in Khuda Baksh Oriental Public Library, Patna* (Patna: Liberty Art Press, 1918); *Catalogue and Index of the Allahabad Public Library* (Allahabad: Indian Press, 1927); *The Bhuleshwar Library Catalogue of Books* (Bombay: Ripon Printing Press, 1895); *The Bombay Native General Library Catalogue of Books* (Bombay: Jehangier B. Marzban, 1898); *The Jamsetjee Nesserwanjee Petit Fort Reading Room and Library, Bombay Classified Catalogue of Books* (Bombay: Captain Printing Press, 1895); *Catalogue of the Delhi Public Library* (Delhi: n.p., 1902); *Calcutta Chaitanya Library Catalogue of English Books* (Calcutta: n.p., 1903); *Duke Public Library, Howrah Classified Catalogue of Books* (Calcutta: n.p., 1931); *Catalogue of Books in the Uttarpara Public Library* (Calcutta: Gupta Press, 1903); *Catalogue of the Calcutta Public Library* (Calcutta: Sanders, Cones, 1855); *Catalogue of the Calcutta Public Library: Part I—Prose Works of Fiction in the English and the French Language* (Calcutta: Bharat Mihir Press, 1894); *Catalogue of the Bengal Club Library* (Calcutta: n.p., 1889); *Catalogue of the Library of the United Service Club, Calcutta* (Calcutta: n.p., 1892); *Catalogue of Books in the Library of the Literary Society at Madras* (Madras: J. B. Pharoah, 1839); *Catalogue of the Madras Literary Society* (Madras: Government Press, 1891); *The Catalogue of Books of the Oriental and Mixed Library, Bangalore* (Madras: Addison, 1899).

of fourteen collections; and a final nine—Ainsworth, Braddon, Collins, Doyle, Harte, James, Lever, Reade, and Stevenson—in eleven out of the fourteen library collections. In other words, all of these twenty-two authors appeared in at least 80 percent of the total libraries surveyed. The fourteen catalogues are a far cry from providing circulation statistics for the entire country; yet what they do provide is a set of trends for the country that we can compare across regions, scrutinize, and evaluate alongside other data such as that on translation that follows.

Scanning the list quickly, roughly 60 percent of the authors are recognizable today, with the remaining 40 percent (figures such as Corelli, Crawford, Marryat, Reynolds, Taylor) known mostly to specialists and experts in Victorian literature. This fact itself merits some attention. Part of what has fueled research into popular fiction and best-sellers is the sense that these non- and anticanonical forms attest to ideological and cultural contestations of their time with great—sometimes greater—clarity and acuity than works that subsequently assume canonical status and stability. These popular forms are frequently seen to represent emerging social formations often before they assume discrete shape, to gesture toward social and ideological frictions of the time in raw and unsophisticated ways that nonetheless explain both their popularity and their historical demise. Moreover, as Jane Tompkins has persuasively argued in her work on the predominance of sentimental fiction in nineteenth-century America: "the work of the sentimental writers is complex and significant in ways *other than* those that characterize the established masterpieces."[48] In returning to study these works, Tompkins has compellingly revealed the sentimental novel's dramatization of contemporary social and political struggles alongside its "solutions" to them, which has helped redirect subsequent understanding of the power of popular, "feminized" fiction in America. In general then, popular literature is supposed to shed light upon its world in a way in which canonical or "high" literature is often not able to: it is about a world in motion, about conflicts, struggles, and issues before they are sorted out, compromised, and fashioned into Historical Events. And, of course, popular literature is popular. It is a literature of the moment, read by those for the moment.

Throughout the nineteenth century many British writers who later became "canonical" were also immensely popular (e.g., Fielding, Scott, and Dickens).[49] "Popularity" and "canonicity" are, therefore, not fundamentally opposed categories, since the market that determines the popularity of a work also often weighs in on canonizing it. The point I therefore wish to stress is that the notion of "popular" highlights a reading response always and only of the moment, while "canonicity" represents the corroborative judgment of a subsequent, retrospective evaluation. Sometimes the two converge, as in the case of Scott and Dickens, to cite two authors from table 2.2; at other times they diverge sharply, as in the case of best-sellers such as G. W. M. Reynolds and Marie Corelli.

To return to the Indian list in table 2.2, then, what is immediately striking is how *safe* and stable a list it is. Sixty percent of its titles are recognizable and still reprinted and read today. Indian readers, it seems, read fairly conventionally; either that or they were very good predictors and perhaps even makers of literary canons. It is tempting at this stage to speculate that Indian readerly taste was pedestrian and imitative and that the colonial grip on culture was so marked that Indian readers stuck to the "good" books of Scott and Dickens that the colonial authorities wished them to read. However, if we compare the Indian list with a list of best-selling fiction in nineteenth-century Britain (I have used Richard Altick's scrupulously assembled and revised lists), we see that again, almost 60 percent of the novelists most available in Indian libraries were also among those most popular in Britain.[50] Here too, it is tempting to carry on the line of speculation above, but there is something in this last comparison that alerts one to its prematurity. The two statistics above appear totally contradictory. The first, on the conservatism of the list, alerts us to the possible fact that nineteenth-century Indian readers were imitative; but the second raises the question: Why only 60 percent of the time? Popular fiction, as indexed by best-seller lists, speaks to its readers in different ways. Comparing the so-called Indian canon with Altick's British list makes one aware that 60 percent is a considerably large percentage of popular books for Indian readers to share with their British counterparts; it is also paradoxically not large enough.

There is something striking in the fact that readers so far apart in culture and sociology as those in Britain and India should share a taste in popular fiction as substantial as the 60 percent figure documents. The disparity in their positions vis-à-vis each other and the unevenness of the cultural situation would suggest that the popular lists would be completely discrepant, which would suggest a zero, or negligible, overlap between the British and Indian most popular lists. However, since Indian readers were reading under a colonial rule, it is tempting to argue they were reading with less of a free hand than they might otherwise have had; that they were reading what they ought to, not what they freely wished to. If this were the case, however, the Indian canon should reveal colonial readers fulfilling the ideological and cultural dictates of their situation and reflecting a close-to-complete overlap with the interests of the colonial state. Poetry, not fiction, ought to characterize their reading.

Something in the Indian taste for English novels—60 percent of which it shares with British counterparts, 40 percent of which it does not—prompts the need to scrutinize more closely not just what Indians were reading in the nineteenth century but how and, if possible, why. Before we address these larger issues, one final set of data on the circulation of novels.

THE NOVEL IN TRANSLATION

Alongside the list of novelists available to Indian readers in English, we also have access to which writers were translated during the nineteenth century. If library catalogues index "vendible" authors, then the translation lists index the most "readable" ones, for they indicate what books were voluntarily translated into Indian languages by particularly devoted readers. In the nineteenth-century cottage industry of translation, with its paltry remuneration, a translator had to be notably enthusiastic about a book, or the book had to promise success before it was worth the expense and exercise of translating it.

The exceptions to this were those volumes translated with the help or support of the colonial authorities. By mid-century, it had become clear that education was leaving a substantial population of Indians behind and that part of the reason lay in the obstacles to mastering English. In 1851 a Vernacular Literature Society was inaugurated in Bengal, in part modeled upon the Society for the Diffusion of Useful Knowledge (established 1827). Its goal was to publish readable Bengali translations of popular English books and to ensure their availability.[51] The Reverend James Long, along with numerous wealthy Indians including Jaykrishna Mukherjee (founder of the Uttarpara Public

Library in 1859), supported the project and selected and supervised the translations. H. Pratt, another founder of the society, expounded upon its wider cultural aims: "To make the acquisition of the English language the sole condition upon which twenty-five millions of people shall obtain access to the stores of valuable information which are in the possession of their rulers is a gross injustice: that such a system must deprive the great mass of the native population of all means of improvement or progress; and perpetuate the great evils which have ever been so prevalent in the East—that of making learning a class distinction."[52] With its intention of broadening the reach of English books into Indian homes, the society flourished for a time, both creating and feeding a taste for certain kinds of popular literature. In 1975 Nilmani Mukherjee assessed the society's work in "[giving] thousands of men and women a shared background of popular culture and [helping] to mould their literary tastes."[53]

Table 2.3 lists the authors, both British and foreign, most translated and "adapted" into Indian languages in the nineteenth century. The list comes from several sources, each reliable but none fully exhaustive. The quarterly *Catalogue of Books Printed* for each presidency, also known as *Appendices to the Gazettes*, were compiled by colonial officials and listed all books published in the particular presidency. These lists were then submitted to the librarians at the India Office and the British Museum, who used them to select Indian books for acquisition in their own collections. The lists became systematic after the passage of the Press and Registration of Books Act of 1867.[54] Additionally, the most useful source to round out our knowledge of what books were translated into Indian languages is the set of meticulous catalogues compiled by J. F. Blumhardt, the legendary, polyglot librarian of the British Museum for works in Hindustani, Marathi, Gujarati, Bengali, Oriya, and Assamese, and by his colleagues, L. D. Barnett and G. U. Pope, librarians for books in Tamil and Telugu.[55] These catalogues only reflect those Indian titles actually purchased by the British Museum, and while the library's purview was wide, it was not exhaustive. Fortunately, however, as we will see in the case of Reynolds, purchases were consistently made of multiple translations of the same title as well as for reissues or new editions of translations even when made by the same translator, each of which is so identified. The Blumhardt and Barnett and Pope catalogues are the best index we have of translated material,

TABLE 2.3 Works Translated or Adapted Into Indian Languages

Pre-19th-Century Writers	19th-Century Writers	Non-British Works
Defoe *Robinson Crusoe (VLS)	Bulwer-Lytton Last Days of Pompeii Rienzi Leila	Aesop's Fables (VLS)
Fielding Amelia	Collins Woman in White	H. C. Andersen Various short stories (VLS)
Goldsmith *Vicar of Wakefield (VLS) Traveller Deserted Village	Reynolds *Mysteries of London *Mysteries of the Court of London *Mary Price *The Seamstress *Loves of the Harem *Soldier's Wife *Joseph Wilmot Rye House Plot *The Young Duchess *Mary Queen of Scots *Rosa Lambert *Faust	*Arabian Nights Boccacio Decameron Cervantes Don Quixote Dumas The Count of Monte Cristo Lésage Gil Blas Hugo *Les Misérables
Johnson *Rasselas		
Swift *Gulliver's Travels Voyage to Brobdignag	Scott Ivanhoe *Lady of the Lake Bride of Lamermoor Kenilworth *Lay of the Last Minstrel *Marmion	Saint-Pierre *Paul et Virginie (VLS) Stowe *Uncle Tom's Cabin (VLS)

TABLE 2.3 Works Translated or Adapted Into Indian Languages (*continued*)

Pre-19th-Century Writers	19th-Century Writers	Non-British Works
	Taylor	Sue
	*Tara	*Les Mystères de Paris*
	Confessions of a Thug,	
	One unidentified by title	Verne
		Twenty-Thousand Leagues
		Under the Sea
		Around the World in
		Eighty Days

Note: Each of the titles was translated into at least three Indian languages.

* denotes titles that were translated into four or more languages.

"VLS" indicates those works translated under the aegis of the Bengal Vernacular Literature Society (though it ought to be mentioned that numerous other works such as Scott's poetry and *Arabian Nights* had the clear approval, if not sponsorship, of the society).

SOURCES: L. D. Barnett, *A Catalogue of the Telugu Books in the Library of the British Museum* (London: British Museum, 1912); Barnett, *A Supplementary Catalogue of Tamil Books in the Library of the British Museum* (London: British Museum, 1931); Barnett, and G. U. Pope, *A Catalogue of the Tamil Books in the Library of the British Museum* (London: British Museum, 1909); J. F. Blumhardt, *Catalogue of Hindustani Printed Books in the Library of the British Museum* (London: British Museum, 1889); Blumhardt, *Catalogue of Marathi and Gujarati Printed Books in the Library of the British Museum* (London: Kegan Paul, Trench, Trübner, 1892); Blumhardt, *Catalogue of the Library of the India Office: Bengali, Oriya, and Assamese Books,* vol. 2 (London: Eyre and Spottiswoode, 1905); Blumhardt, *Catalogue of the Library of the India Office: Marathi and Gujarati Books,* vol. 2 (London: Eyre and Spottiswoode, 1908); Blumhardt, *A Supplementary Catalogue of Marathi and Gujarati Books in the British Museum* (London: British Museum, 1918); *A Catalogue of Books Printed in the Bengal Presidency* [var. years] (Calcutta: Government Printing Press, 1867–1901); *A Catalogue of Books Printed in the Bombay Presidency* [var. years] (Bombay: Government Central Press, 1867–1901); *A Catalogue of Books Printed in the Madras Presidency, Fort St. George Gazette Supplement* [var. years] (Madras: Fort St. George Gazette Press, 1867–1901).

and using the lists in the *Appendices* or quarterly *Catalogues* as correctives, we can arrive at a general profile of books that were either translated or "adapted" (i.e., loosely translated, with names, places, and plots generally Indianized) into an Indian language during the nineteenth century. The compilation is at best a partial one, since the catalogues sometimes failed to identify adaptations (such as O. Chandu Menon's novel *Indulekha* [1888], which was a very loose adaptation into Malayalam of Disraeli's *Henrietta Temple* [1837]).

The translation list in table 2.3 makes several points clear. First, we note the striking persistence of eighteenth-century fiction well into the nineteenth century: all the titles, most especially Defoe and Johnson, continued to be translated throughout the next century and coexisted alongside Victorian writers, some of whom also appear in table 2.2. The continued appearance of the older writers might be explained partly by the assistance and sponsorship that some of these works (*Robinson Crusoe* was a particular favorite) received from the colonial authorities through their aid to institutions such as the Vernacular Literature Society or the regional School Book Societies. Second, the translation list indicates that British fiction, and through it British ideas, penetrated Indian letters and interfaced with Indian readers often removed from the medium of English. When rendered into regional language adaptations and translations, British fiction was indigenized and stripped from the language and culture of its creation. The world opened by these translations did much for Indian readers: Rabindranath Tagore recalls discovering a "pathetic translation of *Paul et Virginie* [1787]" in the Bengali serial *Abodhabandhu* (The Common Man's Friend) in 1868–69, over which he "wept many tears . . . what a delightfully refreshing mirage the story conjured up for me on that terraced roof in Calcutta. And oh! the romance that blossomed along the forest paths of that secluded island, between the Bengali boy-reader and little Virginie with the many-coloured kerchief round her head!"[56] Third, the translation list further corroborates one dominant axis of readerly taste in nineteenth-century India from table 2.2 and renders it strikingly clear: namely, an affection for romance and melodrama, exemplified in different ways by writers as diverse as Reynolds (the most widely translated and adapted of all British writers), Scott (whose poetry was vastly more popular than his novels), Dumas, and Sue.

A portion of this axis of readerly taste is also apparent in the earlier list of fiction most abundantly found in Indian libraries (table 2.2): of the 40 percent of best-selling novelists not found in Altick's British list (i.e., Crawford, Dumas, Harte, G. P. R. James, Lever, Marryat, Taylor, Thackeray), all fall within the categories of melodrama or romance (including historical romances from the earlier part of the century as well as adventure romances from the later half). It appears then that the persistence of translations of eighteenth-century fiction satisfied the demand for didactic fiction in the next century, while newer writers of melodrama and romance as different as Crawford and Reynolds were enthusiastically absorbed through both English and the regional languages throughout the nineteenth century.

Numerous Indian critics have already made something of the colonial interest in reading didactic literature. Balagopal Varma has proposed that didactic fiction served an educative and familiarizing function: "from the point of view of the Indian reader . . . he read the English novel—it was a filtered supply he got—with a view to improving himself in relation to a knowledge of the culture of his masters. This probably accounts for the taste of the educated Indian of those days for didactic literature."[57] Sisir Kumar Das further qualifies this affection for didactic fiction, pointing out that the official sponsorship that often accompanied it in the early nineteenth century underscores the importance that colonial authorities placed on these "good" and "moralizing" works, whose translations they often encouraged for schoolbooks. "Translations from certain texts such as Johnson's *Rasselas*, Bacon's *Essays*, or Bunyan's *The Pilgrim's Progress* were common in many languages mainly because of pedagogical necessity," he has argued.[58] Das is of course right up to a point, and his remarks recall to mind the Anglicist Charles Grant's observations in 1797 that "the easy books used in teaching might at the same time convey obvious truths on different subjects."[59] *Pilgrim's Progress* had already been pressed into this "moralizing" service when it was translated into Tamil in 1793.

Yet, even within this educative function, Indian readers seemed to exercise considerable free will, and well into the nineteenth century as I have indicated, *Rasselas* among other works such as *Robinson Crusoe*, *The Vicar of Wakefield*, and so on, continued to be translated, this time without official sponsorship or assistance. Das acknowledges this point in his encyclopedic and multivolumed *A History of Indian Literature*: "frequent translations of *Rasselas* or *The Pilgrim's Progress* in different languages also indicate their special significance in Indian life and literature. One has to concede that these two works were held in great esteem by the Indian reader" (180).

Few critics have probed why Indian readers held, and continued throughout the nineteenth century to hold these works in such great esteem, or what special significance they carried during this period. A part of that explanation lies, I believe, in the reading taste that Indians also had for melodrama and romance at the same time. From the array of prose that Indian readers had before them (and it was a wide array, from tales, novels, fables, and short stories to numerous forms of the novel such as realist, sensational, historical, romantic, didactic, social, reformist), they made certain choices that they exercised both in the marketplace and in the domestic publishing world. At the risk of reducing the diversity of Indian reading experiences to a single corpus, it seems that the manifold pattern of reading tastes that the archives document is worth scrutinizing as a set of conscious choices made both *for* certain forms of reading and *against* certain others. What I am proposing to do then is to analyze Indian consumption as a pattern of complex but interdependent needs, with each aspect of readerly preference addressing a larger constellation that it both depended upon and satisfied. If Balagopal Varma is right in postulating that didactic fiction satisfied the Indian reader's need to "improv[e] himself in relation to a knowledge of the culture of his masters," then I would argue that it is only a small part of the explanation for the persistence of eighteenth-century writing into the nineteenth and twentieth centuries. To understand the full reason, we need to explore colonial reading tastes in toto and to analyze what the affection for novelists as different as Reynolds, Crawford, Collins, Corelli, et al. satisfied in the nineteenth-century Indian reader's mind. While we can never know exactly how Indian readers read this fiction, we can at least investigate what about these novels worked in India and try to understand how it might have done so in an environment so dramatically different from the one in which the novels were produced.

G. W. M. REYNOLDS AND THE INDIAN READER

G. W. M. Reynolds (1814–79), the most persistently popular of these novelists in India, may be a good place to begin. A prolific novelist and journalist and a prominent Chartist in his day, Reynolds's literary reputation has continued to confound his critics. The founding editor of the *London Journal* and creator of at least two highly successful penny papers after that (*Reynolds's Miscellany* in 1846–69 and *Reynolds's Weekly Newspaper* from 1850 to 1879, which continued publication till 1967), Reynolds was also the author of at least fifty novels, translator of Victor Hugo and Paul de Kock among others, and author of the two-volume, *The Modern Literature of France since the Revolution of 1830* (1839).[60] Anne Humpherys suggests that a biography on him could well be entitled "The Mysteries of G. W. M. Reynolds," playing in part upon the title of his multivolume series of novels, and in part on the many contradictions he embodied.[61] An upper-class Englishman, Reynolds had more sympathy for the French and the working class of England than for his own aristocratic class origins. Despite his radical attitudes that, in the words of Louis James, "show a social conscience lacking in almost all other popular fiction of the time," Reynolds's novels were equally remarkable for their lurid accounts of sexual passion and uncommon sensationalism.[62] And despite being "the most popular writer of England,"[63] who was reputedly "probably twice or three times as great as that of any contemporary author"[64] (including Dickens), Reynolds is virtually unknown by any but the specialist today.

Most of his novels freely used the standard tropes of melodrama: mistaken identity; children switched at birth; fortunes and inheritances usurped; unscrupulous villains; complicated plots embroidered with relentless trials subjected upon the innocent protagonist; striking coincidences; vice and virtue clearly demarcated; and the resolution, reclamation, and restoration of the virtuous and villainous to their respective places. *The Mysteries of London* (1844–48) opens in a heavily editorial tone that establishes its intentions very clearly as it describes the city of London[65]:

> There are but two words known in the moral alphabet of this great city; for all virtues are summed up in one, and all vices in the other: and these words are
>
> WEALTH.   /   POVERTY.

Much of *Mysteries* centers on the intense criminality both wealth and poverty engender upon their denizens, with Reynolds's radical conclusion that "the wealthy may commit all social offenses with impunity; while the poor are cast into dungeons and coerced with chains for only following at a humble distance in the pathway of their lordly precedents" (5). The novel's complex plot with its digressions, subplots, major and minor characters from the city's wealthy to its poor serves to amplify this theme in every possible way. Yet, while Reynolds repeatedly portrays moments of monstrous brutality, he makes clear that greed and money motivate the worst crimes in people even as they always precipitate a retribution commensurate to the crime. In a chilling minor scene, the vicious and abusive Polly Bolter regrets that her infant daughter is too young to be fully exploited in the flesh trade: "What good can she do for us for years and years to come?" she asks her husband, Bill (40). To expedite her daughter's earning potential, she plans to blind the little girl by tying black beetles over her eyes as, "there's nothin' like a blind child to excite compassion" and make her a "successful beggar." A few hours later, Polly gets into a fight with Bill who deals her a vicious blow. She strikes her head upon the corner of a table that crushes her eye in its socket and kills her. "An awful retribution upon her who only a few hours before was planning how to plunge her innocent and helpless daughter into the eternal light of blindness" (44) observes Reynolds's narrator, in one of many such commentaries that follow each scene. Neither Bill nor the children reappear in the rest of *Mysteries of London*, but the economy of retribution, of an eye for an eye, repeats itself many times in the *Mysteries* series, as well as in virtually all of Reynolds's other novels.

Having established this stable moral formula, Reynolds improvised and experimented extensively within it. Works such as *Alfred de Rosann, or the Adventures of a French Gentleman* (1840); *The Loves of the Harem: A Tale of Constantinople* (1855); *Mary Stuart, Queen of Scotland* (1861); and *Omar, A Tale of the Crimean War* (1861) further allowed Reynolds with great imagination to portray for his readers exotic locales, historical plots, and "foreign" ways. *Alfred* is a virtual disquisition on the contrasts between English and French ways, and at one point Alfred has a minor altercation with the banker, Robson, on the boat from Calais to Southampton over just such a comparison. The tone in the narratives is unmistakably that of an editor or savant explaining matters to one far less knowledgeable about these ways with whom he shares the best recipe for mushroom omelettes and to whom he explains appropriate dining etiquette. At times Reynolds used his considerable imagination to try to outdo his betters: *Pickwick Abroad* (1839; also suggested as an appropriate tour guide to France) and *Pickwick Married* (1840) were popular and bowdlerized sequels of Dickens and *Sequel to Don Juan* (1843) of Byron. The *Mysteries* series itself, from which Reynolds's fame arose, was something of an *hommage* to Eugène Sue's *Les Mystères de Paris* (1842–43). In 1839, commenting upon Sue's earlier nautical romances with which he had first made a name, Reynolds provides what must in the end read very much like a particularly astute self-critique of the body of work that came to form his own oeuvre during the 1840s and 1850s:

> It must, however, be observed of M. Sue, that his imagination is only rich in inventing and stringing together a host of improbabilities, occasionally bordering upon monstrosity. To say that the incidents of his tales are *just possible* is to concede a great deal to this author; but then the very improbabilities which spring exotic from his own strange fancy, are so full of deep and absorbing interest, that the reader forgets whether they be natural or revolting to the most credulous mind, in the amusement which he derives from the contemplation of them.[66]

As Donald Kausch further proposes, Reynolds's own fiction did not really restrict itself to any one form:

> Reynolds' popularity came not only from his realism but it also grew because he gave his readers all the major sensations they wanted or were likely to find in writers now more highly regarded. . . . Reynolds' novels provided for the masses almost all the popular fashions of novel writing of that period between the thirties and sixties. He wrote Historical Romances, Newgate Fiction, and Gothic Romance, but his particular brand of radicalism marks his work as unique.   (319)

As testament to the theatricality of his plots, a melodrama, *The Mysteries of London*, based on Reynolds's novel of the same title was produced in London's Marylebone Theatre on May 18, 1846, with other productions following at the Victoria and Pavilion theaters.[67]

Reynolds's popularity among the lower- and working-class readers of

his penny magazines in Britain has frequently been explained by the radical allure of the politics with which he liberally spiced his fiction. In
1852, during a lecture on "Charity and Humour" delivered in New York,
Thackeray quoted a railway bookseller explaining why Reynolds's *Mysteries of the Court of London* (serialized between 1848–56) was "by many
times the most popular of all periodical tales then published, because says
he, 'it lashes the aristocracy.'"[68] Reynolds did not simply lash out at and
ridicule the aristocracy in his novels; he blamed it for the ills that befell
just about everybody else. "Almost all Reynolds's criminals," suggested
Louis James, "have been driven into crime by the evils of society," and
the rich in his novels played a notable role in creating "the moral dung-
heap" that the novels so graphically describe.[69] In a particularly polemi-
cal chapter of *Mysteries of London*, Reynolds intones: "The country that
contains the greatest wealth of all the territories of the universe, is that
which also knows the greatest amount of hideous, revolting, heart-rend-
ing misery. . . . In England, men and women die of starvation in the
streets. . . . In England, the poor commit crimes to obtain an asylum in a
goal," and so on. With little apparent self-consciousness, this part of his
novel devolves into social documentary: the section concludes with a
chart of the annual incomes of various classes, from sovereign (£500,000)
to the aristocracy (£30,000) to the "industrious classes" (£20), and while
Victoria herself is represented in this chapter with considerable dignity
and respect, the "rich man" is uniformly vilified (92–3).

Alongside this radical strain in his fiction, which was often accompanied by the kind of editorializing I have already noted, Reynolds was also
a consummate story-teller who, most critics agree, had a finger firmly on
the pulse of his readers, whom he simultaneously seduced and restrained
in scenes often bordering on the pornographic. In a particularly titillat-
ing passage in *The Mysteries of London* the fallen priest, Reginald Tracy,
spies upon the lovely Ellen Monroe taking a bath with her infant child.
Reynolds skillfully reveals the "treasures of her bosom" as Ellen—
unaware of being watched—slowly undresses, thus unwittingly providing Tracy and the reader with a striptease that Reynolds builds to fever
pitch with each mention of her "small round polished ankles," her "del-
icate waist," "shining hair," and "voluptuous form, naked to the waist."
As the Reverend Tracy watches enraptured while "the fires of gross sen-
suality raged madly in his breast," so does the reader who is further aided
in the voyeuristic act by a suggestive and exquisitely rendered woodcut

illustration. But Reynolds the moralist steps in and closes down the scene just as the Reverend's desires (and presumably the reader's) "were now inflamed to that pitch when they almost became ungovernable" (211). A step is heard approaching, Tracy retreats, and the striptease stops just in time for the reader to pull back, presumably ashamed at his identification with the licentious priest but nevertheless grossly titillated by the scene. At the end of lascivious descriptions such as this, Reynolds often inserted a kind of formal restraint that terminated the scene at its most intense moment, a move that infuriated his contemporaries for being too little too late given the acutely pornographic descriptions that preceded the restraint. It is a criticism, however, that overlooks just how controlled and sedate these sequences really are.

Even as Reynolds plays with soft pornography and titillation in the bathing scene, the tone remains decorous and the threat of sexual violation distinctly contained. He clearly marks Tracy's delirious responses as signs of the priest's particular depravity, a depravity that is linked if only by association to the corruptions Reynolds has painstakingly detailed earlier in the novel. And if Tracy's vocation and vows do not render his conduct despicable enough, Reynolds stages the scene with a direct allusion to the Madonna and child as Tracy spies upon Ellen with infant at her breast stepping into a bath, an allusion underscored by the image on the woodcut accompanying this scene. Rather than coming too late as some of his critics decried, these restraints appear throughout the passage where they mingle with earlier and more directly articulated injunctions such as those condemning Polly Bolter's sadistic treatment of her children. Scenes such as these are consistent and of a piece with the overall moral economy of *The Mysteries of London* rather than an aberration within it. Their alternating pattern of licentiousness and constraint underscores and reinforces the novel's ethical vision rather than, as some have urged, undermining it for cheap effect.

Reynolds's lure as entertainer and edifier was one that his medium of circulation greatly enhanced: *London Journal* and *Reynolds's Miscellany*, in which virtually all his fiction first appeared, were themselves serials devoted to entertainment and uplift (both moral and social), so that Reynolds's fictional installments underscored in the realm of the imaginative what each issue of the serial emphasized in the realm of the "real." The serials, with their advice columns, how-to essays, self-improvement sections, and injunctions on social uplift reflected what Daniel Burt calls the "all-purpose entertainment" of the novels, which also included "practical advice, sentiment, and terror that combine[d] the tabloid and the tract" into a big shaggy bundle that mirrored the form, if not the content, of the serials in which they appeared.[70] The press, like the novels, further participated in the shared enterprise of exposing social corruption, and as Anne Humpherys has shown, the *Mysteries* novels "use some of the same formal devices as the popular press to achieve this goal."[71] What I am proposing then is that the penny magazines that carried Reynolds's fiction in Britain were themselves sources of titillation, exposure, edification, and restraint. In a complex and sophisticated manner, Reynolds's British readers learned to consume his fiction in this larger context in which extensive advice on social and moral uplift and self-improvement initially licensed, then balanced, and even contained the more salacious and sensational elements of his fiction.

The source of Reynolds's continued popularity in India is somewhat harder to describe. No Indian library to my knowledge subscribed to (or catalogued) the penny serials in which Reynolds's fiction initially appeared, and the editions of his works that I located either physically or bibliographically in India were respectable bound volumes published by George Vickers or John Dicks (for the nineteenth-century imprints) or by local Indian presses in twentieth-century imprints. The famous and often risqué woodcuts that inspired Reynolds's less literate readers in England were frequently replaced by more sedate illustrations and sometimes done away with altogether in the imprints found in India.[72] While Reynolds's literary fortunes in Britain declined precipitously after his death, they persisted in India well into the twentieth century, as evidenced by the translations and reprints issued in the Indian domestic press and in the recollections of later novelists such as Mulk Raj Anand. In 1924, almost half a century after his death, the *Times Literary Supplement* ran a column on Reynolds remarking precisely upon this unexpected fact: "An inquiry concerning those of his works in print was lately received in London from an English-speaking native in India—and there can be no doubt that he is by far the greatest and most fertile of a large crowd of authors who, in their fiction in penny weekly numbers and sixpenny monthly parts, reached a class of the Early Victorian community untouched by both Dickens and

Thackeray."[73] Of the titles most available in India, either in English or in translation, *The Mysteries of London* (1844–48) and *The Mysteries of the Court of London* (1848–56) are among those most frequently named in the historical record. Among the other titles present in translation (see table 2.3), a notably socialist vein is apparent in the numerous subtitles that speak of the conditions of the "industrious classes": *Mary Price; or the Memoirs of a Servant Maid* (1851–52); *The Seamstress; or, the White Slaves of England* (1850; renamed after the first number, "A Domestic Tale"); *Rosa Lambert; or, the Memoirs of an Unfortunate Woman* (1853–54, also renamed as "A Clergyman's Daughter"); and *Joseph Wilmot; or, the Memoirs of a Man Servant* (1853–54). At the end of *The Mysteries of the Court of London*, in 1856, Reynolds ran a postscript explaining both of his *Mysteries* novels as, "a fragmentary portion of that which, as one vast whole, may be termed an Encyclopedia of Tales" (quoted in Summers 151).

For Indian readers, this encyclopedia came with a particular provenance: it was a markedly British work, made in, about, and of the culture of the colonizer. If, as Balagopal Varma has argued, "Indians took to fiction as a part of their attempt to familiarize themselves with the language, style, and manners of the ruling race,"[74] then Reynolds's novels, with their combination of "tabloid and tract," entertainment and edification, satisfied this desire particularly well. The edificatory function in his novels might be speculatively, if not entirely, consistent with the taste for eighteenth-century didactic fiction noted earlier in the translation records. Yet the precise nature of what edification Indian readers actually got from Reynolds has never really been fully fleshed out.

In 1883 the Keeper of the Catalogue of Printed Books in the Bengal Presidency annotated a new Bengali serial, *Prabahini*, as "a new serial in which will be published a Bengali translation of Reynolds' *Mysteries of London* and *Mysteries of the Court of London* with the names and characters Indianized. The translator is of the opinion that Reynolds' works are eminently calculated to excite in the minds of those who read them a strong feeling of hatred against vice and social inequality."[75] A fairly literal interpretation of this passage might suggest that the social radicalism that so excited Reynolds's English readers against the ruling classes equally aroused "strong feelings of hatred against vice and social inequality" among his Indian readers.

In this account, the radical themes in Reynolds's novels putatively resonated further with the movement for internal social reform that had been sweeping India, starting with Ram Mohun Roy's pleas to ban *sati* in the 1820s, to the social agitation between 1850 and the end of the century over child marriage, widow remarriage, priestly corruption, and assorted social ills. This straightforward interpretation regarding self-reform clearly operated among a certain segment of Indian readership, who consumed the "Indianized" Reynolds very literally, even to a fault. Annotating *Udasini Raj Kanyar Gupta Katha* (The Secret Story of the Princess who Renounced Worldly Life) by Kailash Chandra Mukharji, the Keeper of the Bengal Catalogue opines: "This is a work in the nature of Reynolds's *Mysteries of London.* . . . The author apparently intends to say that the amount of vice secretly indulged in Hindu society is fearfully large, and that much of that vice finds a safe and easy shelter in sacred places like Benares and Puri."[76] For all the fallen priests and corrupt men-about-town whom Reynolds denounced in his novels of London, his Indian readers found literal equivalents in Benares and Puri to be lashed for their vices.

But there was yet another context in which Reynolds's works were consumed in India. His Subcontinental audience was also reading him under the shadow of a colonial state in which Indians were only ever subjects, never citizens. This context made visible for Reynolds's colonial readers a further layer of vice and social inequality to excite their minds, and it is this layer that the *Mysteries* translator in *Prabahini* may well have been alluding to in the remarks cited by the Bengal Keeper of the Catalogue. The inequities of the colonial state were the moral, if not literal, equivalent of the social and class inequities that Reynolds animated for his British readers. By projecting outward from their own subjection, Indian readers would have discovered a symbolic affinity between their struggles against the colonial machinery and those of Reynolds's oppressed masses in London against the ruling classes. The fact that it was the same class that oppressed both groups was probably not lost upon Indian readers, nor was Reynolds's profound—albeit often contradictory—moral economy. In his epilogue to volume 1 of *Mysteries of London*, Reynolds provided polemic where previously he had provided entertainment, putatively to dispel any misreading of his work or his intentions:

We have constituted ourselves the scourge of the oppressor, and the champion of the oppressed; we have taken virtue by the hand to raise it, and we have seized upon vice to expose it; we have no fear of those who sit in high places; but we dwell emphatically upon the failings of the educated and the rich, as on the immorality of the ignorant and poor. . . .

Crime, oppression and injustice prosper for a time; but, *with nations as with individuals, the day of retribution must come*. Such is the lesson which we have yet to teach. (197; emphasis added)

The remaining volumes of *Mysteries of London* and the immensely popular eight volumes of *Mysteries of the Court of London* that followed it continue with this lesson of justice and retribution to great acclaim.

Numerous critics have ruefully conceded that Reynolds's moral imperatives as articulated in claims such as the one above unfortunately receded in the end against the pull of entertainment and sensationalism to which his fiction succumbed. "His radicalism serves a dramatic rather than a genuinely social purpose," concludes Louis James (*Fiction* 166–67), in a view that is almost uniformly echoed among all Reynolds's critics, both during his lifetime and since. Even Anne Humpherys, in an article subtitled "Popular Literature and Popular Politics," regrets the manner in which "the normative values of melodrama, and the escapism of romance and fantasy undercut the call to action and realism of practical politics" in Reynolds's fiction.[77] The critical disappointment has endured that Reynolds sacrificed radicalism for entertainment, because in the versions he provided in his novels, the two forms were mutually exclusive and they ultimately sabotaged politics.

Reynolds and Melodrama. Whether this was really the case among British readers, I leave for James, Humpherys, and others to decide, but it was far from the case among Reynolds's Indian fans, for whom his use of melodrama and fantasy served precisely as the vehicle for articulating and identifying a call to something that eventually became "practical politics." In the medley of styles that formed Reynolds's fiction of the 1840s, Humpherys is right in calling to mind melodrama, romance, fantasy, even gothic, from each of which Reynolds liberally borrowed conventions and tropes in order to give his fiction what she identifies as "a popular mythic resonance."[78] Yet what marked his fiction beyond these heavily borrowed tropes was a mood and a thematic that played insistently upon an overtly articulated moral economy in which vice was eventually punished and virtue rewarded. This ethos would have undoubtedly proven numbingly boring even amongst the most naive readers if repeated more than once, so Reynolds used the melodramatic conventions of the day in subjecting virtue to unbearable persecution before reward appeared, and vice to innumerable victories before retribution struck (which when it did was usually rendered in grossly marked horrors, including every imaginable form of bodily and mental torture). This is the surface of the novels, of course, but it also gestures toward their deeper content.

In invoking melodramatic form, Reynolds's fiction also invoked the content of melodrama, or what Peter Brooks has called the "moral occult" that undergirds a range of texts that sit upon the uneasy divide between popular forms and a larger social conscience. Melodrama for Brooks is a "system for making sense of experience," and the moral occult, the set of intrinsic values "both indicated within and masked by the surface of reality."[79] For him, as for the earlier generation of critics upon whom his work builds, melodrama is both a theatrical form and a mode for dramatizing moral issues. Melodrama's formal use of easy binaries such as vice and virtue serves in this context to help excavate and restore a moral order upon a universe that has lost it. Reynolds of course exploited the formal elements of melodrama quite extensively (its endless plottedness, its grotesque and exaggerated descriptions, its combination of licentiousness and sentiment, and its appeals to the emotions), but he deployed them within a clearly articulated subtext that insisted on restoring some moral authority to the universe. In his novels, individuals were pitted against monstrous odds, but in vanquishing them, they became rulers of a newer, better, moral order, one that ought to have always been but usually was not. In discussing Reynolds's use of melodrama here, I refer not to his overt use of conventions from what was once a theatrical form but, rather, to the subtext upon which those forms took shape and developed. If melodrama was a sense-making enterprise as Brooks expresses it, then I am interested in pursuing what sense Reynolds and other British novelists made for their Indian readers and why and how.

I have already mentioned the moral axis upon which melodrama revolves, and a few more words are in order. Melodrama is not so much a moralistic drama but, as Brooks so persuasively shows, it is a drama of morality: "it strives to find, to articulate, to demonstrate, to 'prove' the existence of a moral universe which, though put into question, masked by villainy and perversions of judgment, does exist and can be made to assert its presence and its categorical force among men" (20). Yet how might this moral universe assert its presence? In the melodramatic mode, only clearly demarcated conflict can provide moral authority with the opportunity to triumph. Thus, in order to concentrate the conflict in the most dramatic way possible, melodrama places it outward. The hero, Robert Heilman points out in his penetrating study of melodrama, is persecuted by forces entirely and wholly on the outside, over whom he has no responsibility or control. Evil is externalized as is the ensuing conflict.[80]

The outcome of this is manifold, and Heilman further outlines the consequences of placing conflict externally. Melodrama, he argues, provides us with characters who are intrinsically undivided (as opposed to tragedy in which man is divided within). "In tragedy the conflict is within man; in melodrama, it is between men or between men and things," Heilman suggests (79). The apparently "whole" and undivided protagonist of melodrama is thus free from the distortions and doubts that beset the tragic hero. Not only is the melodramatic hero therefore freed from internal conflict, he is also free to act upon the conflict outside, thus becoming a figure of action, one who rights the world, untroubled by any contradictions, doubts, or wrongs within himself. Moreover, in its straightforward moral ethos, its well-defined boundaries, its uncomplicated binarisms, and clear call to action, melodrama is the form both of dreams—and of action. Its model of justice and retribution symbolically assuages a sense of inequity and injustice among its consumers. Furthermore, its own enactment and pursuit of the moral occult occasionally, as in the case of India, served as a call to action that was eventually answered by its consumers.

In consuming melodrama of the kind that Reynolds and other British writers provided them, Indian readers found a world that they could inhabit without contradiction or censure. Reynolds's explanations of the ways of the British upper classes, along with the moralizing and entertainment in his novels, addressed several important needs among his Indian audience. The affection for didacticism that earlier fiction from *Pilgrim's Progress* to *Rasselas* had provided, as well as the psychological need to find a symbolic means to resist empire found both corroboration and inspiration in the melodramatic mode. In its cleaner-than-life modalities, the economy of persecution and justice resonated even among the most unsophisticated Indian readers. In 1884 Ambika Charan Gupta, translator of Reynolds's *Rabart Myakeyar* (*Robert Macaire*) assured his readers that he had "carefully excluded all obscene descriptions."[81] Thus purged of their salacious content, Reynolds's novels became appropriate even for the Indian family, and his moral ethos even more concentrated and applicable, given that there was less to offend than before.

I do not mean to suggest that Reynolds, or melodrama, will necessarily cause revolution. Rather, I would argue that ways of reading these works, at least in nineteenth-century India, might do just that. As many critics of Reynolds in the West have attested, despite his working-class sympathies, his plots often concluded with pitiful and penniless protagonists being rescued and restored to their rightful place as members of the aristocracy.[82] Instead of assessing this contradiction between the fiction's radical politics and its reactionary conclusion as a structural failure, it seems to me to be something that embodies the contradictions of the age *and* is in fact a convention of this fiction that readers were well aware of. The discrepancy between radical plot and reactionary conclusion helped raise questions about the plausibility or adequacy of an ending—*any* ending given what has occurred before—and it is a question readers knew to probe and ask. In the end, of course, neither the radicalism nor the reaction caused or visibly led to revolution among British readers. With Reynolds's predecessor, Eugène Sue, the case is even starker, as Umberto Eco paints it. "The year of Sue's death was the same that saw the publication of *Madame Bovary* . . . the critical account of the life of a woman who read 'consolatory novels' in the style of Sue, from which she learned to wait for something that would never happen."[83]

What Reynolds's popularity in nineteenth- and early-twentieth-century India (along with that of a small handful of other British novelists such as Marie Corelli and F. Marion Crawford) gestures toward then is not so much revolution as the immensely powerful appeal of melodrama in a world that found great symbolic affinities with the psychological structure of the form. The melodramatic mode provided the pleasure and satisfaction of experiencing wholeness, victory, and retribution for all the wrongs that were, in reality or imagination, visited upon the community of readers. Melodrama enabled its readers to conceive of and give shape to the "enemy." It articulated action and projected results, however fictional. As Robert Heilman brilliantly notes, "melodrama has affinities with politics, tragedy with religion . . . [it] is the principal vehicle of protest and dissent" (90, 96).

It was this clarity and singleness of vision that I would suggest most effectively interpellated Indian readers, who discovered in the melodramatic mode not just consolation (as their British counterparts had when Reynolds lashed the aristocracy) but a way of "plotting" and seeing the world that was fully commensurate with their own fantasies. That these fantasies were not just individual ones of personal grandeur and wealth but larger cultural and political fantasies of freedom and liberation in part explains the extended appeal of the melodramatic mode throughout the nineteenth and twentieth centuries in India. "Melodrama is not an exaggeration of our dreams but a duplication of them," wrote Eric Bentley to explain the form's continued success.[84] While melodrama on the English stage from Bentley's example or print quite simply embodied the dream-fantasies of its British consumers, it actually helped enact those of its Indian consumers. What I am suggesting then is that melodrama both sent and received psychological signals to Indian readers, who eventually, as we will see in the next chapters, used its tropes to fashion a liberation struggle that "really" took place, in the world and not just in their dreams.

MELODRAMA IN TRANSLATION

The signals that melodrama "sent" should be clear from the preceding discussion, but *what* precisely was received in India is not as clear, nor how it was received, and it is useful to examine this in greater detail. I have already mentioned that the social context in which Indian readers consumed fiction was different from the one in which their British counterparts did, but it is worth stressing that not only were there differences in contexts, there were also differences in readerly predisposition. The classes of readers who read Reynolds and other popular

British novelists in India were as a whole not the class who read these figures in Britain. Given literacy and reading patterns in nineteenth-century India, it was a small and motley group who read the English novel, from the aristocracy to the educated and professional classes to the lower-middle class, with a somewhat broader section consuming fiction through translation in regional languages. The only common vision shared by such a diverse group of readers was their experience as colonial subjects, and in helping identify and isolate this condition, Reynolds specifically, and melodrama more generally, provided Indian readers with a sense of community and kinship that came from discovering both a shared enemy and a common enterprise.

I have suggested elsewhere that many of melodrama's topoi revealed a symbolic and structural affinity with older literary forms in India and paradoxically helped to bridge the gulf between the premodern world and modernity.[85] The excruciatingly complex plottedness of melodrama that was so pervasive in Reynolds's, Corelli's, and Crawford's novels resonated fully with the circularity and intricacy of the epic plot in Indian letters, so familiar to Indian readers from performances, readings, and recitals of the *Mahabharata* and the *Ramayana*. The edificatory narrative tone that Reynolds assumed toward his reader when explaining banking in his novels, for example, or the working conditions of English miners, or legal issues echoed the familiar didacticism (albeit concerning moral rather than practical matters) ever present in Indian epics. And the coincidence and interconnectedness that Reynolds's characters constantly encountered as they traversed the mazelike urban environment of London in the *Mysteries* series (or the equally alienating geography of France, Scotland, or Constantinople in some of the other novels) underscored the essential, albeit paradoxical, *community* of a world that, despite its enormity, was small enough for characters, treasures, reunions, and murderers to meet and remeet over and over again, as if in a village square. This aspect of community, in particular, resonated for Indian readers with the unwavering bonds of their own world whose closely knit kinship patterns and extended families were a well-established fact of everyday experience that even the colonial apparatus could not diminish. The subtext of community and kinship inherent in the coincidences of family separations and reunions, inheritances lost then found, virtue and evil meeting then parting all in the same house (*Mysteries of London*), room, or wayside inn

(*Alfred*) through many volumes of dense prose may have served to neutralize for Reynolds's penny readers what was in fact for them an ominously over-grown and alienating urban landscape. By giving randomness an order and design, in designating modernity and industrialization "mysteries" to be solved, Reynolds's novels performed the work of wish-fulfillment by assuaging his British working-class readers' worst fears. In India, however, Reynolds's novels did not so much assuage fears as set in motion signs of recognition that were initially only thematic, topical, and familiar, rather than psychological or affective. It was not so much Indian readers' fears that the narratives assuaged; rather, it was their dreams.

While many of melodrama's Western critics have found its "long arm of coincidence a freakish thing" (Bentley 203), for Indian readers exactly the opposite held true. Coincidence of this sort, rather than being freakish, further resonated with tropes from the popular mythic universe so familiar from the epics where curses, spells, vows, planetary constellations, and fate braided together lives and fortunes from one end of the Subcontinent to another. *Shakuntala*, Kalidas's work made famous in Sir William Jones's 1789 translation, is the story of a king destined to love a commoner and a commoner destined to have a royal lover forget her. How they meet, love, part, and remeet across great time and distance is the stuff of the *Mahabharata*—and George Reynolds. Coincidence in the Indian literary tradition functioned much in the same way it did in melodrama: it underscored and affirmed the existence of a divine hand involved in human affairs. The entire plot of *Shakuntala*—or for that matter of all the other stories that constitute the *Mahabharata* and *Ramayana*—revolves around coincidences and interconnections that serve to emphasize a sense of providence and to affirm the presence of a god. Affectively, superficially, and symbolically, there was much in Reynolds that his Indian readers found familiar and recognizable. The dream world of Reynolds's melodrama was closer to the everyday world of his Indian readers than even he could have imagined.

Reading Reynolds under colonial rule gave his Indian readers not only the compensatory satisfaction of dreams but also the psychological and symbolic satisfaction of action. The readers who read him for pleasure also read him for instruction. In his novels their deepest psychological needs were articulated and then vindicated through the moral economy of melodrama. In complicated and paradoxical ways, they found their world symbolically, if not literally, reflected in his. Furthermore, it seems Indians read Reynolds to their own ends, ignoring the conventional ideological vision in his novels (of domesticity, romantic love, social mobility) and concentrating instead on a particular view of the moral order commensurate with their own fantasies. From this act of highly inventive reading and recognition, Indian writers were eventually, as we will see in the following chapters, to fashion a literary corpus that actively responded to melodrama's call to politics. The Indian novel when it emerged in the late-nineteenth century had two major areas of reform at its core: among the early works, the word "novel" was synonymous with domestic social reform. However, as the century wore to an end, in the writings of Bankim Chandra Chatterjee among others, the novel accompanied—and perhaps even inaugurated—the national pilgrimage toward political liberation and an end to colonialism. For some Indians this was a particularly urgent task, as Thakorelal Desai confirmed when he urged in 1919 that "to hope for an India united by a common bond of sympathy and culture, to hope to make a real nation even out of these diverse materials is not an impossible task. . . . If an extensive use be made of the common human fondness for a story and also of the stage, the task will be accomplished all the sooner" (86).

Reynolds, of course, was not the sole writer who inspired this journey into decolonization. He was one of a core of writers whose works elicited this response from colonial readers in India. When H. Pratt, a founder of the Bengal Vernacular Literature Society, explained the need for the society's existence, he almost certainly had little idea of the prescience of his remarks:

There is not only a difference of language between the people of India and of England. We must recognize the far greater difficulty of a difference of *ideas, associations, and literature.* The instruction communicated to the masses requires somewhat more than the mere employment of the vehicle of native language;— the form in which it is conveyed must *appeal to ideas and feelings already existing.* Every possible use must be made of what we *already find in their literature and associations*—consistently with our object of communicating truth.[87]

Neither Pratt nor anyone else in the colonial apparatus could have had any sense of or predicted correctly how the literature that arrived from Britain would appeal to the ideas and feelings already existing. Even in the "safe" titles translated by the Vernacular Literature Society—works such as *Robinson Crusoe* and *Paul and Virginia*—the moral economy of the melodramatic mode is clearly present. In his 1859 *Report on the Native Press in Bengal*, James Long had benevolently noted "the love of orientals for works of imagination" (xxvii), with little apparent notion of what precisely the imagination did with these beloved works.

All the titles translated under the aegis of the Vernacular Literature Society in Bengal, all those translated into Indian languages listed in table 2.3, and just about each of the authors noted in table 2.2 fall within what Peter Brooks so eloquently calls, "the melodramatic imagination." This is not to suggest that all or even most of these authors wrote melodrama: far from it, as examples such as Marryat (adventure romances), Taylor (historical romances), and Bulwer-Lytton (Newgate novels, historical romances) indicate. Yet in the entire corpus of works that constituted the canon of popular novels in India, the psychological structure and the moral modalities of melodrama are almost immediately apparent. Even Scott's poetry, which dominated over his novels in India (with *The Lay of the Last Minstrel* leading), imaginatively reconfigured the social and geographical imaginary of his immediate readers, "in order to make whole a historically traumatized modern present," as Ian Duncan compellingly argues.[88] Reynolds, who mixed popular forms with such panache, serves not just as metaphor but also as index to the wide appeal of the most beloved forms among Indian readers.

The history of consumption that this chapter details invites both a conclusion and a caveat. Indian readers' manipulation of their reading matter was an inadvertent and unpremeditated act of subversion that successfully sabotaged the dominance of the colonial apparatus. It is wise, however, to recall that the historical record also documents a narrative of failure: specifically, the failure of British colonial authorities to understand fully the "ideas, associations, and literature" of their subjects on the ground. In this regard, the record attests less to a history of subjection than to one of invention in which both sides seemed free and able to create the other in the image most commensurate with their own needs. As such, the Indian world survived, and succeeded, by indigenizing the British novel to its own ends. It did so largely by an act of

CHAPTER 3

Readers Write Back: The Macmillan Colonial Library in India

In 1835 Emma Roberts, one of the most insightful travel writers on India, wrote about Calcutta, "Next to the jeweller's shops, the most magnificent establishment in the city is that of the principal bookseller, Thacker & Co."[1] Roberts was hardly speaking metaphorically, for English books at that time were literally prized "next to the jewellers." They were much sought after, extremely expensive (even for the British), and hard to come by. As Roberts further noted in her vade mecum to India, "the profit obtained upon books is more moderate than that of any other European commodity, the retail prices being entirely regulated by those of the London market" (*Scenes* 3:9).

Within a decade or two, however, the situation began to change dramatically. British publishers in London awoke to the realization that there was a lucrative emerging market waiting to be developed among generations of English-educated Indian readers who clamored after new fiction titles but were unable to pay the exorbitant prices of the day. In 1846 John Kaye approvingly noted the publishers' initiative in a glowing essay in *The Calcutta Review* that is worth quoting at some length for the insights it provides into the changed marketplace of novels that was becoming apparent in mid-nineteenth-century India:

India is, therefore, especially beholden to those enterprising publishers, who have undertaken to reduce both the price and the
bulk of the works they put in circulation. There is no country, in
which cheap and portable literature is more required. We are
rejoiced, therefore, to see that some of the principal London publishers are now issuing works of great merit, at a price not equal
to half—in many instances, a third or a fourth of the old conventional charge for similar works; and in a form too, which, whilst
nothing of elegance or convenience is sacrificed, is admirably
adapted for speedy and cheap circulation. Among other series of
works we may especially notice Murray's "Home and Colonial
Library."[2]

Kaye's remarks highlight a transformation taking place in both commodity and commerce: not only are the novels purveyed no longer in
the customary three-volume form (but "reduced in bulk"), they are also
far cheaper than those of the London market (at "a third or a fourth of
the old conventional charge for similar works"). Moreover, the works
are respectable ("of great merit") and the publishing firm (John Murray) one of considerable repute.

Kaye's account locates both the difficulties confronting readers in
India who sought a constant supply of English books for leisure reading and the solution that a group of London publishers developed to
address the perennial problem of low supply and high cost associated
with books abroad. As the century wore on, increased literacy in India
placed growing demand on what had hitherto been a slender stream of
new books entering the country. Starting in 1843, the firm of John
Murray inaugurated a series, mostly made up of reprints, entitled
Colonial and Home Library, initially designated for sale in Britain's
overseas colonies. Despite being a short-lived venture that folded by
1849, Murray's idea of selling English books cheaply to the colonies
was essentially a sound one, and some forty years later it was picked up
by the firm of Macmillan who made it such a resounding success that
virtually every major British publisher at some point in their business
also started their own Foreign, Colonial, or Imperial library series.[3]
Kaye's enthusiasm correctly—albeit somewhat prematurely—identifies
and celebrates one of the great publishing innovations of nineteenth-
century Paternoster Row, one that was eventually to have far-reaching

implications both on the availability and selection of English novels to which Indian readers had access and possibly even upon the production of these works in Britain toward the end of the nineteenth century.

While the previous chapter analyzed how British books, including novels, circulated among readers in colonial India both in English and through translation, this chapter analyzes the particular role that British publishing firms played in recognizing and responding to colonial needs. Since the various colonial library series were directed almost exclusively overseas—often with strict injunctions against sales in Britain—what these series purveyed abroad and how they did so introduces an important commercial aspect into what has hitherto been an account focused on colonial consumption. In part, this chapter is an attempt to test how far the claims of colonial agency from the previous chapter hold up when the vicissitudes of the market are introduced into the story. That the colonial subject was a major consumer is today a truism: indeed, one of the edifices upon which empire rested was the market provided by the colonies. Yet it is worth investigating more closely what role, if any, Indian readers might have played in a mid- and late-century marketplace dominated by British production. How might they have inserted themselves as consumers in a trade cycle that some publishing historians continue to insist excluded or ignored them entirely? And finally, how might one analyze the impact of commercial practices (exporting print to India) that themselves may not have been ideological, even though the commodities that they traded— books and novels—were inescapably implicated in ideology and ideological trade between metropole and periphery?

In order to address these questions, this chapter studies British publishing firms that extended their business to India specifically in the form of colonial library series. For achieving the greatest success in the Indian market, the House of Macmillan is particularly relevant, and this chapter begins with a brief history of the firm in India, then contrasts its success with that of an earlier publisher, John Murray, and a later one, Kegan Paul, that flourished alongside Macmillan but was never able to achieve its success in the Subcontinent. The chapter concludes with an account of some of the complex and unintended consequences of this book trade on both periphery and metropole. Indian patterns of consumption, I show, began to shape British novelistic production at least at the House of Macmillan whose desire to satisfy its

Indian readers came at the cost of disenchanting its domestic ones. Alongside this I demonstrate how the British trade of books and ideas gave rise both to an Indian novel and a new discourse on modernity in the Subcontinent.

MACMILLAN IN INDIA

In 1843, as John Murray III was launching his firm's Colonial and Home Library, two Scottish brothers named Daniel and Alexander published the first book to bear the imprint of Macmillan. Charles Morgan, the firm's biographer, makes much of this modest start: the ninety-two pages of *The Philosophy of Training* by A. R. Craig were something to make the Macmillan brothers very pleased. "They were deeply interested in education, having lacked it themselves; they had published an educational book and were proud of it."[4] In time, the firm's pride in its books extended far beyond education as it produced a robust and highly respected list in fields that included fiction and poetry, philosophy, history, science, music, economics, and anthropology. Within a few decades of its start, the firm's base in Britain was so strong that it began to seek markets farther afield. In 1863 Alexander Macmillan was able to note his efforts in a letter to George Otto Trevelyan, Macaulay's nephew and eventually author of the highly successful *The Competition Wallah* (1864), a thinly fictionalized account of his time in India:

> We are increasing our business with India both in school books and in the supply of Libraries and Book Clubs and private persons, and we could do more if it came in our way. What strides education must be making among the natives! We sell considerable number of our mathematical books, even high ones, every year to India. I should be glad to know something about these same scientific natives. Please write me a longer letter when you next write.[5]

Alexander Macmillan's interest in "these same scientific natives" points to the astuteness with which he recognized possibilities for the firm's advancement in the colonial market. Though he noted the firm's

increasing sales to libraries and book clubs, his prudent eye remained
on the clearly larger opportunities to be had from educational sales. Of
itself this fact is not inconsistent with the house's general policies: it had
built its reputation and esteem in the home market from a basis in publishing educational titles (serving as printers to Cambridge University)
and, despite its success in other fields, the firm was not likely to take
risks in a marketplace as distant and unknown as India was to them at
that time. Lacking education themselves, the Macmillans recognized
its appeal and so tried as best they could to penetrate the Indian market through a means they fully understood and whose success they
could clearly ascertain.

By 1873 the Macmillans had laid the groundwork for what was to
become such a successful business enterprise in India that in 1892 they
had an exclusive agent working for them there and in 1901 began opening book depots first in Bombay, then Calcutta (1907), then Madras
(1913). Up through the 1970s the firm maintained enormous prestige
and market share in India, where its textbooks continued to educate
legions of primary and secondary school students, including this
author. In an 1873 letter to Sir Roper Lethbridge, Director of the Bengal Department of Public Instruction and an author in Macmillan's
Text-Books for Indian Schools series, Alexander Macmillan explained
the source of the firm's success as educational publishers in India: "We
have had letters and communications from all parts of India approving
our scheme, and above all, the fact that we have secured the best men
in each department to make their books, and in several cases asking that
the very authors who have written the books should modify them to
meet Oriental needs."[6] In what was perhaps its most successful innovation in India, the firm was not simply content to market books already
successful at home—or worse, to dump unsellable ones in the colonies
where they might still sell. Ever mindful of its audience, Macmillan
expended considerable resources in producing books appropriate—and
indeed, specific—to Indian needs by signing on the "best men in each
department." "We think that by doing so we best serve the ends of
sound education, and also in the long run they will be most commercially worth doing," Alexander Macmillan concluded in his letter to
Lethbridge (278).

These opening remarks on Macmillan's forays into the Indian market underscore one important point about the firm and its success in

the Indian literary marketplace later in the nineteenth century when it initiated the Colonial Library. The firm was quick to recognize that success in the long run lay with pleasing its consumers, and it was astute enough to recognize that India's "scientific natives" had very specific needs that not just *any* author could satisfy. While Lethbridge himself wrote the history and geography titles in the Series of Text-Books for Indian Schools, the six *Books of Reading* titles were authored by P. C. Sircar, an Indian professor of English at Calcutta's Presidency College. Sircar's special sensitivity to Indian needs might partly explain the success of his *Books of Reading*: five million copies of the series with Sircar's literary selections and commentaries were sold, and generations of Indians learned English the Sircar-Macmillan way. It was this focus on Indian consumers that distinguished Macmillan and gave it an edge in a rapidly growing market. In unpublished notes that he compiled for the house history that Charles Morgan eventually authored, Thomas Mark, a director at the firm, offered a perspective on its success in India: "Macmillan and Co. have reason to take some pride in their bulky Indian catalogue with its range of English text-books specially prepared for the secondary schools, colleges, and the seventeen universities of modern India, its editions of standard works at the low prices necessary to bring them within the reach of the Indian student, and its hundreds of books in twenty-one of the chief vernaculars."[7]

Keeping its eyes on Indian needs, the firm rapidly built a backbone of massively profitable education titles, and by 1885 it came to recognize that purveying fiction directly to Indian readers might also prove lucrative. In launching the Colonial Library series the following year, Macmillan based it on—and to a significant extent subsidized it initially by—the considerable profits that educational publishing in India had already made available. Indeed, the Colonial Library's connection with the firm's educational list is key in understanding how it came about and particularly in why it succeeded so well. "I have a good many friends in India," Alexander Macmillan wrote W. Stigant in 1862 (*Letters* 116–117), and among those he names are many who subsequently became Macmillan authors, writers, or consultants in the firm's India ventures. By the time the firm sought its second overseas expansion in the 1880s, however, it relied not on friends but on family, in the figure of the newly made partner, Maurice Macmillan, son of Daniel and the only Macmillan to that point who had attended university. A school-master at St. Paul's School in London before he joined the firm, Maurice set out to tour India and Australia in 1884–85 in an attempt to see how the firm's education business might be expanded.[8] What he discovered in conversations with Indian booksellers, librarians, journalists, and readers was exactly what John Kaye had urged forty years earlier (and what Maurice's uncle, Alexander, had been mulling over in his letter to Trevelyan twenty years previously): "There is no country, in which cheap and portable literature is more required." Within months of Maurice's return, the firm launched its Colonial Library with forty-three titles, initially made up of both new works and reprints of recent works.

In dozens of letters that Maurice wrote to newspapers and prospective reviewers in India upon his return, he highlighted the Colonial Library as something specifically directed at Indian needs, much as the educational titles had been a quarter of a century earlier. In a letter of February 22, 1886, to the editor of *The Pioneer* of Allahabad urging review of the firm's books, Maurice described the Colonial Library as "volumes which are produced in a cheap form specially to meet the requirements of English readers in India and the Colonies, where the system of lending libraries is not in vogue as it is at home."[9] In another letter he described the series as "chiefly novels, which we are publishing for the benefit of Indian and Colonial readers who are beyond reach of Mudie's."[10] And in 1886 George Lillie Craik, a partner in the firm, wrote Charlotte Yonge about including her *Chantry House* in the Colonial Library: "It is extraordinary how few books go abroad that there must be a public. We are [convinced?] the price must be low to attract either buyers."[11]

I mention these details to underscore how little the Colonial Library departed from practices such as consumer-friendly pricing and book development that the firm was already using in selling educational titles in India, practices it developed in response to an awareness of Indian pocketbooks and particular needs. The evidence from the Private Letterbooks further indicates that Macmillan's target audience for the Colonial Library in India was at best both Indian and European readers ("either buyers," as Craik emphasized in explaining the pricing policy to Charlotte Yonge). It was never exclusively the expatriate community, nor did the list ever exclude Indian readers.

The firm's correspondence further makes clear that the series emerged entirely out of Maurice's India trip for the purpose of developing an educational list for local needs (hence what Mark informs us were Macmillan's "hundreds of books in twenty-one of the chief vernaculars").[12] It was in researching these needs that another demand became apparent and the Colonial Library developed. As Maurice's letter to *The Pioneer* further indicates, the library's pricing and packaging (elsewhere called, "simple and convenient"[13]) were specially directed to meet Indian readers' needs. The "scientific natives" whom Alexander had lauded in 1863 were also literary, Maurice discovered in 1884–85, and the chiefly novels that the firm now added to its exports in response to the pleas Maurice had heard during his visit met with immediate and immense success. They were hailed by British and Indian readers alike, not just by British residents such as John Kaye almost forty years earlier.

In soliciting titles for the library's launch, Macmillan partners carefully and conscientiously outlined their overseas goals to prospective authors. In a letter to Thomas Hardy on May 31, 1886, Sir Frederick Macmillan wrote:

> We have lately begun the publication of a collection of books, chiefly works of fiction printed in quite a cheap form and intended for circulation *only* in India and the Colonies. Colonial readers have no circulating libraries to go to and grumble very much at the difficulties they experience in getting new books. . . . It seemed to us that the right way to meet the demand and at the same time to cut the ground from the people who proposed to import American editions of English books in the Colonies was to start a kind of Colonial Tauchnitz Library which we have accordingly done.[14]

Both the paucity of cheap fiction in India and the need to protect copyright infringements from American piracies were indeed sound reasons to embark on the Colonial Library with guarded optimism as to its success among readers who eagerly consumed new arrivals in any form. In response to Sir Frederick Macmillan's inquiry, F. Marion Crawford, eventually one of the firm's best-sellers in India, proffered the following entrepreneurial encouragement:

From personal knowledge I am aware that a very large sale might be anticipated in India from a good book published at one rupee, and if you can publish at 12 annas (about 1s 6d) a volume like an English shilling edition, you would catch the whole Eurasian (half-caste) population, who read greedily. . . . The cry in India is for cheap books, especially among the Eurasians.[15]

Despite Crawford's enthusiasm, it is worth scrutinizing whether his contention regarding the low price of books, widely echoed during the period, is adequate to explain the success of Macmillan's series in India. Crawford does not mention what it is that the population is "greedy" to read, nor why, and his remarks beg the question of Murray's earlier failure in India. If cheap books were so much in demand among Indian readers, how does it explain Murray's untimely demise in the Indian market forty years previously?

In acquiring permissions and agreements for the Colonial Library, Macmillan had tried to enumerate the commercial possibilities of the venture for their authors much along Sir Frederick's letter to Hardy above, and while the partners were moderate in their promises of the series' success, they were careful to keep their plans under wraps till after the Colonial Library was actually launched. In a letter of January 21, 1886, Frederick Macmillan urged Frederick Fargus (pseudonym of Hugh Conway, who published two titles in the Colonial Library) that "until the series is regularly started I shall be obliged if you will not mention it to anyone else. Other publishers are pretty sure to follow the example but we wish to be first in the field."[16] Indeed, other publishers did follow the example, as Macmillan itself had with John Murray's venture earlier in the century, and in analyzing Macmillan's success, it is vital to contrast it first with a predecessor's attempts and then a competitor's in order to highlight what this particular firm's history in the Indian market tells us about the consumption and circulation of British books in the Subcontinent during the last quarter of the nineteenth century.

Macmillan vs. Murray. Despite the many changes in Victorian publishing that had taken place in the forty-odd years separating Macmillan's venture into colonial markets from Murray's, there were numerous

organizational and structural similarities between the two mostly fam-
ily-held companies that deserve note. Both had initiated their colonial
series in response to changes in copyright legislation: Murray to the
1842 Copyright Act, directed largely at cheap American piracies that
legislated penalties for unauthorized reprints of a British copyright
holder's works, and Macmillan to the 1885 draft of the Berne International Convention and the ensuing 1886 International Copyright Act
that protected the validity of works registered in a colony throughout
the empire.[17] To this initial end, both firms started their series with the
intention of selling reprints and new titles, and both had a respected
name and distinctive market behind them on which they planned to
build: Murray in travel and history, and Macmillan as an educational
publisher in Cambridge since 1843 and India after 1860. In both companies it was the arrival of a new member that inaugurated their respective overseas ventures: with Murray, it was the arrival of John Murray
III as the new head, implementing a plan conceived with his father; and
with Macmillan, it was the arrival of Maurice Macmillan into partner-
ship that, in Charles Morgan's words, "put into practice the ideas that
had been stirring forty years earlier in [his uncle] Alexander's mind"
(187).

As Angus Fraser has argued, Murray's aim with the Colonial and
Home Library was fairly judicious: "the thought of displacing the competition from American piracies, coupled with a sense of obligation
towards the government for the new legislation [the 1842 Copyright
Act], was much more prominent than social engineering in the minds
of the Murrays" (341), a fact that the firm's prospectus on the series
adumbrates. Another important point about Murray's series that the
prospectus also makes clear is how the firm conceived its target audience. As the series' title, the Colonial and Home Library, suggests, the
volumes in it were meant for both colonial *and* home markets, and in
this regard, Murray did not seem troubled that the cheap one-volume
titles priced for overseas sale might undercut the higher priced domestic market for the same title. Macmillan, on the other hand, in model-
ing itself after the Tauchnitz series had very consciously protected
domestic sales from being undercut by cheaply priced Colonial Library
titles by forbidding the sale of colonial editions in the United Kingdom. To this end, the title pages of all Macmillan Colonial Library volumes bore the notation, "Only for sale in India and the Colonies."

Despite Murray's flexibility about having its potential domestic audience include "a large portion of the less wealthy audience at home" (Nowell-Smith, *International Copyright Law* 29), the 1843 prospectus nonetheless reveals a paradoxical narrowness in conceiving its overseas readers: "Mr. Murray's 'Colonial Library' will furnish the settler of the backwoods of America, and the occupant of the remotest cantonment of our Indian dominions, with the resources of recreation and instruction at a moderate price, together with many new books, within a short period of their appearance in England" (Nowell-Smith, ibid. 29). Nowhere does Murray mention a commitment to extending the "resources of recreation and instruction" to the scientific natives whom Alexander Macmillan had so approvingly eyed and identified in his firm's own venture later on. Indeed, even among the settlers and occupants, Murrays' resources of recreation and instruction were found to be short: in its review of the series, *Simmonds's Colonial Magazine and Miscellany* rued that "the selection of works announced for publication does not confirm the new and current works of the day, but only those which have first been extensively circulated at home, until no further sale can be obtained for them."[18] A Canadian review is even blunter: "Instead of issuing cheap editions of his latest works, he [Murray] reissues those that the 'run' is chiefly over for, and which have been reprinted and extensively circulated on this side of the Atlantic long ago."[19] Other reviewers assailed the titles in the Colonial and Home Library for being "too serious for the average colonist looking for light reading" (Fraser 370). Not only were the books apparently ill-suited to readerly needs in the colonies, but Murray was also accused of practicing a form of colonial dumping in which old titles or large print runs were disposed of cheaply overseas in the hope of squeezing a little more profit from them rather than issuing editions of "latest works" that were still turning a profit at home.

John Murray III gestured toward his failure in the colonial marketplace within nine months of the series' launch when he transposed its title in 1844 to Home and Colonial Library. As Angus Fraser further documents, the original audience of the series (settlers and colonists) still appeared in advertisements and prospectuses, but "they now jostled with a range of other suggested recipients or uses: parochial and lending libraries; book societies and book clubs; libraries in schools, factories, workshops and servants' halls; school prizes; travellers on a journey; passengers on board ship; army and navy officers; presents for friends in distant countries; and, finally, the student and lover of literature at home" (371). Murray ceased adding titles to the series in 1849, at which point it essentially ended.[20] Direct Indian responses to it (such as the Canadian *Simmonds's Colonial Magazine* review cited earlier) have been difficult to locate, although extant public library catalogues from the period show very little of the series to be present within holdings of the period or even its titles within Indian translation records. What comprised the Colonial and Home Library and why did it fold?

In the six short years of its existence (1843–49), Murray's Colonial and Home Library published forty-nine titles reflecting the firm's strengths in travel and history. Table 3.1 lists the percentage of holdings for different categories.[21] With Macmillan's Colonial Library, these figures are dramatically inverted: of the 680 titles published between 1886–1916, 93 percent (or 629 titles) were fiction, with history and travel trailing at roughly 1 percent to 3 percent respectively. Despite John Murray III's claim in December 1843 that "I am obliged in the selection of books to study the taste of the middle & lower orders among whom my readers lie in a great degree,"[22] his list did not commit much at all to satisfying the tastes of these readers, providing them with only four fiction titles. Numerous historical sources attest that the home market in the 1840s saw the lower and middle orders enamored with fiction despite concerned attempts to encourage other, higher forms of reading promoted by organizations such as the Society for the Diffusion of Useful Knowledge (which adamantly published no fiction).[23] Despite the prospectus' claims, therefore, Murray's list conveys the firm's preference for endorsing instruction over recreation (or recreation *through* instruction), revealing a general aversion to and prejudice against fiction altogether.[24]

TABLE 3.1 Taxonomy of Titles in Murray's Colonial & Home Library, 1849

Travel writing	45%
History	20%
Memoirs and biographies	18%
Poetry and miscellany	9%
Fiction	8%

In her 1835 account of the pleasures of books in India, Emma Roberts keenly described the particular appeal that the novel held for starved readers in remote locations who chanced upon a well-stocked visitor, "travelling with two or three chests of books as a way of beguiling time in a lonely journey":

> The inhabitants of the station had been accustomed to send to a miserable circulation library, about a hundred miles off, for the "last new work by the author of *Waverley*," and were often fain to be content with the refuse of the Minerva Press: happy were they, when the unconscious passenger deposited at their feet the lucubrations of some popular writer! (*Scenes* 3:8)

Roberts's account marks not only the general paucity of books in India but also the particular demand for novels, be they by the author of *Waverley* or cheap gothic romances published by Minerva Press. More discriminating in taste than those she observes, Roberts nonetheless provides intelligence from the ground of reading conditions and preferences in the decade preceding Murray's Library in India. Provisionally, then, the evidence suggests that notwithstanding the cheapness and portability of books that characterized Murray's venture, the abysmal failure to commit to fiction in its list (a total of four titles only) served to doom it. Indeed, Kaye's review with which this chapter begins praised Murray's library for the production and pricing of its list but not the product itself. Having mentioned Murray in passing in the passage cited earlier, Kaye spent the remainder of his lengthy article reviewing Chapman and Hall's Monthly Series, "to which we now desire to call particular attention . . . [for] its four or five *original* works of fiction and biography" (205; emphasis added). Not only did Murray's Colonial and Home Library fail over the Monthly Series for apparently not providing fiction, it also failed because of the still overwhelming array of reprints that outnumbered new works on the list.[25] In sum, there was not much fiction—nor much that was new—in Murray's list to generate enthusiasm among readers in India who Emma Roberts (in 1835), John Kaye (in 1846), and F. Marion Crawford (in 1886) alert us, were starved—especially for fiction.

Perhaps because of Maurice Macmillan's extensive travels in India in 1884–85, he gathered a better sense of readers' needs than the House of Murray had acquired earlier. Macmillan's correspondence certainly demonstrates this, as reflected in Sir Frederick's letter to Thomas Hardy in which he explains conditions that virtually echo part of Murray's 1843 prospectus: "it seemed to us that the right way to meet the demand and at the same time to cut the ground from the people who proposed to import American editions of English books in the Colonies was to start a kind of Colonial Tauchnitz Library which we have accordingly done." Macmillan of course promised that they would provide both new books and fiction in their Colonial Library, which they did (the letter to Hardy cited earlier is revealing here). However, a glance at the order in which the firm published titles in the Colonial Library indicates how cautious it initially was in departing too widely from a strategy that had already proven so successful in the Indian educational market.

The first two titles from the series were Lady Barker's *Station Life in New Zealand* and *A Year's Housekeeping in South Africa*, books on which the firm already owned imperial copyright and that were apparently intended for settlers of various vintages. The titles had poor sales: 2,000 copies of *Station Life* and 1,000 of *Housekeeping* were printed by the firm in toto.[26] Numbers three and four in the library were William Black's *Princess of Thule* (originally published 1874) and *The Family Affair* (originally published 1885) by Hugh Conway (alias Frederick Fargus), with print runs of 4,000 and 4,500 copies. However, the print runs that exceeded the geometric increase between titles one and four and that suggest something far more complicated was at stake were the runs for the next two titles, F. Marion Crawford's novels, *Mr. Isaacs: A Tale of Modern India* (1882) with a total printing of 12,500 and *Dr. Claudius: A True Story* (1883) at 11,500. Household vade mecums and travel accounts, which ranked among the most popular genres among settlers and Anglo-Indians, clearly failed in Macmillan's Colonial Library despite being both "cheap and recent," while Crawford's novels made and continued to make a big splash.

The reason for this lies in part upon how Macmillan figured its readership at this early stage of the series. In the educational market, the audience for whom the firm produced books was clearly established and the strategy of meeting its particular needs a laudable one that encountered lasting success and consolidated a considerable overseas reputation. However, despite Maurice's assurance to the editor of the

Allahabad *Pioneer*, the firm sought a wider readership for the Colonial Library that included both Indians and Europeans ("either audience" as Craik had written Charlotte Yonge in 1886). Lady Barker's two non-fiction volumes on settler life were most likely intended for the European expatriate market, and their failure partly illustrates both the slimness of this market's share in purchasing books as well as the tepid interest that nonfiction titles generally elicited in India. With the fiction titles on its list, however, Macmillan had immediate success, and the novel eventually came to comprise 93 percent of the Colonial Library, with the bulk being new titles—a sharp contrast to Murray's 8 percent of reprints.

The comparison with Murray's list is instructive in bringing to light which genre sold best in India—and indeed the colonies more generally.[27] Yet much had changed in Victorian publishing between 1843 when Murray started its series and 1886 when Macmillan began the Colonial Library, rendering further comparison between these two firms a bit tricky. On the other hand, Kegan Paul began an Indian and Colonial Series in 1887, within a year of Macmillan's, and the decks are more evenly stacked here for a comparison between the two firms that should highlight what *specific* kinds of novels sold best in India and why Macmillan succeeded to the extent that it did.

Macmillan vs. Kegan Paul. By the 1880s the firm of Kegan Paul possessed all the ingredients to predict success in the colonial market, most notably through Paul's long-standing affiliation with experts in the India trade. Through Henry King, to whom he served as literary adviser, Paul had contact with the firm Smith Elder and Company, in which King was both partner and brother-in-law to George Smith. In the early days, Smith Elder combined what Frank Mumby has called "the oddly assorted business" of running an Indian agency that supplied books to officers of the East India Company (and serving as their bankers) alongside a publishing concern with a strong list of fiction.[28] In 1868 the firm split, with King taking over the India agency and Smith Elder continuing as publishers of a massively successful list, including authors such as Charlotte Brontë, Thackeray, Mrs. Humphry Ward, Mrs. Gaskell, and the serial *Cornhill* (which Thackeray edited). In 1877 King sold off the remaining publishing portion of his company to Paul, devoting himself entirely to the Indian agency but dying shortly afterward, in 1878.

Kegan Paul now had the Indian market open if he chose to pursue it, with all of King's contacts available to him. His close friend and associate, Nicholas Trübner, often called "the Prince of Oriental Publishers" (Mumby x), provided a form of expertise on India if it were needed, although Trübner (whose firm was merged with Kegan Paul's after 1889) had a scholarly, Orientalist bent that did not lean toward fiction at all. Therefore, despite all these possibilities and opportunities, when the firm of Kegan Paul initiated its Indian and Colonial Library in 1887, it appears to have done so with two drawbacks. First, King's market for books in India had largely remained the expatriate one to which Smith Elder had earlier supplied books and stationery, and it was this market that Kegan Paul conceived for its library as it was the only one with which the firm had contacts and real experience. Second, the firm appears to have had some misgivings about putting out a form of publishing (fiction) that it had never fully embraced, and it seemed to have pursued the library out of some sort of copy-cat motive, or what Leslie Howsam has identified as the partners' recognition of it largely "as a source of rich profits to their contemporaries."[29] In short, despite having resources and access to knowledge of Indian conditions to match Macmillan's, Kegan Paul's heart did not seem to lie fully behind its Indian venture, nor was it able to make the shifts in thinking necessary to compete with Macmillan's hold upon a market at this point largely constituted by Indian readers. All this further underscores the irony of a missed opportunity: George Routledge died a few years after Kegan Paul's Indian venture started, and the firm was reorganized into Routledge, Kegan Paul, Trench, Trübner and Company acquiring a hefty list of Routledge's best-selling and reprint fiction (including the massively successful Railway Library). Had Routledge's considerable fiction been folded into Kegan Paul's Indian and Colonial Library, it might have served as real competition to Macmillan's efforts in India, and we might have ended with a very different story altogether.

As it stands, in the two years that Kegan Paul's Indian and Colonial Library Series ran (1887–89), it put out forty-three titles (and nineteen authors) of mostly reprints; Macmillan, on the other hand, put out eighty-eight titles (and forty-one authors) of mostly new titles in the same period, blitzing the market with diversity and real choice. Over a third of Kegan Paul's novels (fifteen titles) were by a single author, the onetime clergyman, George Macdonald (1824–1905), while the number of works by any single author in the first year of Macmillan's list (five titles by Mrs. Oliphant, four by F. Marion Crawford) was kept quite small in comparison. However, these data in themselves are most revealing about the relative success of the two series in India when tested against actual readership and consumption, and the major way to do such testing is indirect.

I examined catalogues of five nineteenth-century public libraries in India where the membership was entirely Indian and compiled a master list of all novelists present in any of these libraries.[30] Typically, most novelists appeared in more than one library; some in all or almost all of them. From this master-list of 207 authors, I identified those novelists who appeared in 80 percent or more of the libraries (i.e., in at least four of the five collections) in multiple titles and copies, arriving at a shortlist of the forty-eight authors listed in table 3.2.

These two lists reveal the following insights: first that authors from Kegan Paul's Indian and Colonial Series comprise 3 percent of the total number of writers found in Indian libraries (i.e., Kegan Paul authors constitute 3 percent of the master list of fiction in the five libraries studied), whereas authors from Macmillan's series constitute 22 percent of the same list. The second and more revealing point emerged when I turned to the shortlist (see table 3.2) of most popular authors in Indian libraries: Kegan Paul authors declined in share from 3 percent to 2 percent (i.e., to a single Kegan Paul author, Philip Meadows Taylor), whereas Macmillan authors *increased* in share to constitute 33 percent of the "most-popular" shortlist (an increase of 50 percent over the initial master list to constitute sixteen of the forty-eight novelists, as indicated in table 3.2).

The fact that fully a third of the most popular authors in India come from Macmillan merits a closer scrutiny of its list. If examining Murray's Colonial and Home Library makes clear that fiction was consumed more avidly than any other form in India, the comparison with Kegan Paul's Indian and Colonial Library makes clear that *Macmillan* fiction was consumed more avidly than fiction from any other single British publishing firm. Holdings in the Bombay People's Free Reading Room and Library (established 1845), where membership was entirely composed of Indians, further reveal that among

TABLE 3.2 Novelists in Indian Library Catalogues, II

AUTHORS	COLONIAL LIBRARY
*Ainsworth, W. H.	
Austen, Jane	
Besant, Walter	Macmillan
Black, William	Macmillan
*Braddon, M. E.	
Broughton, Rhoda	Macmillan
*Bulwer-Lytton, Edward	Macmillan
Caine, Hall	
*Collins, Wilkie	
Conway, Hugh	Macmillan
Cooper, J. F.	
*Corelli, Marie	
*Crawford, F. Marion	Macmillan
Defoe, Daniel	
*Dickens, Charles	
*Disraeli, Benjamin	
*Doyle, Arthur Conan	
*Dumas, Alexandre	
*Eliot, George	
Fielding, Henry	
*Haggard, H. Rider	
Hardy, Thomas	Macmillan
*Harte, Bret	Macmillan
Hope, Anthony	Macmillan
Hugo, Victor	
*James, G. P. R.	
James, Henry	Macmillan

TABLE 3.2 Novelists in Indian Library Catalogues, II (*continued*)

AUTHORS	COLONIAL LIBRARY
*Kingsley, Charles	Macmillan
Kipling, Rudyard	Macmillan
*Lever, Charles	
*Marryat, Capt. Frederick	
Meredith, George	
Oliphant, Mrs.	Macmillan
*Ouida	Macmillan
*Reade, Charles	
*Reynolds, G. W. M.	
*Scott, Sir Walter	
*Stevenson, R. L.	
Taylor, Meadows	Kegan Paul
*Thackeray, W. M.	
Tolstoy, Leo	
Trollope, Anthony	
Twain, Mark	
Verne, Jules	
Ward, Mrs. Humphry	Macmillan
Wood, Mrs. Henry	
*Yonge, Charlotte	Macmillan
*Zola, Emile	

* indicates novelists present in all five library catalogues.

SOURCES: *Calcutta Chaitanya Library Catalogue of English Books* (Calcutta: n.p., 1903); *Catalogue of Books in the Uttarpara Public Library* (Calcutta: Gupta Press, 1903); *The Bombay Native General Library Catalogue of Books* (Bombay: Jehangier B. Marzban, 1898); *The Jamsetjee Nesserwanjee Petit Fort Reading Room and Library, Bombay Classified Catalogue of Books* (Bombay: Captain Printing Press, 1895); *Catalogue of the Delhi Public Library* (Delhi: n.p., 1902).

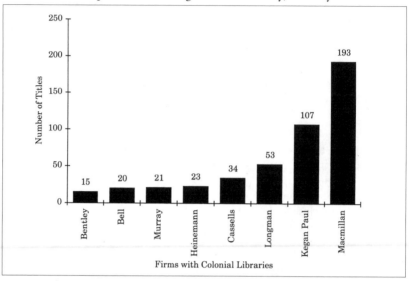

FIGURE 3.1 Number of Titles from Firms with Colonial Libraries in the People's Free Reading Room & Library, Bombay

British publishers who marketed volumes in various colonial libraries to India, Macmillan titles appear most prolifically, towering at almost thirteen times, or 193 titles, over Bentley's 15 titles and Murray's 21, and close to doubling Kegan Paul's 107 titles. Figure 3.1 graphically plots Macmillan's presence in this Bombay public library.

OFFLOADING GARBAGE, THE TWO-HANDED ENGINE, AND AN "ANTI-REALISTIC BIAS": OR, MAKING MACMILLAN'S COLONIAL LIBRARY

In the previous chapter I suggested that, based on public library hold-ings and translations into Indian languages, a particular form of the British novel was most popular among a diversity of Indian readers. Fiction in what I identified as the melodramatic mode interpellated, mobilized, and otherwise resonated among Indian readers, who found in it a world commensurate with their own psychic and symbolic needs. In this mode, as exemplified in the novels of G. W. M. Reynolds, Indian readers found an author whose narrative economy corroborated their own, onto whose moral sensibilities they could project their own dreams and desires. Reynolds functioned among a range of Indian readers as what Gramsci would call a "psychic stimulant,"[31] both stimulating and helping articulate the inchoate mass of dissatisfactions, anxieties, hopes, and fantasies that the indignities of time, place, and empire had heaped upon them.

These patterns of taste in readership persisted throughout the nineteenth century as the previous chapter's data on translation underscores, and it is this reading preference that Macmillan's Colonial Library encountered when it started selling books in India. F. Marion Crawford entrusted forty of his forty-four novels to the Colonial Library series and became one of the library's best sellers, along with Mrs. Humphry Ward (41,000 copies of *Robert Elsmere* were printed for colonial sales; 21,000 of *David Grieve* and 20,000 of *Marcella*) and H. S. Merriman (whose *Barlash of the Guard*, *The Vultures*, and *Last Hope* were printed at 13,000, 12,000, and 10,000 copies respectively).[32]

Crawford, Ward, Merriman—a peculiar canon of best-sellers, among whose oeuvre there is virtually no nonfiction *and* all of whose titles appear in a library whose most popular books, if we can make assumptions from print runs, are all fiction. Herein may lie in part Macmillan's success. The firm initially used its old education strategy with the Colonial Library, producing books they imagined would address wide (i.e., Indian *and* expatriate) readerly interest in the colonies; but each of these titles, which were in the main nonfiction, had poor runs in the first year of the library's existence. Mrs. Oliphant's three-volume *Literary History* had a single printing of 1,500 copies each (numbers 17–19, 1886), as did the anonymously published *About Money and Other Things* (number 38, 1886, 1,500 copies printed). The only nonfiction "success" to have a large and repeated printing was J. R. Seeley's *Expansion of England* (number 118, 1890, at 14,000 copies).[33] Even works with colonial themes animated by the author's personal insights, such as Lady Barker's volumes that inaugurated the series (numbers 1 and 2 at 2,000 and 1,000 copies, respectively) and William Forbes-Mitchell's *Reminiscences of the Great Mutiny* (number 160, 1893) seemed to do poorly, the latter at a total printing of only 5,500 copies.

Fortunately, there was a lot more to the Colonial Library than nonfiction: there was a substantial list of fiction, in which the trio, Crawford, Ward, and Merriman, played a salient and successful role. It has always been something of a conundrum for literary historians to interpret why these writers should have had and maintained both high sales and continuing prestige in India, and a commonplace explanation has been that the colonies were simply a convenient dumping ground for the excess—and excrescence—of the imperial center. According to this account, Macmillan's Colonial Library was a cheap and convenient way for the firm to protect its copyright interest in British authors against American piracies, while dumping quantities of unsold and unsellable books in India and other "undiscriminating" colonial markets, as Simon Nowell-Smith has suggested (*International Copyright Law* 102). According to this explanation, Indian readers read these books because there was nothing else around to read, an explanation that of course fails to consider that Indian readers showed none of this charity of taste toward Murray's or even Kegan Paul's colonial enterprise. Like many implausible arguments, this one too has a certain seductive logic to it— namely, the sense of the colonies as a dumping ground for metropolitan surplus. The argument is simply not borne out in the case of Macmillan in India, however, as the following discussion based on the firm's publishing records, correspondence files, and readers' reports makes clear.

Macmillan expended considerable amounts toward producing the Colonial Library by ensuring a certain look and style and choosing the prestigious and rather expensive printers R. & R. Clark of Edinburgh for the job. Clark was renowned for its speed and accuracy in printing, and the firm had acquired a substantial reputation of its own, so much so that James Frazer expressly requested it for *The Golden Bough* (1890), "as I understand that their work is not surpassed by that of any other printer of the day."[34] Whatever gamble or risk may have been a part of the venture, Macmillan took the Colonial Library seriously enough to get the best printer for the job and to provide it with very explicit instructions of what was expected for Colonial Library editions. Shortly after the inauguration of the series, Maurice Macmillan sent a detailed letter to R. & R. Clark requesting a poster for railway bookstalls in India:

> The special feature about it must be its distinctiveness. The type should be as plain and as large as possible, the larger lower-case as in James' novels and Tales being of a kind that we think would be most attractive. The paper should be blue and the ink a rich

brown. The authors' names should not we think be press on, as they will not be very readable in that form, if they can be arranged in this fashion they will surely attract attention [with a sketch following to illustrate the point]. But we will leave it to you to make the bill as attractive as possible without being gaudy.[35]

The care and attention that Maurice and others lavished upon all aspects of the Colonial Library, including the specification to Clark to make Colonial Library books "as attractive as possible" suggest that there is another, more convincing reason that the firm could simply not have been using a colonial dumping practice for excess stock. Most Colonial Library titles were published to coincide with the British publication date, sometimes even appearing in the colonies a few months *before* their domestic counterparts as Nowell-Smith has shown (*International Copyright Law* 8–12) in the case of George Meredith's *The Amazing Marriage* (1895) and Henry James's *The Tragic Muse* (1890). Waiting to know a book's commercial success could take up to a year and deem the mission of the library null and void: any delay in issuing a colonial edition could mean that commercially successful titles might already have appeared in the colony in pirated American reprints (undercutting the British firm's profit), or that even two-year-old "unsuccessful" titles would be two years old and less desirable in the colonial demand for new titles. The whole aim of the Colonial Library was to be first in the colony, thus disabling potential infiltration by American publishers. In the case of India and the Colonial Library, then, the logic of profit and demand prevailed over the more insidious logic of imperial dumping.

Finally, there is the rather knotty issue of the firm's own selection and attitude toward the titles that went into the Colonial Library. Until Gertrude Mayer joined Macmillan following the purchase of Richard Bentley's firm in 1898, Mowbray Morris was the principal reader of general literature for Macmillan (and between 1891 and 1911 this was in fact his title), a man whose prejudices Gail Chester has eloquently enumerated: "Of course he had an aversion to women, black and Irish people, and working class people, but he also despised old men, young men, journalists, Americans, Australians, in fact anybody who lived outside Central London, and especially, it seems, unknown university extension teachers."[36] This scabrous figure, editor of *Macmillan's Magazine*, has become quite notorious among historians of British publishing for his maledictive dismissals of famous and infamous writers.[37]

Yet, in reading the firm's Readers' Reports in the two decades between 1886 and 1906,[38] the Morris one encounters also appears as a scrupulous reader who held a particularly Olympian standard in selecting titles for the Colonial Library rather than one who used it as a rubbish heap for unsuccessful titles. "From what I have gathered of the qualifications for your Colonial Library, I do not think that either 'The Marble Faun' or its author possesses them," he remarked in one report.[39] On another submission he cautioned, "It would be wiser, I think, to wait and see what the English public thinks of Miss Birell before introducing her to the Colonies"; and about a third volume he wrote, "on its own merits, I should rank the book a long way above the common herd; but when you are asked to take it for both the Home and Colonial Markets, one or two points have to be considered. . . . If the book failed here, that will hardly make for its popularity in the Colonial Library, which on its own merits I think it deserves."[40] Consistent with this logic, Morris dismissed submission after submission because of relative lack of knowledge of the author. In a fairly typical rejection of four manuscripts from the literary agents Messrs. Constable and Co., he bracingly offers: "Mr. Constable, might, I think, be told that for the future he may spare himself, and you, the trouble of offering fragments of stories by unknown and anonymous authors for your Colonial Library. . . . The four do not make a very promising batch for the Colonial or any other library."[41] As Thomas Mark's notes further indicate: "other publishers offered books for inclusion in the [Colonial Library] series, but judging from the reports on works thus submitted, with Mowbray Morris as the two-handed engine at the door, the standards imposed were somewhat exacting."[42]

Mark is undoubtedly displaying his signature diplomacy in assessing Morris mildly as a two-handed engine at the door. Morris was a spirited reader for the firm with strong opinions and exacting standards, and his reports reveal a number of often contradictory attitudes toward its Colonial Library. First, that insofar as his reports reflect the firm's policy, they decimate the garbage-dumping theory altogether. Not only had books for the Colonial Library to be good before being accepted for publication, they often also had to be successful in the home market. Furthermore, simply being "a long way above the common herd" was not good enough: a title apparently had to arrive in the colonies with a dossier of successful reviews behind it before it would be considered seriously for inclusion in what was becoming a very lucrative list. At times, Morris was of the view that "it is of course idle for you or me to attempt to gauge native tastes," as he cautioned Frederick Macmillan in 1896;[43] while at others, he was quite certain that local color would sell well in Australia, though never in India. At yet other times he displayed the conviction that a work with "unreal" formal qualities and a "good, brisk, stirring tale . . . might fare better in your Colonial Library [than at home]."[44]

From among these widely dispersed views, the most consistent conviction apparent in the Readers' Reports is that colonial sales were considerably important to the firm. When in doubt over a work, Morris frequently resorted to assessing authors' reputations as an index to their salability abroad, often displaying a hopeless blind spot even for writers of good, brisk, stirring tales such as Conrad, whose work he pronounced: "clever it is of a kind, certainly, but with a cheerless, unprofitable cleverness, from which I can conceive no pleasure be got."[45] Mercifully, Morris's reports were not always the last word on a manuscript's fate at Macmillan. In some cases, such as Yeats and Hardy, the authors returned to the firm despite searing early rejections; in others, Frederick Macmillan or another reader exercised his own judgment and proceeded to publish a volume Morris had dismissed.

Nevertheless, the reports illuminate a number of important points about the Colonial Library and its success in India. In the crucial early years between 1886, when the Colonial Library started, and 1891, just before Morris became general reader for the firm, most publishing decisions for the library were made by the firm's partners (largely Frederick and Maurice), in occasional consultation with India experts such as F. Marion Crawford and in conjunction with Maurice's own experiences and observations following his extended trip to India and Australasia. There was no question that fiction was to form a mainstay of the library, and the firm was shrewd enough in marketing to learn quickly what sold best and where. The forty-three titles they put out in the first year alone were a substantial enough number to allow for a few failures without the entire list toppling. Of the thirty novels introduced in that first year, Crawford's *Mr. Isaacs* and *Dr. Claudius* were the only works to exceed the 10,000 print mark (the former at 12,500 and the latter at 11,500). In 1887, again it was Crawford's *Saracinesca* whose printing of 10,500 towered over all other titles, which trailed as they had in the previous year at printings of two to three thousand each. It is the popularity of Crawford's fiction that shortly furnishes one explanation for why Macmillan fiction sold so successfully in India.

By 1891, when Morris became a General Reader reviewing manuscripts for the firm, many submissions were made by authors specifically seeking to be included in the Colonial Library. Morris continued the already established and successful publishing practices that Frederick and Maurice had initiated in the 1880s, selecting fiction of a certain kind on which the firm had already made a name and, when in doubt, rejecting the author for his or her lack of established reputation. Charles Morgan has suggested that "Mowbray Morris and other Readers of the 'nineties and of the following years had an anti-realistic bias which was expressed with a perilous emphasis, and led to the exclusion of some of the young lions . . . who might have brought in others of their generation and added to the list of fiction a vitality different in kind from that which it possessed" (144–145). Crucially, Morris's "anti-realistic" bias in fact blended nicely with the firm's already established practice toward fiction, especially in the Colonial Library, a practice that I maintain was pursued because it found expression and repeated approval among Indian readers who made Macmillan their firm of choice, not simply for schoolbooks and educational material as they had already done earlier in the century but also for the novels they consumed voraciously and freely in their leisure.

The firm's willingness to please this audience through "anti-realistic" fiction may in fact have cost it some of the "young lions" of the new century or a vitality it did not possess in fiction as Morgan regrets, but it appeared to be a price the firm was willing to pay, as it clearly cost it nothing in profits or prestige in an overseas market that was increasingly central to the firm's fiscal health. In the decade or so between 1890 and 1902, Macmillan's sales to India more than doubled, from between £15,000 to £16,000 in 1890 to £36,852 in 1902.[46] By 1901 over 80 percent of Macmillan's *total* foreign sales came from the Indian market, exceeding even the sales from the firm's New York branch. By 1903, when J. A. Stagg, the firm's agent in India retired, Frederick Macmillan agreed to keep him on full salary in Britain with the understanding that he would "hold [himself] at our disposal to give us advice and information with reference to any question in connection with our Indian business that might occur," even while having appointed another agent, E. Marsden, to take over Stagg's position on the ground with full salary and commission.[47] It is a striking offer for a firm so careful with its personnel expenses, and it underscores the increasing significance of the Indian market to Macmillan's finances.

Indeed, evidence in the firm's archives not only overturns the garbage-dumping theory toward the colonial marketplace altogether but also, and more powerfully, reveals how crucial the colonial archive itself remains to supplying a more accurate sense of the novelistic world in Britain. While scholars such as Gaye Tuchman have argued that Macmillan compensated its women novelists less than it did men of equal stature, research from the colonial market sheds light on whether this may, in fact, have been so. Between 1886 (when the Colonial Library began) and 1890, Margaret Oliphant received £3,540 from Macmillan, while F. Marion Crawford, a novelist whom Tuchman demonstrates was of comparable status and fame, received £8,950. The discrepancy in compensation (which came from the firm's payment for copyright rather than royalties as would later become customary) is striking, and it appears to corroborate Tuchman's claim of discrimination against women novelists in the Victorian literary marketplace. Yet when we examine Macmillan's Edition Books, in which print runs for all Colonial Library titles are noted, Mrs. Oliphant's payments were quite generous in light of the print runs that her titles enjoyed: 24,500 copies of different titles were printed in total for the Colonial Library during this period while 90,500 copies of Crawford's titles were printed. The largest total print run that an individual Oliphant title claimed in its lifetime with the Colonial Library never exceeded 3,000 copies, while Crawford's smallest total run was 5,000 copies (with a high of 12,500 copies for *Mr. Isaacs*).

These figures, according to which Crawford's total titles were printed almost four times more than Mrs. Oliphant's, help clarify the accuracy of Tuchman's claim regarding a gender-based discrepancy over compensation. Crawford's sales were larger than Oliphant's by almost four times when the colonial market is included in the aggregate computation (90,500 copies over 24,500): his remuneration, however, was only two and half times that of Mrs. Oliphant's (£8,950 to her £3,540). Under the circumstances, at least in this comparison, Macmillan's policies seem equitable, if not slightly favorable, to the woman novelist.[48] If anything, then, the colonial print runs further stress the point that it is not just that Crawford sold better than Oliphant and thus required larger print runs that matters, but that he sold better *in India and the colonies* that matters, as this last fact emphasizes how crucially the happenings in the Indian and colonial market determined Macmillan's policies in the domestic one. It is a story that further highlights how significant the colonial marketplace remains for an accurate understanding of the novel's production and publication in Britain.

In sum, reading this archive underscores the consideration that Indian readerly preferences and colonial sales elicited from Macmillan's management. Indian readers, the evidence demonstrates, were neither passive recipients of metropolitan excess nor compliant coolies in the cultural traffic that originated in Britain. They articulated their needs clearly and persuasively to the Macmillans during Maurice's reconnaissance visit of 1885 and continued to make discriminating judgments of what they liked and did not like to read. The "good, brisk stirring tales" that Morris and others kept supplying into the Colonial Library *and* into the firm's overall fiction list would suggest that it was the overseas readership that eventually determined the firm's accessions in fiction. Yet, while Morgan rues the readers' "anti-realistic" bias in Macmillan's total fiction list, the evidence also seems to suggest that it was Indian and colonial readers who exercised this bias *and* who made the firm ignore alternatives for which the fiscal rewards were not as clear as those from the Colonial Library. The "exclusion of some of the young lions" who might have vitalized Macmillan's fiction list for posterity was never, it seems, regarded as a serious loss: the firm continued to reap a considerable profit from the audience for fiction in India, and in pleasing this audience by providing fiction of the kind it sought, it seems that Macmillan was willing to neglect or ignore other, closer audiences. The firm's reticence toward Conrad and Ford and its rejection of Yeats and Shaw (whose writing puzzled Macmillan's reader for being "without plot or issue" [Morgan 119]) are well documented.[49] Anything resembling modernist—or even modern—innovation took years to be accepted by the firm, to the extent that it took a book war in the 1890s and a world war in 1914–18 for the firm to "grow younger," the title of Morgan's chapter detailing the firm's reluctant advance into newer literary trends. Up through the First World War, the colonial market served remarkably to preserve a particular flavor in Macmillan's overall fiction list, one that included a pronounced "anti-realistic" bias and tended to exclude emerging literary trends of the 1890s and early twentieth century.

The Indian influence was small but steady: it managed to extend the contours and shape of the Colonial Library onto the firm's larger accessions in fiction as well as to render stability in the form of stasis to what ought to have been a dynamic and evolving list. "I think you're out of touch with the contemporary movement in literature," complained H. G. Wells in a characteristically candid letter to Sir Frederick in 1907 (Nowell-Smith, *Letters* 271), astutely pressing the firm to move out of the 1880s and into the twentieth century. The refusal to do so that Morgan, Mark, and others rue has much to do with consumers and a marketplace emanating from India and the colonies whose influence on what Macmillan produced through the First World War ("anti-realistic" fiction of the 1880s mode) remains truly astonishing. In sum, it would appear that it was the Indian and colonial readers who shaped Macmillan's fiction toward the end of the nineteenth century, not just in the colonies but at home as well.

WHY MACMILLAN?

The fullest set of Indian reviews of Macmillan's Colonial Library appear in the *Madras Christian College Magazine*, an English-language monthly for Indian consumption modeled very loosely upon the *Edinburgh Review*. It published lengthy articles by Indian authors and, unlike the *Edinburgh Review*, which never carried fiction, serialized Indian fiction (most memorably Krupa Satthianadhan's two novels [see chapter 4], *Kamala: A Tale of Native Hindu Life* [1894] and *Saguna: A Tale of Christian Life* [1892]). The serial is notable in this period for its unusually outspoken positions on numerous topics, especially those having to do with Britain and Englishness where, instead of blind encomia or bland regard, its writers ventured into brisk and often tart assessments.[50] In a print sample of approximately fifteen years, starting in 1886, the *Magazine* reviewed Macmillan titles both in the Colonial Library and from its education list, alongside reviews of works from other London firms such as Longman, Cassells, George Bell, etc.[51]

Because of their length and continuity, these reviews provide a window into the market that Macmillan had targeted, as well as a sense of how the firm's efforts were being received by a particular corner of that market.

Commending Macmillan's efforts to make cheap books available in India, a *Magazine* reviewer echoed the firm's own market research in the first review of the Colonial Library in 1886:

> Here our public libraries and reading clubs are at best costly and unsatisfactory, as indeed they must be till their constituents are more numerous and centralized. The best managed library in a Presidency town can do little to benefit the mofussil. Here then there is undoubtedly a field for Messrs. Macmillan's bold venture, and if the future volumes of the Colonial Library are as well selected as they have hitherto been, we doubt not they will find a ready sale.[52]

Although it praises Macmillan's list for including titles of a "different and more solid nature" (4:450) rather than only fiction, it is revealing, however, that the *Magazine* exclusively reviewed the fiction in the list, singling out for mention in this first review of the Colonial Library F. Marion Crawford, Hugh Conway, William Black, and Charlotte Yonge. It dismissed Thomas Hardy's *The Mayor of Casterbridge* for being "tedious and vapid" (4:451), and later condemned *Jill and Jack* by E. A. Dillwyn (from whose pen no further volumes were seen in the Colonial Library) with the pithy, "Why such books should be written it is difficult to understand" (5:617 [1887–88]). When Longman's Colonial Library appeared in India, the *Magazine* praised the firm's "attempt to meet the want of India" but insisted that "in the matter of get up, these volumes do not please us quite so well as those of Messrs. Macmillan's well-known Library" (11:486 [1894]).

The major objection to novels of a certain kind was expressed most clearly and forcefully in a review of Mrs. Oliphant's *The Second Son*: "though coming from Mrs. Oliphant's pen, and written in her usual, easy and graceful style, [it] is hardly worthy of a place in Macmillan's excellent collection. Its interest, so far as it has any, is largely the interest of the growing class of novels colored by French *realism*; and if it is free from the baneful influence of even the best of these, its innocuousness springs rather from the tameness with which the subject is treated than from the incidents themselves" (6:58 [1888–89]; emphasis in original). Eschewing realism altogether "for the tameness with which the subject is treated," the *Magazine* also indicates readers turning away from didacticism and moral tales, which had earlier been popular among Indian readers.

In rejecting realism, what the *Magazine* reveals instead is a clear preference among readers for writing of another sort, exemplified by the works of one of the nineteenth century's great writers of entertainment, F. Marion Crawford, virtually all of whose novels were reviewed in its pages. The general and sustained enthusiasm with which Crawford was received in India, and his continued presence in the Colonial Library that published all but four of his forty-four novels, suggest that in him one may find an explanation for the series' success among Indian readers.[53] The *Magazine's* reviewers underscored the pleasure Crawford's novels afforded them. His plots and his settings were inventive enough that he was never chastised for the "the tameness with which the subject is treated," as was Mrs. Oliphant in the same years. Even in novels where he was found to be moralizing more than usual, the reviews concluded with the assurance that "in *With the Immortals* the reader may look both for entertainment and edification" (6:772 [1888–89]).

Part of Crawford's ability to provide both entertainment and edification in a fashion different from the disdained mode of realism may have come from his early experience in India, where he lived for two years from 1879 to 1880 and served as editor of *The Indian Herald*, an Indian-owned opposition daily in Allahabad. His life (1854–1909) often reads like the stuff from a society page or from one of his novels: the son of Thomas Crawford, whose sculpture *Liberty* stands in the dome of the U.S. Capitol, Crawford was born in Italy, educated in New Hampshire, Cambridge, Karlsruhe, and Heidelberg, and reputedly mastered almost twenty languages.[54] Encountering a volume on Sanskrit grammar during a hiking trip in Italy absorbed him so thoroughly that he proceeded to study the language in Rome and eventually traveled to Bombay to master it. After running out of money, he accepted the editorship of an Indian newspaper in Allahabad, reportedly keeping a diary in Urdu, and in the course of his travels in the Subcontinent met one Alexander M. Jacob whose life inspired his first novel, *Mr. Isaacs: A Tale of Modern India* (1882), published by Macmillan to immediate and sustained acclaim.[55]

During his lifetime, Crawford's literary reputation both in the United States and Britain, where he continued to publish with Macmillan, was sustained by forty-four novels, thirty-two articles, four plays, three volumes of history, two books of travel, and a volume of literary criticism. In the 1880s and 1890s he was considered in the United States the literary equal of Mark Twain, William Dean Howells, and that other American expatriate, Henry James. However, as Thomas Mark ruefully remarked in his reminiscences about Macmillan: "[our] fiction list contains names that once counted for a great deal but are almost forgotten today." While literary history has been generous to Crawford's contemporaries, his own reputation in the West declined after his death. Yet a survey of libraries extant in India during the late nineteenth and early twentieth centuries demonstrates extensive holdings of Crawford's novels throughout the country (see table 3.1).[56] He set his novels around the globe—in Italy, Persia, Spain, England, Germany, Switzerland, Turkey, France, and the Arab peninsula—and wrote equally inclusively in his fiction on history, religion, the supernatural, crafts, and politics. Considered a master of entertainment in his time, Crawford, as John Pilkington, Jr., reports, "argued powerfully . . . against the claims of the already entrenched Realism of William Dean Howells and the incipient Naturalism of Stephen Crane" (*Crawford* 191).

In *Mr. Isaacs*, a relatively typical novel written in two months, the narrator, Paul Griggs, encounters a Persian of splendor and mystery in a Simla hotel. Stolen as a child, enslaved, educated, escaped, and well traveled, Mr. Isaacs is a jewel merchant with great powers, who uses his worldly and otherworldly contacts to help an Afghan revolutionary escape from British incarceration before the admiring and sympathetic eyes of Paul Griggs. Along the way, Isaacs falls in love with Katharine Westonhaugh, a perfect soul mate who must die at the end, and also along the way, Griggs (with the reader) is initiated into some of the sports (polo, tiger hunting) and occult mysteries of British India, before Isaacs disappears with a mystical companion quite literally into thin air.

The novel opens with the Second Afghan War (1878–80) as its backdrop, when Griggs, a journalist, travels to Simla, the British summer capital, where he hopes to pick up "the news that oozes through the pent-house of Government secrecy, and failing such scant drops of information, to manufacture as much as is necessary to fill the columns of [the] dailies."[57] The war, however, is almost incidental to *Mr. Isaacs*. Shere Ali, a fictional Afghan revolutionary whom Isaacs liberates, is wanted by the British for murdering one of their officers, yet the intrigue occupies only some of the middle section of the novel in which Isaacs, assisted by Griggs and Ram Lall, an Indian mystic, rescues Shere Ali. Rather than making this plot central or even constitutive of the narrative, rather than having the war's political and historical forces inflect, punctuate, inform upon, or otherwise organize the novel or its characters, Crawford simply makes the Shere Ali intrigue a detail of the larger and more significant point of his novel, which remains the moral characters of Isaacs, Griggs, and Katharine. These figures are not to be understood in relation to the historical moment, nor is the historical to be explained by these characters. The two inhabit separate spheres, and Crawford draws his readers' attention to the biographical and psychic details that create and motivate his protagonists, as this, he insists, is the central point of *Mr. Isaacs*. The actions of John Westonhaugh, a British civil servant who long ago gave Isaacs his start in India with the gift of a rupee, are explained by Westonhaugh's essential humanity—he even turns out to be Katharine's brother—rather than by reference to any broader historical circumstance. In keeping with the ethical economy that Crawford has already illuminated as central, Isaacs returns the earlier debt in true Oriental style, leaving Westonhaugh his entire fortune in gems of inestimable worth. Both Westonhaugh's and Isaacs's actions reveal their shared values in a universe of civility. However, instead of connecting these figures and circumstances to historical atmosphere or social conditions, Crawford anchors them to a theme and thesis that was to dominate all his novels and to form his aesthetic vision of using the novel to create an ideal and idealizing landscape in which the human character mattered more than circumstance of any sort, and ideals mattered more than "reality."

If his tenure in India provided Crawford with the story of *Mr. Isaacs* and "intensified" his interest in what John C. Moran calls the "inexplicable,"[58] it also provided him with a lesson about readership and the marketplace for books that was to serve him for the rest of his professional life and that profoundly resonates with the strategy that Macmillan itself followed in the Colonial Library. Called upon to run an Indian opposition newspaper, Crawford did so with great initial success and to the satisfaction of supporters who included both those British opposed to the government and Indians seeking home rule. However, both the British and the Indians eventually withdrew their support of Crawford and his paper over its position on home rule, the former because home rule was mentioned at all, and the latter because it was not mentioned enough. Despite a very short-lived success, John Pilkington, Jr., Crawford's biographer, considers the experience "a good one . . . [for] he had learned from it that the man who wishes to succeed with the public must not offend too bluntly its tastes and prejudices" (*Crawford* 38).[59]

For the remainder of his writing life, Crawford made pleasing his readers a central credo of his aesthetic practice, and he urged it upon all who would listen, including his editors at Macmillan (who, acknowledging the income Crawford brought them, reciprocated by allowing him use of the penthouse apartment above their offices on Fifth Avenue whenever he was in New York). Crawford provided a detailed and revealing account of his views in a work of literary criticism, *The Novel: What It Is* (1893), which was part of a ongoing debate on realism initiated by William Dean Howells (whose manifesto on realism, *Criticism and Fiction*, appeared in 1891) and taken up by Henry James (whose "The Real Thing" appeared in 1892).[60] For Crawford, realism as a fictional form failed because "it is, generally, a photograph, not a picture—a catalogue not a description" (40). About the novel, he quite bluntly felt, "there is a demand for them and there is a profit in producing them" (8), which he set out to do prolifically, insisting on creating an "art for the buyer" instead of one for the seller. Between these two poles, he argued, lay the conflict between realism and romance (20–21). "Is our province to please those who read our works or to force them to please us by buying them?" (21). The novelist, for him, had one job only, and that was to please those who consumed his work: "We are not poets . . . we are not genuine playwrights . . . we are not preachers . . . we are not teachers or professors nor lawyers, nor men of business. We are nothing more than public amusers. . . . Let us then, accept our position cheerfully, and do the best we can to fulfill our mission," he declaimed (22), and in every one of his novels, this is precisely what he proceeded to do in order to please and entertain his legions of readers around the world.

Crawford gave his Indian readers absorbing stories in exotic locales, often set in past times where heroic deeds and superhuman characters seemed everyday and "normal." He connected his vast oeuvre by having minor characters in one work reappear as protagonists in another, so that *Mr. Isaacs*'s Paul Griggs also makes appearances in *Paul Patoff* (1887), *Katharine Lauderdale* (1894), *The Ralstons* (1895), and *Casa Braccio* (1895, where Griggs's own story takes center stage). As Pilkington, Jr., shows, this fictional device connected novels of India (*Isaacs*) and Turkey (*Patoff*) with those of Britain (*Lauderdale*), America (*Ralstons*), and Italy (*Braccio*), rendering in a single "huge artistic canvas" (*Crawford* 190) otherwise disparate plots in widely different worlds. His readers found in his novels not just pleasure and entertainment but also an entire world that they could inhabit seemingly endlessly, and, crucially for his readers in India, a world where the governing principle was essentially moral and ethical and not circumstantial.

"The foundation of good fiction and good poetry seems to be ethic rather than aesthetic," argued Crawford (*Novel* 86). An aesthetic that appealed to taste would soon "perish as a mere matter of fashion," while the ethical, that which "speaks to man as man . . . must live and find a hearing with humanity so long as humanity is human" (86). With this view, Crawford dissolved the gulf separating his world and that of his Subcontinental readers. Even as they praised him for taking them to Italy, Germany, or Turkey, it was the essentially moral dimension of his writing—Mrs. Patoff's unfathomable dislike for her son, Paul, and the ensuing familial tension, or Isaacs's support for the Afghan rebel whom he helps liberate, or the political and moral dilemmas undergone in the Saracinesca trilogy—that held their attention. In emphasizing character over circumstance as he did in *Mr. Isaacs* and repeatedly thereafter, Crawford emphasized an interior landscape over which the individual had complete control in contrast to an exterior one over whose historical, social, and political circumstances he had none. In this regard, all Crawford's plots, even those about the most fabulously wealthy and far away, were "translatable" into an Indian world where they simultaneously resonated with and empowered his readers into exercising agency from within against an oppressive external world over which they were otherwise powerless.

His was hardly a melodramatic oeuvre in the conventional sense: in fact, in a dismissive essay Ouida faulted Crawford's melodrama because "it does not move us for a minute."[61] Yet his writing moved generations of Indian readers, doing so through a melodramatic mode rather than a literary form—a melodrama in which a visibly ethical economy enabled readers to translate and recontextualize the world they read into the world they lived. The temporal fashions of the day, alien and alienating in India, receded before the ethical and moral economy so skillfully and easily portrayed. Working within what Larzer Ziff identifies as an "ideal" social code, Crawford's novels provided his readers with the comforting sense that honor and breeding could vanquish conflict and preserve harmony in a timeless world, be it sixteenth-century England or twentieth-century New York.[62] The details of the worlds Crawford described receded before the codes that structured them, codes that the fiction seemed to insist were universally shared.

Recognizing Isaacs's love for Katharine Westonhaugh as a problem given their different faiths (Muslim and Protestant) and Isaacs's three wives, the novel nonetheless provides several disquisitions in which Griggs quizzes Isaacs extensively on his intentions and their legitimacy. Isaacs spiritedly defends his marital desires on both religious and legal grounds, to which Griggs concedes: "You have evidently thought it out and taken legal advice; and really, as far as the technical part of it goes, I suppose you have as good a chance as Lord Steepleton Kildare [a rival and a Catholic]" (84). Yet, consistent with his moral vision, Crawford's novel insists that the "technical part" of things is only that—a part—and that the gulf between emotional desire and social acceptability in Isaacs's marriage to Katharine was not inconsiderable. He develops the romance between the two far enough to elicit readerly sympathy before Katharine dies, but rather than letting the novel devolve into maudlin sentimentality at this point, Isaacs soon discovers a higher purpose in life thanks to the timely appearance of Ram Lall, the Indian mystic. Isaacs leaves to pursue this higher calling, which skillfully shifts the novel's emotional focus from grief and loss to spiritual fulfillment. This part of *Mr. Isaacs* provides readers—especially Indian ones—with the considerable emotional reassurance that certain barriers (between religions, castes, or races) and social regulations are not (yet) to be crossed whatever the technical or legal arguments might be. Furthermore, this essentially conservative ending both celebrated individuality and preserved community, conclusions especially familiar and reassuring to readers of the Indian epic tradition. The insistence on Griggs's and Isaacs's moral qualities rather than their circumstances further invited readers of all kinds into Crawford's writing, which pursued this subtext throughout. "The prime impulses of the heart," Crawford insisted in *The Novel*, "are, broadly speaking, the same in all ages and almost in all races" (107).

In one of the most persuasive essays on Indian reading and consumption available in the archive, Ram Chandra Bose provides a powerful account of how Indians may have consumed Macmillan's fiction in the late nineteenth century and why certain writers such as Crawford may have held particular appeal for them. "I read English novels as the plain man reads *Paradise Lost*, skipping over the classical allusions," Bose confessed in a lengthy article on *Robert Elsmere* in the *Madras Christian College Magazine* (7:287 [1889–90]). "I hurry over graphic descriptions of scenes which to me are outlandish; inventories of articles of furniture which it will never fall to my lot even to dream of buying; vivid pictures of costumes which I scarcely expect to see; and portraitures equally realistic of drawing-rooms in which I should probably feel myself and be felt to be a fish out of water," continued Bose (7:288), rejecting a form of narrative description that, despite its scrupulous material detail, was simply too alien ("outlandish" descriptions of scenes)—and alienating (objects beyond his means)—to appear "real" or meaningful to him. Skipping over sections he did not understand, Bose nonetheless found others that he did, "which lifted me above my own self, and stirred up all that was good within me" (7:287). From these fragments, he constructed a novel that he consumed and critiqued with considerable pleasure.

Bose outlines a reading practice striking in numerous ways: despite his apparent sophistication and education (which allow him to take apart Ward's *Robert Elsmere* on numerous theological points), he gestures to a gulf between the social world he reads about and the one he inhabits, a chasm that alienates him from numerous novels he encounters. His objections to the "graphic descriptions" and "realistic portraitures" of drawing rooms and their contents illuminate above all a discomfort with what Ian Watt has called the narrative procedures of the realist novel. For Bose, the very material details that enhance the realist novel's illusion of providing an "authentic report of human experience" (Watt 32) come across as un-real in his Indian social world. The external details end up as obstacles that hinder his subsequent connection with an interior world of character and individuality that also marks the realist novel—and to which the exterior details often gesture.

Acutely aware of this aspect of readership, Crawford maintained that "the reader knows one side of life, his own, better than the writer possibly can, and he reads with the greatest interest those books which treat of lives like his own" (*Novel* 81). Doubting realism, which they eschewed, Crawford's own novels pursued a form of writing that actively encouraged—and possibly even enabled—readers to make just such an identification between the novelistic world and their own.

However, the gulf between certain books and certain readers is not a new one, nor is the preference that readers throughout—and not just in India—indicated for "anti-realistic" forms over realism (itself a carefully constructed form and one relatively recent in literary history). Moreover, since much of Macmillan's Colonial Library constituted what that firm and other British houses already published for the home market,[63] Indian readers' preference for the library's titles at least partly if not wholly overlapped with British readers' own tastes in the home market. What then about the Indian reading public makes it so different from the British one during the same period and worthy of study in its own right? Let me address these questions in turn, starting with realism's "failure" among Indian readers.

REALISM AND ITS DISSED CONTENTS

In *Realism and Reality* (1985), a pathbreaking account of the rise of the novel in India, Meenakshi Mukherjee outlines some of the difficulties confronting Indian readers encountering realism in the nineteenth-century British novel.[64] She makes the provocative argument that realism failed in India because of the discontinuities and aberrations it presented to Indian readers whose world (or "reality") was simply too disjunct from the novelistic world they encountered. The caste, class, colonial, and gender hierarchies in India left little room for social or economic mobility, individualism, romantic love, or domestic autonomy, all dominant themes in British realist novels. Realism's well-made universe was both alienating and defamiliarizing to a colonial reader (as Ram Chandra Bose amply testified), who turned instead to a more familiar, antirealist (or counterrealist, in the case of Crawford) literary landscape for pleasure. Whereas realism in Britain might have explained and "translated" the rapid transformations of an industrializing, urban, and technologizing landscape for its readers who "learned" emerging codes of social conduct, national kinship, and organization from the novel, British realism in India had little explanatory or socializing power to offer.[65]

Indeed, if realism helped emplot a shared social destiny for its British readers, it was also a form that emerged from that very same social world, one that saw its own "plot" distinguished by individual choice and bourgeois or middle-class values. Yet, as Terry Eagleton has cautioned, realism is a particularly *metropolitan* form requiring certain preconditions in order to flourish, preconditions especially present in Britain. Notable among these is the assumption that "the world is story-shaped—that there is a well-formed narrative implicit in reality itself, which it is the task of such realism to represent."[66] Against this sense of settlement and stability (or what Raymond Williams has memorably identified as the confidence that comes from knowable communities), Eagleton describes a widely divergent situation in the colonial periphery where political instability, sustained social unrest, and a very different class structure lend themselves to conditions that are fully amenable neither to the rise of the realist novel nor its popularity among readers. What he shows are the altogether different reading preferences that proliferate instead: "The most ancient literary modes in Ireland are heroic, romantic, fantastic; and the remoteness of such aristocratic forms from everyday life is no fit breeding ground for the novel, which is born of the middle-class's dawning awareness that their own quotidian experience can be dramatically exciting" (149).

While Eagleton's remarks underscore some of the doxa surrounding the British realist novel (as a predominantly middle-class form requiring a sense of stability in order to flourish), they also provocatively link the realist novel's development to extraliterary conditions and allude to the reading preferences that these conditions themselves generate. Places such as Ireland that do not produce the conditions conducive to the proliferation of literary realism tend not to consume realism in their reading either. The preference for heroic and romantic forms in Ireland gestures to this, much as the turn to consuming taxonomically diverse forms that fall within the melodramatic mode serves to underscore the alienation that realism generated among nineteenth-century Indian readers.

It ought to be noted, however, that the prejudice against realism is far from original or unique to Indian readers or even to those in other British colonies such as Ireland. It appears to be one widely encountered elsewhere as well. In his chapter "Narrative Markets, ca. 1850," Franco Moretti maps the diffusion of over 150 popular British and French novels in nine European countries.[67] What he discovers is the widespread suffusion, through translation, of the works of Scott, Bulwer-Lytton, Dickens, sensation fiction, Ainsworth, and G. P. R. James in roughly that order for the British sample, and Dumas, Sue, and Hugo for the French one. "It is a regular, even monotonous pattern: all of Europe reading the same books, with the same enthusiasm," Moretti reports. "All of Europe unified by a desire, not for 'realism' (the mediocre fortune of Stendhal and Balzac leaves no doubts on this point)—not for realism, but for what Peter Brooks has called the melodramatic imagination: a rhetoric of stark contrasts that is present a bit everywhere, and is perfected by Dumas and Sue" (176–177). Indeed each of these novelists popular in Europe also appears widely in Indian records for the same period (even stretching through till the early years of the twentieth century), either in English or in translation into regional languages (see tables 2.2, 2.3, and 3.2).

Although Moretti's work does not explain the pervasive desire for these counterrealist forms, it provides a useful comparative insight for this study. British realism's failure to suffuse the European market in 1850 might of course say interesting things about the market, but it also illuminates the not insignificant insight that in 1850 realism in Britain was still an ascendant form: emerging literacy following the 1832 Reform Bill made numerous other forms such as late gothic and melodrama highly successful and popular among both lower- and middle-class readers who voraciously consumed this fiction, often serially and quite cheaply. According to Raymond Williams, Britain's turn to realism took place in and around 1850: "in twenty months in 1847 and 1848," he argues more precisely, a turning point in the British novel that gave rise to the Dickens of *Dombey and Son* ("and works which now define his achievement"), Thackeray, Eliot, and Hardy.[68] British realism's "failure" in Europe during the period of Moretti's study, then, is one of omission rather than commission: it had yet to ascend to the hegemonic position that it was to reach and maintain through much of the second half of the nineteenth century. To put this differently, during the period of

Moretti's study, British realism was still competing with earlier forms such as war and nautical stories, silver-fork novels, oriental tales, and others that comprise his sample. However, by the time Macmillan and other British firms began purveying novels to India in the latter decades of the nineteenth century, realism was a well-established form in Britain, and as such, its failure in India may be more telling than in Europe ca. 1850. Moretti's European readers chose to read a rhetoric of stark contrasts in the general absence of realism in the marketplace. On the other hand, Indian readers in the late nineteenth century chose the melodramatic mode at a time when realism dominated the market and melodrama's heyday in the 1840s appeared long past.[69]

Furthermore, the literary market in India had one major difference from the European one that Moretti outlines in his *Atlas*: it was a considerably closed market, insulated from foreign imports by British protectionist policies that included a tax on all non-British print. The apparent freedom with which the novel traversed Europe in Moretti's study simply did not exist in nineteenth- and early-twentieth-century India. The supply of books available was a seriously attenuated one: "India's first generation of novelists," Meenakshi Mukherjee writes, "had hardly any access to Tolstoy, Melville, or Flaubert" (17). They had relatively complete access to anything printed in Britain, however, and within this, to the full range of works with which British publishers obligingly flooded the Indian literary market. Translations of European works were generally a very small part of these British offerings. Kegan Paul's Colonial Library series published no translations, whereas Macmillan's Colonial Library provided only three authors in translation, all of whom were French: Amiel's *Journal Intime* in 1888 in a translation by Mrs. Humphry Ward; nineteen novels of Balzac in one fell swoop in 1896; and eight works of Alphonse Daudet, two of which were autobiographies, purchased along with the Balzac titles from Dent and Co., also in 1896.[70] Of the fictional works multiply translated into Indian languages throughout the nineteenth century, the insulation from post-1850s fiction and the general rejection of realism is even starker (see table 2.3): Cervantes, Dumas, Hugo, and Sue proliferate alongside Jules Verne, Lesage's *Gil Blas*, Saint-Pierre's *Paul et Virginie*, and the *Arabian Nights*.[71]

For Indian readers, therefore, the rejection of realism and the preference for the melodramatic mode has to be placed in this context. The novel of ideas, of philosophical interiority, moral reckoning, even Flaubert's protomodernism were simply not part of what was available. It was largely, if not exclusively, the English novel in myriad forms that flooded the market and with which readers had to contend. For Meenakshi Mukherjee, the outcome was regrettable:

> It is perhaps unfortunate that the nineteenth-century Indian novelist had as his model primarily the British Victorian novel; with hindsight after a century, it seems the British model was perhaps the least suitable for the Indian mind in the nineteenth century. The brooding inwardness and philosophical quality of the nineteenth-century Russian novels or the intensely moral preoccupation of the nineteenth-century American writer might have demonstrated to early practitioners of Indian fiction alternative modes of writing novels.   (17)

In this regard, the Indian novelistic world was not one self-created by free-market forces and independent readerly input as the European one in Moretti's *Atlas* may have been; rather, it was one where readerly input exercised itself upon a market already partially constructed and shaped by Anglocentric colonial policies. For Meenakshi Mukherjee, the outcome was to be rued, perhaps rightly, but the story does not end here.

Within this attenuated, artificially anglicist and anglicizing market that they initially had little hand in constructing, Indian readers exercised their choices and tastes through the manner in which they put the market to work for their own ends. I have suggested earlier that Macmillan's willingness to satisfy Indian tastes in the Colonial Library provided the firm with fiscal rewards to the extent that it was willing to eschew or neglect developing its fiction list in any other manner, even to address changes occurring in the home market. Entire forms of emerging fiction lay ignored in the selections the firm made to satisfy its Indian and colonial readership. As an influence upon British production, Indian consumption patterns were decisive but indirect, and their consequences unintended but lasting, at least as far as the history of one of Britain's most esteemed publishing firms goes.

In explaining what Indian readers found so appealing in the novels they chose to read (and that Macmillan so willingly provided), Ian Raeside's history of the Marathi novel suggests that "the popularity of these English writers was doubtless due in part to the fact that they struck a sympathetic chord in their Indian readers."[72] In the previous chapter, I suggested that this sympathetic chord had much to do with the affinities that readers found with certain forms of fiction, both in terms of what they could make of it (it was particularly familiar within their own narrative universe in which epic and orality still functioned in powerful ways) and what they were able to *do* with it. Like British working-class readers of the 1840s and 1850s with whom they at one time shared these tastes, Indian readers too found what Martha Vicinus has identified as "emotional satisfaction" from consuming popular forms of escapism (122). Writers such as Reynolds, Vicinus argues, provided their British readers in the 1840s and 1850s with "forms of and a language for understanding . . . one's own life" (16).[73] She persuasively suggests that the typical Chartist plot that Reynolds frequently exemplified, with its idealistic and honest heroes, passive and virtuous heroines, and fortuitous breaks, held particular appeal among certain British readers in this period: "Unable to control much of their situation, working people found emotional satisfaction in these conventions. They could identify more readily with a hero or a heroine who was largely a victim of circumstances; such a character showed how misfortune was not a reflection of one's own personal worth" (122).

However, if this fiction served as what Gramsci has called a psychic stimulant among its readers, the key point here is that in India it stimulated so many diverse readers into a *single* common pattern. Unlike the reading preferences of British readers whose social and class cleavages were reflected in corollary cleavages in their reading preferences,[74] the conundrum here is that despite wide internal cleavages, Indian readers historically from the 1850s to the 1920s—ranging from the newly urban, first- or second-generation English-educated ones to feudal aristocrats, civil servants to householders, merchants to teachers at both universities and schools, modernizers to traditionalists, women to elders—demonstrated *not* a corollary range or diversity in their reading preferences but a startling consistency in what they preferred to read both in English *and* the regional languages. This immense preference for popular fiction was not lost upon Indian social thinkers, many of whom embraced it for the rich possibilities they saw in it. In a 1919 essay in the august *Calcutta Review*, Thakorelal Desai maintained that "in a big country like India, with its immense diversity of race, religion, common habits, language, politics, where innumerable artificial and natural barriers exist between man and man, a more effective means for the spread of common culture and common sympathy than popularising the study of fiction cannot be imagined."[75] Desai's remarks help contextualize how one might understand the Indian world of popular-fiction readers: not only did certain forms of British popular fiction create a common culture shared among Indian readers both in English and the regional languages, these forms also provided a structure from (and in some cases, against) which Indian *writers* were eventually able to forge a shared narrative universe as I shall make clear in the next four chapters. The reading preferences in the nineteenth century that frame the first section of this study, therefore, not only serve as an index of escape: they are also equally powerfully an index of what readers escaped *from* and what they escaped *toward*.

The extent to which Indian readers shared their common culture with readers in Europe ca. 1850 and in Britain throughout the century gestures toward the invention of a world literature of popular forms uniting a nationally and internationally diverse group of readers who consumed fiction differently, each group to its own ends. Phrased differently, Indian readers read in a manner that Michael Denning has in another context identified as allegorical: seeing the plots of novels not as unique fictional representations of conflict and resolution, but as a general formula or type that was a "microcosm" of a world that the reader recognized or reinvented as his own.[76] It was a form of reading through which readers could script themselves and their concerns into the narrative, in which readerly mastery and control in consuming the text inverted readerly impotence and powerlessness in the colonial world. Through these acts of fabricating meaning in texts that they had no hand in producing, Indian readers laid claims upon the British novel, indigenizing its forms and function to their own markedly different ends.

The chapters that follow in part 2 observe the historical continuation of these patterns of literary indigenization in the emergence of the English novel in India. From vernacularizing the reading tastes that they partly shared with working-class readers in 1850s London, middle-class readers in Paris, and aristocrats in Italy (*pace* Moretti's *Atlas*), Indian writers began to fashion a form of the novel that mutated both the novel and its function in their society. The affinity for melodrama, gothic, romance, and sensation that defined Indian consumption in the nineteenth century gave rise to a powerful form of historical narrative that found a successful and highly influential exemplar in Bankim Chandra Chatterjee (Bengali, 1838–94) whose historical novels defined the world for his readers; in Hari Narain Apte (1864–1919) who brought modernity and social action to the Marathi novel; and in Mirza Mohammad Hadi Ruswa (Urdu, 1856–1931) whose profoundly powerful historical ethnographies of gender and Mughal rule were almost directly the unexpected outcome of his voracious reading and translation of Reynolds's novels earlier in the century.

In a few of these cases, such as Ruswa's, the influence of Victorian reading practices in impulse and in temperament is visible upon the emergence of the nascent Indian novel. But in most others, such as Bankim, as I will show in the following chapter, the consumption patterns from earlier in the century provide no easy or singular roadmap for predicting novelistic production later. The connection between consumption and production that I trace is, therefore, not one of causality. Rather, what the focus on consumption helps illuminate is the manner in which Indian readers exercised agency and authority over an alien cultural product that they interleaved and interpreted through highly local lenses and interests. In a structurally analogous manner, when Indian writers began to produce the novel, they did so by indigenizing both its form and its function in their society, engaging in practices of cultural translation and invention that were similar in impulse to those of readers from earlier in the century. The chapters that follow in part 2, therefore, add a further dimension to the scrutiny of what Indians did with and made of the novel on their own soil.

Toward the end of the century, when Indian novelists started writing in English, they were following several generations of highly successful novelists in regional languages with whom they were in dialogue, much as they also remained in a one-sided monologue with British writers stretching as far back as Defoe through Reynolds, Crawford, and Corelli. From this three-way conversation and the complex circuits of exchange, transaction, translation, and consumption, an

Producing Fiction

CHAPTER 4

By Way of Transition: Bankim's Will, or Indigenizing the Novel in India

There is a striking scene in Bankim Chandra Chatterjee's historical romance, *Chandrashekhar* (1875), in which India's most famous nine-teenth-century novelist provides a vivid picture of what occurs when Englishness and the world of the novel collide with India and its indigenous narrative traditions.[1] The scholarly Chandrashekhar arrives home one day to learn that his beautiful but capricious wife, Shaibalini, has been kidnapped by an Englishman who has become enamored by the woman's beauty. Insistent on finding Shaibalini and bringing her back, Chandrashekhar wonders whether his own abstract and studious ways may partly have estranged his wife from him. He vows to change and sets about doing so immediately:

At nightfall he brought out one by one and collected together all the books, both studied and unstudied and dear as his lifeblood. One by one he began to pile them in the yard; now and again he would open a book and instantly tie it up unread and ultimately collected them all in a heap. When the pile was made up, he set fire to it. The fire blazed up. The Puranas, History, Poetry, Rhetoric, Grammar, everything gradually took fire; the laws of

Manu, Jagnavalka, and Parasara, the Darsanas, the Philosophy of Naya, Vedanta, Sankhya, etc., the Kalpa-Sutras, Aranyakas, and the Upanishads, one by one, all caught the flame and blazed up. Nothing but ashes was left of the mass of invaluable books collected with infinite pains and studied over a length of time.[2]

In this immensely distressing scene of mass bibliocide, thousands of years of Hindu learning from the Forest Books (Aranyakas) to grammars, law treatises to history are reduced to ashes. Not a word from them, the passage seems to suggest, could help in bringing Shaibalini back from her British abductor. On one level, the willful ruin of this massive catalogue of knowledge underscores the urgency for change confronting Indian society in the face of a British onslaught led by different language, learning, and cultural priorities. On another level, the destruction of India's traditional narrative modes of history, poetry, rhetoric, grammar, and philosophy gestures powerfully to the irrelevance of these once classic Hindu forms for organizing knowledge and providing solutions to social problems. In getting rid of them at the start of *Chandrashekhar*, Bankim seems to be highlighting his own aesthetic project as well as alluding to some of its difficulties. While the bibliocide formally and symbolically enacts the death of an entire body of knowledge deemed irrelevant under colonial rule, *Chandrashekhar* also seems to celebrate the emergence of a new, more capable, and possibly more useful narrative form, namely, the novel. However, alongside the mass destruction of Chandrashekhar's library of classical texts, a persistent echo keeps returning as the novel develops not just in Bankim's oeuvre but also in India. How can the new narrative form—which had only recently arrived in the Subcontinent—redress all that has been destroyed of the past under colonial rule? In more general terms, is the novel really capable of replacing any of these other Indian discursive forms in the future?

In posing these questions in *Chandrashekhar*, Bankim (1838–94) was inviting reflection upon a widespread cultural phenomenon in India that had significant implications for his own trajectory as a novelist. Throughout the nineteenth century, all kinds of Indian readers who had never known prose fiction before discovered and enthusiastically consumed the novel, mostly in its British form, which is largely what was available on the market. By the middle of the century, fitful attempts to give birth to an Indian novel became evident in regional languages, but it was not until the end of the century that an anglo-phone novel became visible in Indian letters. In the lively urban capitals of the Indian print industry (Calcutta, Bombay, Madras), major debates and experiments were taking place on how best to vernacularize and make Indian a foreign form that had already proven so successful among readers. Accompanying the experiments at literary indigenization, however, was the anxiety that somehow Indian novelists were unable to weave their social world and its concerns into the imported form. If the presence of domestic narrative forms—which included a living epic tradition—was an obstacle to the rise of the novel in India, Bankim's dramatic bibliocide in *Chandrashekhar* gestures toward one decisive effort at indigenization: the destruction of all anterior modes in order to enable the birth of a new one. Though Chandrashekhar's

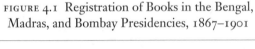

FIGURE 4.1 Registration of Books in the Bengal, Madras, and Bombay Presidencies, 1867–1901

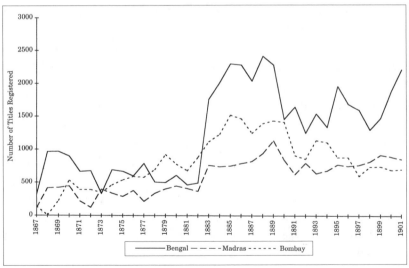

SOURCES: *A Catalogue of Books Printed in the Bengal Presidency* [var. years] (Calcutta: Government Printing Press, 1867–1901); *A Catalogue of Books Printed in the Bombay Presidency* [var. years] (Bombay: Government Central Press, 1867–1901); *A Catalogue of Books Printed in the Madras Presidency, Fort St. George Gazette Supplement* [var. years] (Madras: Fort St. George Gazette Press, 1867–1901).

was largely a symbolic solution, it nevertheless enabled Bankim to articulate his frustration at the slow pace in which he and other writers in India were vernacularizing the novel.

"During my boyhood," wrote Tagore about the 1870s, "Bengali literature was in meagre supply, and I think I must have finished all the readable and unreadable books then extant. . . . I read every available book from one end to the other, and both what I understood and what I did not went on working within me."[3] Alongside the paucity of Bengali fiction in those days, Tagore also rued the inordinate influence of British literature to the extent that "our minds are being moulded from infancy to old age by English literature alone" (132). Yet the world of print in Bengal and indeed the rest of India was already undergoing a considerable transformation that was to become more fully apparent very shortly. As the import of English books into the Subcontinent increased twofold between 1850 and 1880 (see figure 2.1), data from the *Catalogue of Books Printed* help establish that publishing in Indian languages showed a proportional increase.[4] As figure 4.1 demonstrates, between 1868 and 1885 the total number of printed titles registered in Bengal increased more than twofold, by almost 140 percent, and in Madras almost twofold, by more than 80 percent. The percentage increase for the Bombay Presidency was most dramatic at over 340 percent, with the presidency showing the most steady output with few sharp peaks or drastic declines. What these data help illuminate are the beginnings of a period of immense literary and intellectual synergy promoted by an interaction in print among the different Indian languages as well as between them and English, so that while English print continued to be imported into India, it was never able to regain the peak it had marked in 1863–64 of £328,024 (see figure 2.1). What figures 2.1 and 4.1 emphasize, then, is that Indian literacy and the associated demand for print in the second half of the nineteenth century seem to have been sustained by and to have in their turn sustained two different print worlds, one foreign and the other domestic.

Furthermore, the quarterly *Catalogue of Books Printed* records the number of book titles published in each presidency, thus providing some perspective on the nature of Indian print production itself during this period.[5] The largest number of titles published in a single year was in the Bengal Presidency: 2,425 titles in 1888, and the smallest number, 218 titles, was published in 1871 in the Madras Presidency. When book production in the three main presidencies is graphed synchronously, as shown in figure 4.1, the print worlds of the different regions display marked individual characteristics. For instance, between 1868 (the year following the Press and Registration of Books Act) and 1881, publishing activity in Bengal was extremely choppy and marked with numerous sharp increases and declines. In Bombay, on the other hand, print output increased steadily during the same period, suggesting the sporadic nature of press control in British India: Bengal, first to be colonized, was also first to show resistance and, as the uneven output suggests, was the most closely monitored.[6] Furthermore, much as the bulk of British imports was arriving in Bengal and Bombay ports, the bulk of Indian publishing was also taking place in these two regions, a fact partially though not exclusively explained by their commercial and political significance within the colonial apparatus.

Within these regional variations, educational titles formed over half the total published output, followed by government and commercial printing. Literature comprised approximately a third of total book titles published in the three presidencies.[7] Over half the literary titles published in Indian presses were works of poetry; approximately a third were works of fiction; and less than a sixth were dramatic works, often translated or adapted from the ancient epics, the *Mahabharata* and the *Ramayana*.[8] The regional variations in this publishing output are telling: Bombay was the forerunner in poetry production, with Bengal, despite its long-standing tradition in verse, lagging behind by 10–20 percent. One reason for this lapse may lie with shifting Bengali tastes during the same period. In 1868, when poetry was roughly a third of Bengali print, fiction comprised 59 percent of it, and while this figure for the output of fiction diminished considerably to average 32 percent by the end of the century, it begins to record the arrival of a new literary form in Indian publishing. The novel emerged slowly: on average, only 25 percent of Bombay's and 22 percent of Madras's published output was fiction. Included in this output as "fiction" during the period are not just original novels in the regional languages and occasionally in English, but also short stories, chapbooks, tales, and fables, as well as increasing numbers of translations and adaptations from British novels.

If this fact was encouraging to some, it was not so for a distressed Bankim, who laid out the crisis in literary production as he saw it in a speech delivered before the Bengal Social Science Association on February 28, 1870:

> If you look over the quarterly returns published by Government, you will find that the Bengali mind is anything but unproductive. But its productions are remarkable for quantity alone; the quality is on an average contemptible—often they are positively injurious. Excepting a few good books of recognized excellence, they are, when they are nothing more mischievous, either clumsy imitations of good Bengali models, or abject copies of the silly stories of the later Sanskrit writers, or a string of harmless commonplaces.[9]

The title and the internal references in Bankim's talk make clear that his salty description of Bengali literature as clumsy imitation and abject copy applies almost entirely to the nascent novel, for which the characterization was in fact mostly accurate—and not just in Bengal but in other parts of India as well. The avidity with which the form had been consumed following its introduction in the early years of the nineteenth century inevitably led to efforts at indigenous literary production. And yet, as Bankim notes, these had still to breed more than a few notable successes.

Part of the difficulty with the emergence of an Indian novel lay in finding an appropriate fictional *form* to suit Indian needs, and another part lay in finding fiction-worthy material or content. In an introduction to the romance *Manjughosha* (1868), the Marathi novelist Naro Sadashiv Risbud laments some of the difficulties that confronted him: "One finds in the lives of us Hindus neither interesting vices nor virtues, and this is the difficulty which we find in trying to write novels. If we write about the things we experience daily, there would be nothing enthralling about them, so that if we set out to write an interesting book we are forced to take up with the marvellous."[10] And yet, writing the marvelous itself signaled a kind of failure: it was a form not of success but of defeat. Indian epic and oral traditions were already full of fantastic and superhuman stories. The need and interest in the novel lay in discovering through it a new and *different* way of organizing everyday life and its experiences that numerous Indian writers, including Risbud, struggled to articulate, often resorting to "enthralling" ways of doing so. Despite the tools at their disposal, despite the range of forms that they selected and rejected in their own literary consumption, producing an Indian novel did not come easily. Under the circumstances, taking up with the marvelous gestured toward the resignation with which Indian writers returned to the old rather than the confidence with which they mastered and vernacularized a new narrative form.

When the novelist often called the "Scott of Bengal" began his own literary career, it too ran aground with two false starts before finding a firmer literary foothold. Bankim's first false move occurred over the soon-forgotten publication of a volume of minor Bengali verse in 1856 (*Lalita, Purakalik galpa, Tatha Manas*), whose poor reception apparently persuaded him that his literary future might more profitably lie in prose instead.[11] Eight years later he produced *Rajmohan's Wife* (1864), a novel written in English and in self-conscious imitation of the popular Victorian novelists he had consumed in his youth. Its reception apparently persuaded Bankim that greater success might lie with *Bengali* prose. Of the fourteen novels he subsequently wrote, each and every one was written in Bengali, rendering him accolades such as "the man of most literary influence in the country,"[12] and "the best Bengali novelist that Bengal has yet produced."[13]

For almost half a century, beginning somewhere around 1870, Bankim remained the most widely known, widely translated, and widely influential novelist in India. At a time before organized literary sponsorship or institutional support for such activities, his novels were translated into numerous languages including Marathi, Tamil, Gujarati, Hindi, Urdu, Kannada, Telugu, and English. Not only did his work "inspire the growth of the novel in many Indian languages"[14] as Sisir Kumar Das has maintained, it also influenced writers, politicians, nationalists, social reformers, and traditionalists throughout the country.[15] Though Bankim was an essayist, historian, philosopher, and social thinker as well as a novelist, it was largely upon his novels that his popularity and fame rested. As T. W. Clark has suggested, "the stories of Hindu heroes and heroines in his novels served as examples to illumine and enliven the closely-knit and often laborious reasoning of his essays."[16] Under the circumstances, the epithet "first" that many critics apply to him seems appropriate if not fully accurate, as does Bankim's stature as the first truly *Indian* novelist.

Yet this account of Bankim's enormous success partially obscures a more interesting story about the emergence of the novel in India. His achievements did not always come easily, and his literary failures remain extremely revealing about the difficulties that confronted—and that until recently continued to confront—Indian writers in their efforts to indigenize the novel as an Indian form. With Bankim as a case study, this chapter analyzes three moments from his literary oeuvre in an effort to understand the early phases in the development of the Indian novel. I begin with a brief look at Bankim's long-forgotten English novel, *Rajmohan's Wife* (1864), and assess some of the reasons behind its failure. I then place pressure on Bankim's frequent epithet, the "Scott of Bengal," in an effort to discover the extent to which Scott and the tradition of the British novel in fact influenced his formal development. Finally, I turn to Bankim's best-known and most widely translated novel, *Anandamath* (1882), which produced among other things a popular anthem for the nationalist struggle in the form of the poem *Bande Mataram* (Hail Mother). In analyzing Bankim's early novelistic failure in English alongside this successful Bengali work, I trace some of the obstacles to indigenizing the novel in India as part of a larger attempt to connect patterns of novelistic consumption in the early nineteenth century with the emergence of an Indian novel toward the end.

Rajmohan's Wife, THE FORGOTTEN FAILURE

The plot of *Rajmohan's Wife* is both fanciful and straightforward. A young woman, Matangini, overhears her unscrupulous and abusive husband instruct some bandits to rob the house of the local landowner, Madhav, and steal the title to considerable property that he has recently inherited. At great personal risk, Matangini steps out of the *zenana* on a dark and stormy night to warn Madhav (who also happens to be her brother-in-law) of the impending crime. After numerous hair-raising episodes, she manages to prevent it. Her "treachery" discovered, she is kidnapped and imprisoned in a hidden dungeon at the home of a rival landowner who was behind the scheme in the first place. After considerable contortions in the plot, Matangini is found and freed by the grateful Madhav to whom she reveals the unfortunate love she has secretly borne for him since childhood. The novel ends with Matangini's husband being imprisoned and transported; the rival landowner committing suicide in the same dungeon where he had earlier tried to force himself upon the virtuous Matangini; while she herself leaves Madhav's village and returns to her father's house where, significantly, she dies young.

Though the story is supposed to be a contemporary one in which Bankim devotes considerable attention to providing material details of rural Bengali life and domestic customs in the *zenana* and so on, its debt to gothic, crime, and domestic sensation novels is unmistakable. "It is a notorious fact that many eminent zemindar families in Bengal owe their rise to some ignoble origin," claims the narrator early in the novel (14), and expanding upon this thesis the plot revolves around rival claims to property and inheritance, domestic intrigue and disharmony, and a world with intricate relationships between the various dramatis personae. The bloodcurdling journey Matangini makes in the dead of night to warn Madhav, and the crude villainy she encounters from the rival landowner who imprisons her in his dungeon, are recognizable tropes from both gothic and melodrama. Thunderous forces of nature haunt the plot, providing atmosphere in the form of stormy, dark nights, while the sheer excess associated with evil (the extent of corruption and transgression that both husband and rival landowner perpetrate) exaggerates and underscores Matangini's virtue and Madhav's decency. Together, their rational good sense contrasts with the menace they confront, and at key moments in the narrative, hideous shrieks out of nowhere and fears of supernatural interference further emphasize Bankim's debt to gothic topoi.

Yet these familiar conventions introduced considerable problems into Bankim's novel. Matangini's actions were simply too foreign to be believable for contemporary readers. The striking initiative with which she behaves toward a man not her husband and her ability to traverse the strict social apartheid between the women's quarter and Madhav's were extremely alien for a character of the period and especially within the world Bankim's readers inhabited. He seemed to acknowledge how far-fetched his plot was getting when he had Matangini reflect upon her choices in awkward and highly ornate prose: "As the appalling dangers rose before her mind, her noble love expanded and rose also, and she longed to sacrifice at its altar a life whose burden her crushed heart could no longer bear. But still another womanly feeling kept her back. To go to the house of Madhav at midnight and alone! Who would understand her? What would Madhav think!" (38). Unable to develop a compelling and coherent rationale for Matangini's behavior and perhaps equally conscious of what his own readers would think and whether they would understand *him*, Bankim was obliged to explain away his character's actions by awkward plot devices inserted clumsily along the way. Matangini's affection for Madhav (which is initially the source of her daring initiative on his behalf) is hurriedly explained late in the plot by their childhood friendship, placing the origins of their intimacy at a time before the rigid separation between adult men and women was enforced in Indian society. The forbidden love Matangini bears for Madhav, however, is a problem that Bankim cannot (yet) develop or explore, so he "solves" it by having her die young at her father's house rather than remain in Madhav's village as a reproach to the rigid social order she has already challenged.

Bankim could of course have resolved some of the dissonance between his plot and the social world by having male protagonists proliferate as Scott had done before him, but the great pleasure of developing strong female characters and the ensuing tensions that might evolve from their interactions with others were not matters he would easily sacrifice. In the end, despite the wholesale importation of tropes borrowed from gothic and melodrama, Bankim could not make his novel work: it required too many awkward narrative asides to explain the plot and too many ungainly devices to contain it. He gave up with a hasty "Conclusion," which maladroitly tried to tie up loose ends. Earlier details and symmetries in the plot with which the novel opened, or the critiques of feudalism and patriarchy toward which it gestured could not withstand the mandates of making what Risbud called "an interesting book," and *Rajmohan's Wife*, despite all its ambitions, fell short. Its reception in the pages of *Indian Field*, the serial in which it appeared, was so abysmal that the work never appeared as a book during Bankim's lifetime.

Many years later, Bankim counseled an aspiring writer: "Do not try to write like others. Then you will fall between two stools, as we do in our efforts to become Europeans."[17] After *Rajmohan's Wife*, he himself gave up writing like others, abandoning English and the style that had created dialogue such as Matangini's startling and stilted torrent of penitence over her illicit love for Madhav: "'Blame me not,' she said, and then interrupting herself, she bent down her head to hide the tear that gushed again with the current of feeling. 'Yes, reproach me, Madhav,' she continued, 'censure me, teach me for I have been sinful; sinful in the eyes of my God, and I must say it, Madhav, of my God on earth, of yourself' " (55). Possibly aware of how unlikely these utterances and the consciousness therein would have seemed from the mouth of a Bengali village girl, Bankim abruptly ended the novel with Matangini's untimely death. With his next novel, *Durgesanandini* (1866), he kept the strong-willed female protagonist but embraced historical settings, choosing instead to place the work in the sixteenth century and, more important, to render it in Bengali where the split between medium and sensibility—so marked in *Rajmohan's Wife*—was no longer an issue. The historical setting of *Durgesanandini* further allowed Bankim to explain Bimala's and Ayesha's forthright conduct and initiative toward matters of the heart as the manners of women from an anterior age and, therefore, both reasonable and exemplary attitudes toward erotic love and companionate marriage. For Bankim, then, both English and—initially—the contemporary world were obstacles to writing novels: rather than enabling fictional narrative, they hindered it. The issue was less realism as a formal mode than reality: even writing a melodramatic novel in English was impossible for him. He needed to find a different form and a different medium to create a successful Bengali novel.

Constrained by English and unsure about just how much he shared culturally and socially with his readership, who included not just Bengalis but all Indians literate in English as well as the British themselves, Bankim's narrative aims in *Rajmohan's Wife* remained extremely limited in scope and execution. He may have set out to tell more than an entertaining story, yet because it was unclear to him just how much he actually shared with his readers, he was unable to develop serious moral issues or to reflect on meaningful social and emotional complications through critical or narrative instruments within the novel. *Rajmohan's Wife* remains entertaining but unconvincing: there is no sustained or consequential anchor to it to make it particularly relevant to his readers and their lives. Neither the "ignoble origins" of feudal wealth nor the tensions generated from the British rule of property for Bengal (to borrow Ranajit Guha's phrase) prevail in either the narrative or the plot. The opening concerns over the legitimacy of property, the ongoing rhetoric over the propriety of English values in a Bengali feudal order, or the social tensions precipitated by Matangini's initiative dissipate by the time Bankim penned his hasty conclusion. While these issues circulate around his novel, it is not in the end able to be *about* them in any satisfactory measure.

Though Bankim's debt to G. W. M. Reynolds was noted in his lifetime—a sly treatise entitled *Bankim Babur Gupta Katha* [The Mysteries of Bankim Babu] was published by two of his contemporaries in 1891[18]—as were his debts to Scott, Bulwer-Lytton, and Wilkie Collins,[19] *Rajmohan's Wife* appears to have convinced him that a novel in the British mold could not be imported in toto into India without some distortion and translation. The problem was less with the imported novelistic conventions (conventions that Indian readers had already embraced in their avid consumption of British popular fiction) than with Bankim's treatment of those conventions. What had seemed both liberating and inspiring to Indian readers in G. W. M. Reynolds's hands came across as awkward and unnatural in Bankim's. The sonorous narrative interventions and the proliferation of coincidence in Bankim's plot resembled Reynolds' *Mysteries* novels to a degree, but whereas in Reynolds these topoi had spurred Indian readers to detect signs of recognition with Indian epic traditions, in Bankim's novel they appeared to invoke dissonance and distraction. The kinds of imaginative translations that Indian readers could make of a Reynolds novel were less possible in *Rajmohan's Wife*, whose clotted descriptions of a familiar social world clashed with the counterrealist modes that Bankim had borrowed from gothic and melodrama. Bankim's social world and his narrative idiom collided with each other in his one English novel, and nothing he could do to his elaborate plot ameliorated the situation. The solution he needed came partly from abandoning his reliance on British forms. More to the point, it came from the Indian epic tradition from which Bankim borrowed both narrator and "hero" in his efforts to indigenize the novel in the Subcontinent.

SCOTT IN BENGAL

In the Bengali novels that followed this English failure, Bankim's plots become more daring: rather than having illicit desire end by the death of an unfortunate but honorable lover such as Matangini, Bankim now began to write novels that pursued human passion to its often tragic end. In the Bengali novels, socially unsanctioned marriages nonetheless take place and even prosper (between the nursemaid Bimala and the king Virendra Singh in *Durgesanandini*); men take on second wives (such as Nagendra and Kunda in *Bishabriksha* [The Poison Tree, 1873]); beautiful widows live in sin with married landowners (for example, Rohini and Govindlal in *Krishnakanta's Will*, [1878]); and a Brahmin wife such as Shaibalini participates in a complex love triangle in which she loves a man other than her husband while at the same time being pursued by an unscrupulous Englishman who desires her, as well as by the virtuous Brahmin husband who has legal claim to her (*Chandrashekhar*). Yet, rather than becoming more fanciful and marvelous, these novels became in fact far more serious than *Rajmohan's Wife* with its modest, even conservative, ending. In expanding the social and geographical milieu in which his plots now developed—*Rajmohan's Wife* took place in a single village, while all the subsequent novels traversed the length and breadth of Bengal from Calcutta to distant province and often between remote regions—Bankim simultaneously contracted his readership to Bengali-language readers whose values and culture he shared more clearly.

As his plots became more ornate and far-flung, as the emotional and moral dilemmas of the Bengali novels became more intense and socially disruptive, Bankim anchored them by introducing a grave and often serious narrator into his novels. In the face of increasingly racy plots, this omniscient and omnipresent narrator served as a sort of moral counterweight, interrupting the narrative and dispensing injunctions and advice liberally throughout the novels, holding them together by a series of clearly articulated judgments that numerous readers have criticized as heavy-handed didacticism.[20] "The Englishmen of Bengal in those days were incapable of two things only. They could not overcome avarice and they could not own a defeat," the narrator proffers in *Chandrashekhar* (21). In *The Poison Tree*, Bankim's most serious social novel of a traditional society in part ravaged by a collision with the social forces of modernity, the narrator steps closer to the action and directly reprimands the once virtuous Nagendra for his adulterous behavior: "Is this your long-standing good character? . . . Nagendra, it would be better if you were dead. If you have the courage, then go and drown yourself."[21] At yet other times, the narrator stands further back and deposits commonplace nuggets that serve to enhance his intimacy with his readers while also heightening suspense in the plot, as in *Krishnakanta's Will*: "One of the saddest aspects of this world is that no one dies at the right time, that everyone dies at the wrong time—either too early or too late,"[22] and the rest of the plot develops this theme in numerous directions.

With the introduction of this clearly identified narrator, Bankim appears to have discovered a way to bridge the gulf between his narrative mode (the novel) and the social idiom. The highly charged domestic dramas in the social novels, along with protagonists possessing what Sudipta Kaviraj has called "a taste for transgression" could now be contained by the moralizing narrator.[23] He would never let readers forget that though the protagonists confronted and made difficult and emotionally wrenching choices, they also had to accept the consequences of the choices they made, whether these included death by poisoning, heartbreak, or exile and expiation as dictated in the Vedic tradition and amplified repeatedly in the social novels set in contemporary Bengal. The presence of the narrator both liberated Bankim's plots and restrained unruly interpretation, reminding readers that notwithstanding their sensational action, the novels' pleasures still needed to be evaluated from the gravity of a stable social world that the narrator and his editorial asides underscored and represented.

For many readers during Bankim's lifetime, his use of historical settings in numerous novels recalled Sir Walter Scott's to the extent that Bankim was frequently referred to during the late-nineteenth century as the Scott of Bengal.[24] Though the epithet is only partly applicable and often superficial, a comparison with Scott illuminates Bankim's sustained differences from him and helps reveal the considerable adaptations Bankim made in indigenizing the novel in India. Bankim, like Scott, indeed wrote a number of historical novels, yet what he tried to do with history in his novels is dramatically different from Scott. While both created active narrators for their novels, what each *did* with the narrator gestures toward widely divergent formal practices and attitudes toward the social world. Bankim's narrator extensively commented on moral aspects of the plot, Scott's largely upon its social world. Scott's narrator mostly drew attention to his characters, Bankim's toward shaping both the production and consumption of the plot. Through the presence of a relatively weak and passive hero, Scott's narrator helps to explain a history that is already settled and "at peace." Bankim's, on the other hand, uses heroes drawn from the epic mold not to reflect upon a settled history but to shape and inspire an unfolding one. A comparison with *Waverley* (1814) helps illuminate these claims more concretely.

Scott's narrator in *Waverley* frequently intrudes within the narrative to draw his readers' attention toward Edward Waverley and his character: "I have already hinted, that the dainty, squeamish, and fastidious taste acquired by a surfeit of idle reading, had not only rendered our hero unfit for serious and sober study, but had even disgusted him in some degree with that in which he had hitherto indulged."[25] In another scene, set in the thick of the Jacobite uprising and full of a colorful cast of characters, the narrator interrupts again, this time to draw his readers' attention to his method: "It is not our purpose to intrude upon the province of history. We shall therefore only remind our readers, that about the beginning of November, the Young Chevalier, at the head of about six thousand men at the utmost, resolved [and so on]" (389). In both instances, the narrator restricts himself to directing the reader's attention rather than to shaping it. Specifically, in repeatedly referring to Waverley as "our hero," the narrator directs the reader to reflect upon heroism and Edward's role therein. He leaves it to the inimitable Highland chieftain, Fergus Mac-Ivor Vich Ian Vohr, to shape the reader's attitudes when Fergus tells Edward that "you are blown about with every wind of doctrine" (353), or later when Fergus reminds his English friend with a smile that "you are not celebrated for knowing your own mind very pointedly" (405).

When confronted with moral dilemmas, Scott's narrator markedly recedes altogether, leaving it entirely to his characters to supply the perspectives that will shape the reader's judgment of events. In one of the most heartrending chapters in *Waverley*, Edward arrives at Carlisle Castle to bid farewell to Fergus Mac-Ivor as Mac-Ivor heads to the gallows. Most of the chapter is given over to a conversation between the two friends that sheds light on Edward's new maturity and Fergus's brand of romantic heroism that Scott can neither fully embrace nor reject. Even when Fergus mounts the vehicle that will carry him to his execution and conversation between the two friends has to stop, it continues in a sense in Edward's mind as he sees his friend depart and hears him utter, "God save King *James!*" to the Sheriff's "God save King George!" (476). Scott's narrator has virtually disappeared from this scene, appearing only once at the very end to underscore his refusal to comment upon or judge what has occurred as the outcome of a doomed uprising: "I will not attempt," he promises, "to describe his sensations," as Edward grieves his friend's death alone in his bolted room (477).

In this regard, Scott's narrator is predominantly an arranger of the plot rather than its producer. Fergus Mac-Ivor's passions along with those of the age propel the action over which the narrator makes clear he has little control or authority and much less judgment to offer. By having figures such as Mac-Ivor and the Englishman, Colonel Talbot, comment and provide divergent judgments upon the events of 1745 and Edward's role in them, Scott has different and differently motivated characters render the perspectives that an omniscient narrator might otherwise claim. As a result, Scott's narrative, with its multiply delineated human impressions, communicates what Wolfgang Iser has called "a picture of an individualized historical past" that was the product of combining "reality and reaction" into an evocative whole.[26]

In keeping with this assessment, Scott's narrator in the Waverley novels has sometimes been called an unobtrusive one,[27] in sharp contrast to Bankim's narrator who insists above all on raising his voice and asserting his judgments over all matters, *especially* those involving moral issues (an area in which Scott was decisively silent). Whereas Scott's narrator vanishes when Fergus Mac-Ivor is sent to the gallows, leaving all judgment of the decision to his wavering hero, Bankim's narrator asserts himself precisely at each moral juncture in his novels, reminding his readers sometimes playfully and sometimes seriously of what the appropriate behavior might be. As Nagendra's second wife learns of her predecessor's purported death in *The Poison Tree*, she begins to weep, at which point the narrator promptly steps in with a direct address to readers on how to evaluate Kunda's tears: "Hearing this, many of the beautiful readers of this book will laugh to themselves, and will say, 'The cat weeps at the fish's death.' But Kunda was very stupid. It did not occur to her dull mind that the death of a co-wife was to be greeted with laughter. The foolish girl wept a little for her co-wife. And you, lady! You who say, laughing, 'the cat weeps at the fish's death'—if you weep a little when your co-wife dies, I shall be very pleased with you" (149). Liberally sprinkling contempt for Kunda (who was "very stupid") along with advice and encouragement for his readers to show compassion ("if you weep a little . . . I shall be very pleased with you"), Bankim's narrator thinks nothing of guiding and training (by bullying and shaming) his readers into the appropriate moral judgments. When his characters themselves require tutorials or advice, the narrator decisively proffers it repeatedly, as he does when the virtuous Nagendra, besotted by the foolish Kunda, decides to betray his first wife, Suryamukhi, and marry again:

> And Nagendra! Is this your long-standing good character? Is this your long-standing learning? Is this your return for Suryamukhi's self-denying love! Fie! Fie! Look, you are a thief! Even worse than a thief. What would a thief have done to Suryamukhi? He would have stolen her ornaments and gone off with her money, but you have stolen her life. A thief, to whom Suryamukhi has given nothing, simply steals. Suryamukhi has given you everything—and you have stolen more than a thief would. Nagendra, it would be better if you were dead. If you have the courage, then go and drown yourself. (61)

Alternating sarcasm with Socratic explanation, condemnation with disgust, the narrator assumes a distinct identity, voice, and moral vantage point from which to scrutinize and evaluate Nagendra's behavior. His suggestions have the power to transform the plot. Had Nagendra heeded them, he might have saved Suryamukhi the disgrace of his second marriage and allowed her the honorable grief of instead mourning an inglorious husband's death by drowning.

However, Bankim's heroes, unlike Scott's, are larger than life and not easily contained. Whereas Waverley's actions betray his physical and ideological weaknesses in numerous ways, Bankim steadfastly insists upon heroes who single-mindedly pursue their desires to the very end. Passionate, impetuous, and charismatic, Bankim's heroes are closer to Fergus Mac-Ivor than they are to the insipid Edward Waverley, and like Mac-Ivor, most of Bankim's heroes meet their ends all too soon while the dreamy Edward lives on into a comfortable and prosperous old age. Indeed, Edward Waverley's very weakness and ineptitude render him that "mediocre, average English gentleman" whom Georg Lukács famously argued was a perfect vehicle for the historical novel, which requires a protagonist who observes history rather than makes it.[28] For Lukács, the hero who makes history belongs to the epic; for the historical novel to work, it requires heroes who are bystanders not agents of historical action. Neither the decisive Mac-Ivor nor the headstrong Nagendra would be a suitable hero for a historical novel à la Lukács: their characters insist on producing historical action by precipitating its events, whereas Scott's "middle way" (Lukács 32) requires average, mediocre heroes who can observe and make narratively usable the massively opposed extremes that generate historical crises. "Scott's heroes," claims Lukács in one of his most influential remarks on the issue, "bring the extremes whose struggle fills the novel, whose clash expresses artistically a great crisis in society, into contact with one another. Through the plot, at whose center stands this hero, a neutral ground is sought and found upon which the extreme, opposing social forces can be brought into a human relationship with one another" (36).[29]

If Lukács is correct that in purposely displacing his hero from heroism Scott brought him closer to history via the historical novel, then it is equally correct that Scott also distanced his work from that other great protohistorical form, namely the epic. For while Waverley, like Achilles and Aeneas before him, is armed by the gods when the Young Chevalier unbuckles his own sword and asks if Edward will "allow me the pleasure of arming you after the Highland fashion" (298), Scott makes abundantly clear that the comparison between "our hero" and Homer's ends right there. Scott has already indicated that it is not his purpose to intrude upon the province of history, and at no point will he let his hero intrude in that direction either. Unlike Achilles (or even Aeneas) who is the fearless and heroic agent of historical action and its consequences, Waverley is an ordinary spectator at events as he, unheroically, slinks away from duels, slips and sprains his ankle on the unfamiliar Highland terrain, receives concussions, and oversleeps through virtually every military conflagration and sortie in which he is to participate. It is Fergus Mac-Ivor who comes closer to Achilles, for he too has his bard, Mac-Murrough, who appears like Homer at feasts to "sing a catalogue of names of the various Highland clans . . . and an exhortation to them to remember and emulate the actions of their forefathers" (173). Yet, as Scott makes clear, Fergus is not (and cannot be) the hero of his historical novel for he belongs to the epic tradition upon which Scott will emphatically not intrude.

Indeed, Scott's distance from the epic elucidates another distinction between his novels and Bankim's: unwilling to settle for sneaking imbeciles and middling, average heroes as Scott was,[30] Bankim's heroes are closer in stature and temperament to those in the Indian epic tradition whose actions bring crises and disruptions to the social order of which they are part, as will become clearer shortly when we turn to *Anandamath*. Like his heroes, Bankim's narrator, too, shows great resemblance to the ever present narrator of the Indian epics who repeatedly elucidated, explained, commented upon, offered sermons, edited, and judged the events under his purview.[31] In some epics such as Tulsidas's *Ramacharitmanas*, a seventeenth-century vernacular retelling of the second century B.C.E. Sanskrit *Ramayana*, the narrator in the written text initiates his readers into Tulsi's method and even seems to invite them to take over his interpretive function as they consume the work. For instance, when the evil Ravana kicks his younger brother for daring to suggest that he return the kidnapped Sita to her husband, Prince Ram, Tulsi has a frame narrator (the lord Shiva) interject briefly but pointedly to raise awareness of Ravana's appalling behavior:

. . . He [Ravana] struck him with his feet. Still the younger brother clasped them again and again. *[Narrative describes action: Ravana kicks his brother]*

O Uma! Such is the greatness of saints, who always return good for ill. *[Shiva, the frame narrator, comments on action to Uma]*

Well may you, who are like a father to me, abuse me. Yet Lord, your salvation lies in worshipping Ram!32 *[Narrative resumes: the brother addresses Ravana]*

In this brief passage, which Philip Lutgendorf has made available and usefully annotated, the first narrator (who is relatively transparent) simply describes Ravana's actions and his brother's response. Immediately, Shiva, one of the frame narrators addresses an aside to his wife ("O Uma," who is scripted in the *Ramacharitmanas* as one audience hearing the epic), "such is the greatness of saints," a remark that simultaneously characterizes the brother's goodness in contrast to Ravana's own evil and subtly prescribes appropriate conduct to the audience. It is an extremely brief aside, and the narrative promptly resumes with

Ravana's brother's words, and *his* praise of Ram ("Well may you . . . abuse me"). Other narratorial asides and interruptions follow that are longer and more digressive from the main plot and that offer moral commentary by example and excurses, but in each case the narratorial commentaries constitute the very fabric of the epic text and become inspirations for imitation in the oral performances that have kept the epic alive in India.

In a useful reading of the multiple presences of the narrator in Tulsidas's *Ramacharitmanas*, Lutgendorf has suggested that "another frame is implied as well: just as Tulsi is relating the story and commenting on it to his listeners, so they in turn may become tellers of and commentators on his story through the performance genres that have developed around its recitation" (26). The result of the oral and scripted narrator's multiple intrusions and asides generates dramatically different epics throughout India, to the extent that A. K. Ramanujan has argued: "the story may be the same in two tellings but the discourse may be vastly different."[33] Thus Ram, the epic hero, undergoes a considerable transformation from the second-century B.C.E. Sanskrit epic in which he appears as a mortal prince to a full-fledged divinity in the *bhakti*-inspired vernacular interpretations that proliferated in medieval India.

Familiar with the Sanskrit epic and its multiple retellings both in written texts (including the fourteenth-century Bengali version of the *Ramayana* by Krittibasa) and in oral performances through the extensive *kathavachak* tradition, Bankim had before him a narrator figure from both recorded and received texts whose presence was undeniably central to the Indian epic tradition and unquestioned among the legions who consumed the form. It is this figure that Bankim borrows for his novels and places so visibly. In an attempt to domesticate the novel in India, I suggest, he turned to the ancient epics and introduced from them a range of devices including the stature of his heroes and the omniscient narrator who commented, edited, explained, and comforted the audience across the course of each novel. It is this narrator with his moral, didactic, sense-making voice who made sprawling Reynolds-like plots in the sensational mode explicable and respectable in Bankim's novels; it is this figure who provided Bankim with license to develop his Bengali novels in the elaborate manner he did without once being accused of being sensationalist, irresponsible, or opportunistic—as Reynolds had often been criticized for being in his own time. For Bankim, then, the retrieval of the narrator from the Indian epic tradition into the emerging novel served to link contemporary concerns with earlier narrative and social worlds, to connect the new social woes that his novels depicted with earlier solutions, and to make relevant in some form the books that Chandrashekhar had so ceremoniously and methodically burned.

Anandamath. By the time Bankim wrote *Anandamath* (1882), a historical novel that is possibly his most widely known work, he was able to go one step further and almost completely abandon the epic narrator altogether. The setting is eighteenth-century rural Bengal, a time of great famine and suffering when a local insurgency called the Santan Rebellion seeks to overthrow a cruel and unjust political order of British revenue collectors and weak Muslim rulers. Entire communities of men calling themselves *santans* take an oath of celibacy to join a political organization led by the mystic, Satyananda, who invokes for the first time in public memory the figure of India as mother, ravaged by occupiers. Thus united in a common endeavor around a symbol shared by all adherents, the fierce *santans*, who include wealthy landowners along with the lumpen poor, win numerous victories against their British rulers, raising the cry *Bande Mataram* to celebrate each conquest. Bankim, a well-paid civil servant in the British administration, is known to have edited and excised numerous parts of the novel either when confronted with or in anticipation of official displeasure, yet *Anandamath*'s internal contradictions and incoherences notwithstanding, the deep patriotism in the work found immediate and sustained enthusiasm among readers throughout India.[34] Was Bankim's long-standing literary fortune, like G. W. M. Reynolds's before him, a simple consequence of the fact that he "lashed" the ruling power, or was there something more complicated at stake?

Anandamath's immediate success could certainly have derived from its unabashed patriotism, with the historical setting serving as a convention or device upon which contemporary and powerfully held political sentiments could be played out. Yet this explanation is not enough to address Bankim's sustained success with every other novel he wrote, some in which an anticolonial or patriotic theme was only obliquely indicated, if at all (for example, *Durgesanandini, Krishnakanta's Will,*

Indira [1873; rev. 1892], or *The Poison Tree*). Bankim's real achievement, I would argue, lay not just in finding a language in which to write the novel in India (his Bengali, in fact, alternated colloquialisms with highly formal prose) but, more crucially, in discovering a *form of the novel* to suit India. In his historical novels Bankim created imaginary pasts in which his characters portrayed a range of values desirable in the contemporary world. More powerfully, these novels provided not simply a perspective on the present, as Lukács has suggested à propos of novelists such as Scott, but a version of the past itself that was usable in the present.

Confronting a world in which British mastery in all things was unavoidable, Indian readers also confronted a past that was mythic, heroic, timeless—but in the end, one that had few resources to offer in contemplating either empire or modernity. In making this mythic past meaningful (in recasting an actual eighteenth-century Sanyassi Rebellion in contemporary terms; in configuring usable symbols such as Mother India and *Bande Mataram*[35]), Bankim connected the world of the past with that of the present. More to the point, as Sudipta Kaviraj has persuasively argued, Bankim's novels provided his readers with an account of the past in which they were present as actors, not as servile and defeated masses—in other words as agents with proud and meaningful achievements. "[Bengalis] do not lack the events in their past, but the narrative to put some significant order into them," suggested Kaviraj, and this is precisely what Bankim's novels offered his readers.[36] Working from the premise that a people made their own destiny if they first had a knowledge of their history, Bankim used the novel as a space to sort out a usable Indian history from the contradictory strands of positivist European accounts and mythic local ones. "Bengal must have her own history. Otherwise there is no hope for Bengal," he wrote in *Bangadarsan*, the serial he edited in 1880. "Who is to write it? You have to write it. I have to write it. All of us have to write it. . . . Come, let us join our efforts in investigating the history of Bengal. . . . It is not a task that can be done by any one person alone; it is a task for all of us to do together," he concluded in this rousing passage.[37]

Part of Bankim's own efforts in investigating a history of Bengal for *Anandamath* came from a few sentences in a volume by the colonial bureaucrat William Wilson Hunter, entitled *Annals of Rural Bengal* (1868), in which Hunter records two separate incidents, a famine in

Bengal in 1768–70 and a related insurgency of semireligious men in 1771–72. "A set of lawless banditti . . . known under the name of Sanyassis or Faquirs, have long infested these countries; and, under pretence of religious pilgrimage, have been accustomed to traverse the chief part of Bengal, begging, stealing, and plundering wherever they go, and as it best suits their convenience to practise," Hunter recorded.[38] With the famine, he continues, the Sanyassis's ranks grew. They "totally defeated" the British soldiers sent to quell them and two officers (Captains Thomas and Edwards, whom Bankim portrays by name in *Anandamath*) died in the struggle. "The revenue could not be collected, the inhabitants made common cause with the marauders, and the whole rural administration was unhinged. Such incursions were annual episodes in what some have been pleased to represent as the *still life* of Bengal" concluded Hunter in his very brief history of this movement (71–72, emphasis in original).

Building upon an "annual episode" of valor and rebellion such as this one, Bankim sought to fashion a highly patriotic novel from it for his Bengali readers with all sorts of psychic and symbolic incitements against British rule in India. As *Anandamath* went from being serialized to becoming a book in 1882 and in the three editions that followed, Bankim also began the process of softening its anticolonial rhetoric: in numerous places the word "Muslim" replaced "English" or "British," and the enemy went from being the British revenue collectors to the Muslim rulers who enabled the devastation of Bengal.[39] In the novel's conclusion, rather than celebrating the insurgency's victory over the British forces that it routs, Bankim devises a mysterious stranger who suddenly appears and revives Jiban, a *santan* general lying dead on the battlefield. The stranger then proceeds to urge military restraint upon Satyananda, the *santan* leader, with the following completely unexpected speech:

> Unless the British rule this land, there is no chance of the renaissance of the eternal religion. . . . There is not much material knowledge in the country now, there is none capable of teaching it. . . . The English are past masters in the knowledge pertaining to the material world. They are adepts in the art of teaching. So we shall make the British our rulers. Through English education our people attaining knowledge of the material world will also be

made capable of understanding inner knowledge. . . . So long as the Hindus do not become wise, worthy and strong, British rule will endure. The subjects will be happy under the British control. . . . The *santan* rebellion has come only to put the British on the throne.   (190–193)[40]

Rather than celebrating an eighteenth-century victory and using it to continue an insurrection into the nineteenth, *Anandamath*'s astonishing and possibly ambivalent conclusion seems to turn its earlier patriotism on its head by proposing that the British with their material knowledge were actually *good* for India, who needed English education before its people could rule themselves.

The narrative strategy behind this unanticipated ending is borne partly of necessity: whatever glorious past Bankim might describe from Hunter's *Annals* or fabricate from his imagination, he could not remove the palpably present subjection of India from his readers' minds, and the ending connects the eighteenth-century victory with a present reality, albeit in a rather unsatisfactory and incomplete manner. Because its publication came at a moment lacking the settlement that follows historical conflict, *Anandamath*—in contrast to *Waverley*—mostly serves to incite action rather than comprehension. History is still incomplete in *Anandamath*, and Bankim hopes by the insertion of epic heroes to help make it by inspiring its conclusion. If the *santan* insurrection were to continue, the novel's message seems, Bankim's readers first needed to develop themselves as appropriate rulers of their land and for this, the *santan* leader, Satyananda—or someone like Fergus Mac-Ivor—appears to be a better model than a figure resembling Edward Waverley.

However, the celebration of the British as adept teachers and masters of knowledge remains problematic and unconvincing and runs against the passionate patriotism Bankim had already developed, in which the only real enemy of importance was the British. It is a contradiction, however, through which most of his readers easily appeared to have seen. In his memoir of a childhood in turn-of-the-century Bengal, Nirad C. Chaudhuri reports that

Contemporary and later readers argued, though nobody had the courage to put down the opinion in black and white, that the apparent argument of the book was not its real argument, that

Chatterji was concerned really to initiate his countrymen in the doctrine and technique of revolutionary insurrection, and had introduced the peroration about British rule only as an after-thought, as a plea of good faith in case the British rulers took it into their head to prosecute him for preaching sedition.[41]

Chaudhuri's suggestion is persuasive at least in the latter part: an 1883 entry for *Anandamath* in the *Appendix to the Calcutta Gazette* records it as "a story of a highly epic cast. . . . [The insurgents] perceive the necessity and wholesomeness of the English regime in India, and in the spirit of true patriots, break up their armed league."[42] A step ahead of his prospective censors, Bankim's awkward conclusion apparently managed to dissuade them from acting on the suspicion that something untoward was at hand.

However, Chaudhuri's suggestion that Bankim's Indian readers were not so easily duped by the bizarre peroration at the end of *Anandamath* remains provocative and deserves closer analysis. For his contemporaries, Bankim's major contribution lay in making manifest the real claim and urgency of nationalism by embodying it through the figure of a mother, Mother India. The song *Bande Mataram*, "throbbing with enthusiasm" as T. W. Clark writes, did much to relay this message to those who had no direct access to the novel but heard and sang the song in political gatherings and nationalist rallies.[43] For Aurobindo Ghose (1872–1950), a much younger contemporary of Bankim's who admired and translated *Anandamath* during his own journey from an armed anticolonial activist to a pacifist philosopher, it was largely through *Bande Mataram* that "the motherland reveals herself to the eye of the mind as something more than a stretch of earth or a mass of individuals."[44] In an unexpected return to his literary roots in poetry, Bankim finally seems to have found a way of reaching not just the minds but the souls of his compatriots through the verses of *Bande Mataram*, although here too language plays its games: only some of Bankim's readers and singers, even in Bengal, could understand all the words of the song, written as it was half in Sanskrit and half in Bengali.

In another return, however, this time to the epic tradition, he also appears to have found a way of speaking to his readers across the lurking censor's pen. For in *Anandamath*, the narrator from the earlier works remains but only very sketchily: his role has almost entirely been subsumed by that of the *santan's* charismatic teacher, Satyananda, whose omniscience allows him to direct the novel's action and foretell the future. It is he who organizes the *santans* in paramilitary units for their armed struggle, he who develops and reveals the metaphor of the ravaged mother in the novel, he who in the end gives coherence and authority to the novel's anticolonial rhetoric—and he who disputes and weeps at the mysterious stranger's injunctions for restraint that appear at the end of the novel.

For Bankim's contemporary readers raised on the Indian epic tradition, the figure of Satyananda was both familiar and respectable. Like Vyasa from the *Mahabharata*, Valmiki from the *Ramayana*, or Shiva from Tulsidas's *Ramacharitmanas*, the presence of an omniscient teacher lent credibility to the epic plots despite the often supernatural feats he performed. Already introduced in minor ways as early as *Durgesanandini*, Bankim's swamis (wise men or mystics) are not new to his oeuvre: they also appear and function in *Chandrashekhar* and *Kapalkundala* (1866). What is striking is that in those novels the swamis were introduced as devices or dei ex machinae to solve problems that could not otherwise be easily dealt with in the plot. (Hence Abhiram swami in *Durgesanandini* who unites the novel's complex political and romantic plots and Ramananda swami in *Chandrashekhar* who connects the novel's Vedic message with Bengal's history of occupation and insurrection in the eighteenth century.)

In *Anandamath*, however, the swami figure functions neither as an aside nor as an afterthought: here he is a central character in the novel and exists as a moral core around which the entire plot develops. As founder of the *santans* and leader of the armed insurgency, his message is the message of the novel, so that when the mysterious stranger remonstrates on behalf of British goodness in the odd peroration ("the subjects will be happy under British control"), Bankim's readers already had before them the far more powerful and persuasive rhetoric developed and in place in Satyananda's words and figure. "If our purpose was to put the British in control over us as rulers, if British rule was considered beneficent for our country, then why did you engage us in this heartless fighting?" Satyananda queries the stranger (192). Unsatisfied with the response he gets, "sparks flew from Satyananda's eyes. He said, 'I shall drench the mother earth with the enemy's blood and thus make her fruitful'" (193). The stranger grasps Satyananda's hand and leads him away, but Satyananda pointedly does not renounce his vows or his military commitment to India's liberation. Indeed, Satyananda's symbolic value was not lost upon Bankim's translators, who exploited it in unusual ways. In a 1941 English translation, made under particularly vigilant circumstances, Basanta Coomar Roy excised numerous anti-British and patriotic passages altogether. However, he renamed Satyananda as Mahatma Satya, hoping rightly that the honorific "Mahatma" would spur associations among readers of *Anandamath* with the much loved and very present Mahatma Gandhi and *his* well-known anticolonial message.[45]

If Nirad Chaudhuri is right in recording that Bankim's late-nineteenth-century readers consumed *Anandamath* by recognizing the peroration as a convention rather than as a writerly flaw, then I would further argue that the encouragement for this form of reading lies in Bankim's ability to sense and satisfy the pulse of readerly desires through figures such as Satyananda who serve as a tip-off that the more significant ambitions of the novel exceed its narrative ending. In other words, the swami figure, with his recognizable psychic and symbolic stature, both authorizes and connects two gulfs that cannot otherwise be joined. Already anointed in the popular Hindu imagination as a hallowed figure from traditional and everyday practice, the swami refashions and connects the classical past to the present, reconfiguring its resources into more contemporary and pressing needs. In addition to connecting the gulf between the two temporal planes, Satyananda also connects readerly desire with narrative endings, providing closure psychically even when he cannot fully do so narratively.

The swami figure that Bankim fleshed out so compellingly in *Anandamath* gave further license in his novel, as the narrator had earlier, to all sorts of antirealist devices including striking coincidence, supernatural acts, and forms of "magic" such as Satyananda's ability to revive Mahendra's dead wife and child—feats that sometimes produced weakness and incoherence in Bankim's novels. Yet Satyananda's wisdom and his often prophetic enunciations gave meaning and fiber to the novel's ending, linking heroic actions and pyrrhic victories within a larger scheme in which good would eventually, if not immediately, prosper. More important, however, the introduction and transformation of this figure from disembodied narrator in the earlier novels to a named and embodied protagonist in *Anandamath* lent an important dimension to

Bankim's oeuvre. Through it, Bankim fashioned the novel as a form that began to contain an encyclopedic compendium of narrative modes with epic, history, and fiction coexisting in powerful synergy. Both Bankim's narrators and the swamis who came to replace them in the later fiction helped structure the emerging novel into and alongside older narrative traditions (such as the epic) and newer ones (such as history), recombining them by a fitful but successful amount of translation and adaptation into the Indian novel. Though the outcome in the case of *Anandamath* was formally confused with the aspirations of a historical novel rendered in the epic mode, the work asserts its ambitions very clearly at the end when the novelistic register establishes itself following the inability of either history or epic to bring satisfactory closure to the narrative. In this regard, *Anandamath* is both formally and structurally a compromise: suspended between the historical novel and the epic, it gestures toward the multiple narrative forms that accompany and compete with the emergence of the novel in India.

INDIGENIZING THE NOVEL IN INDIA

"No nation can grow without finding a fit and satisfying medium of expression for the new self into which it is developing," wrote Aurobindo Ghose in a 1940 tribute to Bankim. "It is Bankim's first great service to India that he gave the race which stood in its vanguard such a perfect and satisfying medium."[46] Written at the height of the anticolonial movement, Aurobindo's homage further notes Bankim's real gift to Bengal: "he gave us a means by which the soul of Bengal could express itself to itself" (10). That this new self should find itself in and through the novel, in a language both removed from the colonizer's English (which "has something unnatural and spurious about it like speaking with a stone in the mouth," Ghose wrote in an earlier essay on Bankim[47]) and different from the Bengali of "dignified treatises and erudite lucubrations" indicates the linguistic distance the novel had to travel before it could be produced on Indian soil.[48] Even when writing in his native tongue, Bankim was forced to abandon what Ghose calls the "stiff inflexible ponderousness" of the high literary Bengali "of the pundits" and create a language with "the verve and vigour of the vernacular, capable at one end of the utmost vernacular raciness and at the other of the most sonorous dignity."[49] Phrased in the context of the preceding discussion on Bankim's formal innovations to the novel, his contribution and success as a novelist lay not simply in creating a more supple literary Bengali in which to write but also in indigenizing the novel within a vernacular narrative idiom with its own particular needs and expectations.

Bankim's narrative world, and indeed that of all Indian writers, included a still-living oral and epic tradition along with spreading literacy, education, and, in elite and urban sections, anglicization and Westernization. In attempting to write novels along the lines of those they had consumed, Indian novelists were obliged to adapt the form not just to a different print culture but also to a varied literary culture that included in it these preprint forms with their own narrative priorities of order and stability. When Bankim failed to do this with *Rajmohan's Wife*, rather than abandoning the novel form altogether, he adapted and modified a Western convention, the narrator, into its Indian counterpart, almost replacing one with the other. Omniscient and omnipresent, Bankim's narrator most closely resembles his counterpart from the Indian epic tradition who comments, intrudes, and makes asides at will throughout the novel. However, rather than creating difficulties for him as the narrator has often been known to create for the novel in other non-Western literatures,[48] Bankim's retrieval of the epic narrator into the emerging Indian novel liberated him by coming to represent a set of stable values that arranged and anchored his narrative. Jesting, grave, or reprimanding, his narrator organized the unruly parts of Bankim's novels into a single interpretive system capable of addressing and ordering multiple and varied plot twists from the domestic to the financial, the social to the political, and the mundane to the spiritual. Even in novels propelled by issues of statecraft (*Durgesanandini, Chandrashekhar*) and probate (*Krishnakanta's Will*), the narrator underscores the *moral* dimensions of such abstract transactions, holding the protagonists accountable for the choices they make and the roads they travel.

Through the narrator, Bankim reduced a rapidly encroaching modernity and its bureaucratic, administrative practices to a human dimension, insisting that whatever the external impetus, his protagonists still reserved the right to judge and act upon their environments. Rather than an awkward appendage or accretion, the epic narrator in

Bankim's novels served to unify not just the temporal or social aspects of his plots but also the multiple discursive dimensions that those novels often incorporated. History, religion, and romance came to function on a single plane through the narrator's unifying voice and presence rather than as separate and separable discursive spheres. Thus the presence of the narrator resolved many of the "problems" confronting the emerging Indian novel by helping to bridge the gulf between narration and description, traditional themes and contemporary life, social issues and historical practice, myth and religion, the past and its relation to the present. None of these issues ever disappeared entirely; they simply ceased to be problems hindering the Indian novel and became instead its content and its future.

What I am suggesting, then, is that for the novel to flourish in India, it needed to be rendered in indigenous terms that could translate and adapt the British model to Indian needs. For Bankim, that solution lay in retrieving certain narrative devices from the already familiar epic tradition. In his hands the novel became the ordering narrative of Indian modernity, making sense of the diverting past and of an emerging social universe. He sorted through issues of prose, style, and subject from early experiments with the novel and selected a set of themes that were both traditional and contemporary. In a novel such as *Anandamath*, one could further argue that he articulated very contemporary concerns in reassuring and traditional terms from Hindu myth and epic. By drawing upon different aspects of India's pasts for his subject, its explication, and occasionally for the structure of his narratives, Bankim took a foreign narrative form and refashioned it into and alongside an already existing literary tradition. He has been claimed as "one of the first systematic expounders in India of the principles of nationalism,"[49] and while this may well be accurate, the fact that Bankim chose the *novel* to expound the nation is particularly significant to the form's emergence and development. In the absence of such post-Enlightenment discourses as philosophy and history, it was the novel in Bankim's hands that assumed the ambitions of both philosophy and history. The novel was, in other words, not simply an alternative discourse (challenging factual history, for example, through historical romance) but, rather, the *only* discourse available to understand modernity, to the extent that at different times in the nineteenth century the word "novel" itself was used to indicate impulses as diverse as representation, reform, digest, romance, and history.

If Bankim's challenge—shared by all early Indian novelists—lay in indigenizing this Western form on Indian soil, then his achievement lay in making it the only form that could sustain a critique of both modernity and empire. His success is one that Bengal shares with the rest of India, though as the three following chapters show, it took almost a century after *Anandamath* for the Indian novel in English to achieve the stature and self-confidence that Bankim had accomplished within only two decades for the novel in Bengali. The adaptations that Bankim made with such apparent ease in the Bengali novel were a lot harder in the English one, compounding Aurobindo Ghose's contention that for an Indian in the British empire "to be original in an acquired tongue is hardly feasible. The mind, conscious of a secret disability with which it ought not to have handicapped itself, instinctively takes refuge in imitation, or else in bathos, and the work turned out is ordinarily very mediocre stuff" (*Chatterji* 29). Bankim's vernacular solutions such as the insertion of the epic narrator into the novel came across initially as awkward and unnatural in English translation where the language exaggerated the gulf between an Indian narrative idiom, a Western form, and a colonial language. Translations of his novels were frequently poorest in English and often available in that language last.[50] English rendered Bankim's innovations clumsy: they did not yet fit into the narrative universe associated with the language as they did with Bengali or when translated into other Indian languages. As a result, Bankim's innovations seldom really presented themselves as solutions or inspirations for Indian novelists in English.

The chapters that follow track three moments in the emergence of the English novel in India, and while neither bathos nor mediocrity marks them, the secret disability that Ghose speaks of is palpably present, as are a range of solutions—some inspired by Bankim and some in spite of him—that were devised to overcome it.

CHAPTER 5

Reforming the Novel: Krupa Satthianadhan, the Woman Who Did

It is not possible for me to give a work of fiction higher praise than to say that it reminds me of Jane Austen's writings, and that praise is not too extreme for this Hindoo girl's picture of Native and European Christian life together in India.

—Mrs. Fenwick Miller, *The Woman's Signal*[1]

Jane Austen had been dead almost eighty years when a London serial devoted to the New Woman in Britain published this review of two English novels written by a young Indian woman. Krupa Satthianadhan (1862–1894) has exaggeratedly been regarded as the first English novelist in India, but the fact that she was a woman and a Christian was often of equal if not greater importance to her critics, who lavished encomia on her skillful and detailed fictions of Indian life. Satthianadhan's two novels, numerous short stories, and prose sketches appeared in India in the 1880s and 1890s toward the end of what we can now see was an extraordinary century in Indo-British colonial relations. It was a century punctuated by calls for reform on a number of social and political issues and marked above all in colonial India by a representational crisis: not necessarily who represented the contradictions and transformations of Indian society amidst a colonial presence, but how; not which representations were the best, but which were better and why. This was a period when issues of gender had become an especially critical locus of debate and were a crucial site of contestation between various Indian and British groups committed to reform in the name of both modernity and tradition.

Indeed, Partha Chatterjee has famously argued that the Woman's Question was the central and defining issue in nineteenth-century debates on Indian nationalism undertaken on both sides of the colonial divide.[2] For many British, the abject condition of India's women affirmed the need for a colonial presence as protectors and guarantors of female uplift and advancement. British feminists played a particularly significant role in this endeavor, seeing in the condition of Indian women a cause that they could use to enhance their own participation and status within empire. Meanwhile, Indian activists were split between those who regarded the Indian woman as belonging to a sacrosanct sphere untouched by empire and its ways and so insisted that women remain veiled and isolated as they were expected to by "tradition," and those who insisted that the anticolonial struggle required the modernization of Indian society in which addressing the Woman's Question and pursuing social reform were critical. It is for the many positions under debate and the extent of cultural and social scrutiny undertaken in the mid-nineteenth century by and about Indians and Indian self-representation that this period has frequently been referred to as the decades of reform in India.

The range, contrariness, and complexity of issues brought up, and the question of who was raising them, how, and for whom formed part of what was clearly a major representational crisis. Another question of course is where and in what medium the crisis took place. Through a reading of Krupa Satthianadhan's novels and their reception, this chapter examines how the so-called representational crisis and its discrepancies were addressed in the literature of the period. The first Indian novels began appearing in regional languages in the late 1850s and 1860s, and the historical convergence of the appearance of a new genre in a period of social turbulence merits some attention. I am not proposing that the novel caused turmoil in India, nor necessarily that it calmed it. Rather, I am interested in exploring how the novel was used in India and what role it might have played in this period of representational ferment.

Written in English and appearing almost half a century after the consolidation of the novel in several regional languages, Satthianadhan's work participated in complex and multiple transactions that simultaneously corroborated, challenged, and shaped some of the most intense issues surrounding narratives of nation, empire, gender, and the emergence of the English novel in India. When *Saguna*, her first novel, was serialized in the rather staid pages of the *Madras Christian College Magazine* in 1887–88 and published to acclaim as a single volume in 1892, reviewers during her lifetime and literary historians since have, with some hyperbole, claimed it to be the first English novel written by an Indian woman. However, for inexplicable reasons that this chapter attempts to elucidate, Satthianadhan's distinction of being "first" seems to have guaranteed her little subsequent longevity in public memory. No critical accounts of her writing exist yet, and while she is frequently mentioned in most literary histories of the Indian novel, none dwell upon the substance of her literary output beyond invoking the unseemly metaphor of an athletic race and mentioning her apparent success in being "first" in producing an English novel.[3] By most standards, Satthianadhan's failure to sustain critical memory is a dismal omen with which to begin the story of the English novel in India. Yet forgotten tomes and literary failures still carry their stories with them—indeed, sometimes on them—and Satthianadhan's novels exemplify among other matters the pleasures and rewards of literary recovery and restitution.

Both the form and content of her novels, as well as their production and reception, reflect amply upon the complex literary and cultural landscape in which the novel—in English—was indigenized and naturalized in India in the latter decades of the nineteenth century. Indeed, Satthianadhan's subsequent failure to make the Indian canon gestures toward the uneasy and vexed position of the anglophone novel in India that was to persist into much of the twentieth century as well. Unlike Bankim's apparent intimacy with a Bengali readerly community that he wrote into being and whose values he simultaneously shared and shaped, Satthianadhan's novels betray no such easy intimacy with her readers, to whom she literally and figuratively introduces and explains her social world in considerable detail. Written in English, and perhaps because of this linguistic fact, her novels were immediately claimed by all sorts of communities including educated Indians, Christian converts, British colonialists and educators, Indian and British missionaries, and British women interested in reform both in India and in Britain. For the majority of these groups, it was the fact of Satthianadhan's production, rather than the product itself, that marked her for praise and attention. Satthianadhan's own concerns as novelist were obscured in the agendas that claimed her. Through a reading of her novels, this chapter sets out to address two linked issues surrounding early novelistic production in India. First, in an attempt to probe the issue of failure that is associated with her arguably foundational but nonetheless forgotten novels, this chapter provides a long-overdue appraisal of Satthianadhan's novelistic ambitions, as well as the social worlds that were part of them. The larger preoccupation behind this critical reading is an investigation into the origins and trajectory of the English novel in India, specifically, its emergence, shape, and forms that Satthianadhan with considerable prescience identified and sought to address. Looming over these two themes of inquiry is the specter of colonial literary culture and the Indian novelist as consumer and agent engaged in a series of transactions with forces both above and below, outside and inside a changing literary landscape. As I argue in this chapter, Satthianadhan's multiple audiences and their reception of her work were only one part of her difficulty as novelist: far more apparent and acute obstacles were the purportedly unifying English language in which she wrote and the tension between narrative and fiction with which her novels continually wrestled. Her failure in the literary canon, then, is consistent with the general difficulties confronting other English novelists in India, while her skill in navigating these obstacles indicates a common strategy of literary production that was followed by many subsequent Indian novelists in English.

THE NOVEL AS "FAITHFUL PICTURE"

Krupa Satthianadhan was one of fourteen children born to Brahmin parents who, in a striking departure from their caste, had converted to Christianity before her birth. Despite her parents' subsequent work in promoting women's formal education through *zenana* schools, most of Satthianadhan's own early education was conducted at home.[4] At the age of fourteen she enrolled at the Zenana Mission School in Bombay, where, encouraged by an American missionary doctor, she eventually won a scholarship to study medicine in London. Fears of the toll that medical education in a foreign land would have upon her health kept her in India, where she was among the first group of women admitted to Madras Medical College. A scholarship endowed in Satthianadhan's memory at the medical college shortly after her death attests to her success there, although she quit medical studies after the first year due to her failing health. She began publishing occasional pieces in Indian periodicals in the 1880s, and her first novel, *Saguna: A Story of Native Christian Life*, was serialized in *The Madras Christian College Magazine* in 1887 and 1888 and appeared as a bound volume in 1892; her second novel, *Kamala: A Story of Hindu Life*, appeared in the same magazine in 1893–94 and was published in a single volume shortly after her death in 1894. In 1896 a collection of her writings and prose sketches was published as *Miscellaneous Writings*, and in the same year, her newly remarried husband, Samuel Satthianadhan, riding on the back of his late wife's considerable literary popularity, published *Sketches of Indian Christian Life*, jointly edited with his new wife, Kamala, and containing a dozen entries of which six were short stories by Krupa.[5]

Much of what we know of Satthianadhan's life comes from a lengthy memoir, written in 1894 by Elisabeth L. Grigg, wife of the Director of Public Instruction of Madras. Grigg's memoir was published as a preface to Satthianadhan's second novel, *Kamala*, some months after the author's death. It is a sympathetic portrait of the novelist, claiming her as the product of efforts by British women on behalf of female education in India. More than seeing Satthianadhan simply as an example, however, Grigg expresses solidarity with her achievements, pointing out "how much there is in common in the waves of thought which have stirred the women of East and the women of the West."[6] Her account of Satthianadhan's life is part of a short but intense moment in what one might call late-nineteenth-century feminine social hagiography in which British feminists and travelers such as Mary Frances Billington and Mrs. E. F. Chapman excavated the lives of remarkable Indian women, subsequently recording and publishing them to considerable attention and review in the British feminist reform press.[7] The hagiographies had their own complex agendas that included inspiring further activist work on behalf of Indian women and enhancing the literary prestige and feminist status of the hagiographer. Through the attention she received from the British feminist press and figures such as Mrs. Grigg (who claimed that Queen Victoria herself had read *Saguna* and "was graciously pleased to request that any other work by the authoress should be sent to her" [i]), Satthianadhan's novels were part of an inadvertent but significant transaction with a world far outside the Madras Presidency where she lived and wrote.

Grigg's "Memoir" frames the first edition of *Kamala* at one end, and at the other end are printed excerpts from several dozen reviews of Satthianadhan's writing, a pattern begun in the publication of her earlier novel, *Saguna*, and carried out in the posthumously published *Miscellaneous Writings*. The reviews come from both the British and the Indian press and reflect a variety of opinions regarding the interest of her work. Indeed, given the physical layout of Satthianadhan's books (which was supervised by her husband, Samuel), to read her work was first to learn *how* to read it (from Mrs. Grigg) and then *what* to make of it (from her reviewers). Sandwiched between these sometimes contesting narratives is Satthianadhan's own writing, and it is worth examining her novels more closely before scrutinizing the claims that were made upon them.

Of the two novels she wrote, *Saguna* appeared first. The "novel" is largely autobiographical, and as if trusting no one else with her story Satthianadhan crafts a first-person narrator for the work, which frequently renders the novel more akin to testimonial than fiction. Its opening lines betray the considerable tension Satthianadhan felt as she attempted to function as both narrator and subject: "In the following pages I shall in my own way try to present a faithful picture of the experiences and thoughts of a simple Indian girl, whose life has been highly influenced by a new order of things—an order of things which at the present time is spreading its influence to a greater or less extent over the whole of her native land" (1). Within the course of the novel's opening sentence, the first-person narrator "in my own way" distances herself from the subject, "the simple Indian girl," and the remainder of the sentence records "her" testimony of growing up in a Christian household, working in *zenanas* with a pair of European missionaries, going to medical school, mating, and marrying. The promise of self-disclosure gestured in the opening "I" rapidly shifts to remoter description in the move between the narrative "I" and the narrated "she" that also signals the move from scrutiny inward to interrogation outward.

This shift between narrative subject to object marks a larger discomfort with fiction and fabrication: the exemplary fictional lives that Bankim and other regional language novelists (such as O. Chandu Menon [Malayalam], S. M. Natesa Sastri [Tamil], and Srinivas Das

[Hindi]) developed and portrayed with such apparent ease within worlds inspired by imagination and history were evidently obstacles for Satthianadhan who instead chose "real" lives and testimonies to place at the center of her novelistic universe. In this regard, *Saguna* draws upon her own biography and *Kamala* partially upon that of her mother. Yet within this insistence upon the authority of autobiography lies a persistent narrative timorousness that frequently flees the testament of the "real" for the apparent reassurance of fiction, as *Saguna*'s opening sentence demonstrates. Indeed, the movement in this novel from its opening to its closing lines is consistently one between the revelation of the self and the outside, between self-investigation and the investigation of the world.

Saguna's plot lends itself well to this strategy of critical vacillation and its numerous possibilities. As the daughter of Christian activists, Saguna lives in different microworlds, both Indian and British, Hindu and Christian, male and female all of which come under her scrutiny. Precocious, studious, and highly sensitive, Saguna's observations unfold and give depth and texture to what constitutes "India," what kinds of social relations are possible in its changing cultural and political landscape, and where a woman of her erratic background and independent mind might fit in. Early in the novel she describes a conversation with her older brother and mentor, Bhasker: "He talked of doing great things, and, forgetting that I was a mere girl he poured out the ambition of his life and grew eloquent over the great work that had to be done for India. He was a Brahman, he said, a Brahman to the backbone, and he would show his countrymen what it was to be a real patriot to live and die for one's native land" (11). In a novel so clearly marked from its subtitle as a "story of native Christian life," Bhasker's assertion of his father's repudiated religion and caste is striking: on the one hand, it serves as an index to the persistence of caste in nationalist politics. On the other hand, the very claim to Brahmin status serves to contest the nationalist fantasy of a homogenous India in which few in fact *are* Brahmins and fewer still could lay claim to the caste as a matter of birthright. Throughout the novel Satthianadhan both reveals and obliquely critiques her larger social world with this delicacy of touch. While nowhere in her oeuvre does Hinduism come under direct critique, its caste practices frequently do, as, paradoxically, do Christian social practices in India as well.

Through conversion, Satthianadhan and her alter ego, *Saguna*, exist at the fault line between Hindu and Christian, Indian and British cultures, which provides Satthianadhan with the occasion for a critical practice directed at both religious and secular spheres, nationalist and colonial priorities. With her family's embrace of Christianity, Saguna receives an English education, carried out in an unorthodox and informal manner where she is let loose among the volumes in Bhasker's study. Isolated from contact with others of her own age, Saguna develops an imaginative interpretive apparatus liberated from prevailing shibboleths and free to construct alternatives at will. "My brother described some of the works of the great poet and grew eloquent over some of the grandest passages in *Paradise Lost*. I did not understand much of what he said, and in my simplicity thought Satan quite a hero in his having waged eternal war with heaven" (8). Profoundly moved by Bhasker's rendition of the poem, Saguna recognizes that the passages her brother recites are "some of the grandest ones" in Milton's epic, but she misses the rest of the point of the work and remarks on it revealingly. She recognizes that there is a correct reading but attributes her critical shortcomings in not getting it to her "simplicity." Undaunted, however, her interpretation overturns religious orthodoxy on Satan's "heroism" for an aesthetic and political end, and this passage is striking in part because it helps illuminate the flexibility of the convert's belief in Christian doctrine. Liberated from both Hindu *and* Christian orthodoxies, Saguna's imagination exercises a creative independence that is free to dissent against both faiths and to invert and inscribe alternate readings where it will.

There is a further element in Saguna's literary *Bildung* that gestures to the critical gulf between her interior and exterior worlds, one that is often apparent more widely. Sitting on an isolated beach, she is approached by an Englishman who asks what she is reading. Spenser's *Faerie Queen*, Saguna replies. "You are very clever to understand it. An English girl twice your age would not understand it," the stranger remarks (165). "I don't know what you mean by understanding. I guess the meaning. I am not at all clever, though I want to be clever," Saguna confides as she ends the conversation. It is a remarkable admission from a young woman desperately precocious and anxious beyond everything to fit in. It is an even more curious admission of readerly practice in a novel in which virtually all the works the protagonist remarks upon and devours are British. Saguna's reading of British literature, we realize, is fundamentally an act of fabrication: consuming texts within her reach, she "doesn't know what [it] means by understanding" and simply "guesses" at their meaning. In part this representation of reading fleshes out in the realm of fiction what the theoretical argument on consumption claimed earlier, demonstrating a practice in which readers actively produced the books that they read. More important, Saguna's bewilderment gestures far more acutely to the considerable gulf between the British literary texts she consumes and her uncooperative social world—and this, it seems to me, remains the point of the repeated literary references.

The imported works Saguna reads are neither about nor do they apparently always speak to the world she inhabits. Contrary to the Department of Public Instruction's insistence that English literature provides the best gloss to empire—and at its most successful *glossed over* the disjunctions enforced between empire and its subjects—Satthianadhan's novels demonstrate a different process at work. Saguna is passionate about the books she consumes, taking them to mean what she thinks they say; yet, rather than socializing her into the hierarchies of a colonial landscape as the Macauldian model for English education would have it, the English literature she imbibes actually renders her ill equipped to deal with the world she inhabits. Her wider education helps her even less. Early in the novel she records learning from Bhasker about "great men, heroes, patriots, philosophers, and about Greece and Rome" (3). Later, when her British missionary teachers ask her what she is reading, her response is critical: "I have finished *Landmarks of the History of Greece*," she begins, at which they scoff, "What have you to do with Greece?" Deflated, Saguna confides, "I had loved this little book. *It was like a story book*" (149–150; emphasis added).

It is a revealing insight she proffers, for it vividly explains Saguna's perceptual apparatus. Educated and socialized by imported values and narratives whose worth lies mainly in their quality as "story" rather than shared public memory or national pride, she appraises her wider social landscape too as "story book." The history and geography she reads are predominantly of Greece and Rome and as such have nothing whatsoever to do with her lived environment. When describing her own travels in western India, she resorts to invoking fables and folklore of saints and *satis* rather than using a more discerning discursive apparatus influenced by Indian history or sociology. "Stories" and novels we realize are Saguna's main way of apprehending her world, and while they serve her well at times, they render her socially bereft at others. "My daughter is alone at home. She learns a little too much, so I have brought her here to be like other girls" (169), begins Saguna's mother as she deposits her at the missionary boarding school. However, Saguna is so unlike other girls that being unfit for, and unfittable into, the school's pedagogical apparatus (or its "story"), she ends up having to take lessons on her own.

To an extent, Saguna herself is aware of this discrepancy between the British world she encounters through her reading and her family's missionary work and the community of "native" Christians and Hindus she lives within. She pushes against the prevailing tide that considers these worlds the same by trenchantly remarking upon those who are unwilling to see the two worlds as completely separate. Describing a young Christian girl, who like her lives in her books, Saguna records: "Like many a novel-reading girl, she lived in a world of her own making and enjoyed it. She knew that the native Christian community was very small, and that there was no society to speak of, neither *long skirts* nor *short skirts*. Her mother wore a *saree*. But she attended an English school, and her thoughts were influenced by those with whom she mixed" (97). The swift and stern aside that despite the length of skirts in fashion in the English novel "her mother wore a *saree*," puts the matter in perspective to a point. Satthianadhan's is a sharp reminder that notwithstanding claims to the contrary, British influence on Indian secular and religious matters needed to be balanced by vernacular practices and perspectives that ought never to be abandoned for anglicist ones.

And yet, while she is so clear on marking her dissent from a full-fledged embrace of British priorities and social customs, there is a particular area of Indian practice against which Satthianadhan's entire oeuvre rebels and that frequently allies her with her British promoters. The condition of Indian women receives its fullest critique in *Kamala*, a novel about a child bride and eventually girl widow married into an orthodox Hindu family. Yet even in *Saguna*, the more "modern" novel in which the female protagonist avails herself of and flourishes under the freedoms of English education, travel, and professional training, first as teacher then as a prospective doctor, Satthianadhan's critique of the Woman's Question is pointed. If a woman's lot in the Hindu household is one of bone-numbing work and alienation where "the only diversion Radha [Saguna's mother] and girls of her age had was in the way of ceremonies and temple visiting during festival times. The cramped houses and the drudgery of home work were trying . . . and the girls longed for freedom and a little diversion" (26–27), then the situation of educated women like Saguna is paradoxically not much better. In a powerful passage that strikingly echoes Jane Eyre's famous lines at the Thornfield balustrades, Saguna reflects upon her lot:

> I had chafed under the restraints and the ties which formed the common lot of women, and I longed for an opportunity to show that a woman is in no way inferior to a man. How hard it seemed to my mind that marriage should be the goal of woman's ambition, and that she should spend her days in the light trifles of a home life, live to dress, to look pretty, and never know the joy of independence and intellectual work. The thought had been galling. It made me avoid men, and I felt more than once that I could not look into their faces unless I was able to hold my own with them.[8]   (178)

As soon as Saguna is offered the opportunity to pursue medical studies with its "large and noble possibilities" (178), she grasps it, only to be pursued by an ill-fated trio of marriage proposals pushing her back toward dreaded domesticity. Each comes within minutes of the other from Indian men recently returned from England who propose to Saguna at a social gathering of Indians and Britons associated with the missionary school. Saguna's initial amusement at the attention her academic success is drawing among suitors who include a barrister, a doctor, and a student turns quickly to disappointment then anger. One sweetens his offer by saying, "it is not necessary for all girls to earn their own living and devote their lives to study. It is only those who cannot get husbands that must do this" (204); another by noting that in marrying him, she would be better off than pursuing her medical studies since "a bird in the hand is worth two in the bush" (206). It is after this proposal that Satthianadhan locates her real anger with the Woman's Question: it is no different, she seems to argue, between India and

Britain; therefore, the resources to redress it cannot be sought abroad but must be cultivated at home. "It is really disgusting," she exclaims, "to see how many of you imitate the English in manners, dress, and other superficial things without imbibing their liberal spirit—that spirit which gives to a woman equal privileges with man, and credits her with noble and disinterested actions" (207). While this passage praises the British for their "liberal spirit," there is nevertheless an emerging sense in Satthianadhan's writing that India needs far more than a superficial application of Western modernity to reform the condition of its women. The reform needs to be initiated from within rather than applied from without if it is to avoid reproducing attitudes like those assumed by the England-returned barrister, doctor, and student.

If *Saguna*'s promise lay in delivering a female *Bildungsroman* as its protagonist literally and symbolically journeys across colonial India searching for independence, Satthianadhan's second novel, *Kamala*, is set in a far more traditional and circumscribed environment. Unlike Saguna, *Kamala*'s protagonist has no direct contact with the Indo-British world or its institutions such as the church, schools, and libraries: the novel deals with a young woman's upbringing and child-marriage in a small, highly orthodox Hindu community. It is an intensely written, tightly woven romance that combines the "new order of things spreading over the native land"—the pressure to reform the condition of Indian women—with an exquisite style amalgamating Austenesque social observation with plot conventions derived from British melodrama and sensational fiction. In contrast to the earlier novel of a Christian life, this one dwells on a young motherless Hindu girl, brought up by a scholarly, Brahmin father. Kamala has no formal schooling as such nor contact with books; she is functionally illiterate and grows up in an isolated and idyllic pastoral world without many adults or supervision. She has no idea of her mother's identity except for fleeting visions she gets. Shortly after puberty, according to tradition, she is married into a traditional, upper-caste Brahmin family. We learn that her husband, Ganesh,

> was come of a learned family. His father and his grandfather were *shastris*, noted for their learning and bigotry. But in these days Sanskrit learning is not appreciated . . . Sanskrit learning is despised and English learning is all in all, for it pays best. So,

much against his will, the old *shastri* of Sivagunga sent his only son Ganesh to an English school. The old man in his inmost heart had the greatest contempt for English learning, which he regarded as not only superficial but also as antagonistic to the Hindu religion. But he was forced to yield to the influences of his times, and he felt no doubt some satisfaction at the success of his son, though he had his own misgivings as to the influence the new training would have on the young man's religious belief and conduct.   (50)

Ganesh makes a short-lived attempt to have a modern, companionate relationship with Kamala: "With the English ideas he had imbibed regarding a woman's love and education, he thought of striking out a new line and developing Kamala's mind and so training her to be a real companion to him" (79). The Hindu joint-family responds with fear— of the shame that an educated daughter-in-law might bring—and then jealousy—at what it perceives is a spell their new daughter-in-law has cast upon their son—and they make the couple's life miserable, so that Ganesh soon abandons Kamala's lessons. If there is any question as to how far the "new order of things"—personified by English education and English ideas—have pervaded the native land, the passage above reveals the speed with which the new order moves from colonizing social institutions (English education replaces Sanskrit learning even in a Brahmin family) to intruding into the domestic sphere and disrupting it.

This new order renders other matters irrevocable too: an English education brings with it a civil-service job, and Ganesh soon moves out of the traditional joint-family home and into a house of his own with Kamala. Nothing in Kamala's training to be a good Hindu wife prepares her for her new surroundings, and when Ganesh, freed from the restraints of his extended family, brings a prospective mistress into the house, the meek Kamala storms out to return not to her own father but to her in-laws. The dénouement comes soon thereafter: Ganesh, who is named after the elephant-headed god of auspicious beginnings, dies of cholera shortly after Kamala's flight; embracing modernity is clearly *not* a good beginning in this novel. Kamala almost simultaneously learns of her mother's aristocratic identity from her in-laws and finds out that her austere, mendicant father has left her an immense fortune that he had absent-mindedly forgotten about at the time of her wedding. The messenger of this fortuitous news is none other than Ramchander, her father's former disciple, a man whom we now learn has secretly adored Kamala from afar all her life and to whom we further learn she was once herself betrothed. He asks her to share his life, but Kamala declines—abandoning tradition is no good either, even though widow remarriage may now be legal. She spends the rest of her life as a childless widow "in unselfish works of charity" (207) and upon her death, leaves her fortune "for the sole benefit of widows and orphans" (208).

For all the novel's romance conventions—Ganesh's mistress, we learn, was once engaged to Ramchander before he was engaged to Kamala, and her affair with Ganesh is part of a complicated revenge on the unwitting Kamala for "stealing" her man; the mysterious loss and retrieval of Kamala's fabulous fortune; miraculous coincidences that link Kamala to Ramchander and a mysterious cult of learned *swamis*—there is a startling seriousness in its social vision. Despite the vivid descriptions of Kamala's degradations and privations as Ganesh's wife in his large and intrusive joint-family, Satthianadhan seems unwilling to dismiss the family presence altogether, for as she insists following one description of the rhythms of the Hindu domestic structure: "others know nothing of the luxury of this life" (131). The remark is neither ironic nor facetious as Satthianadhan underscores when she has Kamala return to her in-laws' house after storming out of Ganesh's, or when Kamala spurns Ramchander's proposal for a companionate marriage. Indeed, in rejecting Ramchander's proposal, Kamala most confounds the novel's romance origins: in sharp contrast to the weak-willed Ganesh, Ramchander appears to be a mate worthy of her and one who corroborates a moral code learned from the *Puranas* that "good deeds were rewarded and bad deeds punished" (57).

However, in rebuffing him as she unexpectedly does, Kamala invokes another code, also learned from the ancient *Puranas*, which "had taught her one great lesson, the great lesson of humanity, love for others and the need of doing one's duty at any cost" (57). It is Kamala's adherence to *dharma*—that hardest of Hindu concepts to define meaning both religion and duty, social custom and individual interpretation—upon which this novel turns. Far from *Saguna*, the idealized

Bildungsroman, with its fairy-tale ending in which Saguna eventually finds a prince who is both Christian and profeminist, *Kamala* portrays the hardships of Hindu child marriage, which she insists be reformed, but she will not do away with the larger Hindu religion and its customs, which she insists are important. The novel's chaste ending insists on reforming practices within Hinduism rather than rejecting the religion altogether, and it is this aspect of Satthianadhan's restraint that partially frustrated her evangelical British supporters while winning attention from Indian readers who praised her "realism" and integrity. In this regard, *Kamala* is not just an anti-romance, but a serious and thought-ful anti-*family* romance. Even when Kamala is miraculously provided with an unimaginably large fortune and a lover who shares her values, she rejects the alternate, idyllic, and ideal world that she could now lay claim to for one that is familiar and traditional. Tempering the rush to unmake Indian society from within in the name of "reform," Satthi-anadhan proposes a slower alternative that is both less radical and more sustainable. In this regard, *Kamala* veers closer to the work of an Eng-lish novelist once forbidden to her: "I have also learnt a new lesson which has changed my horizon and given me a new glimpse of life. The lesson has been conveyed partly in the shape of books . . . I had lately been devouring with intense delight George Eliot's works—once for-bidden books" (223), she reveals at the conclusion of *Saguna*, with its fairy-tale *Jane Eyre*-ish ending in which Saguna gets her feminism and her marriage plot too. By the time of *Kamala*, however, a more serious vision—possibly inspired by Satthianadhan's reading of Eliot—had set in, and for all its romance and melodramatic borrowings the novel reins itself in order to provoke a critique not so much of Hinduism but of a colonial modernity that implicates Christianity and the British in its purview.

"ISSUES THAT SEIZED US . . . AND WOULDN'T LET US GO"

Satthianadhan's novels touch on a number of social issues that were the focus of debate between reformers and traditionalists throughout most of the nineteenth century in India: she writes about female education in India, invoking the *zenana* movement; on the plight of child-widows, invoking the controversial Widow Remarriage Act of 1856; and she places *Saguna* within an ongoing discourse of missionary activity and Indian conversion. Furthermore, her novels' focus on female subjectivity as both the source and the substance of reform aligns her most immediately with New Woman fiction in Britain, to the extent that the Madras Presidency *Catalogue of Printed Books* describes her work as "showing the native New Woman beside the old."[9]

While Satthianadhan's novels on these subjects can hardly be called controversial, what became increasingly contested in the 1890s was Satthianadhan herself. To whom did she belong? Or, more to the point, who could lay claim to her writing: the missionary organizations to whom this successful young novelist provided the best proof of their own achievements in the field; or the aristocratic British matrons such as the Marchioness of Dufferin and Ava whose efforts toward female education in India had found a prize pupil in her; or her British readers in the radical press to whom she represented the successful native New Woman; or indeed Satthianadhan's Indian readers who looked up to her as a model, one even insisting that "every educated Hindu ought to buy this book, nor only for the purpose of encouraging Indian literature, but also for the purpose of laying well to heart the lessons it contains."[10] Satthianadhan was claimed by these groups and others, and while it was her work as a novelist that brought her to prominence among those committed to social reform, it is ironically her literary achievements that are today conspicuously unknown at a time when increasing scholarship and research are being conducted on the archives of reform in nineteenth-century India.

In order to understand Satthianadhan and the Indian novel in English today, one needs to invest something in understanding the cultural and political context that produced them, as well as the intellectual and social practices that preceded them and subsequently appropriated Satthianadhan's writing. I have already mentioned the social transformations taking place in nineteenth-century colonial India: Satthianadhan was very much a product of this period of reform, yet her writing robustly and unequivocally contests the emerging forces overtaking her world. She is both outcome and proponent of female education, for instance, yet her novels animate a powerful critique of the social costs continually extracted and incurred in the process. Whereas her British readers and patrons claimed her work as a contribution to the landscape of their efforts, Satthianadhan's novels give voice to entirely separate concerns, indicating the vast territory of female subjectivity untouched by domestic and colonial reform efforts on their behalf.

Given the almost immediate and enthusiastic response that her novels elicited in India, the absence of sustained or serious critical engagement with her writing is a glaring lacuna in Indian literary history. To have achieved such an articulate public voice and to have been such a visible participant in the debates of her period required Satthianadhan to confront the major axes of reform and to adapt and rearticulate them from within the female subjective consciousness she crafts in her novels. Her use of both English and the English novel inserted her writing into a wider (and more international) context and was undoubtedly part of her appeal in the 1890s.[11] However, to understand Satthianadhan's use of the novel from within the larger culture in which reform constituted a single, albeit powerful, portion is also to investigate the possibilities that the genre might have offered to a writer committed to addressing the social and historical transformations overtaking her world. Despite her success then, does the fact that Satthianadhan wrote a *certain kind* of English novel offer any explanation for her absence from Indian literary history today or explain her failure to produce a literary movement or corpus around the English novel in India in the way Bankim had already accomplished in Bengali?

Both of Satthianadhan's novels privilege childhood as a sacrosanct period marked by a kind of prelapsarian innocence. For Kamala, that era ends on her wedding morning, when for the last time (at the age of eleven or twelve) she "ran and jumped and sang out in her joy whatever came to her lips" (25). Adulthood and maturity appear shortly thereafter in the novel as "a new and dreadful world" (37) punctuated by injustices and an awareness of gendered inequities. Both the novels' formal affinities with women's autobiography invite one to regard them as particularly female *Bildungsroman* with an emphasis on process rather than on product. And indeed, it is the *process* of growing up, rather than *being* grown up that establishes Satthianadhan's bond with New Woman writing in Britain, which, as Kate Flint has pointed out, "presents a woman's life as process, stressing the value of continuity, even endurance, and of adhering to often painfully learnt principles: principles which are self-generated and rationally arrived at, rather than being imposed by dominant social beliefs."[12]

Indeed the great tension in British New Woman fiction was precisely between what Flint calls "dominant social beliefs" and alternatives proposed by the New Woman. The fiction's major themes arose from reformist debates in Britain over jobs, votes, and contraception for women. Dissolute (often syphilitic) husbands, self-taught protagonists, occasional New Men, a restrictive social order, a gradual coming to consciousness, and an increasing openness about female sexual education characterize these works. Grant Allen's *The Woman Who Did* (1895) was the best-known of this genre, which included among others the work of Mona Caird, Sarah Grand, and Emma Francis Brooke.[13] Beginning with the passage of the Married Woman's Property Act in 1870, a vigorous output of reformist periodicals also appeared alongside New Woman fiction in Britain.[14] Read together with the New Woman fiction, the reformist press provides a fuller idea of the range of issues tackled in the fiction, functioning as a kind of reality effect to some of the often lurid New Woman novels. Reading the radical press today reminds one, for instance, that the New Woman novel appeared in Britain to readers already familiar with—though not always particularly sympathetic to—many of its themes from hosts of public agitations, reform meetings, temperance groups, and suffragist teach-ins. In the words of Gail Cunningham: "Violently abused by many, ridiculed by the less hysterical, and championed by the select few, the New Woman became a focal point for a variety of the controversies which rocked the nineties."[15] The fiction appeared among readers already primed by Ibsen's *A Doll's House*, which had its first London production in 1889. Recalling her response to seeing the play for the first time, Elizabeth Robins remarks on its acutely *familiar* quality for her: "The unstagey effect of the whole play . . . made it, to eyes that first saw it in '89, less like a play than *like a personal meeting—with people and issues that seized us and held us, and wouldn't let us go.*"[16]

I cite Robins's comment and mention the women's radical press in Britain to point out the immensely localized nature of the period that existed alongside its many overtly global ambitions: namely, its voracious ability to absorb and appropriate a plurality of conditions whose functions were sympathetic to its causes. For one, the New Woman novel made no attempt to mask its contemporaneity: it was a fiction for women, about women, *today*. Furthermore, there was a powerfully self-referential quality between the press and the fiction: much of the latter was serialized in the weeklies, but more acutely, the mandate for reform operated—much as high imperialism did a quarter century earlier—with a carte blanche to take over the globe. Virtually any topic anywhere in the world that was relevant to the spirit of British reform could be included for circulation among the meeting halls, the weeklies, the fiction, and subscription notices for reformist causes. Mrs. Fenwick Miller's review of Satthianadhan in *The Woman's Signal* is part of this trajectory of what one might call reformist colonialism: Indian women had, after all, long been the object of reformist activity among their well-meaning British sisters in India. On one level, it is true that their stories validated and endorsed the energies of their British sisters. For this purpose, however, certain stories clearly functioned better, and here one could cite the considerable archive of what I call testimonial writing that circulated especially around the *zenana* movement: namely, the inscription of stories of Indian informants confirming the use and success of missionary activities in education and conversion.

Yet, as I have already mentioned, there were other kinds of testimonies published in the late-nineteenth century, those that I have earlier termed feminine social hagiographies. The most significant of these was Mrs. E. F. Chapman's *Sketches of Some Distinguished Indian Women* (1891), whose portraits, read critically, appear to extol their subjects for *simply being women*.[17] Harriot, the Marchioness of Dufferin and Ava, Vicereine of India (1884–88) and longtime champion of women's education, has this to say in her preface to Mrs. Chapman's *Sketches*:

> No one will read these *Sketches* . . . without a feeling of intense sympathy and admiration for the subject of each one of them; or without pride and pleasure in the fact that so much talent, perseverance, and determination should be found combined with so much gentleness, and with so many truly feminine qualities. One might, perhaps, have feared that women who had to break through the hard and fast rules of caste and custom would have lost their more lovable characteristics in the struggle; but one rises from the perusal of each one of these biographies with as much affection for the woman as admiration for the student.

(v–vi)

For the Marchioness at least, what makes these women "distinguished" is that even after "breaking the hard and fast rules of caste and custom," they remained with "so many truly feminine qualities"—in other words, they remained women. Furthermore, in a more subtle subtext to her reading, by abandoning the traditional Hindu ways of "caste and custom" these women become more modern and more like their English compatriots, i.e., truly feminine. However, Mrs. Chapman, who assembled the biographies, is slightly more circumspect about the sketches, while at the same time making even wider claims for them:

> Happily there is now a brighter side to the picture. The appeal to English sympathy and interest has not been in vain, and thanks to the energy, the courage, and the perseverance of many noble-minded men and women, this sympathy and interest have found expression in many well-directed efforts to extend to the women of India the blessings of civilization and of education and to secure for them at least *a share of that liberty and honourable respect, which we are accustomed to consider as among the most valuable and incontestable "rights of women."* (1–2; emphasis added)

For Mrs. Chapman, the Distinguished Indian Women are made so by the blessings of "civilization and education" extended to them by her own "noble-minded" countrymen and women. Her comments bring to mind the rhetoric of the civilizing mission transplanted to the particular cause of women's education in India. It should, therefore, come as little surprise that *Sketches* as a whole appears to function by legitimating the efforts of the entire mission and by appealing for further English "sympathy and interest" in continuing the cause.[18]

If Mrs. Chapman's comments stopped here or persisted in this vein, they would continue to reside in a substantial but otherwise today unremarkable archive of *coloniale oblige*. However, they do not. *Sketches* has a more complicated mission, one alluded to obliquely toward the end of Mrs. Chapman's "Introduction," from which the quote above comes. In the passage already cited, Chapman makes particular note of that "liberty and honourable respect, which we are accustomed to consider as among the most valuable and incontestable 'rights of women.'" Read from the perspective of the civilizing mission, the passage rather straightforwardly appears to endorse Britain (for extending the rights of women) over India (who keeps her women in the dark). However, about a third of the way through the introduction, Mrs. Chapman makes the following deeply revealing remark, one that divulges an entirely different set of concerns underlying her writing and, indeed, the archive of which it is part:

> So rapid indeed has been the development of female education in India, that the Indian universities actually threw open their degrees to women before any English university did so. The University of Madras threw open its degrees to women in 1876, Calcutta followed in 1878, and it was not till 1879 that the University of London accorded them the same privilege." (7–8)

Mrs. Chapman's comment here betrays less enthusiasm for the efforts of her "noble-minded" country and a genuine anxiety about the glaring inequity of female educational opportunities between London and Madras. "So rapid indeed has been the development in India"—and so slow in Britain, her passage suggests. Her careful and precise chronology of female higher education exposes the immense paucity of her earlier claim, namely, of education as an "accustomed and incontestable right" in Britain. However, rather than taking away from the achievements of the female education movement in India, Chapman's comparison reveals a more complex intervention at work: on the one hand, her collection of sketches endorses reformist efforts toward the colony, but on the other more powerful albeit less visible hand, her collection about "distinguished" Indian women works to generate possibilities for women in Britain, possibilities that reveal themselves from within remarks such as the comparison above.

I would argue that the archive of what I have been calling feminine social hagiography in late-nineteenth-century India performed a vital function for the British reformist movement: its skillful deployment of biography with cultural history in the works operated both to inspire and to introduce transformative possibilities for women in Britain. The Indian biographies both function as and reveal sublimated narratives in which the struggle for reform emerges victorious. As such, the disguised narratives functioned for British women as a stage on which to enact certain kinds of agency: in dramatizing the lives of Distinguished Indian Women, the biographies relive and underscore struggles contemporaneous to their British readers, thus further operating as idealized sites where social problems have already been resolved. Like all hagiographies, these too combine didacticism with inspirationalism and, almost like textbook cases, contain within them a visual image of saint-as-icon, usually a photograph or portrait on the front flyleaf. In Satthianadhan's case, *Saguna* comes with her photograph and a careful signature below, further corroborating the image of these women as living legends worthy of imitation.

In short, what is unusual when reading these biographies alongside their accounts and reviews in the British reformist press is a recognition of the immense reversal at work: it is the narratives of India and her women that become sources of resistance and resolve for British women in *their* struggles for social and legislative equity at home. In first creating then colonizing the narratives of their Indian counterparts, British reformers articulate then stage their own claims for liberation, a liberation only possible in terms and narratives borrowed from an unexpected and unacknowledged transaction implicit in the colonial encounter. There is a small—albeit revealing—reference to the extent of this reversal in an anecdote printed in *The Woman's Signal* in 1894: "A correspondent writes us that one of the ladies now canvassing for the Suffrage Petition received this answer from an old man, 'Give women votes? Why, you will be wanting to give them to the animals next.' *This was in England not in India!*"[19] Once recognized and catalogued, the sins of the child become a lot harder to bear in the parent.

Paradoxically, recent feminist historians uncovering the imperialist roots of Western feminism have committed many of the same omissions as the nineteenth-century reform press and have largely ignored the voice of Indian women. Scholars such as Antoinette Burton, Barbara Ramusack, Leslie Flemming, and Kumari Jayawardena have drawn considerable attention to the efforts of numerous nineteenth-century feminists such as Josephine Butler, Mary Carpenter, Annette Ackroyd Beveridge, Margaret Noble (Sister Nivedita), Margaret Gillespie Cousins, Eleanor Rathbone, the Marchioness of Dufferin and Ava, Annie Besant, Madeleine Slade (Mira Behn), and Mirra Alfassa who used their marital statuses, institutional networks, religious or secular passions, and wealth toward decades of work on behalf of women in India.[20] Some of these British reformers established schools while others agitated for legal reform on matters of marriage and inheritance;

some traveled, stayed on, and died in India while others never visited it (Butler); some went native and found a new faith in the Subcontinent (Noble, Slade, Alfassa) while others remained devout and adamant that the only real uplift was through Christianity. Yet, without exception, all of these women used the press and the printed word to agitate for their causes and to win support for the cause of India's women. It is this voluminous archive that scholars such as Burton and others have culled in their research into the labor of Victorian feminists on behalf of the Indian woman in the nineteenth and early-twentieth centuries. Considerable as their findings have been, these scholars are curiously silent on one crucial aspect of the historical and textual record of which they nevertheless seem well aware. Not a single one of them explains, exposes, or otherwise considers the effect upon or the *response of* Indian women to the massive efforts extended on their behalf.

Although the volume it appears in is subtitled *Complicity and Resistance*, Leslie Flemming's 1992 essay nonetheless concludes by regretting that "what is clearly missing is an assessment of Indian women's *response*" (204; emphasis in original). Furthermore, Antoinette Burton, despite her critique of what she calls "feminist imperialism" (167) and the way in which Indian women were used as ciphers by both Indian nationalists and British feminists, nonetheless dismisses the women of India from serious purview herself: "While images of a colonized Indian womanhood were the linchpin of British imperial feminism, this book is not about contemporary Indian women, except insofar as they were imagined by British feminists and manipulated as types in the service of Western feminist strategy" (30).

If the Victorian feminist accounts in the reformist press misrepresented the Indian woman in order to claim her for a higher cause, then recent scholarly accounts of Western women and imperialism ignore her altogether. Indeed, Burton's excavation into the involvement of British women in empire usefully complicates what she identifies as a triumphalist and male-dominated account of colonialism. Yet, in retrieving women's history from the imperial archives, she largely ignores the voice, participation, and practices of Indian women altogether. By making Western women the center of her important study, she entirely overlooks their Indian counterparts in what ends up being an account of empire that replaces the exploits and triumphs of European males with those of European females. In attempting to gender colonialism, her work, like that of Ramusack, Flemming, and Jayawardena, essentially colonizes gender as a singularly Western category while reducing empire to a neutered monolith in which the colonized woman has neither voice nor agency.[21]

However, the very colonial archives that Burton, Jayawardena, and others have culled for their rewritings of empire are rife with accounts in which Indian women such as Krupa Satthianadhan not just talked back but also shaped and informed increasingly intense efforts during the late Victorian and Edwardian period regarding their "condition" and uplift. Whether encouraged by families or isolated in their communities, these Indian women spiritedly participated in the debates on Indian womanhood, published articles, edited serials, and authored books, and by the early decades of the twentieth century established women's organizations associated with the anticolonial movement such as the Bharat Mahila Parishad (established 1905), the Bharat Stree Mahamandal (established 1910) and the Women's Indian Association (established 1917).[22] Educated (sometimes formally), well read, and well informed, the Indian women who emerge from this abundant record in the colonial print archives are far from figures who "humbly accept their misery, and are, to outward seeming, contented with their lot" as Mary C. Holdsworth represented them in a front-page essay of 1894 in *The Woman's Signal*;[23] nor are they purely the oppressed and enslaved masses who appealed to the *coloniale oblige* of British feminists such as Josephine Butler, Annette Ackroyd Beveridge, Sister Nivedita, and countless others. By the early decades of the twentieth century, the political and social organizations that Indian women had formed began to play a major role in issues of national and nationalist importance. For instance, when the American Katherine Mayo published *Mother India* (1927), her sensationalist and racist account of women in India, the Women's Indian Association acted promptly and decisively in using the ensuing controversy for its own reform efforts. As Mrinalini Sinha persuasively documents, the association immediately issued a statement that read in part: "while we repudiate the book as a whole we must turn every ounce of our zeal towards the rooting out of those social evils [such as child marriage] which are undoubtedly in our midst."[24]

The pattern of decisive engagement is far from restricted to the twentieth century. Accounts of Indian women participating and shaping debates on what would come to be known as the Woman's Question proliferate even earlier from the second half of the nineteenth century onward.[25] Rosalind O'Hanlon has analyzed a passionate and powerful monograph on the condition of Indian widows authored by Tarabai Shinde, entitled *Stri-Purush-Tulana* ("A Comparison Between Women and Men," Marathi 1882); Veena Oldenburg has written a brilliant ethnohistory on the manner in which the courtesans of Lucknow organized into a formidable social and economic force in the aftermath of the 1857 Mutiny; Vir Bharat Talwar, Partha Chatterjee, and Malavika Karlekar have analyzed Indian women's writings in the serial press, in autobiographies, and in memoirs at the turn of the nineteenth century.[26] The Indian woman who emerges from these accounts is a far cry from the kind "contented with their lot" as depicted in Holdsworth's essay in the British press. At the same time, she is also far from the "exceptional" women depicted in Mary Frances Billington's glorified hagiographies. The women whose autobiographies Chatterjee reads were self-educated homemakers and actresses; Tarabai Shinde was the daughter of a head clerk in the Central Provinces; and Oldenburg's courtesans were women increasingly excluded from respectable society. These women belonged to an altogether different milieu and class than the women described by Billington or by other British works such as Mrs. Chapman's *Sketches of Some Distinguished Indian Women*: they were neither royalty like the Maharani of Kuch Behar, nor international travelers like Pandita Ramabai or Dr. Anandibai Joshee, both of whom had traveled to the West and had become celebrated poster women in the British reformist press.[27] I mention this detail to underscore how exceptional even the unexceptional women of Victorian India were and to suggest that they were far from the meek and mute figures that Holdsworth and others would have British readers believe them to be. The gulf between the descriptions proffered by the British reformist press and the practices retrieved from the colonial archive by scholars such as O'Hanlon, Oldenburg, and Chatterjee highlights how central the Indian woman was to nineteenth-century debates on social reform, empire, nationalism, India, and modernity.

In an effort to resist ignoring or silencing her for the third time, as recent scholars such as Burton and Flemming have done in their research on feminism and empire, this chapter continues to examine how an Indian women such as Satthianadhan participated in her own

textualization. Recognizing the centrality of this figure to both nationalist and imperial histories, my account further probes how the Indian
woman herself articulated her condition, how she responded to the
efforts in her name and behalf by her reformist sisters, and in what language and form she shaped the representational debate.

SATTHIANADHAN, HER "TRUTHFUL PICTURE," READERS, AND READING

Writing about *Saguna* in the British-Indian press shortly after the
novel appeared, a reader in the *Madras Mail* enthused: "The most valuable part of it is the truthful picture which it represents of the *vie intime*,
as *Amiel* would call it, in Hindu and Native Christian families. It has all
the claims to praise which we recently shewed Mrs. Chapman's biographies of *Some Distinguished Indian Women* to have, and it has the additional qualifications of being written by an Indian lady instead of by a
foreigner."[28] Though Mrs. Chapman's work was praised in Britain, it
was somehow marred by her race (i.e., being a "foreigner"). Satthianadhan's writing, however, was scripted for its authenticity: being
Indian makes her account a "truthful picture." Apparently, by 1894,
when the *Madras Mail* review appeared, the voice of the native inform-
ant had become especially useful.

The *Malabar and Travancore Spectator* is more direct about Satthianadhan's particular qualification as a writer: "[*Saguna*] is not the sec-
ond-hand description of a foreigner that we have here. A native Christian lady herself writes of Indian life, so that we get an accurate idea of
such life." Being an Indian writer is an "additional qualification," rendering a more "accurate" idea of life in India. The English reviews
underscore an immense concern that the accounts of Mrs. Chapman
(or any other "foreigner" for that matter) be corroborated by a native
lady herself, and on this level at least, Satthianadhan's use of biographical form achieves an affiliation with her readers. Not only do her
British readers identify with her story, *they make it their own*: her
account of native life became their trophy to use in their own reformist
struggle (or, in the more conventional reading, a validation of the colonial presence). As such, Satthianadhan's novels fall neatly into English
accounts of what they *should* be about, and the *Madras Mail* has *Kamala*

"bear witness to the ennobling power of true English culture on a highly talented Indian lady." In the early British reviews, then, Satthianadhan's writings were received in clear concert with the more conventional readings of biographies like Mrs. Chapman's, namely, as part of the archive of *coloniale oblige* to instantiate New Woman developments in India. Indeed, in Satthianadhan's case, her British reviewers— who are by far the more articulate majority—reveal more about themselves than about her in their reviews of *Saguna* and *Kamala*. Her writing becomes part of *their* transactions with British social reform rather than with the Indian conditions to which Satthianadhan refers. As we will shortly see, her writing was appropriated into one particular narrative at the expense of other, more urgent ones.

For her Indian reviewers, on the other hand, Satthianadhan's greatest achievement was her stylistic and formal mastery over the novel in English. The *Madras Christian College Magazine*, which serialized both her novels and published a number of her short stories, writes of *Saguna*: "The writer has acquired a command of English which is rarely found even in the case of graduates, and which many Englishmen might well envy her, and she tells her story in an exceedingly interesting way"; while the Madras daily, *The Hindu*, praised *Kamala* for its fairness: "The authoress, though a Christian, shows a singularly accurate knowledge of the social and domestic customs of Hindus, and is free from any endeavour to present the moral and spiritual effect of the Hindu religion in an unfavourable light." To both Indian reviewers, she is a model, and neither seems troubled by the complexity or singularity of her work. For them, she is neither New Woman nor Everywoman, but simply a Christian novelist of whom the *Madras Christian College Magazine* reviewer concludes: "We can all hope, however, that the example set by Mrs. Satthianadhan will be followed by others, and that she may have many successors in the work of revealing this country and its people to the rest of the world."[29] Not only does Satthianadhan's English style draw admiration from her Indian readers, but her "realism" is one they identify with and wish to celebrate.

On this level, one could take issue with Meenakshi Mukherjee's contention that English was somehow inadequate for enabling a meaningful subjective consciousness among early Indian writers. Not only does the English language enable Satthianadhan, but an until now English form—the novel—sustains her writing. Her use of biography reaches outward, including her readers in the intimate and hitherto closed world of an Indian woman's consciousness. Crafting *Kamala* as a *Bildungsroman*, in particular, invites a subjective solidarity among its readers who participate in the process of Kamala's growth. The fulcrum of both Satthianadhan's novels is her protagonists' emerging consciousness: like the New Woman novels to which hers were frequently compared, Satthianadhan's novels encourage both a participation in and a critique of the worlds that her protagonists inhabit. As Kate Flint suggests, "the [New Woman] novels themselves encourage an interrogative manner of reading, not just developing one's rational powers in relation to the printed word, but in relation to society more widely" (296).

But, what *is* the relation of the printed word to society more widely? Satthianadhan's style and her use of realism—so successful among her readers that her novels were printed at twice the usual print runs of other fiction titles of the period—suggest that her work approximates the "reality" of the out there. Yet, if we read her work against the grain, another pattern altogether emerges. Nothing in Satthianadhan's writing endorses even the remote possibility of a shared consciousness among the English printed word and society more widely in colonial India. One recalls that Satthianadhan was among the early English novelists in India; one recalls as well that she was one of several early generations born into a literary, cultural, and intellectual landscape overwhelmingly dominated by the British novel. Mrs. Fenwick Miller praises Satthianadhan in this chapter's epigraph for reminding her of Jane Austen; granting Miller a reviewer's license for hyperbole, it remains worth recalling how Satthianadhan herself regards the world of English letters to which she is commended and from which she takes at least some of her craft. For her, it is a baffling and occasionally bewildering universe in which she is made to doubt her intelligence ("I am not at all clever") and to "guess" at meanings that elude her.

Her alter ego, Saguna's, greatest misunderstandings, ironically, take place with two European missionaries whom she helps in their *zenana* work. They simply do not understand her, nor she them; reacting to Satthianadhan's clear-eyed critique of missionary behavior in India, Mrs. Grigg's "Memoir" hastily explains Satthianadhan's unflattering portrait of the British with: "Christianity has been taught to her with an apostolic simplicity utterly free from the Shibboleths and conventionalities of the nineteenth century. . . . Precocious in mind and thought and terribly in earnest, she was a prey to self-consciousness and to an almost hysterical over-sensitiveness" (xxii). For Satthianadhan, the Bible lies (the missionaries are apparently closer to God than their Indian flock); for Mrs. Grigg, the novelist's nerves do, making her prey to "an almost hysterical over-sensitiveness."

The point I want to highlight is twofold. One, which I think is quite clear from the instances I have cited, that despite colonial efforts to claim otherwise, there remained a massive and unbridged gulf between Indian "reality" and the world of English formal realism that neither the Department of Public Instruction's literary prescriptions nor its proscriptions was fully capable of bridging. Second, in her use of realism, particularly in her use of certain forms of realist fiction (*Bildungsroman*, confession, autobiography), Satthianadhan's was a project invested in creating a subjective consciousness that reached out to a community of readers in order to bridge this gulf through the novel. What her novels create in the process is a particular form, combining memoir, confession, and polemic in an attempt to engage in a dialogue with her world; what they reveal as well is the immense difficulty of the task at hand. Satthianadhan's work, as we have already seen, was almost unanimously championed by her British readers for its insights on the condition of Indian women; for them, no other issue merited attention. Praising her "exquisite description of scenery," her enthusiastic British readers looked no further to the larger canvas of which it was a part and toward which Satthianadhan vainly gestured. Furthermore, while the New Woman might be abused, ridiculed, and pilloried in Britain as Gail Cunningham earlier reminded us, she was a figure of inspiration and resolve in India, and some of the same British readers who might have responded with derision to New Woman concerns in England were promoting them in Satthianadhan's account in India. She was commended for her reformist credentials, while her work, exceeding its critics, was in fact on to another project. What was it in Satthianadhan's novels that her British readers were unable—or unwilling—to see?

RE-FORMING THE NOVEL

I began this chapter by referring to a representational crisis in nineteenth-century colonial India, stressing that the crisis was one of Indian *self*-representation during a period of turmoil and increasingly rapid social transformation. This project's focus on literary form in general and the novel in particular underwrites its interest in the role of the novel in this contest of representation. One of the central issues, indeed *the* single issue, that confronted the development of the novel in India was the issue of subjectivity: finding a form that could create and sustain an exploration into subjective consciousness; a form that could refer with confidence to the social world of its readers; a form that in structure, sign, and play could also take on the colonial world in which it was shaped.

Yet the issue of creating and sustaining a subjective voice that could balance the interiority of Indian experience with the objective conditions of empire and encroaching modernity persists. It comes as little surprise that testimonial writing, or novel-as-autobiography, were the modes that have endured longest in the Indian novel in English: indeed, in the case of women's writing, the repeated use of the first-person narrator further helped offset some of the formality of literary narration by encapsulating it within more "natural" oral story-telling forms, which in India had historically been the woman's provenance. Certainly Satthianadhan pursued these possibilities to the fullest in her fiction. Her novels resisted hagiography, though as I have already indicated, they had their own investment in biographical form. In *Saguna*, she exploits autobiography; in *Kamala*, biography as *Bildungsroman*. I say "exploit" for Satthianadhan uses biographical form for its ability to carry the reader into her novels from the outset by encouraging an identification with the subject. With its intimate recording of her protagonist's emotional and intellectual growth, her autobiographical novel enables a further closeness between reader and fiction, and indeed the integrity of her accounts was noted by her early Indian reviewers. However, one also observes a great tension in having her newly created subjective consciousness speak with confidence to the conditions of its construction. The only access one has to the world of Satthianadhan's novels, for instance, is through the consciousness of her female protagonists; yet the world her protagonists take us to is an eerily bichromatic one, infused with the singular, unidirectional tension between the female narrator and the rest of her world. Moreover, Satthianadhan's is a world where female solidarity has been thoroughly ruptured: a rupture we learn that is the product of a relentlessly voracious modernity that accompanies empire. "Ramabai, Toru Dutt, and Cornelia Sorabji have all borne witness to the debt they owe to their mothers," Mrs. Chapman informs us in her hagiography (13), citing three important nineteenth-century women. There are no mothers in *Kamala*, only grotesque mothers-in-law; and in *Saguna*, the mother is someone whose simplicity and lack of education confine her movements largely to a minuscule domestic sphere, which Saguna does not enter, nor the mother leave. To venture beyond this space, as Satthianadhan's protagonists must, is to venture alone, and both novels dwell on the unavoidable pain of abandoning the home in both the domestic and the symbolic sense.

In reforming a tradition-bound India and its customs, in embracing modernity, what has been lost for the women in particular is a means of going back to their pasts and of carrying their histories with them into the future. Each generation of women that moves forward does so at the expense of the past, of literally and metaphorically losing contact with its mothers, and here I think is where Satthianadhan's resistance to embrace modernity in her novels becomes so remarkable. She *will not* abandon the joint-family in *Kamala*, for "others know nothing of the luxury of this life"; tutored by both the sensation novel and realism, she creates a character such as Kamala's long-time admirer, Ramchander, but goes no further and will not let her accept his proposal of marriage, for though there is a new law in the land allowing widow remarriage, she knows that to embrace it will, for Kamala, at least, mean irretrievably abandoning her community altogether. Her suitor's proposal is a heady one: "It is the land of freedom I want you to come to. . . . We shall create a world of our own and none dare interrupt our joys" (204–205), he pleads. Kamala stands firm and refuses: "she felt that her life would have been an unending remorse and misery; and thus she freed herself once and forever" (ibid.). Much of what I have already detailed from *Kamala* makes clear the sensation novel's influence on Satthianadhan's writing: the enigma of Kamala's birth, her unknown matrilineage that reveals itself in the course of the novel, the mysterious fortune that appears when she most needs it. Yet these are elements of the plot that Satthianadhan restrains toward the end of her novel. Ramchander's proposal is one last twist that would certainly have been accommodated in the sensation plot; it could also have easily been accommodated in the New Woman novel as well, for by now Kamala is widowed and legally able to remarry. Yet, in her refusal to have Kamala marry her long-time admirer, a man clearly her equal in virtue, Satthianadhan seems to be reminding us that she is writing neither a sensation nor a New Woman novel, her critics' impressions notwithstanding.

Her realism exposes the suitor's "land of freedom" as an artificial and idealized one from which the past—in the form of custom and lived tradition rather than recorded injunction—has been completely sundered, and from which Kamala can never return. Such a state, theoretical prescriptions aside, is marked for the woman especially as a state of exile, of "unending remorse and misery." This ending is hardly a repudiation of Satthianadhan's position on social reform, although I believe it is her caveat to it: reform works only if it carries its constituents with it; legislative acts make sense only in communities that themselves promote them, not in colonial states that enforce them. Satthianadhan's is an impossible vision, simultaneously soliciting reform but preserving tradition; yet hers is also a singular vision. In the half-century-long clamor for social reform, Satthianadhan's was one of the very few voices—raised in the novel—inquiring: change from what, precisely? to what, precisely? For her, gender was not simply a site of change in a transitional period; rather, gender was a crucial actor negotiating between tradition and modernity during a century of reform, and Satthianadhan chooses the novel to depict the complexity and contrariness of the transaction. The world without mothers that she depicts is both a caution to and a prediction of the reformist zeal in nineteenth-century India. Her own writing resists the claims made on it by her British readers for whom her mission is solely to reveal the "native New Woman beside the old." Satthianadhan's work both claims its own agency and constructs its own platform from which to launch female social uplift, a platform that *includes* both the "native new woman" *and* the old. But to read Satthianadhan's novels and to understand this from them is first to *unlearn* how to read the English realist novel and to learn how to read an Indian novel in English.

For Satthianadhan's purposes, the novel, which was seen as a powerful, albeit misleading, tool of English self-representation in colonial India, was also seen as most appropriate for her own project of inserting an alternative voice and vision into the maelstrom of representation in late-nineteenth-century India. Indeed, the possibilities offered by the novel toward Indian social reform were not apparent uniquely to Satthianadhan: in the 1930s when the English novel took off in Indian letters, it did so around the early socialist realism of Mulk Raj Anand and the gentle social irony of R. K. Narayan, writers we will examine more closely in the next chapter. Yet Satthianadhan's was also a doomed vision: she has resided untouched in a colonial archive not because she failed to articulate a compelling position on social reform but because social reform failed altogether. By the early years of the twentieth century, the centrality of social reform was replaced by political reform, and Satthianadhan's voice was abandoned along with that of her self-serving critics. In this new century and in this new period, the only feminine hagiography permitted was that of Mother India, unilaterally deployed and maintained by the nationalist movement, in which the woman and the nation are one. Satthianadhan's subtlety and independence had little place in this new platform, which was to contain Indian women for almost another century.

CHAPTER 6

The Exile at Home: Ahmed Ali's Twilight in Delhi

PROGRESSIVE WRITING AND THE INDIAN NOVEL IN ENGLISH

English has become ours: it is not less ours for being primarily the
Englishman's or the American's; and Indo-Anglian literature too is
our literature, the literature, which, with all its limitations, still
taught us to be a new nation and a new people.[1]

When Professor K. R. S. Iyengar, the dean of Indian writing in English, delivered these lines in a crowded lecture hall at the University of
Leeds in 1959, he was quietly but triumphantly making the assertion to
his audience of British academics that English had finally become an
Indian language and was no longer something gifted or loaned to India
by "them." By transforming English thus, the Indian "we" had created
a literature "our" own that in turn had actually created a new nation
and a new people. I mention the quietness of this assertion because
implicit—but certainly not explicated in it—is the entire history of
anglicist policy in India starting with the 1835 English Education Act
and culminating in the Orientalist Horace Wilson's dire predictions:
"By annihilating native literature, by sweeping away all sources of pride

and pleasure in their own mental efforts, by rendering a whole people dependent upon a remote and unknown country for all their ideas and for the very words in which to clothe them, we should degrade their character, depress their energies, and render them incapable of aspiring to any intellectual distinction."[2] Macaulay's strategies of a century ago articulated in his notorious Minute on Indian Education with its infamous proposal to use English and its literature to "create a class of persons, Indian in blood and colour but English in taste, opinions, morals and intellect" had had their effect of colliding Indian priorities against anglicist ones.

However, if we are to believe Iyengar, somewhere in or around 1959 Indian English had changed. It had ceased to be British; it had liberated itself from the taste, opinions, morals, and intellect of its shadow motherland. It had come of age, creating its own literature and its own nation. As Frantz Fanon had argued a few years before Iyengar, "to speak [a language] . . . means to assume [its] culture, to support the weight of [its] civilization."[3] In claiming English as its own language, India was asserting its own culture ("Indo-Anglian literature") and its civilization ("the new nation"). What Iyengar's otherwise exhaustive study of the Indian novel in English that follows the text of this lecture does not do satisfactorily is to document precisely when and how India created its own language and literature. He suggests quite rightly that the new nation had something to do with this process, but that is not the complete story. Although the desire for national sovereignty was indeed one of the major catalysts for the new literature, it was not enough to create and to sustain it. For this we will have to understand a whole body of efforts made by several generations of Indians educated under Macaulay's policies, who were working and writing in English and a borrowed form (the novel) and whose literary concerns were not exclusively defined by or confined to nationalism.

In 1932 in Aligarh, four friends in their early twenties—Ahmed Ali, Rashid Jehan, Mahmuduzzafar, and Sajjad Zaheer—published a collection of daring and innovative short stories entitled *Angarey* [Burning Embers], which, in the recent assessment of one of its contributors, "[gave] the first great jolt to the whole social order . . . and they awakened."[4] The stories were in Urdu, itself an unusual event, for Urdu till then had a scarce tradition in the short story. *Angarey* attracted immediate critical attention and notoriety for its frank depiction of sex and its general irreverence toward religious subjects, particularly for a story by Sajjad Zaheer in which a man has a wet dream while taking a nap with his head on an open Koran. In a case startlingly similar to Salman Rushdie and *The Satanic Verses* (1988), the collection and its writers were condemned from Aligarh mosques and pulpits as being "un-Muslim" and a threat to Muslim culture. Fearing that the protests would spread and lead to riots, the British government of the United Provinces installed a ban on *Angarey* (which incidentally remains on the books today) and indexed the four contributors in the Central Intelligence Department in New Delhi.[5] In response to this attention and the ensuing civil inflammation, the four writers published a manifesto of their literary and intellectual aims in an Allahabad newspaper on April 5, 1933, which became the first document of what has come to be known as the All-India Progressive Writers' Association.[6] In the words of Ahmed Ali, the last surviving member of the original group of four:

> [the Progressive Writers'] Movement was essentially an intellectual revolt against the outmoded past, the vitiated tendencies in contemporary thought and literature, the indifference of people to their human condition, against acquiescence to foreign rule, enslavement to practices and beliefs, both social and religious, based on ignorance, against the problems of poverty and exploitation, and complete inanity to progress and life.[7]

It is an impressive catalogue of claims for the movement, its scope undoubtedly embellished by the forty-odd years that had elapsed between its recollection in 1974 and the 1933 manifesto, yet two themes occur consistently in almost every item: "revolt" against an "outmoded past" and the "vitiated" tendencies of contemporary Indian social practice. It is a manifesto both for and against modernity: *for* the social and political equality of a liberal democratic state (proposing an end to ignorance, piety, exploitation); but *against* the forms of modernity ushered in by empire (the contaminated, perverted "vitiated" tendencies in contemporary society). The movement's aims were directed severally, equally against internal orthodoxy and ignorance that had their origin and source in India, as well as externally against foreign domination. Ali's description is for a Herculean project, one far greater than simply a "writers' movement" as it was called, though, as we will see, this scope, initially at least, energized rather than enervated Indian letters in the 1930s and 1940s.

Between 1933, when the first manifesto appeared, and 1936, when the first national meeting of the association convened, a number of developments had taken place. The original membership of four had expanded to include virtually every single major writer from a number of Indian languages.[8] Representatives from the association had participated in the 1935 Writers' Congress for the Defense of Culture Against Fascism in Paris and had received the attention and encouragement of other writers such as Louis Aragon, André Gide, Henri Barbusse, and Alexy Tolstoy.[9] By the time of the first national meeting in 1936, the Progressive Movement (now called the All India Progressive Writers' Association [AIPWA]), whose goal was to use literature in order to raise the fragmented social castes and classes of India and unite them against the British, had found ideological and practical support in Communism. At this juncture, "progressivism" as an aesthetic practice became a kind of euphemism for socialist realism, and amidst the practical aims of the movement, which included translation, publication assistance, freedom of expression as a fundamental right of all writers, and so on, the formal manifesto from the 1936 meeting was firmly and primarily committed to "rescu[ing] literature and other arts from the priestly, academic and decadent classes in whose hands they have degenerated so long; *to bring the arts into the closest touch with the people*; and to make them the vital organ which will register the actualities of life, as well as lead us to the future" (emphasis added).[10]

I mention these stages of the AIPWA from *Angarey* to the 1936 manifesto for several reasons. One is to explicate that even in its genesis in the pungent, albeit adolescent, literary project of *Angarey*, its members were acutely conscious of the vital need to connect literature with everyday life in order to transform some of the "vitiated tendencies" of an "outmoded past" into a new and more equitable social order. Literature had to be rescued from the elites, and the manifesto's usage of "priestly, academic, and decadent" alludes to an entire sociology of the Indian literary landscape against which the AIPWA articulated its project, and a landscape against which a quarter of a century earlier Satthianadhan too had been writing. From the start, the project was one that sought to create a social consciousness in India where one may not have existed, a consciousness that would challenge both colonialism and domestic power elites as much by the mind as by arms. In Tom Nairn's keen phrase, the mandates of the AIPWA were written "to invite the masses into history; and the invitation-card had to be written in a language they understood."[11] The notion of using a language the masses understood should not underestimate the extent to which the AIPWA's project was equally to endorse writing that dwelt on issues relevant to particular social groups. In the minds of the Communist members of the 1936 meeting, these groups were the Indian peasant and the proletariat; in the minds of the creative writers of the group, however, the "field of progress could not be narrowed or confined; . . . the middle class, the bourgeoisie was as fit a subject for a progressive writer as the working class . . . for exploitation has many faces."[12]

The differences in the descriptions of the meanings of "progressive" were eventually to fragment the association, but till this happened in 1938–39, the AIPWA had launched a literary magazine named *Indian Writing*[13] and had created a community of writers, translators, reviewers, and publishers united by an urgent need for reform of all kinds—social, intellectual, aesthetic, political—all of which are accomplishments that cannot be underestimated for their contribution to the development of modern Indian letters. By 1936 the association had ushered in a period of significant literary production in a number of Indian languages. Perhaps because of its origins in *Angarey*, a formative and far-reaching impact was felt in Urdu. However in English as well, the sense of reform initiated by the AIPWA introduced added possibilities: Macaulay's anglicist edicts of the previous century had created a substantial population of middle-class Indians with proficiency in English. The Indian writer of the 1930s could, therefore, choose to write in English if only to reach the widest possible readership and to help make the case before what Ahmed Ali hoped might be a "world-wide audience."[14] The AIPWA created a mood and moment in the literatures of a number of Indian languages that had an impact well beyond the decade that initiated it. The literary and intellectual possibilities it enabled, along with the debates and dialogue it generated, make it among the single most important events in the history of modern Indian letters. The reach of this movement was substantial, so much so that the progressive tendencies it mandated in the 1930s—the insistence on a language the masses understood—persisted in the Indian novel in English for so long that another jolt would be needed to liberate Indian letters from what had become the often stultifying literary decades of the 1950s, 1960s, and 1970s.

But for the moment, it is not surprising that the environment of the 1930s saw the emergence of a number of important Indian writers of English. The four most important figures of this period were R. K. Narayan and Raja Rao (neither of whom was a member of the AIPWA, though both had close literary and personal associations with the movement) and Mulk Raj Anand and Ahmed Ali.[15] Apart from being the cofounder of the Progressive Writers' Movement in 1933, Ali was later the AIPWA's literary guardian, as his nomination in 1936 to the editorship of the Progressive journal *Indian Writing* attests. In the words of one critic, "Ahmed Ali was really the only real writer in the *Angarey* group, the others being social reformers who used literature as a means for their particular ends."[16] The *Angarey* group, however, had expanded quite rapidly, and a number of other "real writers," including Anand, had entered the ranks of the AIPWA. Yet, of the four English writers mentioned above, Raja Rao and R. K. Narayan never joined the movement. Rao eventually left literature altogether, turning to philosophy, in which he currently holds a chair at the University of Texas, and R. K. Narayan's prolific novels and stories are realist portraits of the imaginary rural town of Malgudi, arguably containing little demonstrated sensibility to wide-scale reform.

Mulk Raj Anand, the other major writer of the 1930s, is best known for his searing novel, *Untouchable* (1935), which exposes the inhumanity of the Hindu caste system toward its victims and perpetrators alike. Recalling *Untouchable* in 1972, Anand writes that he chose the novel as a form for his narrative because "the novel is, for me, the creative weapon for attaining humanness—it is the weapon of humanism."[17] Since *Untouchable*, Anand has continued to use the novel as a "weapon" to depict the many social ills of Indian society. Perhaps because of the zeal for social reform in his fiction, his writing has tended to be socialist realist and somewhat mechanical rather than literary or innovative. Anand's role in Indian letters is an important one: he has demonstrated more than once that literature should and could deal with a society in transition in a direct and unequivocal fashion and that modern Indian literature could do so perfectly competently in English. Reminiscing about the 1930s when the Indian novel in English took off, Anand adumbrates: "The English-writing intelligentsia in India was thus a kind of bridge trying to span, symbolically, the two worlds of the Ganga and the Thames through the novel" (15). If the anglicist edicts of the previous century deployed the British novel to create a one-way traffic of ideas and ideals from metropolis to colony, Anand's (and Narayan's and Ali's) appropriation of the novel in English a century later was an attempt to force the traffic both ways, an exchange that was to occur fully with Indian writers of the 1980s. Without underestimating the importance of Anand's contribution to Indian letters, I would argue that his writing did little to develop, explore, or create a form or language for Indian literary expression. Anand appropriated the novel in order to further his ends: he placed a certain previously invisible population of Indian society on the map (untouchables, tea pickers in Assam), but in his fidelity to the "watchful revolutionary censorship" of the Communist Party, Anand's stories are interesting, useful, even vital social documents, but less notable for ground-breaking literary merit.[18] As he remarks in his recollections of the 1930s, "We did not produce propaganda tracts, but showed the revolutionary transition, in all its contradictions, crises, and struggles, of rigidity against reversal, of fear against hope, of lies against the possible truth, of death against rebirth" (14).

It was Ahmed Ali in the 1930s who took on the creation of a language and literary form for the Indian novel that was independent of the hegemony of English "taste, opinions, morals, and intellect." Between 1932 and 1938 Ali had published a number of short stories in Urdu that played with literary consciousness and genre in ways that had barely existed before. He had already begun to experiment with structure and language in his celebrated Urdu short story, "Hamari Gali" [Our Lane] (1936), but it was when he took the same story from the lanes of Delhi into its houses in his first English novel, *Twilight in Delhi* (1940), that Horace Wilson's calamitous predictions of a century before began to be vindicated. In choosing to write his first novel not in the Urdu of his acclaimed short stories but in English, Ali both fulfilled and overturned a century of British domination in India that for him also included a palpable cultural and psychic burden. As he wrote in 1993, shortly before his death:

In spite of Bentinck's Westernization and Macaulay's painting our faces brown with a pigmentless brush of anglicization, ignorance had increased a hundred fold and people had forgotten their own mother tongues. Ashamed and demoralized by the distorted pictures of India presented by British historians, Orientalists, and trained propagandists from missionaries and civil servants to Anglo-Indian journalists like Rudyard Kipling, we suffocated in an atmosphere of inferiority. . . . In the process of transformation from Indian to "brown Englishman," I found that I had lost not only my freedom but also my culture and individuality, and I have been engaged ever since in search of my self, my identity. Where between the heart and the mind had it been waylaid? Slowly, through the years, light began to filter through the pictures of Delhi to which I turned for my past.[19]

Dismissing as propaganda British forms of knowledge such as history and journalism and setting aside literary forbears such as Kipling, Ali nonetheless used a British form, the novel, and the English language to retrieve a past that no history book had included in order to restore a lost sense of identity for India and to urge it upon readers everywhere else. The Delhi he names in his novel's title serves as the repository of stories that once thrived in a pre-British India even as the city is replaced and rebuilt by British urban planners who now lay claim upon it as the new capital of the Raj.

"If presented in Urdu," he lamented about his novels, "their concerns would die down within a narrow belt rimmed by Northwest India" (xvi). Therefore, Ali's use of English is partly to reach the widest possible audience both in India and abroad. However, if writing a novel in Urdu would doom it to a shrinking number of North Indian readers, Ali imports into his English novel Urdu forms borrowed from poetry and ghazals that are themselves the product of borrowings from Arabic, Persian, and Hindustani, thus involving *Twilight in Delhi* in a complex transaction with both anglicist and Oriental priorities combined in a project to reinscribe a new history of India on terms different from and even irrelevant to the versions presented by the colonial state.

His was a form of literary indigenization that had severed all ties with the Victorian literary world and in which empire is represented largely as a distorting and corrosive power rather than a productive cultural influence. Unlike Satthianadhan's novels before or G. V. Desani's after, *Twilight* was a singular attempt at vernacularizing the novel with almost exclusively local preoccupations. Unlike Anand who recalls Reynolds and Corelli as literary influences or Rushdie whose debt to Kipling comes through in characters such as Wee Willie Winkie in *Midnight's Children*, Ali's formal and cultural influences in *Twilight* tend to be from the Urdu and Persian poetry that flourished in Mughal India. The transaction he engages within *Twilight* is an oddly paradoxical one, freely utilizing an imported language and form but vigorously eschewing other cultural influences from them altogether. Few Indian novels before or since *Twilight* have been as sternly selective.

AHMED ALI AND *Twilight in Delhi*

In 1940, between a printer's charges that the novel was subversive of law and order and the positive intervention of E. M. Forster and Virginia Woolf, Hogarth Press published Ahmed Ali's *Twilight in Delhi* in London. Ali had begun to write the novel in 1938 at the age of twenty-eight after a bitter disagreement with the AIPWA over what constituted "progressive" literature. For him, progress was "essentially an attitude of mind,"[20] while for the majority of the movement, particularly Sajjad Zaheer and Mulk Raj Anand, representations of the struggles of the proletariat alone were progressive and everything else was decadent. Ali broke with the AIPWA over this dispute and began writing *Twilight in Delhi*. According to him, the novel was to "depict a phase of [Indian] national life and the decay of a whole culture, a particular mode of thought and living, now dead and gone already right before our eyes."[21]

The culture Ali refers to is Muslim culture in Northern India, but as he insisted in a recent interview with this author, "it was a book about India, though written through the eyes of Muslims—of a Muslim family—but it's the story of India."[22] It is a remarkable story of India because it dwells on the silence and slow time of a culture that has every sense of its past greatness but little of its ongoing demise. Ali records the effect of the so-called decay on a Delhi Muslim family, in particular on its patriarch, Mir Nihal, during a period when colonial rule seemed invincible. In *Twilight*, Mir Nihal has a son closer in age to the twenty-eight-year-old Ali who is writing the novel, yet the consciousness in the work is defiantly Mir Nihal's, and it is uncanny how often Asghar, the son and emblem of modernity he comes to represent, are sidelined in the work by author and protagonist alike. In depicting the story of India through the eyes of Mir Nihal, Ali seems to confirm the particularly novelistic code that the individual is in the end the culture with all its limits and ideals, and we will see shortly how irrevocable this position is. The action of the novel begins in or around 1911 and ends in or around 1919 with the passing of the Rowlatt Bills and the beginning of the nationalist Home Rule movement and the riots that followed. Three major historical events mark the novel: the 1857 Mutiny when Indian soldiers revolted against their British officers and tried to restore the Mughal Bahadur Shah II as emperor of India (the Mutiny was brutally put down and Bahadur Shah exiled to Rangoon by the British); the coronation in Delhi of George V on December 7, 1911; and the passing of the Rowlatt Bills in 1919, which allowed British judges to try cases without juries and permitted provincial governments to hold suspects without trial.

The historical markers are relevant to Ali's method: seldom has a novelist with ambitions of depicting a "whole culture" done so by having as the centerpiece of the novel a family as completely removed from, and most of its members even indifferent to, the political and social changes around them. The sprawling family is absorbed in its quotidian banality, and Mir Nihal's days are taken with his mistress and his hobbies: pigeons, fine china, alchemy, and medicine. In the first third of the novel, which is largely devoted to the Nihal family, it is difficult to locate exactly when the action takes place, and despite Mir Nihal's antipathy toward specific English fashions in clothing and footwear, it is hard work identifying the period by these fashions. The historical markers, it seems, are needed to do this.

Mir Nihal begins to notice change only in local and domestic ways at first: when his son, Asghar begins to wear English shoes or, more ominously, when he wishes to marry a woman of his own choice despite his parents' objections. Hearing of Asghar's plans, Mir Nihal thunders at his wife with the old language of feudal patriarchy and class interest: "How can my son marry Mirza Shahbaz Beg's daughter? You don't want to bring a low-born into the family? There are such things as the family honour and name. I won't have the marriage" (48). At one point his wife also echoes Mir Nihal's objections to Asghar's choice because of the woman, Bilqeece's, birth and class: "Money is not everything. It's blood that matters. Their blood and our's can never mix well" (43). Neither Mir Nihal nor his wife conceive of values other than those of blood and birth, circumscribed by the Koran and their social background. For them it is still vitally important to remember that they are Saiyyeds of Arab stock, direct descendants of the Prophet, whereas Bilqeece comes from a family that has the blood of a maidservant or prostitute in it. In the Nihals' mind, their culture is sustained by maintaining the purity of blood, something that Asghar's marriage to Bilqeece would dramatically threaten. After all, as Begam Nihal intones, "the good-blooded never fail, but the low-blooded are faithless" (43).

Even when Mir Nihal's world literally begins to die, bit by bit, he still refuses to give up his old feudal values or to adapt them to the changing environment; he chooses instead to separate himself altogether from the world around him. When his mistress and prize pigeons die on the same night, Mir Nihal's grief dwells on the impermanence of life. Yet, rather than modify the values of the past that he holds so dear or find a new mistress and pigeons in order to stay part of the changing world around him, Mir Nihal stubbornly maintains his attitudes and chooses to break with the present instead. Rejecting the changes that overwhelm his family as irrelevant to him, Mir Nihal withdraws into himself: "It mattered little whether Asghar married a low-born or a girl with blue blood in her veins. He would not be in it, anyway. He had lived his life, good or bad, done all he could for the children and the purity of his stock. Now it was their look-out whether they flourished or decayed" (86).

It is at this point, after the domestic drama of marriage and the future of the Nihal descendants has settled down, that the narrative space of the novel begins to widen. George V's absurd coronation in Delhi takes place within fifteen days of Asghar's wedding, and the events of the family story begin to parallel the world outside. Asghar's delight in his marriage to Bilqeece begins to turn sour not long after the wedding, auguring as it were the final disillusionment with empire that followed George V's farcical ceremony. While the enclosed quarter of old Delhi begins to discuss the foreign king and British India, Mir Nihal begins to retreat more and more into the world of the past, for it is the only world that has meaning for him.

The lyrical opening of *Twilight in Delhi* outlines the city that Mir Nihal claims as his heritage. The Delhi built after the battle of the Mahabharata in 1453 B.C.E., seat of the great Hindu and (even greater) Mughal dynasties who ruled Delhi with bloodshed and poetry (4), is the glorious—and lost—past. "Until the last century [Delhi] had held its head high and tried to preserve its chastity and form. . . . But gone are the poets too, and gone its culture" (4). Built and rebuilt seven times, Mir Nihal's Delhi from the novel's opening is really Ali's protagonist. It is a heroic city, capital of earlier empires of which "only some monuments remain to tell its sad story and to remind us of the glory and splendour—a Qutub Minar or a Humayun's Tomb, the Old Fort or the Jama Mosque" (4).

A number of readers of *Twilight in Delhi* have responded to the suppleness of its language and its poetic rhythms that combine the slower story-telling pace of Indian oral narratives with the cohesiveness and structure of the novel. Yet only a few readers have responded to *Twilight*'s intense preoccupation with the city, which is, I think, Ali's greatest innovation in the novel. His Delhi is not so much the scene of Mir Nihal's ruminations on decline as it is *itself* the novel's protagonist on whose decline the form dwells.[23] In staging the city as the center of subjective consciousness—indeed *as* subjective consciousness itself—Ali goes back to far older influences. Harish Trivedi, perhaps the only critic to address the Delhi of *Twilight* systematically, quite rightly points out that "both the theme and tone of [the novel] derive directly from the Urdu verse form, *shehrashob*, [which is] a lament on a misgoverned, depraved, or ruined city."[24]

As an Urdu poetic form that developed in the eighteenth century, the *shehrashob* emerged following the Persian Nadir Shah's rapacious sack of Delhi in 1739, an attack intended in part to loot the city's famed treasuries and in part to restore a "pure" Islam to India. With the subsequent consolidation of British power over Mughal India, Urdu culture, particularly poetry, went into a slow decline (one that *Twilight* gloomily laments), yet the *shehrashob* bled into other genres. Ali's use in *Twilight* is one; another is in Premchand's powerful Hindi and Urdu short story, "The Chess Players" (1924), in which "Lucknow was plunged deep in luxurious living," while the East India Company's armies march in and depose Wajid Ali Shah, its Muslim ruler.[25] Wrapped in decadent living and intoxicated by the game of chess, Avadh's aristocracy seems impervious to the British military threat upon their city. None can grieve the loss except the city itself: "The broken archways of the ruins, the crumbling walls, and dusty minarets looked down on the corpses and mourned" (192) is how Premchand's story ends.

The city mourning for that which its citizens will not or cannot yet feel: Premchand's short story highlights one of the central tropes in the Urdu form that make it so richly suggestive and appropriate for Indian writers in this period. Theirs are cities whose social structures have historically developed and sustained community and individual practices within the larger group: Mir Nihal's hobby in pigeons is maintained, indeed enabled, by the urban landscape of Delhi where owners taunt each other and compete from rooftop to rooftop. Their cities go into decline not simply because of an external threat—Delhi has after all already remade herself seven times—but because this time, the threat penetrates further than it has ever before into the very soul of the city. In *Twilight*, the assault on Delhi is made not simply by the colonial presence but also by the modernity it brings with it, and Ali's novel makes clear that the two are not always easy to keep apart. With the impending coronation of George V, Delhi was deemed cluttered and dirty, and armies of British architects and builders were brought in under the supervision of Edwin Lutyens to tear down the old walled city and build a new, imperial one outside it.[26] "The residents of Delhi resented all this, for their city, in which they had been born and grew up, the city of their dreams and reality, which had seen them die and live was going to be changed beyond recognition. They passed bitter remarks and denounced all the Farangis" (*Twilight* 143). Indeed the new Delhi that Lutyens designs for the new British bureaucracy condemns the old spaces that had once nurtured the Nihal ways of life. To its inhabitants, the new city increasingly resembles an alien, foreign, environment in which the individual is pitted in a contest against the metropolis, a contest that, we will see shortly, takes its toll on what Simmel has called the individual's mental life.

The contrast I have been making here between Mir Nihal's Delhi and that of Lutyens is clearly between Weber's notion of the medieval and renaissance city whose social structures emerge from within and whose environment sustains its citizens; versus Simmel's of a retrograde, enervating, modern, urban space that extracts a toll on its citizens by making them seek protection from its constant and unwanted stimuli.[27] Weber's account of twentieth-century European metropolises is a chilling one in which the complexity of capitalist and bureaucratic systems has reduced the environment into abstract and disconnected units. The city then becomes not just an alien force, but an *alienating* one as well, penetrating into the mental life of its inhabitants from whom it extracts the price of their full consciousness, or what Simmel calls a "blasé attitude."

In Ali's Delhi, the city's transformation is heightened by the degree of colonial intervention into its citizens' lives: Mir Nihal's confrontation with both empire and modernity does not occur as an obscure principle in an abstract realm; rather, it takes place *within* the urban experience that is unmistakably changed. "The gutters which were deep and underground from the times of the Mughals to this day were being dug and made shallow, and the dirty water flowed very near the level of the streets . . . the expansive peepal trees which had given shelter to the residents and the poor from the scorching rays of the sun, were cut down. . . . This affected the people more deeply than anything else" (143). The dissonance that follows, however, moves from the paved spaces of the city into the Nihal household, and thence into the imaginative realm that structures the Nihals' social relations. How the new Delhi will end up still remains to be seen, but it becomes apparent that despite his complete withdrawal from public life after the deaths of his mistress and pigeons, Mir Nihal is to be at least emblematically a counterpoint of the new Delhi even as he vigorously eschews any involvement with it. His derision for the invasion of modernity is acerbic: all forms of the new are labeled "farangi," a derogatory word which has its origins from the time of the conquests into Europe by the Muslim Turks who regarded the French-speaking Normans as barbarians and called all of Europe west of Byzantium "firangistan," or Frank-land.[28]

THE ADVENT OF MODERNITY

The intrusions of modernity that Mir Nihal most heatedly abrogates appear at first to be small ones: the leather shoes, English furniture, silk dressing-gowns, and hairstyles that his son, Asghar, sports—he clearly ascribes these to the British presence in India. But as the extent of English claim to India is enacted in George V's farcical coronation, where the so-called subjects can scarcely distinguish the king from his coterie, Mir Nihal experiences the full import of the changes that the British have ushered in. They have spayed the culture of Delhi, rendering it incapable of regenerating itself or the city. While the advent of modernity may have been inevitable, as was the jeopardy it placed upon traditional forms, what is completely unexpected is the way this novel responds to the change. For Mir Nihal the most painful change under the British is that poetry is dying. "That relation which existed between the society and its poets and members was destroyed" (176). The old nights spent in long symposia discussing various poets are over. Now Delhi has gone from being the center of poetry to its grave, and as he leaves the coronation in a rage, Mir Nihal has a particularly poignant encounter with a beggar, who turns out to be the youngest son of Delhi's deposed ruler, Bahadur Shah, whose lineage goes back to Changez and Timur and who now sweeps the streets of Delhi with his lame feet, reciting verse for money.

Modernity in Delhi has done more than banish poetry, however: the Farangis have deposed its patrons, and even as the heirs to the Mughal throne roam the streets of Delhi singing their sad fate, this new poetry is not enough to preserve or even to keep alive the glorious tradition. The once vital culture of the seventh Delhi is adulterated and maudlin now, and all that remains to recall its vital past is Asghar Nihal who sentimentally spouts Urdu verse to celebrate his highly formulaic love for Bilqeece. Whereas poetry under its Mughal patrons inhabited both public and private realms—all of the Mughal emperors from the first, Babur (ruled 1526–30), to the last, Bahadur Shah II, (ruled 1837–58) were themselves great poets whose courts were as much forums for reading and discussing poetry as adjudicating laws—with the banishment of Bahadur Shah, a division occurred between public and private spaces. In Mir Nihal's feudal world of landed income where the time and spaces of work have no more claim than those of pleasure, the spatial division between the two is scarcely visible. By Asghar's generation, however, work has assumed an entirely separate space from the home as well as nine-to-five rigors, and what time is left for pleasure or solitude is shared with the demands of the nuclear family. In a world so excruciatingly divided, the shared medium of poetry, which was at once public (in the recitals that both generations of Nihals once frequented) as well as private (a language of inwardness that exists only in the listener's mind) ceases to be possible. It is this new world that has exiled poetry that is politically and ideologically corrupt for Mir Nihal:

> The richness of life had been looted and despoiled by the foreigners, and vulgarity and cheapness had taken its place. The relation that existed between a society and its poets and members was destroyed. Perhaps the environment had changed. Society had moved forward, and the people had been left behind in the race of Life. New modes had forced themselves upon India. Perhaps that is why that unity of experience and form, which existed in Mir Nihal's youth, had vanished. (176)

Mir Nihal's nostalgia for another, earlier life that preserved the unity of experience and form annotates the extent to which the changes overtaking him have also transformed *all* public relations in his society. Whereas at one point the seclusion, and therefore to some extent, preservation, of Mir Nihal's Delhi was the product of British policies that sequestered then ignored the Muslims for their "betrayal" during the 1857 Mutiny, it is clear that now these very policies have somehow magnified modernity's intrusion into their homes. The generational unity that enclosed past and present is ruptured seemingly within days in this world, and suddenly the validity of *all* experience comes under question.

Writing about the transformation of subjective experience at the advent of modernity, Reinhart Koselleck posits,

> the future of this progress is characterized by two main features: first, the increasing speed by which it approaches us, and second, its unknown quality. "Unknown" because this accelerated time, i.e., our history, abbreviated the space of experiences, robbed them of their constancy, and continually brought into play new, unknown factors so that even the actuality or complexity of these unknown quantities could not be ascertained.[29]

Twilight's narrative rhythms heighten the rupture that occurs as the colonial "future" moves into the past: Ali's attempt to contain Mir Nihal's experience of an encroaching modernity imposed from above within older forms—the *shehrashob*—first makes it impossible to identify its temporal setting, then makes it impossible to ignore it, underscoring the profound transformation at work. Not only are the changes comprehensive within Delhi in that they pervade both public and private life, but the novel takes pains to show that they are incomprehensible as well, for the means to understand them have already been destroyed when the old culture was spayed. Modernity is not supposed to make us mad, if we are to believe Marx or Adam Smith, simply breathless by making us run faster to keep up. Yet what we see here are the beginnings of Mir Nihal's homelessness in a society where all familiar rituals and relationships have been made impossible. Even the customs of this life—the passion for pigeon-flying, poetry readings, arranged marriages—are challenged, and it becomes a central question whether the incursion of modernity denies traditional forms their place in culture, or whether the two can coexist productively.

For the novel, there is no compromise between forms of tradition—i.e., Mir Nihal's world—and the forms of modernity—i.e., Asghar's world. In the struggle to preserve the old world, Asghar is literally displaced, and he moves to a separate house when he marries Bilqeece, while Mir Nihal pursues, at least for some time, a life even more traditional and hidebound than before. He turns to alchemy and his house becomes a center for wandering sages of the old art. He consults hakims (herbal doctors) in the face of his eldest son's growing cancer. He becomes a tutor of sorts to his grandchildren, disciplining them with his sword rather than, more conventionally, with his belt. All the spaces of the traditional home that are being hollowed from within by the institutions of the modern world (hospitals, schools, work, clubs for hobbies) are reintroduced in the Nihal household in the most vigorous attempt yet by Mir Nihal to retain some part of his old world, or at least to contain the new world in familiar forms of the old.

In trying to preserve the seventh Delhi further, the Delhi of Bahadur Shah and the 1857 resistance to the British when the Muslims in the city fought General Metcalf's cannon with naked swords (106–107), Mir Nihal invokes the most legitimate of claims for dynastic rule: blood ties. If Delhi is to remain "chaste," its bloodlines must remain pure and unadulterated: Bahadur Shah and his legitimate heirs must keep the throne, and Mir Nihal's heirs must do their part in preserving the culture by maintaining the purity of *their* blood. For Mir Nihal, Bilqeece the "low-born" has no part or place in this mission, and Asghar's marriage to her is something his father will never fully accept.

There are some remarkable moments in Ali's use of this logic. One is its resonance with a rhetoric of conquest and empire that precedes the Raj. Before the British in India came the Mughals, and as a product himself of this earlier colonization, Mir Nihal denounces the newer wave by invoking the legitimacy of the old colonizers' caste over creed and blood over bonds. But even before the Mughals in India came the Greeks: Alexander's genius led him to maintain his massive conquests across Persia and northern India by marrying his governors to the daughters of Asian kings, thereby literally letting the flow of Greek blood chart the course and extent of his empire. His strategy was not entirely successful, and Alexander died of athlete's foot or curry (it is not clear which) shortly after his "conquest" of India. What could have been the greatest strategy of his conquests was ultimately unable to maintain his empire, but in the end it made another, more durable empire possible elsewhere: glorious Rome. And, if we are to believe Virgil, Rome happened because Aeneas, unlike Alexander, did *not* remain in Carthage and mix his blood with the foreign Dido but heeded his mother's wishes and moved on to found Rome where Jupiter approved the mixing of Trojan blood with the native Rutulians, predicting that "the race to come, mixed with Ausonian blood, will outdo men and gods."[30]

I offer this anecdote not to suggest in any way that empires prevail because of the purity of their blood but, rather, to show how the restrictions on mixing and unmixing blood are strategically deployed at different times either to restrain *or* to propagate dynastic influence. Even royalty in Europe, which always intermarried to extend itself, faced the discomfort of its mixed blood at times and tried to undo or erase it at such moments. George V, for instance, gave up his German names in 1917 and went from Saxe-Coburg-Gotha to Windsor when his German lineage was more a burden than an asset. In its colonies as well, Europe played out its attitudes of dominance and mastery by first ignoring then vigorously legislating specific injunctions against the mixing of European blood with that of the natives. The Marriage Act in India disapproved of marriage between the races, and a strictly observed social apartheid *on both sides* maintained the separation further.[31] One realizes that Mir Nihal's recalcitrance regarding miscegenation—and the language of his objections, redoubtable as it is, is exactly one that abhors miscegenation—has a wider context and practice. It is a part of the reality of the "out there" that is upheld equally by natives and rulers.

If, however, one scrutinizes the social practices of the time beyond doxa and legislative decree, it becomes apparent how spurious the claims of racial purity are on both sides. Mir Nihal's beloved Mughals happily and successfully followed the Alexandrine practice of marrying into Hindu royalty in order to consolidate their command over India. Meanwhile, after the British settlements, an increasing Anglo-Indian or Eurasian population silently began to become apparent across India.[32] The taboo against the mixing of bloods that flourished alongside the actual practice becomes for Mir Nihal (as for British legislators) a defense against changes that are already taking place. The more Farangi Asghar becomes, the more Mir Nihal denounces his choice of a wife. When Asghar finally marries Bilqeece, Mir Nihal becomes fully absorbed in the pastimes of another era—alchemy, herbal medicine— renouncing, as it were, the world of change around him. Paralyzed by a stroke toward the end of the novel, Mir Nihal loses even the solace of nostalgia and as the "sole guardian of years that had gone" (175), he decides:

> New ways and ideas had come into being. A hybrid culture which had nothing in it of the past was forcing itself upon Hindustan, a hodgepodge of Indian and Western ways which he failed to understand. The English had been beaten by the Turks at Gallipoli. Even this had not affected his heart. He had become feelingless and was not interested whether the Caravan stayed or moved on. The old had gone, and the new was feeble and effete. At least it had nothing in common with his ideals or his scheme of things. (175)

Mir Nihal's most evident grief is that the changes sweeping across Hindustan—and he deliberately uses the ancient Mughal name for India—are a "hodgepodge" that have created a hybrid culture. Hybrid, bastard, mutant, half-caste—each of the words could equally be applied for all Mir Nihal feels about the new culture. Like the child of mixed-race parents whom neither race will claim, the hybrid culture Mir Nihal sees around him is so far mutated from its Hindustani roots as to have "nothing in common with his ideals or schemes of things." It is "new" for Mir Nihal in as much as it is in fashion as a novelty, but beyond that it shares no tradition or values with his own past. Furthermore, Mir Nihal is not the only one to feel this way: both races—the English as well—reject the "hodgepodge" they have produced, but yet it keeps getting produced at a rate to dismantle the "unity of experience and form" of Mir Nihal's youth and to make him feel that he is not part of the new at all.

HOMELESSNESS AND MODERNITY IN EMPIRE

The outcome of this mixing is somewhat anticlimactic. One would expect the vigorous old culture of martial valor and naked swords at least to stand up and protect something of its glory in the face of modernity's intrusive "hodgepodge," but this is not to be. Asghar who is the product of this new culture and wears it with ease is the man to do the job. But, as Muhammad Hasan Askari retorts, Asghar is a man "whose life had neither depth nor expanse, nor balance nor uniformity, who is culturally a mongrel, and in fact, a hybrid and somewhat contemptible [man]."[33] As such, he is hardly inclined to stand up to modernity. Moreover, Mir Nihal, in the most crucial ways, is exiled from the world taking shape around him. He responds to the changes of modernity as one destroyed by them, recalling the Old French origins of "exile," meaning to ravage or devastate. Instead of being forcibly evicted from his native land as the contemporary definition of exile denotes, Mir Nihal's exile is more acute for it actually displaces his native land from around him. The Delhi Mir Nihal has known is replaced by a new Delhi built outside it, the so-called eighth Delhi (today known as New Delhi), and Mir Nihal finds himself in a world with which he shares neither connection nor values:

A new Delhi meant new people, new ways, and a new world altogether. That may be nothing strange for the newcomers: for the old residents it was a little too much. . . . The old culture, which had been preserved within the walls of the ancient town, was in danger of annihilation. . . . [Delhi] would become the city of the dead, inhabited by people who would have no love for her nor any associations with her history and ancient splendour.   (144)

Not only does Mir Nihal reveal the complex pain of being un-landed, his state highlights the distinctions between the experiences of being at-home and being in-exile. The exile typically both lives a life outside his land *and*, more important to subjective experience, lives out of time, and maybe even *without* time. He inhabits the time of the old land even when he is in the new: the values and associations, however symbolic, of the old land, remain with him in the new, and it is appar-ent here that being marooned in these aspects of the old, the exile is in fact living in time past and in so doing has little imagination or sense of future. The state of exile, therefore, is not only a state of being in the past: in being exiled from land, one is exiled from time as well. From Mir Nihal's perspective, it will never be possible to feel at home in the world that is replacing his. What memories he holds of Delhi's ancient splendor have no place in the new Delhi, and what value he placed on the old culture and practices is deemed out of place in the modernity the new city had begun to embrace. To be at home in New Delhi would mean eliding too many differences.

For Mir Nihal, it did not take learning Macaulay's edicts of a gener-ation earlier to confirm that no identification, however symbolic, with Europe would ever be possible for him. Macaulay's doctrine of "men-tal miscegenation"[34] was instrumental in displacing an entire popula-tion from its cultural origins. Not only were the priorities of English-ness replacing native culture, but the systematic implementation of Macaulay's policies across time was making it more and more difficult to remember and *retrieve* the native culture that had been replaced. At the same time, the invitation to be culturally "at-home" in Britain ("English in taste, opinions, morals and intellect") was voided of any fidelity to the concept of "home," which etymologically recalls a place *and* a space. As illusory a concept as home is, it was made more so by British colonial policies toward their Indian subjects: no part of Macaulay's policies involved or offered a sense of place so essential to a feeling of belonging or claiming a homeland, much as the assertion of Delhi as the Raj's new capital abducted the city's physical spaces from its inhabitants.

In making *Twilight in Delhi* above all a novel of *place* and *about* a par-ticular place, which he names in the title, Ahmed Ali exposes several important aspects of a modernity complicated by empire. The first, that no amount of elegy or dirge can undo the breakdown of communal and cultural integrity that occurs once a sense of place is taken away. As Lutyens's army of architects and builders tears down the seventh Delhi to make room for theirs, the culture of old Delhi is torn down as well. Mir Nihal has never for a moment considered it even imaginatively possible to inhabit the cultural or physical world of British India. When he retreats into the empty cocoon of the past, he affirms that at least one more time the harmonies of the past can offer him some respite from the dissonance and "hodgepodge" of the new. His exile at the end of the novel is the culmination of a complex of attitudes, choices, restrictions, and contingencies placed on *all* colonial subjects, which anticipate in unexpected ways a period when a hodgepodge, hybrid culture with no center and no place would become pervasive, and perhaps the norm.

However, Ali's description of exile is still just that: a description. The *experience* of exile that was to mark entire populations after the fall of empire is extremely remote in the novel. Whereas Mir Nihal laments the particular problematics of being homeless *at home*, the generation of writers after Ahmed Ali engages with something else altogether: the experience of being homeless in the world, where the confrontation with modernity is always complicated by the residues of colonialism. For these writers—and here one thinks of Salman Rushdie and V. S. Naipaul and Amitav Ghosh and the many others who have written in the last several decades—migration is a matter of fact. Being at-home is always and only provisional; a homeland, then, becomes the imaginary place of symbolic meanings and associations that are woven together to render place to displacement, and meaning to memories. "Meaning is a shaky edifice we build out of scraps, dogmas, childhood injuries, newspaper articles, chance remarks, old films, small victories . . . perhaps it is because our sense of what is the case is constructed from such inadequate materials that we defend it so fiercely, even to the death," wrote Salman Rushdie in an intellectual testament of sorts entitled "Imaginary Homelands."[35] The past, so sanctified in *Twilight in Delhi* for its purity, is cherished by the generations after Ali precisely for the hybridity of its "scraps."

Ali's novel in the end identifies both the subjective outcome of empire—the feeling of homelessness and exile—as well as the site of its greatest infliction—namely, history. Not only does the city's destruction at the end of *Twilight* underscore its separation from the lives of its citizens but, more poignantly, its rupture symbolically enacts a *histori-*

cide—specifically, the killing of history altogether as a meaningful category of experience and survival in the once colonized world. In the novel, the perpetrator of this historicide is not simply modernity, as Koselleck posits in an earlier explanation, but empire, whose penetration critically severs the continuity between the past and the future. The imaginary homeland so adroitly conceived for the colonial masses through English language and literature ends up a calumny, evacuating the existent homeland and taking with it both path to and parcel of the past. Yet we also realize that Ali's description of historicide is also his way of reclaiming history, even though it be in these newer, hybrid forms combining verse *shehrashob* with the English novel. The narrative *Twilight* deploys, seeped in nostalgia and despair, nevertheless posits an alternate way of apprehending historical rhythms and preserving them within the once alien forms of Macaulay's literary legacy that serves this time to connect Ali's world with the British rather than to alienate one from the other.

CHAPTER 7

The Other Modernism, or The Family Romance in English

1885 was a mixed year in India. It saw the founding of the Indian National Congress and the height of Bankim Chandra Chatterjee's fame following the publication of his nationalist novel, *Anandamath* (1882). However, it was also the year in which Barada Mitra, an Indian contributor to the *Calcutta Review*, lamented the continuing difficulties confronting Indian literature in its attempt to claim cultural and literary independence from Britain's dominating influence:

> They [the English and their literary influence] have partially denationalized our literature. As we depend upon Manchester for our clothing, and upon Sheffield for our cutlery, so we depend upon Byron and Shelley for our poetical inspiration, and upon Macaulay for the rounding off of our prose periods. We have not as yet been able to assimilate and make our own the various influences of Western civilization. . . . Our literature has been made to advance by forced marches; instead of developing from within, it has gathered accretions from without.[1]

For Mitra, both the matter ("poetical inspiration") and métier ("prose periods") of Indian writing had been denationalized into a foreign mold that was increasingly constraining and limiting. Neither growth nor development or even transaction was possible in the forced literary march to a foreign drumbeat. The only available means of expression was through yet another accretion acquired in a one-way cultural traffic originating in Britain. Though he does not mention it, his reference to Byron and Shelley makes clear that the difficulties Mitra refers to are felt particularly acutely for an Indian literature seeking to be born in the English language where the presence of British titans and traditions towered over and intimidated innovation.

A century later, Upamanyu Chatterjee began his irreverent, comic novel about an urbane, twenty-four year old, pot-smoking, masturbating Indian civil servant who is posted to a remote provincial town by celebrating just what Mitra had earlier bemoaned: "'Amazing mix, the English we speak. *Hazaar fucked*. Urdu and American,' Agastya laughed, 'a thousand fucked, really fucked. I'm sure nowhere else could languages be mixed and spoken with such ease.'"[2] Somewhere between Mitra deploring the accretions and forced acquisitions in Indian English in 1885 and Upamanyu Chatterjee coolly celebrating them a hundred years later, a revolution had taken place in Indian literature—and this time it was in the novel in English. The awkwardness and tensions with idiom that caused Mitra and others, including Bankim, such discomfort in the past were now accepted and celebrated. Almost a century after the first novels began to appear in English, a dramatic change had taken place in the Indian novel in English. It no longer espoused or aspired to a worldview suggested by the colonial mandates of a century ago. It was fiction written in a robustly vernacular English that was manifestly hybrid, gleefully mixing the diverse narrative and linguistic forms of the Indian past into what it would announce was an "Indian novel."

This chapter traces the impetus behind this most recent revolution in Indian letters and argues that what the 1980s inaugurated in Indian literature is a liberation from the cultural and linguistic anglicization that persisted among Macaulay's Children well into the 1970s. The arrival of Salman Rushdie's *Midnight's Children* in 1980 delivered an international attention and destiny to the Indian novel in English, and while its Western readers have made much of Rushdie's postmodern credentials and his affiliation with García Márquez and Günter Grass, this chapter probes something only Rushdie's Indian readers and critics have noted: namely, his confident claim of English as an Indian language, alongside his indigenization of the novel into an Indian form. With *Midnight's Children*, the landscape of the Indian novel in English changed to the extent that a dozen years after its appearance the critic Rajeswari Sunder Rajan insisted: "to write fiction in English in India today is to write in the shadow of Salman Rushdie's *Midnight's Children*."[3] This chapter begins by taking stock of Rushdie's shadow and probing what precise vacuum "Salman Rushdie" filled in Indian letters. Alongside a reading of *Midnight's Children* and its innovations in the Indian novel, the chapter considers a few of Rushdie's children, the writers after Midnight who, I argue, literally and symbolically, in form and in content (re)turned the Indian novel in the 1980s to a very specific form of the romance, namely the family romance. In doing so, I implicitly ally Indian novels of the 1980s alongside and within two useful conceptual categories: the first, modernism, and the other, Goethe's now unfashionable concept of *Weltliteratur*, or world literature.

Let me begin by suggesting that what the decade of the 1980s has wrought in Indian letters is a phenomenon akin to literary modernism in Europe during the interwar period. The experiences of modernity and modernization—including industrialization, urbanization, an increasingly visible market economy, new technologies of production and representation, unsettled communities and migrating labor, exile, war, secularization—that characterized European efforts at modernization and shaped its literary modernism in the early decades of the twentieth century began to become apparent in Europe's former colonies shortly after decolonization. Yet the attendant literary production in these emergent nations that addresses the tensions of their incomplete and nonsynchronous modernization is variously labeled postmodern, third-world, etc. Insisting that this contemporary output recalls some of the earlier modernism's political and revolutionary tendencies as well as its investment in critiquing the dominant, "official" culture of capitalism and its modernities, I would argue that postmodernism, with its opaque nonhistorical strictures, is conspicuously inadequate as a description of this literary phenomenon. The term neither accounts for the critical and oppositional motivations of the literary output from the periphery nor addresses how centrally this output, by grounding itself in a specific literary locale and defying the conventions of its earlier models and masters, denies the temporal logic of "post" anything as it creates a literature that is genuinely Indian.

What I am suggesting is that in peripheral spaces such as India where modernity was initially associated with empire and often impossible to abstract from it, modern*ization* followed decolonization both with a bang and a whimper. Unevenly spread between the urban and the rural, north and south, literate and illiterate, male and female, its advent exaggerated quite dramatically the contrast between "new" and "old," past and present, ushering in a heightened awareness of what had occurred and a critical, often oppositional, stance toward what was to come. Modernism for me is the name for the impulse that characterizes this critical and oppositional stance, one that is capable of apprehending the rhythms of the past while it anticipates the onset of a "future." It is an impulse that was predominantly defined in the West during the interwar period, but it is by no means confined to this geographical or historical location.[4] I should specify that I do not claim the two modernisms—European and Indian—to be the same. Rather, what I see are a set of motivations and manifestations that, despite their many historical and geographical differences, are nevertheless connected at various points by a scrutiny and critique of modernity and its many forms. The critique of modernity is greatly compressed in India, much as the experience of modernization occurs in severely truncated form there. As one writer usefully described the denizens of these peripheral spaces: "They've lived through centuries of history in a single lifetime—village-born, colonized, traditionally raised, educated. What they've assimilated in 30 years has taken the West 10 times that number of years to create."[5] The modernist tendencies that I claim for the Indian novel of the 1980s, therefore, are just that: tendencies and impulses of critique rather than a fully fledged literary movement.[6]

To the extent that postmodernism is an abdication of many of modernism's oppositional impulses, it is also a practice that arises out of a new economic and social order in which commodification takes precedence over the product, imitation replaces innovation, and the critical impulse has been amputated into what Fredric Jameson has so compellingly identified as the proliferation of pastiche. For Jameson, one of the predominant features of the postmodern aesthetic remains pastiche, in sharp contrast to modernism's parody: for him, pastiche flourishes "without parody's ulterior motive, without the satirical impulse, without laughter, without that still latent feeling that there exists something *normal* compared to which what is being imitated is rather comic.

Pastiche is blank parody, parody that has lost its sense of humor."[7] Postmodernism for me rehearses modernist form without its more serious political motives or content, serving as a particularly capacious signifier in which everything and nothing belongs.

Curiously, despite obviously agreeing with Jameson's influential characterization of postmodernism and providing a detailed outline of third-world "cosmopolitan" writing that includes Salman Rushdie alongside Günter Grass, Vargas Llosa, and García Márquez, the critic Timothy Brennan nevertheless claims Rushdie as a postmodern writer, albeit one with what he calls a "revisionist spirit."[8] Brennan's important reading (his was the first book-length study on Rushdie) identifies Rushdie's postmodern credentials based almost entirely on the "formal similarities of his work with postmodern trends as a whole . . . [which] suggest not so much an exception to, as a different type of postmodern writing" (141). Yet the so-called differences Brennan cites (which include the storyteller's digressions, the parody of political villains, attempts to write a "history of the present" within the novel, the glorification of art's "functional role in political and social life," and Rushdie's encyclopedic compendium of narrative modes) vividly recall the oppositional and critical mandates of modernism rather than those of postmodernism. Rushdie, as Brennan's catalogue makes clear, is a novelist writing very much in sympathy with modernism's aesthetic and political tendencies: rather than creating historical amnesia or succumbing to cynicism (which Brennan includes in his catalogue of postmodernist impulses), he addresses and inspires what Ernst Bloch, hoping to revive modernism, optimistically called the principle of hope. The "different type of postmodern writing" that Brennan identifies is thus in fact modernist rather than postmodernist. Therefore, while I do not wish to quibble with Brennan's scrupulous catalogues or thoughtful characterizations, I will argue for a very different reading of Rushdie, one that places him within an Indian literary tradition that stretches as far back as the epic from the fourth century B.C.E., the *Mahabharata*, rather than a tradition that includes the contemporary cosmopolitan writers whom Brennan insists are Rushdie's "tradition."[9]

By a similar logic, the appellation "postcolonial" is increasingly vexed as a general description of this writing, for a significant impetus behind the "amazing mix" in the new Indian novel is precisely that it reorients and decenters the emphasis of colonial priorities in defining

Indian writing. While some of the new writing indeed takes on the aftermath of empire for which postcolonial would be an accurate, albeit temporal, description, a significant measure of the new work takes on other themes, and to continue to approach it from the logic and temporality of the colonial would be at the cost of losing what the novels of the 1980s have brought to Indian fiction. The persistent critical reference to writing from once colonial lands as postcolonial does precisely this. Even when the logic of temporality might be the only meaningful justification for using the term, there is a recurrent unease: When does it end? For how many years after empire ends does writing have to be "post" before it can become itself? Indeed, one might fairly ask, *does* it ever end or does all literature from once colonized lands always bear the stamp that comes with the appellation "colonial"? These are questions that "postcolonial" raises but does not satisfactorily address or resolve. As Anne McClintock has persuasively argued in describing her own unease with a term that continues to reproduce the binarisms and power structures once deployed in empire: "colonialism returns at the moment of its disappearance."[10] The danger, therefore, of preserving any part of the term "postcolonial" is that it ultimately eviscerates the possibility of conducting a historically grounded or specifically directed study. "Indian" literature becomes in some way primarily defined for having once been "colonial"; or, more to the point, having been "colonial" once, certain—say, Indian—literatures forfeit the possibility of making any original theoretical contribution outside a colonial sphere. In following this line of reasoning, we see that rather than clearing new ground, the term, with its deeply contradictory conceptual apparatus, limits any meaningful engagement with writing from once colonial worlds. Furthermore, it marginalizes this writing to the extent that though empires were transnational, once imperial subjects are, and at best remain, hopelessly national.

The Indian novel of the 1980s (including the work of Rushdie, Upamanyu Chatterjee, Amitav Ghosh, Shashi Tharoor, I. Allan Sealy, among others) was part of a literary phenomenon in English writing that had its roots in the "prose works of imagination" of the previous century. However, in language, tone, structure, theme, and content, its contributions mark a radical split with the earlier anxieties and influences of the Indian writer in English. Rather than reading these novelists and the literary phenomenon they generated as isolated incidents, this chapter demonstrates the extent to which this development (akin to the Boom in the Spanish American novel of the 1960s and 1970s) is part of the category of world literature and can best be understood from that perspective. Indeed, while the origin of the novel in India was a nineteenth-century phenomenon dominated by English culture in general and the English novel in particular, the development of the Indian novel was an uneven process marked by temporal divisions between early experiments in English versus the other languages of India. The unevenness was heightened with the introduction of other Western prose models in the early twentieth century (most notably with Russian and American novels) and the declining hegemony of British culture as the new nation was born. The novels of the 1980s are the literary product of this tangibly widening world space. I say "widening" because the Indian literary world went from having a bipolar imaginary in the nineteenth century (Britain and India) to a multipolar one after Independence in 1947, and the emerging literary forms reflect the interaction with this larger world system. In asserting the centrality of certain social and material conditions for understanding the Indian novel—namely, in invoking modernization and its by-products as I have done earlier—the chapter concludes by extending the grounds on which theoretical debates about culture and literature in the metropolitan West may be usefully extended to and invigorated by writing from the periphery.

SWALLOWING THE WORLD

"In order to understand just one life, you have to swallow the world," asserts Saleem Sinai, Rushdie's first-person narrator in *Midnight's Children* (1980), and the rest of the novel goes about doing just that.[11] While "swallowing the world" is in many ways the governing logic behind the digressive, sprawling structure of the novel, it also has a particular resonance in understanding the world outside *Midnight's Children*, particularly the Indian literary world in which the novel appeared. I think it would be perfectly fair to say that in many ways the Indian novel had already seen its heyday prior to the arrival of *Midnight's Children*. The vitality of the imported form had invigorated all the languages of India: Malayalam experiments of the 1880s inspired Hindi fiction of the 1940s and 1950s; experiments in English of the 1930s spawned Urdu writing for another generation; Bengali fiction of the 1870s and 1880s inspired Tamil fiction up till a century later; and so on. By the 1960s, however, it seemed as if the Indian novel had had its season, and the end of the decade saw the form, especially in English, stagnating in an awkward and discomfiting entropy—stagnating that is, until *Midnight's Children* appeared in 1980.

Reading back from *Midnight's Children*, of course, the temptation to find a precursor is strong and not an altogether empty exercise. In 1948, at the heels of Independence, G. V. Desani published *All About H. Hatterr*, which he elusively subtitled "A Gesture."[12] The work was a significant eruption on the literary landscape, introducing an aesthetic and linguistic modernism to Indian letters, but it failed to take root or, more significantly, it failed to *give* root to the extent that it today appears more a sport of nature without clearly discernible offspring rather than an important originary moment in the English novel from India. Though Rushdie among others has credited Desani for refreshing Indian fiction and bringing it to new terrain, insisting that "*Hatterr*'s dazzling, puzzling, leaping prose is the first genuine attempt to go beyond the Englishness of the English language . . . my own writing, too, learned a trick or two from him,"[13] Desani's work has remained a literary curiosity at best. The novel is narrated by H. Hatterr, born of a European merchant seaman ("from which part of the continent? Wish I could tell you" [31]) and a Malay mother, who spends his youth in an English missionary school in India. Largely self-taught, Hatterr writes in flawless malapropisms with perfect idiomatic Hinglish that he spices with words and phrases picked up from the missionary school headmaster's "own-authored *Latin Self-Taught* and *French Self-Taught*" (32). Though in the course of the novel Hatterr travels east and west in search of Truth, his view of the world essentially remains that learned from the five hundred slides of the school's stereoscope that he has stolen. Hatterr is, in other words, the perfect colonial subject. He (and the novel as a whole) seems to have stepped out of a V. G. Kiernan history book: Kiernan is famously known for his transhistorical account of empire, which concludes, "Europe was throwing the other continents together, sending Indian sepoys to China, Chinese coolies to South Africa, African slaves to Brazil. In one sense these peoples were being brought in closer, in another sense more deeply divided."[14]

Desani appears to take his cue from this colonial precondition, and he makes Hatterr a kind of prototypical imperial subject: the mongrel product of imperial expansion whom no nation will claim. Culturally he is more English than Malay or Indian, perhaps even more English than the English. His entire experience of the world is mediated by the extent to which his notion of "Englishness" exposes the English: "I was sitting in my humble belle-vue-no-view, cul-de-sack-the-tenant, a landlady's Up-and-do-'em opportunity apartment-joint in India. On the walls were hanging many home-framed photo-gravures of well-known passenger boats of the mail lines; and on the top of the only shelf, a stuffed crocodile, the six foot of which yours humbly once shot in the Baluchistan borders" (33). If Europe used its languages and through them its literatures to bring culture to the colonial masses, Hatterr's scrupulous usage exposes the dissemblance at work: "belle-vue" promises but does not provide a view; nor does "cul-de-sac" recreate privacy and affluence in the dingy boarding house with its rapacious landlady; and the glory of England's naval might is reduced to cheap reproductions of mass transit mail lines. In Hatterr's usage, which he insists is "conditioned by his past, his experience" (16), the colonizers' language and through it their literature are exposed for their complicity in camouflaging the truth rather than conveying it, for cloaking meaning rather than clarifying it. "To one," explains Hatterr of his usage at the novel's opening, "*M.P.* stands for *Member of Parliament*. To another, it might mean *major parasite*. Depends on his experience. That's all why this book isn't English as she is wrote and spoke" (16). And, for Hatterr, it is not just language that is part of this duplicity; it is also the entire arsenal of images by which the empire recreated its glory for its subjects on foreign shores. After his first glimpse of England, Hatterr is dismayed:

> There was no transparent amber and cider sunshine-glow, which I had accustomed myself into imagining as a perpetual God's gift aura over England, from stolen peeps into Rev. the Head's privately-owned Our Lovely Homeland type of sunny Devon-Cornwall illustrated in tricolour publication (and confirmed by the Society's stereoscope). No: instead by Pitt and Gladstone! Clang o'doom, thunder, and Glasgow fury!   (35)

Even the pictures lie, a thousand times perhaps, because they carry that many more lies than words do.

Despite this, it is the words that make *Hatterr*. Anthony Burgess, introducing a newly revised edition of the novel in 1970, exulted: "It is the language that makes the book, a sort of creative chaos that grumbles at the restraining banks. . . . It is not pure English: it is, like the English of Shakespeare, Joyce and Kipling, gloriously impure" (10). *Hatterr*'s is of course the glory of impurity that comes from throwing the continents together with the mixture of English as she is wrote and spoke the world over, and Burgess is not alone in dwelling on the glory of Desani's language or in likening it to Joyce. K. R. S. Iyengar calls the novel "a Joycean exercise in seeming incoherence and total comprehension,"[15] and to some extent his critical acclaim suggests two things. One, that any kind of linguistic experimentation ("chaos," "incoherence") post-1922 is immediately likened to Joyce. And second, I would argue that by calling *Hatterr* "Joycean," Iyengar and others mean a particular Joyce: the Joyce of linguistic virtuosity, not the bard of exile; the author of Bloom's bumbling peregrinations, not the critic of colonial underdevelopment; the Joyce celebrated by semiotics not by sociologists; in other words, the structuralist Joyce over the poststructuralist.

This critical reception did two things: it acknowledged the novelty of Desani's style, but it ignored its deeper implications. Desani was championed for bringing modernist form and experimentation to the Indian novel, but not its content, and while this initial assessment is entirely disputable, as the excerpts above with their willfully combined sociology of bazaar-speak, Queen's English, and Babu-talk make clear, it did much to contain the novel's impact. *Hatterr*'s inventiveness with language was regarded in the "Joycean" reading (which, incidentally, still holds sway in studies of the Indian novel) as a cerebral game rather than as the product of the colonial experience. The character's journey from colony to metropolis and across class boundaries is regarded as the privilege afforded to a freak rather than as the often painful fallout of being exiled in one's own land, or worse, unlanded by the changing geography of empire as Hatterr, insisting "biologically, I am fifty-fifty of the species" (31), reveals. In other words, the novel's brilliance was ascribed to its formal elements only: content was divorced from it. If the modernist novel was to exist in India, it seemed to be able to do so only in form. Somehow, history, sociology, ideology—what I would argue were the vital *political* dimensions of modernism as we know it— were kept out of an entire generation's reading of *Hatterr*.

They were kept out, that is, until *Midnight's Children* came along, initiating a mode in the Indian novel where content was not just relevant to form but *determined* form. If the form of *Midnight's Children* was narratively directed at "understanding just one life," then the content forced one "to swallow the world" in order to do so, a strategy that opened up a whole range of possibilities for the Indian novel. The method of Rushdie's novel takes its cue from the adage that sometimes in order to go forward, one has to go back, which Rushdie does, going back to a period when the storyteller eulogized by Benjamin held sway, and when the meaning of a narrative still resided inside it, not outside "enveloping the tale as a glow brings out a haze."[16] In this moment from the cultural past, stories came from tellers, epics, songs, not from the novel, and this is where *Midnight's Children* begins. It takes its narrative clue from the circular structure and oral nature of the Indian epic tradition that provides the general composition of the novel.

Eschewing a linear narrative or one recorded in the third person, Rushdie abandoned an early draft of *Midnight's Children* with just these features for a structure and form that recall the oral epics of India with their multiple digressions and recurrent improvisations. "I became a writer at the moment I found a narrative voice for *Midnight's Children* and that was finding a literary equivalent of that oral narrative from India that had kept the audience rapt for thousands of years," Rushdie explained.[17] When Saleem Sinai begins his story with the conceit that an entire world can be understood from his life, his conceit is perfectly amenable to an audience raised on the *Mahabharata* and that has conceded to one of its signal premises: that the story of the House of Pandu is the story of the world, a theme echoed in the commonplace, "whatever is in the *Mahabharata* can be found elsewhere; but what isn't in it can be found nowhere."[18]

The main story of the *Mahabharata* deals with a conflict several generations long over dynastic succession in the Bharata family that is told in approximately twenty-four thousand stanzas. However, the epic in its textual form contains numerous accretions and commentaries on matters of religion and philosophy, genealogy, history, folklore, and myth that quadruple its length to roughly one hundred thousand stanzas. Three generations of reciters are credited internally with transmitting the bulky text that opens with the bard Ugrasravas reciting the version he claims to have heard Vaisampayna reciting to the king Janamejaya, which itself originated from the mouth of one Dvaipayana, or Vyasa:

> I shall speak the entire thought of that great seer, Vyasa, of limitless brilliance. Poets have told it before, poets are telling it now, other poets shall tell this history on earth in the future. It is indeed a great storehouse of knowledge, rooted in the three worlds, which the twiceborn retain in all its parts and summaries. Fine words adorn it, and usages human and divine; many meters scan it; it is the delight of the learned.[19]

Embedded within Ugrasravas's preamble is the entire compositional and reception history of the epic. Passed on from poets "before" to those "now," the work anticipates a long journey of oral and written transmission in which each reciter and scribe wove into the epic his own additions, commentaries, and summaries. Indeed the recorded text of the *Mahabharata* itself bears this out: each retelling and recitation carries the marks of the audience that inspired it and of the teller who intervened on his audience's behalf, to the extent that scholars believe the numerous Brahminical commentaries that today constitute much of the epic text are a result of this group's investment in what was initially a succession story of interest mostly to kings and the baronial classes. In other words, the ascendance of Brahminical classes gave the recorded text of the *Mahabharata* the particular flavor in which the epic battle is subsumed within lengthy commentaries on other matters entirely. This view persuasively accounts for the reflective and explanatory mode of the accretion known as the *Bhagavad Gita* in which the lord Krishna justifies the massive battle to the warrior Arjuna who shies away from raising his bow to kill members of his extended family. As J. A. B. van Buitenen puts it, "the Brahmins were hardly hearing the story of the epic for the first time; they already knew of the miserable course the war would take. What could be more appropriate than to add a moment of pause . . . a moment of reflection on whether the warriors should really do it?"[20] This moment leads to Krishna's extended counsel, which in turn has become a major text of Hindu religious practice. Therefore, not only do the many commentaries, written and oral, insert the audience into the epic, they also redirect its main plot (the battle over the throne of

Hastinapur) and diminish its authority before the needs and interests of each narrator and his particular audience.

Some of these needs have made it into the recorded texts of both Indian epics. One recalls here the burlesque moment when Ram's brother Laxman chops off Shurpnakha's nose in a fit of rage in the *Ramayana*, or Draupadi's shameful disrobing after the game of dice in the *Mahabharata*, which has been rendered in all possible modes from comic and tragic to erotic. Others are more commonly enacted in the many oral retellings of the epic and its numerous performances. The recorded text has very little authority in these venues; the oral narrator continually improvises, relates, digresses, comments, updates, and even upstages the recorded text to suit his audience's desires. Whereas Bankim's narrator in the Bengali novels I have discussed in chapter 4 takes his cue from the serious and judgmental narrator of the recorded epic, Rushdie's clearly comes from the jesting, jocular figure known and beloved from the oral tradition. Unlike the recorded form that (perhaps because of its Brahminical influence) allows its narrator few mistakes, the oral form allows the narrator more leeway in error and fallacy, both of which Rushdie exploits fully in *Midnight's Children* as will come into view very shortly when Saleem, the cheerfully unreliable narrator, presumes to record the political history of India from roughly 1914 to 1979. Whereas the particular epic narrator in Bankim's novels helped stabilize meaning, Rushdie's narrator, taking his inspiration from the oral tradition, intentionally multiplies it. In much the way that the figure of Ram is dramatically reconfigured from prince to divinity in the vernacular retellings of the *Ramayana*, Rushdie's method too takes his epic subject (the political history of India) and refashions it considerably in his vernacular version.

The story Saleem tells is the story of Independent India, "born" like Saleem himself at midnight of August 15, 1947. Rushdie fleshes out the one-life-whole-world conceit on several levels with events in Saleem's life explaining, commenting, or reflecting events in the nation's. In order to do this, Rushdie appropriates a number of epic conventions into the novel, the most startling of which is his narrator. High realism in the nineteenth century perfected novels with what Fredric Jameson has called "depersonalized authorial voices," and much has been made of this so-called depersonalization: that it is more than simply an aesthetic choice, that it in fact marks the limits of realist narrative, which, confronting a world to which it *has* no moral meaning to offer, recedes from center stage into the disembodied narrator. Sharpening the contrast between the epic narrator (or "storyteller") and the novelistic one, Benjamin has proposed: "What can be handed on orally, the wealth of the epic, is of a different kind from what constitutes the stock in trade of the novel. . . . The birthplace of the novel is the solitary individual, who is no longer able to express himself by giving examples of his most important concerns, is himself uncounselled and cannot counsel others."[21] While Benjamin's account of receding narrative authority that combines declining social cohesion with the loss of cultural wisdom and "counsel" is compelling for realism and certainly so for the post-Independence novel in India, Rushdie's blithe appropriation of the dominant figure from Indian oral epics forces us to ask what the slightly irritating, know-it-all Saleem-narrator is actually doing in *Midnight's Children* after all. As a narrator, he does indeed know it all, and knows it so well that he frequently scolds himself in the text for letting the story get ahead of him. And yet, like a narrator from the high realist tradition of *L'Education sentimentale*, Saleem-narrator *cannot do anything* with his knowledge: history will crush him and consume his story, and Saleem also knows this only too well.

It does not stop *Midnight's Children*, however; the narrator has a job to do. The world of the novel might be depraved, and independent India revealed to be betraying each of its promises. In the chapter entitled "Midnight," Saleem's sperectomy—what he calls "the draining-out of hope" (521) that follows his forced castration—corresponds with Indira Gandhi's Emergency, one of the most egregious violations of democratic process in India when Mrs. Gandhi, who was found guilty of election fraud, responded by clamping a twenty-one-month state of Emergency during which constitutional rights were "temporarily" rescinded, freedom of the press was denied, and many of Mrs. Gandhi's real and imagined critics were summarily jailed or dismissed. The period of the Emergency forms one of the most horrific chapters in the novel, taking place (like "Circe") at midnight, the time of nightmares that persistently haunt the subject's waking moments. It is also significant that in this chapter, the narrative, like Saleem, breaks down: Rushdie writes much of "Midnight" in a kind of stream of consciousness (or, more appropriately, *scream* of consciousness) bringing the style back to its beginnings as a representation of collapse and mental breakdown. However, despite the political and personal collapse, Saleem-the-narrator has a job: to make sense of the story he is telling. And to do this, Rushdie's appropriation of epic conventions grants him a certain license. Epic, in India, still exists after all in the form of myth, far richer than religion and far more pervasive as well. So be it that the matter of *Midnight's Children* is history, real events lived by the millions in India; its métier is still fiction, and in Hayden White's keen reminder, "mythic narrative is under no obligation to keep the two orders of events, real and imaginary, distinct from one another."[22]

Midnight's Children exploits epic-myth as a means to enable its storytelling, by which I mean that in the realm of the real, none of the events that Rushdie recounts has conclusively ended: independent India is still searching to fulfill the promise of its birth without disintegrating as the novel's enigmatic ending suggests. Yet the scheme of the novel borrowed from the oral epics allows, indeed insists that, the events in the real be moralized as if they had a conclusive meaning that was apparent all along in the plot. The narrator of epic has the privilege and the responsibility of making sense of the world to his audience. The novelistic narrator has no such obligation, putatively because his world *has* no unifying sense to it. In inserting the epic narrator into the novel, Rushdie opens up new ground for the genre. He does not stand by, representing reality; rather, he *shapes* it. His narrator brings to the novel an interpretive function that insistently makes meaning and connection out of lived events even as they are taking place, to the extent that each event in the private domain explains and is explained by an occurrence in the public sphere:

> History books newspapers radio-programmes tell us that at two p.m. on June 12th, Prime Minister Indira Gandhi was found guilty, by Judge Jag Mohan Lah Sinha of the Allahabad High Court, of two counts of campaign malpractice during the election campaign of 1971; what has never previously been revealed is that it was at precisely two p.m. that Parvati-the-witch (now Laylah Sinai) became sure she had entered labour.   (497)

As Parvati delivers the boy who is not-quite Saleem's son, "the Prime Minister was giving birth to a child of her own" (499), and as Saleem greets his son, "at exactly the same moment, the word Emergency was being heard for the first time." The infant Aadam is born with "elephant ears" that Saleem informs us have heard late-night shrieks protesting the Emergency and its atrocities, and Aadam, as a result, is "rendered dumb by a surfeit of sound" (501).

In dozens of accounts such as this that connect Saleem's biography with the nation's, Rushdie self-consciously inverts the earlier modernist aesthetic of parataxis: rather than rendering innumerable unconnected and unconnectable events meaningless, his narrative insists that an intrinsic and organic logic connects and relates together what would otherwise be a series of bewildering and alienating occurrences. In this regard, Saleem-the-narrator does not simply personalize Indian history (i.e., amplifying the boast of his birth paralleling the nation's; the peaks and valleys of his life causing peaks and valleys in the nation's): he also interprets public events with a logic that integrates isolated private actions into them to create a gigantic tapestry of meaning in which everything makes sense and thus affirms the presence of providence in what would otherwise be randomness. Alongside the numerous gaffes, factual errors, and oversights he commits (many of which his Indian readers gleefully pointed out to Rushdie), it is above all this aspect of Saleem-the-narrator's sense-making function that most renders a moral where chaos and futility would otherwise reign. What Rushdie finally achieves through his epic insertions into the novel is to give meaning to Indian modernity and to rescript it within more persuasive terms that are both deeply personal and magical.

If Naipaul is right when he laments, "the novel as a form no longer carries conviction. Experimentation, not aimed at real difficulties, has corrupted response, and there is great confusion in the minds of readers and writers about the purpose of the novel,"[23] then *Midnight's Children* shows that Rushdie's particular experimentation with India's epic precedents actually enables response (and responsibility, as well), making meaning where none existed. *Midnight's Children*'s excursus into the Indian literary past empowers the novel to take on the present, which becomes the content of the work. India, its colonial history, Independence, Partition, democracy, development, and political betrayal determine the plot of the novel, and while the use of Indian literary tradition commissions this conceit, it also in a very real sense takes the question to another realm: to whether cultural tradition in a more general sense enables modernity, or is antithetical to it.

In *Midnight's Children*, for instance, the narrator, Saleem, plays up the conventions of the oral epics that he has appropriated, and at some point he begins to *speak* his story to an auditor—in this case, to Padma, his so-called "dung goddess" (21). I intentionally use the word, "speak," for even as Rushdie stages Padma as a fictionalized audience from the oral tradition that he has smuggled into his novel, he restricts her role in the novel to that of a character whose understanding of Saleem's story is limited to his literal utterances. Padma listens for the plot, expressing dismay and impatience at different times as Saleem unveils one or another detail of his story: "Arré baap . . . just tell what happened, mister!" (507), she exclaims in irritation at yet another digression. In other words, she hears only what Saleem speaks, being unable or unwilling to take the narrative on to any degree of abstraction. And yet, as we know from Rushdie's insistent one-life-whole-world opening, abstraction is exactly what the novel demands, functioning on some level as an allegory. But, if Padma the auditor cannot (or will not) understand the story for this, it is fair to ask what role she plays in Rushdie's narrative other than being a vestige from the epic tradition floating in the generic smorgasbord that makes up *Midnight's Children*.

Alongside her, the novel stages another reader, this one to whom the narrator appears to address his concerns and to whom he sends regular dispatches such as the opening I cited earlier: "To know me, to know just the one of me, *you'll* have to swallow the lot as well" (4). Who is this "you," one might ask? It is not Padma, one realizes quickly, since the narrator addresses much of his impatience with her to the second reader as well. This second figure, I would argue, is Rushdie's ideal reader (and audience), framed as a kind of textual mise-en-scène within the novel. It is this ideal reader to whom the narrator addresses his concerns and from whom he invites a response. Having recognized the presence of an ideal reader, however, makes it increasingly difficult to maintain the distinction between the narrator and Rushdie in the novel, so much so that Saleem's rather flimsy identity begins to disintegrate. How, for instance, can one be sure that it is the ideal reader to whom Saleem addresses himself when he says, "we are a nation of forgetters" (37)? "We" indicates a speaker and a spoken, but who is the speaker? And more to the point, to whom is he speaking? One reading, perhaps Padma's, would be that Saleem and the implied reader are the "nation of forgetters"; another would interpret the declamation to imply that Rushdie speaks through Salem via the ideal reader to a larger audience, and that *all* his readers are "forgetters"; and a third, slightly at an angle to this one, would be that readers from the *particular* nation staged in *Midnight's Children* suffer the exceptionally modern malady of collective amnesia.[24] I will discuss these last two readings in turn shortly, but for the moment the interpretive confusion generated by the "we" deserves some scrutiny.

When Homer began his magnificent catalogue of the Achaean army in book 2 of the *Iliad*, he first addressed himself to his muses: "Sing to me now, you Muses who hold the halls of Olympus"[25]: "me," the singer; "you," the Muses. A few lines further, he continued, "You know all things—all we hear is the distant ring of glory, we know nothing" (2:574–575). Homer's "we" has been famously interpreted as a representation of the unselfconscious unity between the ancient Greeks and their culture, a unity that allowed Homer to identify in a full and uncomplicated manner with his audience. His "we" literally includes all his listeners, for, according to this reading, Homer and his listeners shared their assumptions about the world they inhabited. The assumptions of this world in turn provided the basis for the form of the epic, so that Homer's innocuous "we" becomes the *unambiguous* interpretive key by which a later reader—Lukács, for instance—would understand antiquity, its outlook, and its cultural forms. Indeed, this unity and easy solidarity between narrator and audience has come to represent one of the defining tropes of the epic in both Western and non-Western traditions. According to this thesis, the epic is a form that takes as its point of departure community and kinship, in contrast to the novel that, *pace* Lukács and others, laments the loss of community in its representation of "transcendental homelessness."[26]

If we apply this strategy to *Midnight's Children* and its ambiguous "we," several things become clear. First, that its ideal reader is made to play a role that the novel simply cannot sustain. When Homer (or Vyasa or Valmiki) sang, his audience understood what it heard, to a large extent because it accepted Homer's interpretive authority as a story-teller. The novel as a genre, on the other hand, has lost this authority, and its reader is asked to assume an interpretive role that exceeds the novel's capabilities. When Rushdie stages an ideal reader within *Midnight's Children* to whom he gives the responsibility of making sense of the novel's world, he seems to be playing on a number of registers. On one, the ideal reader extends the epic ambitions of the work, performing what I have earlier called a textual mise-en-scène of an epic audience, so that unlike Padma, this reader actually gets the story and is able to organize its disparate, shaggy details into a narrative that is ordered and coherent. On another level, the presence of this figure goads one into asking precisely what *Midnight's Children* really is. There is a substantial gulf between the two registers: either the work is an epic with its singular capabilities, or it is a novel with *its* reach—but it surely cannot be both. The insertion of a fictionalized reader in the text allows Rushdie to suggest both and to manipulate the ensuing indeterminacy with powerful effect. The greatest confusion it seems to me lies in the ambiguous nature of the "we." In as much as Saleem is addressing himself to the textual reader, the novel's actual readers have no idea of the imaginary reader's response, and this silence is telling, particularly since the "we" signals—indeed, demands—a response.[27] In *Midnight's Children*, the actual reader's identification with an authorial or narrative "we" becomes muffled in a confusion that, I would argue, is at the core of the novel's reach. "We are a nation of forgetters" invites both the interpretations I have mentioned earlier: one, that *all* Rushdie's readers (East and West) fall under the collective "we"; and the other hand, that the readers of the particular nation in the novel do so. Certainly, if the latter reading is to hold, it would also further imply that it is to his actual readers in the Subcontinent that Rushdie addresses his concerns, and the "we" becomes a manifesto or a particular *cri de colère*.[28]

If *Midnight's Children*'s use of literary tradition permitted the novel to make forays into economic and political modernization (the "world" of Independence), the validity and contradictions of anchoring an understanding of modernity within categories and terms borrowed from anterior traditions persist among Rushdie's literary offspring writing in English. Shashi Tharoor's *The Great Indian Novel* (1989) appeared almost a decade after *Midnight's Children* and takes on some of these issues in a self-conscious continuation of *Midnight's Children's* "project." Its title and theme are directly inspired by the epic *Mahabharata*, which literally translated means, "great India."[29] Further literalizing Rushdie's earlier borrowings, Tharoor's novel grafts the entire plot and characters of the ancient epic onto twentieth-century Indian political history. His first-person narrator is no other than Ved Vyasa (reputedly the original composer of the *Mahabharata*), whose professed aim in the novel is "transcribing the Song of Modern India in my prose" (18). The battle from the ancient epic becomes a battle for India's soul—democracy—who, played by Draupadi, wife of the five Pandavas, suffers fits of asphyxia as the novel progresses. While much of Tharoor's novel revels in the clever turns of phrase and puns that have relegated it to a realm closer to parody than allegory, it drops its playfulness toward the end when it takes on the issue of tradition in the broadest sense. Confronted by yet another political betrayal, the narrator, Ved Vyasa, mourns:

> How far we have travelled from the glory and splendour of our adventurous mythological heroes! The land of Rama, setting out on his glamorous crusade against the abductors of his divinely pure wife Sita, the land where truth and honour and valour and *dharma* were worshipped as the cardinal principles of existence, is now a nation of weak-willed compromisers, of leaders unable to lead, of rampant corruption and endemic faithlessness. Our democrats gamble with democracy; our would-be dictators do not know what to dictate. *We soothe ourselves with the lullabies of our ancient history, our remarkable culture, our inspiring mythology. But our present is so depressing that our rulers can only speak of the intermediate future—or the immediate past.* (411; emphasis added)

Tradition, in Vyasa's lament, has failed to renew the culture it serves. At best, it is a salve deployed by the power elite to contain dissent or used as a trophy of past grandeur to deflect criticism of current failures. Its "glory and splendour" are mythic. Quite simply, it has ceased to matter. Or has it? In one of the novel's most stunning reversals, the eternally righteous Yudhishtir, whose observance of *dharma*[30] ultimately guides his victory in the *Mahabharata*, renounces tradition altogether. "If there is one thing that is true today, it is that there are no classical verities valid for all time. I believed differently and have paid the price of being defeated, humiliated, and reduced to irrelevance. . . . No more certitudes. . . . Accept doubt and diversity. Let each man live by his own code of conduct, so long as he has one. *Derive your standards from the world around you, and not from a heritage whose relevance must be constantly tested*" (418; emphasis added).

Earlier I noted that Yudhishtir's words were a reversal, and they are indeed so in the tradition of the *Mahabharata*, where the epic Yudhishtir's unwavering abeyance to *dharma* inspires even the gods. However, the words above appear not in the epic but in this novel where they are disturbingly ironic. "Derive your standards from the world around you," Yudhishtir exhorts. Yet, as the novel makes clear, the world around him *has* no "standards." "Accept doubt and diversity," he commands to an audience confronting a modern nation fragmenting before its eyes. On the surface, Yudhishtir's words echo the sentiments of just about any modern politician in the developing world just at the moment when the politician is about to sell out massively to some third party and wants to quell dissent. "Move on, modernize, don't cling to the outmoded past" the politician urges, and one could spin this embodiment in any number of ways to see the devastation this rhetoric can—and has—unleashed. The novel concludes with Vyasa writing, "I woke up . . . to today's India. To our land of computers and corruption, of myths and politicians. . . . To an India beset with uncertainties, muddling chaotically through to the twenty-first century" (418).

NONSYNCHRONOUS NARRATIVES

Tharoor's novel is hardly one of revivalism or fundamentalism: much of the work embraces aspects of modernity (exemplified by simple "advances" over British rule such as democracy, education, health care, redistribution of wealth), balking only when it comes at the cost of the past. Like Rushdie before him, Tharoor's project in *The Great Indian Novel* is a self-conscious appropriation of history whose uses and abuses lie at the crux of the long-current Indian political climate. Moreover, both Rushdie's and Tharoor's annexation and refashioning of history in their narratives underscore the urgency with which they assume (and are respected for) a certain voice in contemporary Indian politics. "The very fact that [*Midnight's Children*] is being discussed constitutes a unique tribute to its author. No other novel about India has had such an impact," reminded Tariq Ali in an argument that continues to remain valid for Salman Rushdie and for some of his literary offspring in India.[31]

Even for readers who capitulate to Saleem's obstreperous insistence on his role in Indian history and who can suspend disbelief when reading his highly personal and fabulous version of it, two things become clear. The first, as David Lipscomb points out in a brilliantly insightful reading, is Rushdie's ability to make the novel's version of events appear the normative one while destabilizing and rendering as "exotic other" the official, expert, Western historiography on India of the kind exemplified in texts such as Stanley Wolpert's *A New History of India*, which recounts many of the same political events that Rushdie narrates in *Midnight's Children*.[32] Lipscomb demonstrates that in a novel liberally sprinkled with entire passages lifted from Wolpert's textbook, *Midnight's Children* nonetheless questions the credibility of "objective" historical discourse by rendering it as parody when placed alongside the deeply personal, even fallible version Saleem provides. Saleem's version of history is made up partly from family myths and personal boasts, partly from scraps of gossip and innuendo picked up from the streets, and partly fantasized, all into a compendium of what Lipscomb shows are nevertheless "stories that perhaps tell a kind of truth . . . that is not found in verifiable accounts" (178). The official, verifiable details (*pace* Wolpert) behind Mrs. Gandhi's Emergency or the 1971 Bangladesh War are far flatter and less meaningful than Saleem's account of these events, which interprets them through Parvati's labor and his own castration or through the paramilitary CUTIA unit that, despite being officially unproven, claims a special "truth" in Rushdie's harrowing narrative of the Bangladesh War. History in *Midnight's Children* is not so much rendered fantasy, as fantasy and fabulation are rendered respectable forms of acquiring historical knowledge and interpreting it. In this regard, official, textual history has no greater claim to authenticity than the recorded epic does: both lose their authority in the narrator's retellings to suit the audience's needs and interests. Furthermore, Rushdie extends his epic narrator's sense-making responsibility to include an interpretive and explanatory role that eschews Western historiography's insistence on the referential illusion—or what Benjamin has called the authority of facts and "information"—to embrace instead all the things that derive from experience: "wisdom," counsel, community.

It ought to be underscored that Rushdie's and Tharoor's insistence on using fiction to complicate and amplify Indian history is a striking choice, though one by no means original. In seeking politics and history as its provenance, the Indian novel in English follows a trail already cut in numerous regional languages, from Bankim's *Anandamath* (1882, Bengali), to Premchand's "Shatranj ke Khilari" ("The

Chess Players," 1924, Urdu and Hindi), Saadat Hasan Manto's Partition stories of the 1940s and 1950s, Shrilal Shukla's *Raag Darbari*
(Hindi, 1968). Earlier anglophone novelists further make clear that
even the "history" they dwell upon is a particularly indigenous one. As
Raja Rao explained in his foreword to *Kanthapura* (1938), the particular form of history he uses in the novel was *sthalapurana*, which mixed
local legends with political events as it describes a Karnataka village
caught in the Gandhian movement preceding Independence.[33]

More striking than the use of history, however, is the status fiction
generally has been able to claim in wider debates on Indian modernity:
Partha Chatterjee draws on Bankim's and Tagore's novels to craft an
influential theory of Indian nationalism; in an attempt to document
Bengal's emerging public culture in the late 1870s and 1880s, the political theorist Sudipta Kaviraj has written extensively on Bankim's novels; and the social theorist Veena Das, writing about the unresolved
trauma of the Partition, largely dismisses the 1949 parliamentary hear-
ings on the matter and draws instead upon Manto's version in stories
such as "The Return," which details the Partition's unspeakable and
unnamed violence by leaving unspoken and unnamed a young woman's
serial rape during a border crossing.[34] In this regard, the English novel
of the 1980s has followed the lead of earlier regional language novels
in commenting, analyzing, complicating, and developing issues related
to the nation and modernity. I would argue, however, that the English
novel pursues its project with a difference.

The instability in its generic boundaries—the works call themselves
novels, yet significantly include epic, journalism, history—represent
above all the nonsynchronism in once colonial societies. "Not all people exist in the same Now," Ernst Bloch wrote in a powerful essay of
1932. "They do so only externally, by virtue of the fact that they may
all be seen today. But that does not mean that they are living at the same
time with others."[35] Written in the shadows of Hitler's political ascen-
dancy, Bloch's essay addresses the persistence of multiple, older "times"
in the present, which manifest themselves in stark contrast to the Now
that he associates with capital. The more thoroughly societies are integrated into capitalism, the more synchronism or temporal "sameness"
they exhibit. Modernization, Bloch concluded, assimilates "contradictory" nonsynchronous elements and remnants of an older economic
and social order into temporal homogeneity, but where it fails, the

presence of these nonsynchronous fragments exhibits itself as a problem that "impedes" the future from occurring (33). The process of full synchronization, however, has clearly yet to come to the India of the novels where nonsynchronism persists—and perhaps even multiplies. Few people inhabit the same Now: most because they are kept out of it (the colony of magicians in Saleem's ghetto, for instance), and some because they simply cannot get into it (such as Mary Braganza, Saleem's former ayah, despite her class mobility and eventual ownership of a financially successful pickle factory).

However, rather than being a cause of dismay as it was for Bloch in 1932 Germany, nonsynchronism in Rushdie's novel is a matter of fact and a powerful and persuasive principle of alterity. Saleem's dislocations in *Midnight's Children* from scion of a powerful family to dispossessed ghetto dweller place him within some of the temporal disunities that proliferate in decolonized India, and the contradictions within the multiple nonsynchronous elements he encounters offer themselves as alternatives to the dominant political vision the novel contests. There is a comical moment in the magician's ghetto when a Congressman (a caricature of Sanjay Gandhi, Mrs. Gandhi's zealous younger son) arrives to give a speech: "Brothers-O! Sisters-O! What does Congress say to you? This—that all men are created equal" (475), he begins. His is the language of the Now, of liberal democracy being travestied in the ghetto during election time, to which the snake charmer, Picture Singh, responds with a show: *his* formidable skill with a poisonous king cobra that he charms to terrifying effect. "You see, here is the truth of the business: some persons are better, others are less. But it may be nice for you to think otherwise" (475), Picture Singh calmly tells the cowering politician when he finishes his show. The snake charmer's view of unequal excellence comes from his world, depicted as surviving precariously in the shadow of Old Delhi's Jama Masjid. And yet it is a view that can see through the contradictions of the Now as well as articulate its own stance to counter the duplicity of the Congress Party's rhetoric. This is what I mean when I say that nonsynchronism in Independent India is a principle of alterity: living in a different Now means living with other meanings, other values, and maybe even, a vision of other possibilities. Rather than being a burden, the existence of different historical moments offers a means of survival: it *makes most sense*, and as such, it exists as a choice rather than as a sentence. Like Picture

Singh, those living in different times keep alive different stories and possibilities that a totalizing Now has yet to incorporate. Whereas in Bloch's Europe, nonsynchronism tends to be problematic, in the India of the novels, it is prescriptive and possibly even liberating.

It is to these prescriptive possibilities that the novel of the 1980s—what I have earlier called the modernist novel in India—applies itself. Its use of forms from epic and history, with their discursive and narrative possibilities, enables it to apprehend other historical rhythms *and*, I would argue, to proffer other critical possibilities to an unfolding political drama. If by dropping politics, European modernism in a sense dropped history from its provenance, the Indian novel's insertion of history advances the potential of rescuing an oppositional, *political*, modernism from decline. Its depiction and celebration of an exaggerated nonsynchronism is as much a matter of representation as it is a strategy: insisting on the presence of multiple consciousnesses in a once colonial world underwrites the appropriation of multiple discursive and narrative styles, which in turn sense and stress a wide range of critical issues. Here again, Rushdie's insistence on swallowing the world becomes the practice of these self-consciously encyclopedic narratives that encode not just the major and minor forms of knowledge in once colonial India (oral epics alongside street magic, pickle recipes next to tutorials in democracy), but a critique of those forms as well.[36] It is not just the willful representation of the minor beside the major that exaggerates the presence of nonsynchronism but also the pleasure and possibilities that this representation of oppositions provides that renders them so crucial to the novel's political vision of Emergency-era India.

As such, the novel's reception in India was considerably different than in the West. "In India, people don't really treat my story as fantasy. The fantasy elements in it are relatively minor, and are only enabling devices to talk about actuality," Rushdie explained in an interview that a survey of Indian critical responses to the novel corroborates.[37] To a considerable extent, I would argue that *Midnight's Children*'s borrowings from the epic tradition are in fact achievements in fully and literally indigenizing the novel as an Indian form able to apprehend and advance rhythms commensurate with Indian reality. The earlier gulf that plagued the development of the Indian novel between form and content, or what Meenakshi Mukherjee called realism and reality, finally seems to have vanished with *Midnight's Children*, and it is this vacuum in Indian letters that Salman Rushdie helped to fill.

BY WAY OF EPILOGUE: THE FAMILY ROMANCE, IN ENGLISH

Comparing Rushdie, father of the twentieth-century Indian novel in English, with Bankim, father of the nineteenth-century Indian novel, can be profoundly instructive. Like Bankim's *Rajmohan's Wife* (1864), Rushdie's first novel, *Grimus* (1975), was also an abysmal failure. It too was an attempt to write seriously in a popular form—in Rushdie's case, in science fiction. While many of the most successful qualities of Rushdie's later fiction are to be found in it—his fluid prose and verbal games, the intoxicating evocation and complete control over an imaginary landscape named Calf Island where Flapping Eagle, the man who cannot die, washes ashore—the novel had minor sales of approximately eight hundred copies in its initial printing and was pulped by its publisher shortly after release. Looking back at it after the success of *Midnight's Children*, Rushdie provided what remains a persuasive explanation for both *Grimus*'s failure and *Midnight's Children*'s success: "The thing that I disliked about my first novel . . . was that it's a complete fantasy. It's not placed in a real place . . . and after finishing it, after some distance had been established from it, it seemed to me that . . . fantasy is not interesting when you separate it from actuality, and it's only interesting as a of mode of dealing with actuality."[38] Like Bankim before him, Rushdie's later success also came from absorbing an earlier Indian literary form into his work and grafting historical narrative onto the novel, thus indicating that both *Grimus* and *Rajmohan's Wife* failed in part because of their ostensible divorce from what Rushdie calls "actuality," while the other works succeeded for their successful marriage of fictional form with social concerns. Whereas Bankim stopped short after folding the epic narrator into the Bengali novels following *Rajmohan's Wife*, Rushdie's importation was far more wholesale. *Midnight's Children* takes the narrative idiom, circular structure, oral and performative qualities, and overall rhythms of the Indian epic tradition and places them largely unchanged as the organizing topoi of his novel.

If to this point Rushdie's distinction is in degree only, one aspect of his literary ascendance marks his originality from Bankim and for that matter from most of his Indian literary forbears with the exception of G. V. Desani: namely, his insistence that English "as she is wrote and spoke in India" was a language all its own that deserved to be represented in the novel without apology or embarrassment. Unlike Bankim, who abandoned English altogether as a language of composition, Rushdie stuck with it. Rushdie's Indian readers reacted immediately to this aspect of *Midnight's Children*[39]: Rustom Bharucha promptly called Rushdie's language "*Angrezi*," exulting, "it is almost as if the Queen's English has been 'chutnified,' fried in sizzling ghee, and dipped in curry."[40] "Not only has Rushdie grasped the absurdities and contradictions of my post-Independence India, he has represented my world in a language totally unprecedented in the history of English literature," Bharucha concluded (236). Despite prolific Hindi terms such as *arré baap*, *yaar*, *futafut*, *ekdum*, *janum*, *chi-chi*, *crorepati*, or hybrid expressions such as writing-shiting, cho-chweet, and Indianisms such as "Eat, na, food is spoiling" or "Catrick Sahib, it would be so shaming if my mother found out," Subhadra Sen Gupta wrote in relief that "thankfully this book does not carry the compulsory glossary at the end. Rushdie has allowed Indian English the respect it deserves."[41] Reviewing the growth of the Indian novel a decade after Rushdie, the novelist Ranga Rao concluded: "The number of Indianisms in Rushdie confirms that this genre has entered the age of self-confidence. The early novelists [of the 1930s and 1940s] used Indianisms to reach their regional audiences; their successors of the '80s are accepted, Indianisms and all, everywhere in the world."[42]

I invoke some of these accolades to Rushdie's linguistic achievement to underscore the extent to which *Midnight's Children* liberated the Indian novel from the considerable anxiety and undue influence to which it had been subject following the Macauldian mandates from a century and a half earlier. Having said that, Rushdie's achievements are neither really as an insurgent nor as a fugitive. His is not quite the success of what Homi Bhabha in a different context would label sly civility, nor what Shashi Tharoor would praise as the ability to smuggle his writing "past the immigration inspectors of English literature."[43] On the contrary, Rushdie does not so much translate Indian languages and idioms into Queen's English as he occupies and commandeers the English language much the way its users in India have historically done. According to data in reports gathered by the census commissioner, the population of India using English today is equal at least to the total population of the United States and Britain.[44] When examined in the context of sheer numbers then, to write English as used and spoken by this substantial population of close to four hundred million people is perhaps considerably less striking an achievement than the recent critics I cite above have made it out to seem.

It is something of a paradox to realize that the Indianisms for which Rushdie was given credit have their own considerable history of transaction and exchange: despite years of learning Indian languages in Haileybury and Fort William, British civil servants nevertheless arrived in India only to be confounded by the *English* their subjects *and colleagues* were speaking. The extent to which Indianisms had seeped into and shaped the language during the colonial encounter was so vast that a best-selling dictionary was produced made up of the most indispensable of these "outlandish guests" into the English language. In 1886 Colonel Henry Yule and Dr. A. C. Burnell published *Hobson-Jobson: A Glossary of Colloquial Anglo-Indian Words and Phrases, and of Kindred Terms, Etymological, Historical, Geographic and Discursive*.[45] Claiming that the dictionary compiled "the words . . . that have washed the shores of India during twenty centuries and more" (xvii) from Arab, Turkish, Persian, Portuguese, Burmese, and English visitors, *Hobson-Jobson* is a peculiar and peculiarly motivated lexicon that "standardized" and *legitimated* a bastard, hybrid, colloquial English that claimed its legacy from twenty centuries of accretion into a distinct form as she is wrote and spoke in the Subcontinent.

Words such as *bungalow* and *cummerbund*, *thug* and *toddy* have become well anglicized, but others such as *dacoit*, *curry*, *verandah*, and *palanquin* still bear traces of the exotic East from where the dictionary makes clear they originate. If *Hobson-Jobson* is a testament to the accretions of Indian usage into the English language, it also testifies to an early and vigorous transaction between the languages and peoples of Britain with those of India. In a sense then, *Midnight's Children* updates the Indo-British transactions of the first twenty centuries with developments of the last twenty decades. Even when using the language of colonial masters, *Midnight's Children* often playfully alludes to its Indian influences and requires an Anglo-Indian dictionary to be fully understood by those who brought the language to India in the first place. And if the dictionary conveyed the language as she is spoke in

India, then Rushdie's novel insists in conveying it in a form as she is wrote there as well. In the end, the combination of formal and stylistic qualities that characterizes *Midnight's Children* (of which language is just one aspect) together inverts and refashions both the order of "English" literature *and* the novel as a form. Let me explain how this occurs, with a minor digression through Europe.

Toward the end of his life in what was one of his final notes on world literature, Goethe wrote: "All nations, thrown together at random by terrible wars, then reverting to their status as individual nations, could not help realizing that they had been subject to foreign influences, had absorbed them and occasionally become aware of intellectual needs previously unknown."[46] If world literature is what happens when "intellectual needs" and "foreign influences" are realized, a pressing and intervening step remains how, in fact, to represent this new world order. It must be done not just by crafting a new language but also by creating a new logic, an immense project under any circumstances, but an especially acute one as well. When it happened eventually, it took place on the level of narrative, touching all forms of knowing, telling, and ordering by remaking them afresh.

There is a crucial moment in *Ulysses*, one of the great modernist disruptions of the twentieth century, when Joyce, who has waited till the end of the novel's long day, begins to render its complex narrative accounts, a classic nineteenth-century device perfected by Trollope, respected by Flaubert, and scrupulously followed—however parodically—even by Joyce. It takes place in the "Ithaca" chapter: Bloom and Stephen are in Number Seven Eccles Street, and an omniscient narrator goes over, in catechism, the day's events, explaining them, filling in gaps, and generally renarrating "what happened" in the novel. Looking at his scattered library reflected in a mirror, Bloom affirms, "The necessity of order, a place for everything and everything in its place."[47] The chapter putatively settles *Ulysses*'s balance sheet: everything is put in its place, and a tally is literally and symbolically rendered, starting with the events of Bloom's life and ending with a calculation of his budget for the day that reassuringly adds up in two columns to £2.19.3. Debits equal credits; "[Bloom] rests. He has travelled"; and the section ends in a dot (737). As a whole, this chapter renders narrative order to the text. It affirms an account comprehensively settled as it could only be in a world ordered around double-entry book-keeping and single-term accounting. Everything, even banality, comes together at the end of *Ulysses*.

Midnight's Children and other modernist novels from the periphery changed this easy accounting practice forever. Once daily, double-entry narrative bookkeeping, calculated by simplifying exchanges of cultural debt and credit to "equal" each other in two columns is no longer possible, and these novels proceed with a far more complex accounting, computing balance sheets obsessively—often leaving them unreconciled—compounding interest with painstaking frequency, narratively reproducing a world of complex hedge transactions and futures trading rather than the simple exchange of debit and credit circa Dublin 1904. Narrative in *Midnight's Children* moves in the manner capital does, reflecting its multinational circulation and inflected by the complexity and multiplicity of its real and symbolic transactions. It takes a part of its compositional cue from capital, which remains the singular example of the cosmopolitan spirit. *Midnight's Children* opens with self-conscious rewritings, announcements of coming attractions, extensive foreshadowing, belabored gestures at making connections (at a synchronicity that evades it), and within a few pages, Saleem gives up, lamenting, "I can already see the repetitions beginning" (7).

Accounting makes sense of expenses; the massive summaries, plot condensations, and prefigurations in *Midnight's Children* are a way of making sense of its world, but the complexity of this world requires an entirely new kind of narrative accounting than before: it can no longer be contained easily even by the Joycean catechism that partly spoofs narrative closure in *Ulysses*. The outcome is the proleptic, sense-making, circular narrativizing that characterizes not just Rushdie but also other modernist novelists from the periphery, including García Márquez and the early Carlos Fuentes. Therefore, while the formal origins of *Midnight's Children* lie in India (much the way that García Márquez's lie in Colombia or Fuentes's in Mexico), its narrative innovations participate in a wider, transnational conversation that recalls Goethe's poignant call in 1827: "National literature is no longer of importance; it is the time for world literature, and all must aid in bringing it about" (224). In this regard, the modernism of *Midnight's Children* does not so much "reenchant" the West as Franco Moretti has suggested, as it reconfigures Western forms of telling into a far wider critique of modernity than is included in its narrative space of sixty-six years.[48]

Saleem's insistence on reordering twentieth-century Indian history to fit his family's biography and his own fantasies of grandeur recalls another attempt at ordering lived experience that is perhaps the originary impulse of all narrative. *Midnight's Children* brings to mind Freud's theory of the family romance that identifies a moment occurring in late childhood when all children begin to author a narrative that liberates them from their parents. In this childhood fiction, the child replaces less than perfect everyday parents with better fantasy parents who *may* be of higher birth and social standing, or may not: the key is that they are *better* (more loving and more responsive) in the child's eyes. In other words, the child rescripts his everyday life into a narrative more amenable to his wishes and so fulfills his psychic desires for love, stability, and authority through the help of a fantasy in which he not simply rewrites his parents, but—inasmuch as the parents constitute his past and all that comes before him—he symbolically revises and rewrites his entire history as well. The healthy child, Freud claims, could dismiss this childhood romance by adulthood; in the neurotic, however, it would persist through numerous layers of repression and would come to mark not liberation from his parents but a form of subjection to them and to his past.

This relatively straightforward account of Freud's notes on the family romance[49] marks perhaps one of the most theoretically provocative speculations on the nature and origins of fiction. The biographical fantasy that constitutes the family romance is also aligned with the sense-making function inherent in *all* forms of narrative. To the extent that the child reconfigures his lived experience into a more amenable fantasy, the family romance links forms of knowing (from "narrative," *narrare* [Latin], to know) and telling to psychic needs, desires, and wish-fulfilments. As such, the family romance stands as a marked challenge to objective reality, to history, and even maybe to the "facts" that Saleem invokes when he insists: "sometimes legends make reality, and become more useful than the facts" (48). The powerful narrative impulse driven by the willful child's desire to power his destiny pulverizes the objective world into another order. The authority and charge of the stories that the child fabricates into the family romance arise in part from their complete necessity: "the whole progress of society rests upon the opposition between successive generations," wrote Freud (237), and the family romance forms an absolutely crucial juncture in the child's separation from his parents.

From this perspective, in impulse and in affect the family romance is a liberation narrative (a particular liberation narrative of the weak, one might add) that resolves the crises of human development. Furthermore, it is a form of sense-making and narrating that bears a particular relevance to the colonial context. While critics such as Françoise Vergès have applied the family romance to reading colonial history, their focus has been placed quite differently than mine. Vergès posits the family romance as a fiction deployed by the colonizer to control and curtail its dependencies into ideological and political submission.[50] I, on the other hand, see the family romance as a narrative very much authored by the colonized themselves against the colonial state and its cultural and ideological apparatus through which the colonized seek their own destiny and autonomy. For me, the family romance that the colonized imagines is both a critique and a replacement of an inadequate and oppressive world that the colonized substitutes with a world more conducive to his needs. It is in this regard that the family romance gathers its psychic and historical power as a liberation narrative. It is a narrative that defines and separates the past from the present; indeed, one might conclude that it is a narrative that at some point and in some form is crucially required to enable the very possibility of a present.

Moreover, along with functioning as a liberation narrative, the family romance also attests to individual agency: even though the narrative it produces to replace "reality" remains a fiction after all, the family romance is a celebration of the subject's ability to narrate himself to freedom if not to procure it fully. Rather than a narrative that dupes the weak (the child, the colonized) as Vergès claims, I therefore see the family romance as something the weak develop in order to flee their subjection in symbolic if not real ways. I see the family romance in some of the same terms that Lynn Hunt does in her use of it to understand the French Revolution: as a series of "creative efforts to reimagine the political world," rather than a set of pathological and pathologizing impulses of dominance and aggression.[51] Indeed, one of the spaces in which these creative efforts were imagined and organized in India remains the novel, especially in English, which bears some of the most visible traces not just of a dominant cultural and ideological regime that it sought to challenge. The Indian novel in English also exposes a complex set of attitudes and inclinations that help explain its particular status in Indian social life.

An important aspect of modern Indian literature in which the novel has played an increasingly key role is the extent to which it has addressed issues surrounding modernity. Philosophy generally, and social theory more precisely, embraced the task in the post-Enlightenment West. In India, however, where it eschewed modernity altogether as being tainted by colonialism, philosophy abdicated this function completely. Perhaps as a result of the earlier disengagement, political and social philosophers on India have recently increasingly turned to literature for evidence in constructing broader theories of modernity, particularly around issues such as citizenship, subjectivity, secular identity, community, and even nationalism. With the expansion and increased involvement of its reading public from the mid-nineteenth century on, the novel participated unreservedly in social and political debates of the period, shaping and collaborating, complicating and developing issues much in the manner that Enlightenment philosophy had done in eighteenth-century Europe. It is to this cultural world that *Midnight's Children* addressed itself with its relentless critique of the modern nation state on a number of registers, from philosophical, political, historical, to satirical, parodic, and mocking.

Not surprisingly, *Midnight's Children* inaugurated what seemed like an endless stream of "nationsroman" in the 1980s—novels of the nation, including I. Allan Sealy's Parsi version, *The Trotter-Nama*, Ghosh's *The Shadow Lines* (1988), Tharoor's *The Great Indian Novel*. Paradoxically, however, the most striking feature of this wave of "nationsroman" is exactly how *un*nationalistic they are. Unlike Bankim's unmistakable albeit contradictory nationalism or Tagore's more probing version of almost a century earlier, the English novelists of the 1980s seem more elegiac over than celebratory of the nation. These are national novels, yes; but hardly national*ist* ones. Each in its own way and together collectively these works have remade the English novel into a particularly Indian form, and yet it is almost as if the nation had to totter before the genre could take off.

If the novel was a form whose ascendance was twinned to the consolidation of the nation-state in Europe, the story is subtly different in India. In the early years of the twentieth century the novel's rise in Indian letters could be understood by its immense explanatory capacities. It was seen as the form most capable of consolidating anticolonial sentiment, of resisting orthodoxy, and of promoting social change. It is fair to expect that the novel might also have been the literary form best equipped for nationalism, but this we see was not to be. The novel in India seemed better equipped for liberation than for nationalism, and the boom in novelistic output that has subsequently occurred in the 1980s has taken place at a time when the future of the Indian nation-state is being questioned; when Rushdie's enigmatic ending in *Midnight's Children* of a "broken creature spilling pieces of itself into the street" (552) is echoed in communal unrest and increasing separatist violence. If, in their obsession with the nation-state, these novels of the 1980s formulate or expose what Timothy Brennan has called a collective "myth of the nation," then theirs is a curious obsession: to mythologize the nation not at its moment of birth when it was the glorious victor of a liberation struggle, but in its unglamorous middle age, riddled by the maladies of modernity and despair that the novels proceed to catalogue in painstaking detail.

What fictions and what fantasies do these novels then assuage? On any interpretive level, the content of the national novels inaugurated and exemplified by *Midnight's Children* recedes far from the idealizing nature of the family romance, or even the traditional romance with what Gillian Beer has identified as the impulse to "remake the world in the image of desire."[52] By contrast, the function of these fictions tends to be less wish-fulfilment than exorcism, less the projection of an ideal world than a lament to a collapsing one. Even if *Midnight's Children* is a liberation narrative, it is not fully clear immediately from what it seeks this freedom, since the depiction of its worlds is arguably so relentlessly bleak and full of dread.

No, the family romance is not quite so straightforward here. In seizing the authority to tell their own versions of history, sociology, politics, *Midnight* and its children recall the child's earlier urge to master his destiny by authoring his own fantasy. As such, I would argue that the *fact* of their enunciation is initially the liberation narrative, rather than the content of the narrative itself. It is *that* these novels exist that marks their liberation and autonomy from "objective" and "official" reality much as it marks their autonomy from the stifling anglicist priorities of a century and a half ago. Having said this, the content matters too. The instability in these novels' generic boundaries (flirting with epic, history, journalism) outlines alternative, deeply personal, indeed prescriptive accounts of Indian history (all six hundred and thirty million versions, according to *Midnight's Children*) that reconfigure and represent an entire and entirely new calculus of modernity. Rushdie's play with faulty memory and historical "facts" (he gets all sorts of dates wrong, such as the date of Gandhi's assassination); Amitav Ghosh's insistence on relying almost entirely on different characters' personal memories to recall a riot in Dhaka in *The Shadow Lines* (1988); I. Allan Sealy's dismissive, "People want to hear stories so you make them up" (572)—all these ways of ordering the past render a profound dislocation to the discourse of historiography itself, defamiliarizing it and its authority upon the referential illusion. In these versions of India's history, there is no referential illusion, no authorizing center, no grand narrative. These are just "legends that make reality" and worlds that have to be swallowed. As such, these novels may be the first works that in Dipesh Chakrabarty's keen phrase provincialize Europe by provincializng its forms of knowledge and narration.[53]

This then for me is the relevance of the family romance to Indian literary modernism: individually and as a corpus, these novels are fantasies in a very formal sense, celebrating first the fact *that* they can create. And when we turn to *what* they articulate, their account of the nation is a sound critique of the Enlightenment myth of a unified nation whose citizens inhabit a single homogenous plane by remembering and forgetting the same things (paraphrasing Renan). In contrast, Indian modernist novels celebrate the nonsynchronism of postcolonial India as a space from which alternatives might emerge in a language that is fully liberated from an enervating British culture and its ensuing expectations. Observing this phenomenon repeat itself around the former empire, Rushdie triumphed in an essay in the *London Times*: "The instrument of subservience became a weapon of liberation."[54]

What I have earlier called the elegiac mood of these novels can now be explained as the mood befitting the demise of one political and narrative order, even as these novels struggle to give voice to the possibility of an alternative one.

NOTES

1. THE POETICAL ECONOMY OF CONSUMPTION

1. Q. D. Leavis, *Fiction and the Reading Public*, p. 4.

2. Gauri Viswanathan, *Masks of Conquest*. For a vigorous critique of her position, see Harish Trivedi, "Reading English, Writing Hindi," pp. 176–179.

3. Harish Trivedi, *Colonial Transactions*. Lata Mani's brilliant work on *sati* illuminates another dimension of the transaction model when she shows how Indian priestly informants seized the power to interpret Hindu law for Governor General William Bentinck and provided a version of it that did not simply fabricate "tradition" in colonial India but also consolidated their own position within the hierarchy of native elites in the colonial state. See Mani, "Contentious Traditions," pp. 88–126.

4. See for example: Partha Chatterjee, *Nationalist Thought*; Ranajit Guha, *Dominance without Hegemony*; Ashis Nandy, *Intimate Enemy*; Nicholas J. Thomas, *Colonialism's Culture*; Frederick Cooper and Ann Laura Stoler, eds., *Tensions of Empire*; Nicholas B. Dirks, ed., *Colonialism and Culture*.

5. John L. Comaroff and Jean Comaroff, *Of Revelation and Revolution*, vol. 2, p. 219.

6. See Nandy, *Intimate Enemy*, especially pp. 29–48 for a fuller discussion of this theme.

7. John M. MacKenzie, *Propaganda and Empire*, p. 2, passim.

8. The most vivid example of this remains Edward W. Said, *Orientalism*. See also: Patrick Brantlinger, *Rule of Darkness*; Martin Green, *Dreams of Adventure*; Abdul R. JanMohamed, *Manichean Aesthetics*; Anne McClintock, *Imperial*

Leather; Benita Parry, *Delusions and Discoveries*; Suvendrini Perera, *Reaches of Empire*.

9. The Comaroffs' *Of Revelation and Revolution* is scattered with literary references; more than half of Nandy's monograph takes on literary texts to substantiate his claims; and MacKenzie has a chapter specifically on juvenile literature in his book.

10. Said spent almost half of *Culture and Imperialism* (a work published fifteen years later that he calls "not just a sequel to *Orientalism*") on documenting and theorizing the "historical experience of resistance against empire" in readings of literary figures including Césaire, Yeats, Fanon, Tagore, Achebe, Ngugi, and Rushdie.

11. The story of soap's consumption in colonial Africa is thoughtfully accounted for in the work of the anthropologist Timothy Burke, *Lifebuoy Men*.

12. Mary Layoun, *Travels of a Genre*, p. xii.

13. Robert Darnton, *Business of the Enlightenment*; Darnton, *Forbidden Best-Sellers*; see also Roger Chartier's more qualitative account of similar intellectual terrain in Chartier, *Cultural Origins*, pp. 67–91.

14. For examples specific to the history of the book, see: Fernand Braudel, *Structures of Everyday Life*; Roger Chartier, "Intellectual History"; Chartier, *Cultural Uses of Print*; Chartier, *Culture of Print*; Lucien Febvre and Henri-Jean Martin, *Coming of the Book*; Henri-Jean Martin, *Livre*.

15. Edward W. Said, *Culture and Imperialism*, p. xiii.

16. A few pages earlier, Said states his case about the novel and imperialism more bluntly: "Without empire, I would go so far as saying, there is no European novel as we know it, and indeed if we study the impulses giving rise to it, we shall see the far from accidental convergence between the patterns of narrative authority constitutive of the novel on the one hand, and on the other, a complex ideological configuration underlying the tendency to imperialism." See *Culture and Imperialism*, pp. 69–70.

17. On the regulatory function of the novel, see Franco Moretti, *Way of the World*; D. A. Miller, *Novel and the Police*; David Lloyd, *Anomalous States*.

18. T. W. Clark, "Introduction," *Novel in India*, p. 11.

19. Balgopal Varma, "Some Thoughts on English Fiction," p. 6.

20. Meenakshi Mukherjee, *Realism and Reality*, p. 6; also pp. 3–18, passim.

21. Chapter 2 provides details on libraries and users; for details on newspaper advertisements, see my preliminary findings in Priya Joshi, "Culture and Consumption," pp. 196–220.

22. For a discussion of the transactions between India and Britain along the consolidation of religion in the mid- and late-nineteenth century, see Vasudha Dalmia, *Nationalization of Hindu Traditions*. For useful documentation on the manner in which English educational priorities were manipulated by Hindu scholars during the same period, see Dalmia's, "Sanskrit Scholars," pp. 321–337.

23. For a useful discussion of the British empire and print, see the excellent

chapter, "Imperialism and Textuality," in Elleke Boehmer, *Colonial and Post-colonial Literature*, pp. 12–59.

24. Benedict Anderson, *Imagined Communities*, p. 37.

25. The Sahitya Akademi, with an army of distinguished specialists, has begun this task in their multivolume, *A History of Indian Literature*, of which two excellent volumes have appeared under the formidable editorship of Sisir Kumar Das. A multivolume German series also entitled *A History of Indian Literature* on the development of literature in select Indian languages has also appeared under the editorship of Jan Gonda with each volume authored by an expert in the language. See for example, Dusan Zbavitel, *Bengali Literature* and Ronald Stuart McGregor, *Hindi Literature*.

26. James Joyce, *Portrait*, p. 205.

27. "The Ministry of Fear," in Seamus Heaney, *North*, p. 59.

28. Trivedi's remarks refer to Hindi writers and thinkers such as Bharatendu Harischandra and others who followed him. Trivedi is careful to distinguish their unease with English in the late-nineteenth century from the "exuberant capitulation to things English expressed in an earlier period by writers in some other linguistic areas, as for example in Bengal by Michael Madhusudhan Dutta, or by Ishwarchandra Vidyasagar" (186). It is wise, therefore, to note that the regional responses to anglicization sometimes varied quite substantially at different periods, as did individual responses across time.

29. Upamanyu Chatterjee, *English, August*, p. 1, emphasis in original.

30. Karl Marx, "Introduction to a Critique of Political Economy," pp. 124–152.

31. Somewhat ironically, in a dialectical move, Marx anticipates the deficiencies in his own argument along much the same lines as I locate them here in sentences such as: "Consumption produces production in two ways. Because a product becomes a real product only through consumption. . . . Because consumption creates the need for *new* production" (131–132). Significantly, however, despite sentences such as these, he never quite gives up on the centrality of production to economic history as his numerous examples underscore insisting at the end that "Consumption without an object is not consumption, in this respect therefore, production creates, produces, consumption" (132). For a critique of this aspect of Marx's emphasis on production over consumption, see Walter Benjamin, "The Work of Art in the Age of Mechanical Reproduction," in his *Illuminations*, pp. 217–252.

32. Michel de Certeau, *Practice of Everyday Life*, p. 34.

33. There is a useful literature critiquing Marx's position on consumption. Baudrillard, for instance, memorably remarked, "Marx made a radical critique of political economy, but still in the form of political economy." See his *Mirror of Production*, p. 50. See also Arjun Appadurai, "Introduction: Commodities & the Politics of Value," in Appadurai, ed., *Social Life*; Daniel Miller, *Material Culture and Mass Consumption*.

34. De Certeau fully intended his description of consumption to resonate

with Claude Levi-Strauss's concept of bricolage. He uses the same verb to express the ways in which users make (*bricolent*) transformations to the system as they adapt it to their interests (see pp. 174–176). On a methodological note, he underscores why tactics such as bricolage only became apparent to Western ethnographers when studying anterior or exterior cultures: "Our 'tactics' seem to be analyzable only indirectly, through another society: the France of the Ancien Régime or the nineteenth century, in the case of Foucault; Kabylia or Béarn, in that of Bourdieu; ancient Greece, in that of Vernant and Détienne, etc. *They return to us from afar, as though a different space were required in which to make visible and elucidate the tactics marginalized by the Western form of rationality*. Other regions give us back what our culture has excluded from its discourse" (50; emphasis added). For further evidence of indigenous responses to Spanish colonization, de Certeau cites J-E Monast, *On les croyait Chrétiens: Les Aymaras* (Paris: Cerf, 1969); and his own "La Longue marche indienne," in *Le Réveil indien en Amérique Latine*, ed. Yves Materne and DIAL (Paris: Cerf, 1976), pp. 119–135.

35. See Daniel Miller, *Material Culture*, pp. 176ff.

36. See Thorstein Veblen, *Theory of the Leisure Class*; Pierre Bourdieu, *Distinction*.

37. Homi Bhabha, "Of Mimicry and Man," in *Location*, pp. 85–92.

38. See his "Minute on Indian Education" (1835), p. 241.

39. Homi Bhabha, "Signs Taken for Wonders," in *Location*, where see especially pp. 117ff.

40. Vicente Rafael, *Contracting Colonialism*.

41. Put another way, opposition may be intransigent, admirably so, but it is never intransitive: grammatically and politically, opposition (as verb or action) *always* requires a direct object, one who receives its actions and to which it remains tied, often for very long stretches of time. Production anew, or another production, under these circumstances is difficult, for oppositions all too often (re)produce phantoms of what they oppose.

42. In addition to Q. D. Leavis, see also: Ian Watt, *Rise of the Novel*; John J. Richetti, *Popular Fiction Before Richardson*; Michael McKeon, *Origins of the English Novel*; Nancy Armstrong, *Desire and Domestic Fiction*; Nancy Armstrong and Leonard Tennenhouse, *American Origins of the English Novel*; Lennard Davis, *Factual Fictions*; Jane Spencer, *Rise of the Woman Novelist*.

43. This is largely true only for the novel from England. With the novel from Scotland or Ireland, things are quite different, and questions of the kind I raise with the English-language novel in India persist there as well. For instance, writing about the forms the Anglo-Irish novel has *not* taken, Terry Eagleton questions: "How is one to produce realist narratives from a history which is itself so crisis-racked, hyperbolic, improbable? How can even the most spectacular of tales not find itself trumped by the lurid theatricality of the actual events it records, which offer to beggar imagination in their epic violence, romantic bravado, or tragic despondency?" (181). Earlier, explaining

Joyce, Wilde, and George Moore, Eagleton argues: "In discarding or transgressing realist conventions, these distinctly non-popular writers were in a curious way aligned with the great bulk of Irish literature, which belongs to that species of magic realism known as folklore" (154). See Eagleton, *Heathcliff and the Great Hunger*; see also Penny Fielding, *Writing and Orality*.

44. Catherine Gallagher, *Nobody's Story*.

45. Gilles Deleuze, and Félix Guattari, *Kafka*. Deleuze and Guattari's argument on minority literature requires some qualification before being appropriate to the Indian context. As in the case of Kafka, the minority status of the Indian novelists in part 2 of *In Another Country* refers both to a political and a cultural context. The "majority" that these writers address, however is a shifting one: on the one hand, it refers to the world of anglophone novelistic production originating with the colonial state and continuing in postcolonial writing (where their contributions have been notably visible in the last decade or so). On the other hand, their "majority" also includes the particular character of Indian nationalism today where these novelists, by virtue of religion and gender, are "minor" in most ways. There remain, of course, those who would contest this characterization and argue that writing in English, however, is not writing in the language of an Indian majority. To them, one would have to reply that such a narrow application of Deleuze and Guattari's argument misses their central point on minority writing altogether.

46. Salman Rushdie, *Ground Beneath her Feet*, p. 43.

2. THE CIRCULATION OF FICTION IN
INDIAN LIBRARIES, CA. 1835–1901

1. I realize a claim that Indians were *never* represented reading can be something of a generalization, but it seems a judicious one to make. There is rare evidence to the contrary, and when it appears it is far more damning of the British for their depiction of Indian reading practices than no representation would have been. Consider Dr. Veraswami in chapter 3 of Orwell's *Burmese Days* (1934): an ardent Anglophile babu consuming classics from his "rather unappetising little library" of the "Emerson-Carlyle-Stevenson type" without really getting them, Veraswami comes across as a *Punch* cartoon figure—one that fortifies the Englishman's fantasy of Indians as indifferent mimic men rather than even remotely conceiving of them as active consumers with critical and creative reading habits. See *Burmese Days*, p. 37.

2. Thakorelal M. Desai, "Study of Fiction," p. 333.

3. Anand's description of this meeting comes from the chapter, "Tea and Empathy from Virginia Woolf," in his *Conversations in Bloomsbury*, p. 105. Later in the reminiscence, he makes clear that he has been playing with Virginia: "I felt that if I was honest about the bad taste of my youth, Virginia Woolf might also acknowledge some blunders she had committed. Actually, I wanted to dethrone her from the perch of the goddess to the common clay in

which her husband had revealed himself [to me] under the chestnut tree in Tavistock Square" (105).

4. "The novel," wrote Anand, "is for me, the creative weapon for attaining humanness—it is the weapon of humanism." See his *Roots and Flowers*, p. 36.

5. Elleke Boehmer, *Colonial and Postcolonial Literature*, pp. 12–13.

6. Graham Shaw, *South Asia Bibliography*, p. 5. Shaw details the not uninteresting history of print in India from its inception in 1556 to 1800, a period during which "printing was almost exclusively the preserve of Europeans from missionary presses to an increase in government printing then commercial and finally journalistic publications" (3). See also Katharine Smith Diehl, *Early Indian Imprints*, p. 63; and Lucien Febvre and Henri-Jean Martin, *Coming of the Book*, pp. 212–213.

7. Shaw, *South Asia*, p. 7.

8. Benedict Anderson, *Imagined Communities*, especially the chapter, "Cultural Roots," pp. 9–36. Salman Rushdie's *Midnight's Children* provides a powerful amplification in fiction of the persistence of oral culture in India: in many ways, *Midnight's Children* is a work about competing discursive registers—oral and written—in which myth, novel, epic, and history jostle for recognition. See chapter 7 for a fuller discussion of these themes.

9. The sharp decline of book imports shown in figure 2.1, beginning in 1866, is something of a conundrum: the passage of Act XXV of 1867 (the Indian Press and Registration of Books Act that mandated the registration of all books and periodicals with a central authority) would suggest an *increase*—or stabilization—of book imports from Britain at a time when publishing activity in India was being scrutinized, yet what we see in fact is a decline in imports that has yet to be fully explained. Trade figures were assembled from *The Annual Statement of the Trade and Navigation of British India* (1850–1901). The figures for trade in "Books and Printed Matter including Stationary, Maps and Charts" are compiled under the heading "Imports." I have used the word "exports" to emphasize both the source of this print and the fact that it was *sent in* from overseas.

10. Thomas Babington Macaulay, "Minute on Indian Education," see p. 241.

11. Charles Grant, *Observation*, p. 151, emphasis added.

12. Given the attention with which some aspects of print were scrutinized by colonial authorities, it is striking that no records have yet been found that detail the content of book imports into India, neither among records at the India Office, nor in the customs records at the Official Publications Library, London.

13. D. Natarajan, ed., *Extracts from the All India Census Reports*, p. 18, table D. Natarajan also points out that although the 1881 census is considered the first reliable census for India, its literacy figures for males and females are extremely problematic because of the manner in which "literacy" was defined, and he hazards, as do most historians on the subject, that a more reliable figure for male literacy in 1881 is 6.6 percent, and for women 0.3 percent, rather

than the 9.05 percent and 0.39 percent literacy that the census records for males and females, respectively (i). Using these corrections, total literacy in India for 1881 was 3.5 percent.

14. Rev. James Long, "Report," p. ix.

15. Though their work illuminates women's participation in print at a much later stage, see Malavika Karlekar, *Voices from Within*; Vir Bharat Talwar, "Feminist Consciousness." See also Partha Chatterjee's accounts of selective women's reading and writing practices in *Nation and its Fragments*.

16. Janice A. Radway, *Reading the Romance*.

17. Cathy N. Davidson, *Revolution and the Word*.

18. Carlo Ginzburg, *Cheese and the Worms*.

19. Michael Denning, *Mechanic Accents*, especially pp. 27–46.

20. Fredric Jameson, *Political Unconscious*, p. 106, emphasis added.

21. India Office Library, Board's Collections no. 72538, F/4/1768 (1838–39), p. 20.

22. *Report of the Maju Public Library* (1913).

23. India Office Library, Board's Collections no. 76498, F/4/1838 (1839–40), n. p.

24. *Annual Report on the Administration of the Madras Presidency* (1887–88 and 1899–1900), pp. clx–clxiv and pp. clxxviii–clxxxix, respectively; also *Thacker's India Directory*. Indian public libraries, as these sources document, existed within a constellation of other social institutions variously called "Literary Societies" or "Reading Rooms." It ought to be noted, however, that both these terms are partly misnomers: "Literary Societies" often had less directly to do with literature or with maintaining print collections than with the "political improvement of the people of India," as the Triplicane Literary Society indicated in its mission statement; and "Reading Room" often included the corollary activities, "to deliver lectures; to afford amusements as billiards, &c.," as the Vizagapatnam Hindu Reading Room maintained in its charter statement. In this regard, many of these reading rooms and societies were more like the Mechanics' Institutes that proliferated (then failed) in Britain in the 1830s and 1840s, motivated by good intentions for civic improvement but indifferent to local needs. Like the Mechanics' Institutes, these Indian institutions too were often what R. K. Webb calls "clubs to local vanity" and places of essay recitals, rather than public libraries of the kind mentioned in this section. For more on the Mechanics' Institutes, see R. K. Webb, *British Working-Class Reader*, p. 64; see also Richard D. Altick, *English Common Reader*, pp. 188–212.

25. In a recent essay, Robert Darnton, a noted historian of French publishing in the eighteenth century, claims quite the opposite. He calls the army of scribes who maintained the colonial print archive in India "literary policemen," a characterization that few book historians of India to my knowledge would confirm because while there is no doubt that the presence of print and print establishments was extensively documented, it is not clear that this

observation was a form of censorship (as the robust content of the print archive would establish). However, what Darnton does show with great nuance is the manner in which *certain* forms of print were placed under surveillance. In a gripping analysis of early-twentieth-century trials of authors accused of "disaffection," Darnton shows how the colonial courtroom essentially became "a hermeneutic battlefield, where each side acted out its interpretation of the other and imperialism appeared . . . as a contest for symbolic dominance through textual exegesis" (p. 156). What is remarkable is that the trials were never for novels; all the cases Darnton documents were prosecutions for literary forms that had a pronounced oral component to them (such as poetry or drama). See his "Literary Surveillance in the British Raj."

26. Rev. James Long, "Report," pp. i, ii; all emphases in original.

27. C. A. Bayly, *Empire and Information*; see especially pp. 340–343 in which Bayly describes some of the "severe but flexible controls" the colonial government introduced toward newspapers (341). Despite the surveillance that Bayly indicates increased after the Mutiny, he is right to insist on the highly conflictual attitudes the government had toward this task as it remained reluctant to restrict or close down an important source of information on native sentiments toward the Raj. Long's beliefs on the freedom of print were put to the test shortly after his "Report" was published. In 1861 he found himself tried in a highly publicized case for his promotion of a translation of *Nil Darpan*, a Bengali melodrama about the oppression of Indian peasants by British indigo planters. He repeated his views on press freedom during his defense and was condemned to a month's imprisonment and a fine of Rs. 1,000.

28. *Appendix to the Calcutta Gazette* (1883), n. p.

29. Bankim, however, as many biographers point out, never received a single promotion in his job as deputy magistrate for the colonial state. In the end, this seems a paltry and ineffectual form of censorship if it was one, since the dead-end job gave the novelist plenty of leisure to write and edit the Bengali journal *Bangadarsan*, which published a robust set of nationalist articles and stories in its pages with apparent unconcern. See also chapter 4. Some critics even go so far as to suggest that Bankim's stagnation on the bureaucratic ladder was the principal reason that he turned to writing. See Anil Seal, *Emergence of Indian Nationalism*, p. 118.

30. *Appendix to the Calcutta Gazette* (1884), n. p. This is one of at least ten different translations for Tod's *Rajasthan* since 1883, the year that the Bengal catalog started listing books by subject heading.

31. For more on the Indian press, see also Margarita Barns, *Indian Press*; Milton Israel, *Communications and Power*; S. Natarajan, *History of the Press in India*.

32. Paul Kaufman, "Some Reading Trends in Bristol, 1773–84," in *Libraries*, p. 28; see also Kaufman, *Borrowings from the Bristol Library*. Other scholars who have worked with borrowing patterns in single libraries include Mechtild Raabe, *Leser und Lektüre im 18. Jahrhundert*, 4 vols. (Munich: Saur, 1989) and Jan Fergus, "Eighteenth-Century Readers."

33. F. J. G. Robinson, and P. J. Wallis, *Book Subscription Lists*.

34. Darnton, *Forbidden Best-Sellers*, pp. 23–24.

35. Paul Kaufman, "The Community Library: A Chapter in English Social History," in his *Libraries*, p. 197.

36. See for example Simon Eliot, *Measure of Popularity*; Eliot, *Some Patterns and Trends in British Publishing*.

37. See for example John Sutherland, *Victorian Fiction*.

38. For the twentieth century, data seem more forthcoming. Q. D. Leavis has some sets for Britain that she uses in her *Fiction and the Reading Public*; for the United States see Bernard Berelson, *Library's Public*; Douglas Waples, Bernard Berelson, and Franklyn R. Bradshaw, *What Reading Does*.

39. These nineteenth-century trends, in which loans of fiction tower over everything else ("general literature"), were consistent with British public libraries of the same period, though they are in marked contrast with reading tastes visible in the eighteenth century. During that period, Paul Kaufman notes that history, antiquities, and geography maintained the lead among Bristol subscribers, followed by belles lettres, then theology, and that poetry dominated over fiction. Using Kaufman's data, John Brewer concludes, "the picture conveyed by these data is therefore highly conservative. Religion and theology dominate, poetry far exceeds any new literary forms of prose, classics lord it over the modern languages." See Brewer, *Pleasures of the Imagination*, p. 172; Kaufman, "Some Reading Trends," pp. 28–35.

40. From Sir John Kaye, *Life of Lord Metcalfe* (1854) as quoted in Barns, *Indian Press*, p. 222.

41. India Office Records, Board's Collections, no. 72538, F/4/1768, 1838–39, p. 20.

42. *All the Year Round*, 5 April 1862, p. 80 as cited by Krishna Dutta and Andrew Robinson, *Rabindranath Tagore*, pp. 25 and 382n.

43. *Report of the Calcutta Public Library for 1847*, p. 19.

44. For Britain, see Altick, *English Common Reader*, especially chapter 10; for the United States, see James D. Hart, *Popular Book*.

45. Kalpana DasGupta, "The National Library," p. 5.

46. *Report of the Bagbazar Reading Library for the 19th Year Ending on June 1902*.

47. For the preliminary findings from this research, see my "Culture and Consumption," especially pp. 210–211.

48. Jane Tompkins, "Sentimental Power," p. 23, emphasis in original.

49. Q. D. Leavis remarks on the shift between popular and canonical that occurred in the twentieth century and explains it thus: "When a Mrs. Haywood sat down to write a novel, she could produce admirable fiction because she was in touch with the best work of her age. . . . The bestsellers of the twentieth century do not change their courses because D. H. Lawrence, Virginia Woolf, or James Joyce has written; indeed they have probably never heard of these novelists." See Leavis, *Fiction*, pp. 131–132.

50. Altick, *English Common Reader*, pp. 381–390; Altick, "Nineteenth-Century English Best-Sellers: A Further List," pp. 197–206; Altick, "Nineteenth-Century English Best-Sellers: A Third List," 235–241.

51. In its translation of novels, the Bengal Vernacular Society was in marked contrast to the SDUK, which specifically excluded fiction from its publishing activities.

52. H. Pratt as cited in Rev. James Long, "Report."

53. Nilmani Mukherjee, "A Bengal Zamindar."

54. Prior to 1867, information on publishing from this source is erratic and depends upon compilations of earlier periods made in Bengal (where composite lists of all books published in the presidency between 1830 and 1867 appeared); and Bombay (where J. B. Piele compiled a list, though only from 1865 to 1867); or from other annual surveys made by the colonial authorities and recorded in the voluminous *Administration Reports* (beginning in 1850 and shelved under "V/10" at the Oriental and India Office Collection of the British Library). J. B. Piele, *Catalogue of the Native Publications of the Bombay Presidency*. See also *A Catalogue of Books Printed in the Bengal Presidency* (var. years); *A Catalogue of Books Printed in the Bombay Presidency* (var. years); *A Catalogue of Books Printed in the Madras Presidency, Fort St. George Gazette Supplement* (var. years).

55. J. F. Blumhardt, *Catalogue of Hindustani Printed Books*; Blumhardt, *Catalogue of Marathi and Gujarati Printed Books*; Blumhardt, *Catalogue of the Library of the India Office, Bengali, Oriya, and Assamese Books*; Blumhardt, *Catalogue of the Library of the India Office. Marathi and Gujarati Books*; Blumhardt, *Supplementary Catalogue of Marathi and Gujarati Books*; L. D. Barnett, *Catalogue of the Telugu Books*; Barnett, *Supplementary Catalogue of Tamil Books*; Barnett and G. U. Pope, *Catalogue of Tamil Books*.

56. Rabindranath Tagore, *My Reminiscences*, p. 89.

57. Balgopal Varma, "Some Thoughts on English Fiction and the Reading Public," p. 7.

58. Sisir Kumar Das, *History of Indian Literature*, vol. 8, p. 180.

59. Charles Grant, *Observation*, p. 151.

60. Reynolds founded or edited a total of eight serials, including the short-lived *Reynolds's Political Instructor* (which ran from November 1849 to May 1850). Since most of his novels first appeared serially in the penny press and complete editions are hard to find, it is especially difficult to compile an accurate and full bibliography of his writings. Montague Summers has what appears to be the most scrupulously assembled bibliography of Reynolds's novels in his *Gothic Bibliography*, pp. 146–159, though even he confesses this to be, "intricate and complicated to the last degree" (147). Donald Kausch has compiled a further checklist, correcting many spurious titles and works inaccurately ascribed to Reynolds, in "George W. M. Reynolds," pp. 319–326.

61. Anne Humpherys, "G. W. M. Reynolds: Popular Literature and Popular Politics," p. 3.

62. Louis James, *Fiction for the Woking Man*, p. 166.

63. Anon., "G. W. M. Reynolds, Obituary," p. 660.

64. Anon., "Reynolds and Penny Fiction," p. 56.

65. The first series of *Mysteries of London* has recently been usefully edited by Trefor Thomas. All citations are from this edition. See p. 4.

66. George W. M. Reynolds, *The Modern Literature of France*, vol. 1, p. 80.

67. See Summers, *Gothic Bibliography*, p. 150 and James, *Fiction*, p. 165.

68. W. M. Thackeray, "Charity and Humour," *Collected Works* (London: Smith Elder, 1896) vol. VII, p. 772 as cited in *TLS*, January 24, 1924, p. 56.

69. Louis James, "View from Brick Lane," p. 98; G. W. M. Reynolds, *Mysteries of London*, 2 vols. (1846).

70. Daniel S. Burt, "Victorian Gothic," p. 153. Anne Humpherys cites a seventeen-part series Reynolds wrote for *London Journal* entitled "Etiquette for the Millions" in which he counseled his readers on matters such as table manners, proper behavior in different social situations, proper dress, even handwriting. See her "G. W. M. Reynolds," p. 12.

71. Humpherys, "Generic Strands and Urban Twists," p. 64.

72. See Trefor Thomas on the power of Reynolds's woodcuts in his "Introduction," Thomas, ed., *The Mysteries of London*, p. xvi.

73. Anon., "Reynolds and Penny Fiction," p. 56.

74. Varma, "Some Thoughts on English Fiction and the Reading Public," p. 6.

75. *Appendix to the Calcutta Gazette for 1883*, n.p.

76. Ibid.

77. See for instance Margaret Dalziel, *Popular Fiction*; Humpherys, "G. W. M. Reynolds"; James, *Fiction*. Dalziel notes, "It is a pity that the undoubted righteousness of his cause, a cause taken up by people like Shaftesbury, should be obscured by Reynolds's artificial and declamatory style, so that it is hard to avoid suspicions about his sincerity" (42).

78. Humpherys, "Geometry of the Modern City," p. 72.

79. Peter Brooks, *Melodramatic Imagination*, pp. xii, 5.

80. Robert B. Heilman, *Tragedy and Melodrama*.

81. *Appendix to the Calcutta Gazette*, 1884.

82. In a useful reading of Reynolds's *The Seamstress*, Catherine Gallagher argues that "to object that once the seamstress is recognized as the daughter of the aristocracy she is no longer a representative worker is to overlook the peculiar logic of melodrama and its affinity with the peculiar logic of social paternalism. Melodramas typically strain away from the literal facts of their narratives toward some more universal significance . . . melodrama allows the social-paternalist metaphor to be literalized without being destroyed." See her *Industrial Reformation of English Fiction*, p. 133.

83. Umberto Eco, *Role of the Reader*, p. 140. Having said this, Eco seems to wish it both ways, for he goes on to cite Jean-Louis Bory's "excellent work," *Eugène Sue: Le roi du roman populaire* (Paris: Hachette, 1962), which "proved" the influence of *Les Mystères* on the events of 1848, "an irresistible saturnalia

celebrated by Sue's heroes, the labouring classes and the dangerous classes in the Paris of *Les Mystères*" (Eco 141).

84. Eric Bentley, *Life of the Drama*, p. 205. It is no coincidence that more than a century after Reynolds, Salman Rushdie used melodrama's powerful Manicheanism to develop a political allegory of modern India in *Midnight's Children* (1980), while popular Bombay films since Independence churn out hundreds of highly successful melodramas each year.

85. Priya Joshi, "Culture and Consumption," p. 213.

86. Thakorelal M. Desai, "Study of Fiction," p. 335.

87. As quoted in Rev. James Long, "Report," pp. lv–lvi; all emphases in the original.

88. Ian Duncan, "Scott, Hogg, Orality," pp. 56–74.

3. READERS WRITE BACK: THE MACMILLAN COLONIAL LIBRARY IN INDIA

1. Emma Roberts, *Scenes and Characteristics*, vol. 3, pp. 8–9.

2. John Kaye, "English Literature in India," p. 205.

3. A partial list of these libraries with dates where available would include Bentley's Imperial Library (1878–81), Cassell's Colonial Library, Kegan Paul's Indian and Colonial Library (1887–89), Sampson & Low's Favorite and Standard Novels for the Colonies, and Frederick Warne's Colonial Library, among many others. Sometimes, as in the case of Cassell, the library appears to have been a local cottage industry with new title sheets sewn on to editions for colonial sale; in this case, few records of sale or distribution appear to have been maintained in the home office—to the extent that even the firm's house history makes no mention of it. See Anon., *Story of the House of Cassell* and Simon Nowell-Smith, *House of Cassell*.

4. Charles Morgan, *House of Macmillan*, pp. 1–2.

5. Letter to G. O. Trevelyan, April 14, 1863, in George A. Macmillan, ed., *Letters of Alexander Macmillan*, p. 138.

6. Letter to Sir Roper Lethbridge, November 29,1873, in Macmillan, ed., *Letters*, p. 277.

7. Thomas Mark was a legendary and long-standing figure at the firm, and his notes on its history are invaluable in part because they provide insights and details into how a family firm conducted its most private business, details that are often entirely absent from the firm's correspondence archives. Since almost all the partners were family members, business decisions and matters of policy were frequently hammered out in conversation or at home, and it is difficult, for instance, to know with certainty some of the firm's thinking behind its India expansion. In this regard, Mark's unpublished notes become particularly useful. He spent his entire working life with the firm from 1913 to 1959, starting with a position in the foreign department but moving on to become secretary to the board before assuming a directorship. As Lovat Dickson notes in his

obituary of Mark: "This office [of the Secretary] . . . provided its occupant with drama-packed moments, and called on him for the exercise of great discretion, and to perform feats of memory which can only be described as phenomenal. For the Board in those days was only the family, and the discussions and arguments were of the forceful kind usually reserved for the intimate family circle" (see Dickson, "Thomas Mark: Obituary"). Having this rare insider's knowledge, Mark's notes on Macmillan and Company were written to assist Charles Morgan (a well-known author, but an outsider) in writing a history of the firm: Morgan found them so useful that many of Mark's insights found their way into his *House of Macmillan*. "I am greedy for all I can get," wrote Morgan enthusiastically in a signed, undated page in the Macmillan Archives. "Probably I have marked too much, but Mark's notes are so good that they tempt me to be greedy." Morgan Source Files, Macmillan Archives, British Library, box M75d.

8. Given the number of Macmillans in the firm, it has become common practice among those who work on it to refer to each brother, uncle, or son by his first name only. "Macmillan," on the other hand, refers to the firm. Due either to the schoolmaster's discipline or the family's Scottish prudence, Maurice combined the trip to India and Australia with his honeymoon.

9. Macmillan Archives, British Library, Add. Mss. 55421, vol. 2, p. 622. The collection includes letters in Maurice Macmillan's hand to the *Madras Mail*, *Bombay Gazette*, the *Englishman* (Calcutta), the *Times of India* (Bombay), and the *Statesman* (Calcutta).

10. Letter to the Editor, *Madras Mail*, March 19, 1886 (Macmillan Archives, British Library, Add. Mss. 55421, vol. 2, p. 865).

11. The word "either" appears to be underlined for emphasis (Craik's hand, among all the partners, is hardest to read in the Macmillan Letterbooks). Letter to Charlotte Yonge, January 4, 1886 (Macmillan Archives, British Library, Add. Mss. 55843, Private Letterbooks, p. 108).

12. Maurice Macmillan's 1884–85 trip included Australia as well as India, but the particular importance of the Indian market to the firm is undeniable from the records. The firm had three offices and half a dozen agencies in India, and only one in Australia (in Melbourne), and while Morgan's house history devotes a single paragraph to Australia, concluding with its "unbounded promise for the future" (166), the India section of the book spells out in detail over four pages the great importance the company placed on that market, both in education and for general books (see pp. 186–189). Maurice followed his exploratory trip to India with two more (in 1914 and 1920), while the Australasian market was delegated to George Brett, Jr., son of Macmillan's partner in the New York office.

13. Letter in Maurice Macmillan's hand (signed, "Macmillan and Co.") to the *Statesman*, Calcutta, March 19, 1886 (Macmillan Archives, British Library, Add. Mss. 55421, vol. 2, p. 867).

14. Letter to Thomas Hardy, May 31, 1886 (Macmillan Archives, British

Library, Add. Mss. 55422.357J, vol.1, p. 104, emphasis in original). Tauchnitz's series, on which Macmillan modeled theirs, consisted of cheap reprints of English novels for sale on the Continent, though there was no injunction against the sale of Tauchnitz editions in Britain. However, as John Sutherland reports, "only a surprisingly small number of Tauchnitz reprints seem to have seeped back into the British market, despite their cheapness and attractive format." See John Sutherland, *Stanford Companion to Victorian Fiction*, p. 619.

15. F. Marion Crawford Correspondence, Macmillan Archives, British Library, Add. Mss. 54935, letter dated January 8, 1886.

16. Macmillan Archives, Private Letterbooks, British Library, Add. Mss. 55843, p. 105.

17. Murray's intentions are made most clearly in a September 1843 prospectus on the Colonial and Home Library, which claims, "it is called for in consequence of the Acts which have recently passed the British Parliament for the protection of the rights of British authors and publishers, by the rigid and entire exclusion of foreign pirated editions." As reproduced in Simon Nowell-Smith, *International Copyright Law*, p. 29. See also Angus Fraser's excellent article, "John Murray's Colonial and Home Library," charting, among other matters, Murray's close ties with their politician-authors such as William Gladstone and Philip Henry Stanhope, the latter who ushered the 1842 copyright legislation through the lower house of Parliament.

18. "Murray's Colonial and Home Library," *Simmonds's Colonial Magazine and Miscellany* 1:1 (January 1844): 108–9; as cited in Fraser, "Colonial and Home Library," p. 359.

19. The views are those of the Montreal bookseller, William Grieg, as cited by Fraser, ibid., p. 370.

20. In 1861 Murray's series was "reissued" in cheap editions domestically, though as Richard Altick observes, "The unctuous trade-journal advertisement heralding this public spirited gesture is typical of those that sought to disguise publishers' efforts to liquidate an unlucky speculation as a contribution to the grand cause of cheap literature." See Altick, *English Common Reader*, p. 297n. Despite the series' demise (no further titles were added to it beyond the forty-nine that constituted it as of 1849), Graeme Johanson has shown that Murray's Library continued to circulate in remote stations in Australia in the form of traveling bookcases. See Johanson, "A Study of Colonial Editions in Australia." Edward Petherick, who ran a bookselling agency with offices in Australia in the 1890s, continued to hope for more from Murray. "When will Mr. Murray add to it? What a revival the Series would experience from the addition of Mr. Smiles's Industrial Biographies and the "Self Help" Series! Or Livingstone's Travels, Gordon Cumming's Lion-Hunter, Bates's Amazons, Layards' Nineveh, or the Travels of Du Chaillu, Vambery, Hübner, and Isabella Bird." Revealingly, Petherick's suggestions for new titles remain in travel and moral literature, Murray's own preferences in the 1840s, even though Petherick made a handsome fortune in Australia (which he soon lost)

purveying up-to-the-minute fiction of a kind Murray would never carry. See Edward Augustus Petherick, *Colonial Book Circular*, p. 3.

21. The taxonomy in virtually all categories, with the exception of fiction, is slippery: Murray sometimes included "biography, history, and historical tales" as a single category, and "voyages, travels and adventures" as another. In my own count above, I have separated biography from history and made a number of decisions such as placing *Lives of British Poets* under poetry, not biography. This shakes the figures out somewhat, but leaves the figures for fiction (four titles, or 8 percent of the list) absolutely unchanged. A different form of classification would render higher percentages for both travel and history than those I have calculated, lower for memoirs and biography, but it would leave the percentage of fiction as I record it in table 3.1, at 8 percent.

22. As quoted in Fraser, "Colonial and Home Library," p. 358.

23. Useful accounts of British reading habits during the nineteenth century can be found in Altick, *English Common Reader*; Margaret Dalziel, *Popular Fiction*; Louis James, *Fiction for the Working Man*; R. K. Webb, *British Working-Class Reader*; Jon Klancher, *Making of English Reading Audiences*; Martha Vicinus, *Industrial Muse*. See Dalziel's chapter "The Moral Issue," for how contemporary concerns aroused by forms of popular fiction were addressed in the late 1840s and 1850s (46–54).

24. Or, to put this aversion in perspective, the father-son duo cast what Angus Fraser calls "a jaundiced eye on both poetry and fiction, a disposition fully shared by his son [John Murray 3d]." See Fraser's, "Publishing House and its Readers," p. 10.

25. Fraser reports that "in the end, just under half the titles in the series would have some claim to newness . . . and almost three years passed before new material began to predominate over reprints" (359).

26. Colonial Library titles usually began with a print run of one thousand; subsequent printings depended upon sales and demand. Each of the print figures reported above records the *total* number of books printed by the firm over time. These figures were compiled by John Handford, archivist at Macmillan, and verified by me in the firm's Editions Books kept at Macmillan's archives in Basingstoke.

27. The following studies further attest to fiction's popularity in other colonies: Carole Gerson, *Purer Taste*; Wendy Griswold, "Writing on the Mud Wall"; Johanson, "Study of Colonial Editions in Australia." See also, Paul G. Bator, "Entrance of the Novel into Scottish Universities."

28. Frank Mumby, *House of Routledge*, p. 181.

29. Leslie Howsam, *Kegan Paul*, p. 125. In enumerating the difficulties in reconstructing the history of the series, Howsam concludes (as Mumby had in his earlier history of the firms that eventually came under Routledge's imprint): "In any case [Kegan Paul's] preference was clearly for publishing, in series format, serious original non-fiction works of high quality" (p. 126). In short, the fiction in the library was simply not where the firm's publishing heart lay.

30. The libraries I investigated include the Delhi Public Library, the Chaitanya Public Library (Calcutta), the Uttarpara Public Library (Uttarpara, West Bengal), and the J. N. Petit Library and the People's Free Reading Room and Library, both in Bombay.

31. Antonio Gramsci, *Cultural Writings*, p. 368. Gramsci used the phrase in the context of Jules Verne's popularity among early-twentieth-century Italian readers.

32. Another big seller from the 680 titles in the Colonial Library was Rolf Boldrewood (alias T. A. Browne), the Australian policeman turned novelist, whose *Robbery Under Arms* (1888) had fifty-two thousand copies printed, though he is almost entirely an Australian phenomenon, with single titles of his works appearing in only two of the fourteen Indian libraries studied (see table 2.2).

33. The other nonfiction work to be moderately "successful" was the first series of Matthew Arnold's *Essays in Criticism* (#40, 1886, of which seven thousand copies were printed).

34. As cited in Charles Morgan, *House of Macmillan*, p. 172.

35. Macmillan Archives, British Library, Add. Mss. 55328–819c, p. 893, letter dated May 10, 1887.

36. Gail Chester, "The Not so Gentle Reader," p. 17.

37. See Gaye Tuchman with Nina E. Fortin, *Edging Women Out*, where Tuchman and Fortin suggest that Morris was a "veritable curmudgeon," and "to put it kindly, ambivalent about women writers" (71). They further argue that the firm exercised a subtle form of discrimination against women writers, particularly as the century wore on and the gentleman writer gained in status and authority. For Macmillan's now well-known dismissal of Yeats, see the excellent essay by Warwick Gould, "'Playing at Treason,'" especially pp. 40–43 detailing Morris's review of four books of Yeats' poetry, which concludes with: "I should be sorry to think that work so unreal, unhuman, and insincere would be found to have any permanent value, nor do I believe that it will be found to have it, any more than Maeterlink's will be or Ibsen's, or, in another realm of art, Burne-Jones's or Rossetti's" (p. 42; also quoted in Morgan's *House of Macmillan*, p. 220). On William James's *Principles of Psychology*, which the firm eventually published to acclaim, Morris nonetheless demurred: "His power of exposition is *not* of the very highest. . . . There are queer little streaks of what I should call literary commonness. . . . I should incline toward the smaller of the two figures you mention." Macmillan Archives, British Library, Add. Mss. 55944, 1890–91, p. 1, emphasis in original.

38. Morris's readers reports are catalogued in the Macmillan Archives, interleaved with other readers' reports and copied by scribes for the firm in British Library, Add. Mss. 55939 to 55973; Morris's own notebooks with reviews in his hand and tallies of the number of submissions reviewed appear in Add. Mss. 55977 to 55982, 1891–1911.

39. The remarks come, respectively, from a review of G. Colmore's *The*

Marble Faun, March 23, 1900, Macmillan Archives, British Library, Add. Mss. 55961, pp. 121–123.

40. Review of Olive Birell's *The Ambition of Youth*, March 17, 1898, Macmillan Archives, British Library, Add. Mss. 55957, pp. 102–103; review of Mrs. Archibald Little's *A Marriage in China*, ibid., pp. 260–262.

41. Macmillan Archives, British Library, Add. Mss. 55954, 1895–96, pp. 225–226.

42. Thomas Mark, "1886" in a folder entitled "Odd Notes, 1873 on," Morgan Source Files, Macmillan Archives, British Library.

43. Review of Lal Behari Day's *Bengal Peasant Life*, Macmillan Archives, British Library, Add. Mss. 55955, 1896, pp. 199–201.

44. Review of Francis Francio's *Wild Rose: A Tale of the Mexican Frontier*, Macmillan Archives, British Library, Add. Mss. 55953, 1894–95, pp. 174–175.

45. Review of *Almayer's Folly*, which the firm nonetheless accepted, Macmillan Archives, British Library, Add. Mss. 55953, 1894–95, pp. 171–172. On Conrad and Ford Maddox Hueffer's *Romance*, Morris again displayed what Charles Morgan has called his blind spot: "One feels all through how much better a story it would have been with a simpler style and less intricate setting, had [R. L.] Stevenson written it, for instance, or [Anthony] Hope; but one cannot deny it some virtues, originality both in the characters and the situations, good local colour, and clever scene-painting. *The question of its admission into your Colonial Library depends of course on Conrad's value overseas*, which, as he has been writing for some time now would not be difficult to ascertain." Macmillan Archives, British Library, Add. Mss. 559667, 1903–1904, pp. 157–60, emphasis added.

46. Maurice Macmillan quotes the firm's sales for 1890 as "amounting to between £15,000 and £16,000" in a letter offering J. A. Stagg the position of Macmillan agent to India (Macmillan Archives, British Library, Add. Mss. 55843, Private Letterbooks, p. 357, letter dated June 8, 1892). The 1902 figure comes from the firm's Private Ledger for 1901, p. 299 (courtesy of the Macmillan Archive, Basingstoke).

47. Macmillan Archives, British Library, Add. Mss. 55844, Private Letterbooks (1895–1905), p. 608, letter dated August 21, 1902. The firm was well known for its sound business sense, and the insistence in 1902 on retaining Stagg in retirement at his full Indian salary (£200 per year) while also hiring the skilled Marsden at 1 percent commission with a guaranteed minimum of £300 per annum strikingly emphasizes the Indian market's increased importance to the firm on which they were now spending more than twice Stagg's original salary.

48. Tuchman's scrupulous research in *Edging Women Out* is inspiring for all those working on gender and the literary marketplace, including this author who remains warmly allied to the work's larger claims on the presence of women novelists in the late-Victorian world of letters. The differences I raise here ought to be noted in this spirit. As Tuchman judiciously points out in her

comparison between Crawford and Mrs. Oliphant, she did not consult information on print runs for Mrs. Oliphant from Macmillan's Edition Books in making her argument on the critical double standard between men and women novelists. Therefore, she notes, she is open to the idea that "perhaps Crawford received more money because his novels sold better than Oliphant's" (p. 200).

49. See nn. 37 and 45 above.

50. The *Magazine* was well known for its robustly phrased views, eschewing colonial positions and anglocentrism with élan. For instance, Samuel Satthianadhan, senior officer in the Madras Department of Public Instruction, was taken severely to task in a review for the anglocentrism and unexamined criticism of India and Indian education in his memoir of his student days at Cambridge. This asperity is particularly unexpected, given Satthianadhan's status in Madras as well as in the *Magazine* where he and his wife, Krupa, were frequent contributors.

51. The *Magazine* reviewed Macmillan's English Statesmen, English Men of Letters, Men of Action, and various Textbook Series, alongside reviews of books from Hodder and Stoughton, Longmans, T. Fisher Unwin, the Christian Vernacular Education Society, Longman's Colonial Library, the Clarendon Press (Oxford), and Cassell, in a fifteen-year print sample from vol. 3 (1885–86) to vol. 8 (1890–91); from vols. 11 and 12 (1893–95); and from the New Series 9 and 10 (1909–11).

52. *Madras Christian College Magazine* 4 (July 1886–June 1887): 450. The author sets up the distinction between functioning libraries in the presidency capitals (Madras, Bombay, Calcutta) and those in remote stations (the mofussils), as well as indicates an acute need for English books throughout.

53. Typically, however, even here the *Magazine* made discriminations in its generally enthusiastic reviews of Crawford's oeuvre. Some novels, such as *Paul Patoff*, were praised with reservation: "surely the novel would have been a better one had the author denied himself the pleasure of writing the last seventy pages" (4:61 [1888–89]); while others such as *Marzio's Crucifix* "does not seem to us . . . [to] fulfill the promise held out in *A Roman Singer*" (4:59 [1888–89]).

54. Edward Wagenknecht, "Novelists of the Eighties," pp. 166–71.

55. For details on Crawford's remarkable life and his first novel, see Maud Howe Elliott, *My Cousin*, and John Pilkington, Jr., "Genesis." Elliott in particular provides extensive and useful details from family letters, now housed at the Houghton Library at Harvard University. The best critical biography on Crawford remains Pilkington, Jr.'s *Francis Marion Crawford*. In the 1970s Crawford's reputation revived somewhat with the establishment of an F. Marion Crawford Society, with headquarters in Nashville, Tennessee.

56. Between ten and thirty titles from Crawford's pen are listed in catalogues of the Chaitanya Public Library, Calcutta; the Uttarpara Public Library; the J. N. Petit Library and the People's Reading Room and Library, both in Bombay; the Delhi Public Library; the Calcutta Public Library; and the Madras Literary Society. Catalogues from other libraries throughout the

country record him in smaller numbers or record him but not his titles in their holdings.

57. F. Marion Crawford, *Mr. Isaacs*, p. 6.

58. John C. Moran, *F. Marion Crawford Companion*, p. 3.

59. Upon his return from India, Crawford wrote a number of searing pieces in the American press that were critical of the British mismanagement of Indian affairs. "The question is, whether the establishment of extravagant colleges for educating a small number of natives into nondescript atheist malcontents is a just compensation for the loss of national personal estate. . . . Reviewing the history of the last fifty years, it is beyond the power of any upright human conscience to believe that England has done her duty by her Eastern subjects." See F. Marion Crawford, "British Rule," p. 3; see also Crawford, "Press in India," p. 3.

60. F. Marion Crawford, *Novel*. Pilkington, Jr., provides other participants in this debate on realism, including Hamlin Garland, Henry Blake Fuller, and Frank Norris. See Pilkington, Jr., "F. Marion Crawford."

61. Ouida, "Italian Novels," p. 91.

62. Larzer Ziff, *American 1890s*, p. 242.

63. Macmillan solicited numerous novelists for the Colonial Library whom the firm did not already publish for the home market, such as Mrs. Humphry Ward, Anthony Hope (whose *Prisoner of Zenda* came from Arrowsmith and was number 184 in the library in 1894), George du Maurier, Rhoda Broughton (who became a highly popular Colonial Library author and Macmillan's "property" after the purchase of Richard Bentley's list in 1898).

64. Meenakshi Mukherjee, *Realism and Reality*.

65. Numerous works have made this argument about the novel and its socializing effects, the most useful of which remain D. A. Miller, *The Novel and the Police*; Franco Moretti, *The Way of the World*. On the novel and the forms of specifically national kinship it engendered, see Benedict Anderson's *Imagined Communities*, especially chapters 2 and 3.

66. Terry Eagleton, *Heathcliff and the Great Hunger*, p. 147.

67. Moretti, *Atlas of the European Novel*, pp. 174–185, especially the maps on pp. 178–179.

68. Raymond Williams, *English Novel* p. 9; the quote on Dickens is from p. 27.

69. It ought also to be underscored that "antirealist" forms never disappeared from the British market altogether in the second half of the nineteenth century. They proliferated in their own way under realism's shadow, giving rise to sensation fiction, neogothic, and Corelliesque melodramas, among others. A number of influential theorists of the novel, such as Lukács, Ian Watt, Raymond Williams, and continuing to an extent through Edward Said and Nancy Armstrong, have tended to focus upon realism and to sideline the other popular forms that coexisted or predated its ascendance. Meanwhile, the work of scholars such as Peter Brooks (on British and French melodrama), Ian Duncan

(on romance in Britain and Scotland), and Margaret Cohen (on sentimental novels in France) has begun to shift the critical emphasis on realism and to give sustained attention to what Franco Moretti has called the "great unread" of the nineteenth-century fiction industry. My description of realism here should, therefore, be placed in context. It addresses the market phenomenon of realism's ascendance in Britain and should not be viewed as a critical affinity for or against it, an affinity evident in the first and still rightly influential group of theorists I have just mentioned. In short, my interest here is in studying patterns of consumption as they relate to the overall profile of the market. Realism's relative obscurity in India highlights a major difference between the British market and the one constructed by Indian readers—it is this fact that propels the inquiry of *In Another Country*.

70. Since translations, permissions, and probably plates for Balzac and Daudet were acquired from Dent, no print numbers for them were kept in Macmillan's Editions Books. Amiel's *Journal Intime* had a total printing of three thousand copies only, though it is believed to have circulated widely in translation, where the work's great introspection had a particular appeal among Indian readers. In Tagore's *The Home and the World* (1916), a novel where what each character reads self-consciously illuminates an aperture into the soul, Nikhil, the intellectual landowner, is seen to gain solace from Amiel's *Journal* when his domestic life begins to disintegrate.

71. The circulation of European titles in Australia provided a considerable contrast to the situation of literary insulation in India. Edward Petherick, the London agent who had wide sales to Australia between 1888 and 1894, published extensive monthly catalogues of stock for his overseas business. According to these, contemporary French writers had a small, but not insignificant niche: Petherick included works by Sand, Flaubert, the Goncourt brothers, Malot, Hugo, Daudet, Ohnet, alongside Loti, Maupassant, and Anatole France in his lists and in a special list, "Petherick's Collection of European Authors." Tolstoy was the only non-French writer to appear in these lists. In a signed, dated holograph *Catalogue* at the British Library, Petherick claimed that "the average value of stock 1892–1894 was above £45,000. . . . The total sales aggregated a quarter of a million pounds in five years." See *Petherick's General Catalogue*.

72. Ian Raeside, "Early Prose Fiction," p. 91. In a note on the same page, Raeside mentions that "the novelist, G. W. M. Reynolds, who is not worthy apparently of an individual entry in the encyclopaedias, had more influence in India than almost any other nineteenth-century Western writer."

73. On the unifying possibilities available in certain forms of popular fiction, see also Janice A. Radway, *Reading the Romance*.

74. The correlation between class cleavages and reading preferences is extremely well documented in Britain between 1790 (when literacy was still emerging) and 1950 (when almost complete literacy existed). See, for instance, work that deals with the specific tastes of working- and lower-class readers:

Dalziel, *Popular Fiction*; Richard Hoggart, *Uses of Literacy*; Louis James, *Fiction and the Working Man*; Vicinus, *Industrial Muse*; Webb, *British Working Class Reader*.

75. Thakorelal M. Desai, "Study of Fiction," p. 334. Desai concludes startlingly: "Newspapers cannot bring this about for two reasons. They are not yet so cheap as to find their way into every household, and their style, the absence of continuity in the many topics that they deal with, and their more or less prevalent party note are most likely to defeat this object."

76. Denning, *Mechanic Accents*, p. 72.

4. BY WAY OF TRANSITION: BANKIM'S WILL, OR INDIGENIZING THE NOVEL IN INDIA

1. Bankim is almost always referred to only by his first name. Given the manner in which Bengali names were anglicized, his last name is variously rendered Chatterji, Chatterjee, or even Chattopadhyay.

2. Bankim Chandra Chatterjee, *Chandrashekhar*, p. 34.

3. Rabindranath Tagore, *My Reminiscences*, p. 87.

4. It should be noted that the data on book production in figure 4.1 come from the publication lists found in the quarterly *Catalogue of Books Printed*, or *Appendices to the Gazettes*, put out by each presidency. The *Annual Reports* compiled subsequently for each presidency by a different battery of civil servants based their profiles of print upon these sources as well. However, the composite statistics for print that appear in the *Annual Reports* are so far removed from the more easily verifiable figures in the *Catalogues* and *Appendices* that they are neither reliable nor useful for research purposes. I have, therefore, used the *Annual Reports* for their qualitative assessments only, preferring to rely on the *Catalogues of Books Printed* for raw statistics on book publishing, print runs, and so on, which further allow me to compute statistics on publishing by taxonomy and form that follow in these pages. See *A Catalogue of Books Printed in the Bengal Presidency* (var. years); *A Catalogue of Books Printed in the Bombay Presidency* (var. years); *A Catalogue of Books Printed in the Madras Presidency, Fort St. George Gazette Supplement* (var. years).

5. In this regard the annual reports are different from the trade data on British imports, which record aggregate value of total books, not the number of single titles.

6. However, as figure 4.1 also demonstrates, publishing in Bengal increased dramatically beginning in 1881, a factor very possibly related to two events: the serialization that year of Bankim's deeply nationalistic *Anandamath*, with the poem *Bande Mataram* that soon became the anthem of the anticolonial movement, as well as the 1883 Calcutta conference of the nascent Congress Party (which was formally founded in 1885).

7. The ratio of literature to total output of 30 percent is the average for all three presidencies, although occasionally regional variations were considerable.

In 1876 and 1881 literary titles made up more than 50 percent of the total titles published in Bengal. Madras, where educational printing was far higher than in the other regions, saw an average 20 percent literary titles overall, of which the lowest dip, of 13 percent, was recorded in 1881.

8. Tapti Roy has argued that "dramas significantly came to outnumber prose fiction" in Bengal during the nineteenth century. She bases this erroneous claim upon data gathered from an incomplete source, namely, J. F. Blumhardt's *Catalogue of the Library of the India Office. Bengali, Oriya, and Assamese Books*. While Blumhardt's catalogues of the India Office Library's collections have many uses for book historians (see my chapter 2), to base national or even regional print production upon any library's very selective purchases is simply incorrect, especially when each presidency's quarterly catalogues and appendices to the *Gazette* provide exhaustive, complete, and more detailed reports of all titles published, rather than simply those that Blumhardt records the India Office Library having purchased. See Tapti Roy, "Disciplining the Printed Text," pp. 49–52.

9. Bankim Chandra Chatterji, "A Popular Literature for Bengal," p. 100.

10. As quoted by Ian Raeside, "Early Prose Fiction," pp. 89–90.

11. Scott, too, began his literary career as a poet. Unlike Bankim's poetic career, however, Scott's was far more illustrious and included an offer to become the Poet Laureate in 1813, an offer he declined. Fearing that his eventual foray into the novel could possibly damage his considerable stature (and revenues) as poet, Scott insisted on the long anonymity that surrounded "the Author of *Waverley*." As is well known, the success of Scott's novels did nothing of the kind. As Jane Austen somewhat crossly noted, "Sir Walter Scott has no business to write novels; especially good ones. It is not fair. He has fame and profit enough as a poet, and ought not to be taking the bread out of other people's mouths." See J. E. Austen-Leigh, "A Memoir of Jane Austen" (1870) in *Persuasion*, ed. D. W. Harding (Harmonsdsworth: Penguin Books, 1965) p. 332.

12. Anon, "Bankim Chandra," pp. xxiv-xxv.

13. See "Translator's Preface" in Bankim Chandra Chatterjee, *Chandrashekhar*, p. iii.

14. Sisir Kumar Das, *Artist in Chains*, pp. 21, ix.

15. In 1951 Nirad Chaudhuri compared Bankim to two of his famous countrymen and suggested that "if today Bankim Chandra Chatterji is not as highly rated in his country as Tagore or Gandhi, it is largely because he received less European recognition than them." See Nirad C. Chaudhuri, *Autobiography*, p. 480.

16. T. W. Clark, "Role of Bankimchandra," p. 437.

17. As cited in Tapan Raychaudhuri, *Europe Reconsidered*, pp. 123 and n.

18. Bhuban Chandra Mukharji and Krishnadhan Vidyavagish, *Bankim Babur Gupta Katha* [The Mysteries of Bankim Babu] as listed in the *Appendix to the Calcutta Gazette*. Much earlier, in 1874, Nilkanta Goswami, a lesser Ben-

gali novelist, wrote a preface to his *Ami Tomari* [I Am Only Yours] with an obvious dig at Bankim's reading tastes in English: "That I will be regarded as among the leading authors is also beyond my expectations since Scott or Reynolds are not my companions." As cited in Tapti Roy, "Disciplining the Printed Text," p. 59.

19. In a preface to *Rajani* (1877), Bankim wrote: "In that excellent novel by Lord Lytton, *The Last Days of Pompeii*, there is a blind flower girl named Nydia. . . . The character of Rajani is built on this foundation." Later in the same preface, he continued: "It is not common in the construction of a popular novel to make the hero and the heroine speak for themselves, but it is not new. It was done first by Wilkie Collins in his *Woman in White*." See "Preface," *Rajani* (Calcutta: Banga Sahitya Parishad), p. 8, as cited in T. W. Clark, "Bengali Prose Fiction," p. 70.

20. See for instance, Partha Chatterjee, *Nationalist Thought* and Sudipta Kaviraj, *Unhappy Consciousness*.

21. Bankim Chandra Chatterjee, "The Poison Tree [*Bishabriksha*]," p. 61.

22. Bankim Chandra Chatterjee, "Krishnakanta's Will," p. 284.

23. Kaviraj, *Unhappy Consciousness*, p. 1

24. The epithet is interesting and somewhat unexpected for it most evidently recalls Scott the historical novelist and not the poet who was far more popular among Indian readers (see table 2.3).

25. Walter Scott, *Waverley*, p. 50.

26. Wolfgang Iser, *Implied Reader*, p. 98.

27. Among other critics who have claimed this, see especially Katie Trumpener, *Bardic Nationalism*, p. 151. The *Waverley* narrator is also in sharp contrast to Thackeray's narrator in *Vanity Fair* (1848). Calling himself the Manager of the Performance, Thackeray's narrator serves much like a character in the novel, teasing the reader with ironic suggestiveness and commenting at some length upon the other characters, whom he calls, for example, "the famous little Becky Puppet" and the "Amelia doll." However, like Scott's narrator, Thackeray's also pointedly refuses, despite his claimed omniscience, to deliver moral judgments at key moments, as the aftermath of the Curzon Street catastrophe indicates: "Was she guilty or not? She said not; but who could tell what was truth which came from those lips; or if that corrupt heart was in this case pure?" W. M. Thackeray, *Vanity Fair*, p. 535.

28. Georg Lukács, *Historical Novel*, p. 33. For amplifications on this theme, see also Franco Moretti, *Way of the World*.

29. Not only do Scott's heroes provide the "neutral ground" on which history can be resolved, it seems that history itself for Scott was a neutral ground on which opposing positions are worked out, resolved, and compromised. Edward Waverley and the Baron of Bradwardine take pleasure in each other's company "although their characters and habits of thinking were in many respects totally opposite," the narrator alerts us (108). Edward's judgments have been influenced by poetry, toward which he is particularly disposed, the

Baron's by "simple prose." "Yet," avers the narrator, "they met upon history as on a neutral ground, in which each claimed an interest" (109). Indeed, it is not just the subject of history (as a discursive practice) but its very nature that provides the neutral ground on which opposed forces express themselves and are worked out into stable and far-reaching compromises. Thus while *Waverley* extols the vividness of events, characters, and motivations Sixty Years Since, it does so from the tranquil, retrospective, and *neutral* position of 1814 when the union with Scotland seems far more established and settled than it did in 1745–46 when the Jacobite uprising was still taking place.

30. The phrase "sneaking imbecile" is Scott's well-known assessment of Edward Waverley, made in a letter of 1814.

31. Though frequently scripted into the recorded texts, the Indian epic narrator emerges most vividly in the numerous oral performances that characterize the epic's long life in Indian culture. Here, the narrator-figure updates, explains, and otherwise reinterprets the written text for the needs of his immediate audience. The persistence of the narrator in the epic's oral performances gestures toward a distinction between the recorded text (to which few had access and perhaps even interest) and the received one (that many knew intimately and consumed repeatedly). This dual structure, in which the oral narrator—inspired by the presence and changing nature of the audience—repeatedly produced a new text at each moment of consumption, leads some to call the oral narrator (or teller) the second author of the Indian epics. Velcheru Narayana Rao has suggested that the narrative itself in its recorded form appears to invite and urge reinterpretation in the hands of *both* teller and audience: it is not too tightly constructed and leaves plenty of space for a second "author" to come into play. Narayana Rao calls this the systematic flexibility of the Indian oral epic, and he shows how it engenders radically different responses from male and female audiences. See Narayana Rao, "A *Ramayana* of Their Own," pp. 114–136. Salman Rushdie has played extensively with many of these oral practices and the ensuing expectations in *Midnight's Children*, and chapter 7 explicates his borrowings from the Indian oral tradition in greater detail. As I show there, while Rushdie, like Bankim, borrowed from the epic tradition, he does so largely from the oral epics, while Bankim seems to have relied largely upon the written ones.

32. Tusdidas, *Ramacharitmanas*, as cited and translated by Philip Lutgendorf, *The Life of a Text*, p. 25.

33. A. K. Ramanujan, "Three Hundred *Ramayanas*," *Many Ramayanas*, p. 25. In an immensely illuminating and influential essay on the many *Ramayanas* in South and Southeast Asia, Ramanujan continues: "No text is original, yet no telling is a mere retelling—and the story [of the *Ramayana*] has no closure, although it may be enclosed in a text" (46).

34. Tapan Raychaudhuri even suggests that Bankim was summarily demoted from the single promotion he received shortly after a particularly offending part of the novel was serialized in *Bangadarsan* in January 1882. See

Raychaudhuri, *Europe Reconsidered*, pp. 117–119. The following sources provide extensive descriptions of the changes Bankim made in numerous editions of *Anandamath* in order to stay one step ahead of the colonial censor: Sisir Kumar Das, *Artist in Chains*, especially pp. 141–144; Bimanbehari Majumdar, "Ananda Math and Phadke." See also Meenakshi Mukherjee, *Realism and Reality*, pp. 51–52.

35. *Bande Mataram* itself has a fascinating history. Bankim originally composed the lyric around 1875 to fill a blank page of his serial, *Bangadarsan*, but he never published it till *Anandamath* appeared in 1882. Tagore set the verses to music and sang them in public for the first time before the twelfth session of the Indian National Congress in 1896. During the 1905 riots surrounding the proposed partition of Bengal and the related Swadeshi movement, *Bande Mataram* became a rallying cry and anticolonial anthem. However, by the 1920s the song had acquired particularly Hindu overtones and, as Sisir Kumar Das writes, "from this time onwards Vandemataram began to be used as the war-cry of the Hindu fanatics" a status that the song maintained through the 1970s and 1980s (*Artist in Chains* 220). As a result, a Tagore composition (*Jana, Gana, Mana*) was adopted as India's official national anthem. With the fiftieth anniversary of Independence in 1997, however, in a moment of delightful irony, the highly popular Bollywood music director, A. R. Rahman, reclaimed *Bande Mataram* and produced a best-selling album with riffs on it, including versions in Hindi, Tamil, Urdu, and English, alongside the original Sanskrit. Not just Muslim, but South Indian as well, Rahman was doubly marginalized in the Hindu fanaticist hierarchy, yet his audacity and courage returned *Bande Mataram* to national status from the purview of Hindu communalists. In a final irony, Britain's oldest bank in India, Grindlay's (now under Australian ownership), handed out compact disks of Rahman's *Vande Mataram* (Sony Records, 1997) to all account holders in New Delhi during the month of Independence celebrations.

36. Sudipta Kaviraj, *The Unhappy Consciousness*, p. 125 and passim.

37. From *Bankim Rachanabali* vol. 2 (Calcutta: Sahitya Samsad, 1954) as translated and quoted by Ranajit Guha, *Indian Historiography*, p. 1.

38. See W. W. Hunter, *Annals of Rural Bengal*, pp. 70–71. For a more recent critical account of these martial sadhus, see William R. Pinch, *Peasants and Monks*, especially pp. 24–30.

39. In muting its anticolonial rhetoric, Bankim made the novel distressingly anti-Muslim, and this fact eventually lent *Bande Mataram* its edge in the fanatical cause of greater Hinduism. Yet it is equally worth noting that Bankim's rhetoric kept lines such as the following: "All *santans* belong to the same caste. In this great vow, we do not distinguish between Brahmins and sudras." See Bankim Chandra Chatterjee, *Anandamath*, trans. Aurobindo Ghose and Barindra Kumar Ghosh (1905), p. 100. All future references to *Anandamath* come from this English translation. In a later and more uneven English translation, by Basanta Koomar Roy, this passage is rendered more specifically (and

with greater license): "All Children belong to the same caste. In our work we do not differentiate between Hindu or Moslem, Buddhist or Sikh, Parsee or Pariah. We are all brothers here—all Children of the same Mother India (78)."

40. Bankim's English translators have done about as much violence to his text as he himself did in muting its anti-British rhetoric. In the only translation of *Anandamath* in print today (made in 1941 during a particularly tense period), Basanta Koomar Roy has thoroughly excised this passage along with numerous other overtly anti-British ones, no doubt in fear of the increasingly vigilant censor of those days.

41. Chaudhuri, *Autobiography*, p. 420. Chaudhuri himself claims that Bankim's contradictory ending in *Anandamath* was a legitimate one and that he simply held two separate, incompatible views on the British presence in India—on the one hand, admiring and emulating the British for their vigor and productivity, and on the other, despising them for India's subjection. Given the subtlety and intelligence with which Bankim depicted other explosive issues in his novels (such as polygamy and widow remarriage), it is difficult to find Chaudhuri's conclusion—coming as it does on page 420, the number for deception and subterfuge in Indian numerology—fully persuasive. It seems more likely to me that Bankim's contradictory ending for *Anandamath* was a carefully planned ploy on his part along the lines I have argued above.

42. *Appendix to the Calcutta Gazette for 1883.* See also chapter 2.

43. T. W. Clark, "Role of Bankimchandra," p. 438.

44. "Rishi Bankim Chandra" in Aurobindo Ghose, *Bankim-Tilak-Dayananda*, pp. 12–13.

45. See Bankim Chandra Chatterji, *Anandamath*, trans. Basanta Koomar Roy.

46. Ghose, *Bankim-Tilak-Dayananda*, p. 9.

47. Ghose, *Bankim Chandra Chatterji*.

48. Ghose, *Bankim-Tilak-Dayananda*, p. 9.

49. Ibid., p. 10.

50. See for instance Henry Y. Zhao's excellent monograph on the topic in Chinese fiction at the turn of the century: "The huge amount of directions trying to explain the newly adopted techniques betrays the narrator's uneasiness about the stability of his status," Zhao argues in his survey of late Qing fiction (*Uneasy Narrator* 69). "Never before had the narrator in Chinese fiction felt the need of this kind of desperate self-defense. Never before had the narrator been so worried about the effectiveness of his communication. One feels that the narrator of Chinese fiction now finds himself in a much more vulnerable position," Zhao concludes (71). Other scholars who have researched the gulf between foreign literary consumption and indigenous production of the novel include Doris Sommer, *Foundational Fictions*; David Derwei Wang, *Fin-de-Siècle Splendor*; Ato Quayson, *Strategic Transformations in Nigerian Writing*; Emmanuel Obiechina, *Culture, Tradition, and Society in the West African Novel*.

51. Partha Chatterjee, "The Moment of Departure: Culture and Power in the Thought of Bankimchandra,"in *Nationalist Thought*, p. 54.

52. In their recent English translations of three Bankim novels, S. N. Mukherjee and Marian Maddern record the limitations of earlier attempts in translating Bankim. Recalling Miriam Knight's 1895 translation and J. C. Ghosh's 1962 version of *Krishnakanta's Will*, Mukherjee writes that he is "well aware of the narrow Victorian moral attitudes of these two otherwise good translators," who excised entire passages from a scene where Govindlal revives Rohini by mouth-to-mouth resuscitation on her "juicy, cherrylike lips" ("Translators' Preface" xv). Meanwhile, in his 1880 translation of *Durgesanandini*, Charu Chander Mookerjee does not even attempt to translate a number of Sanskrit aphorisms and Bengali proverbs, leaving them in the original language in the "translation." In other novels and at other times, for example, Basanta Koomar Roy's 1941 translation of *Anandamath*, characters are renamed and entire sections eliminated, this time for political not prudish reasons. The difficulty with rendering Bengali literature in responsible and supple English translation is not restricted to Bankim: Surendranath Tagore's 1919 translation of his uncle, Rabindranath's, *The Home and the World* (1916) combines Bimala's two sisters-in-law into a single figure, while English translations of Tagore's poems were so abysmal that Robert Bridges repeatedly urged Macmillan, Tagore's British publishers, to do whatever it took to improve them short of a law suit (Tagore Correspondence in the Macmillan Archives, British Library, Add. Mss. 54788, p. 117, letter from Sir Frederick Macmillan to his cousin, George, July 7, 1915). Aware of these limitations, I have read multiple translations of Bankim's novels where available and checked my own readings with scholars of Bengali literature.

5. REFORMING THE NOVEL: KRUPA SATTHIANADHAN, THE WOMAN WHO DID

1. Mrs. Fenwick Miller, "Book of the Hour." The masthead on the *Woman's Signal* carried the following announcement of its mission: "A weekly record and review of Woman's Work in Philanthropy and Reform," with a motto that insisted, "For all the World."

2. Partha Chatterjee, *Nation and its Fragments*, p. 116.

3. See, for instance, mentions of Satthianadhan in K. R. S. Iyengar, *Indian Writing*; Dorothy M. Spencer, *Indian Fiction*. Susie Tharu and K. Lalita did much to generate interest in Satthianadhan by providing a useful biography and excerpt from *Saguna* in their important anthology, *Women's Writing*. Inspired by Tharu and Lalita's anthology, Oxford University Press (India) recently reissued both novels under the uneven editorial guard of Chandani Lokugé, whose supervision has involved changing *Saguna's* subtitle to *The First Autobiographical Novel in English by an Indian Woman*. In keeping with this inexplicable renaming, much of Lokugé's introductions to the two novels force

upon them a limited set of interests gleaned from postcolonial criticism. The introductions, therefore, provide little critical or literary insight to Satthianadhan's work other than clothing her in overused and once fashionable categories such as hybridity. See "Introduction" *Saguna*, p. 16. Krupabai Satthianadhan, *Kamala. The Story of a Hindu Life* (New Delhi: Oxford UP, 1998) and Satthianadhan, *Saguna. The First Autobiographical Novel in English by an Indian Woman* (New Delhi: Oxford UP, 1998).

4. *Zenana* literally means "women's quarter" and refers to the separate space in the house where women lived and where men outside the immediate family were not allowed. The Zenana Movement took various forms in its approach and outreach to women in India: at its most energetic, it was associated with missionary activities of education and conversion. Later, in the 1880s, particularly under the sponsorship of the then British Vicereine, the Marchioness of Dufferin and Ava (1884–88), the movement began to promote wider education for women, and in particular the training of Indian women to be doctors in the service of their sisters. At the call of Pandita Ramabai (1858–1922), an organization called the National Association for Supplying Female Medical Aid to the Women of India—popularly known as the Dufferin Movement—was inaugurated by the viceroy's wife in 1885. See Harriot Georgina Blackwood, Marchioness of Dufferin and Ava, *A Record of Three Years' Work*. There remains a massive literature on *zenanas* that includes numerous journals, tracts, testimonies, how-to books, memoirs by *zenana* workers, novels, tales, poems, and romances.

5. Krupa Satthianadhan, *Saguna*, 2d. ed., 1895; Krupa Satthianadhan, *Kamala*, 1894; Krupa Satthianadhan, *Miscellaneous Writings*, 1896; Samuel Satthianadhan and Kamala Satthianadhan, *Sketches of Indian Christian Life*, 1896. References to Satthianadhan's work in this chapter come from these editions.

6. Mrs H. B. Grigg, "Memoir," *Kamala*, p. vi.

7. For other examples of this genre, see Mary Frances Billington, *Woman in India*; Margaret Bretherton, *Ten Noble Women*; Mrs. E. F. Chapman, *Sketches of Some Distinguished Indian Women*; Lady Glover, *Famous Women*; Mrs. E. J. Humphrey, *Gems of India*.

8. Jane's lines in the famous chapter 12 read in part: "Women are supposed to be very calm generally: but women feel just as men feel; they need exercise for their faculties, and a field for their efforts as much as their brothers do; they suffer from too rigid a restraint, too absolute a stagnation, precisely as men would suffer; and it is narrow-minded in their more privileged fellow-creatures to say that they ought to confine themselves to making puddings and knitting stockings, to playing on the piano and embroidering bags." Charlotte Brontë, *Jane Eyre* (1847) Ed. Q. D. Leavis (London: Penguin, 1966), p. 141. I have found no reference to Brontë in Satthianadhan's writings, so for the moment, this striking echo will remain just that.

9. *Report on the Administration of the Madras Presidency During the Year 1894–95*, 3d. quarter, p. 62.

10. From the *Christian Patriot* (Madras, 1895) as reprinted in Krupa Satthi-anadhan, "Reviews of Kamala" in *Miscellaneous Writings*.

11. In addition to her British readership, Satthianadhan's work was trans-lated into German in 1898 and Danish in 1921, languages of two other major missionary churches in India.

12. Kate Flint, *Woman Reader*, p. 295.

13. Allen himself is of more than incidental interest here: he spent three years as a colonial educator in Jamaica, which had a lasting impact on his views toward empire. He wrote several works about the colonies, including one on India, *The Devil's Die* (1888) featuring a Hindu doctor. Allen was also far from the only male writer of the genre, which also included the works of Hardy, Meredith, and Gissing. His particular success in this form of fiction has recently been attributed to the essentially conservative endings of his novels, which could claim to challenge prevailing social beliefs but conclude by falling in line with them. See Sarah Wintle, "Introduction," in Grant Allen, *The Woman Who Did*.

14. Some of the first periodicals that followed the 1870 Act and agitated for further reform were *Woman, A Weekly Journal Embodying Female Interests* (1872); *Social Review* (1872); *Woman's Opinion* (1874); *Woman and Work* (1874–76); and the aforementioned *Woman's Signal* (1894–99). See also the collection, *The Social and Political Status of Women in Britain, 1870–1928: Radical and Reforming Journals for and by Women* (Brighton: Harvester Press Micro-form Publ., 1983).

15. Gail Cunningham, *New Woman*, p. 1.

16. Elizabeth Robins, *Ibsen* , pp. 10–11, emphasis added.

17. Mrs. E. F. Chapman, *Sketches*. *Sketches* includes biographies of Pandita Ramabai Sarasvati (active in widow reform and education); Dr. Anandibai Joshee (the first Indian woman to receive a medical degree); Maharani of Kuch Behar; Toru Dutt; and Cornelia Sorabji. Only two of the women were converts (Ramabai and Joshee), although all of them had visible public roles as either writers, social reformers, or royalty.

18. Mrs. Chapman is clearly canny about her readers: she concludes her introduction by enumerating the considerable generosity of Americans toward the cause of Indian female welfare: "Surely these things should stir up the hearts of English men and women to emulate the generosity shown on the other side of the Atlantic, towards those who have so much greater claim on us, and are bound to us by so many ties of duty and of common interest" (25). Between pressing the button of anti-Americanism and invoking *noblesse oblige*, Chapman is sure that at least one of these tactics will open up her readers' pocketbooks!

19. *Woman's Signal*, February 8, 1894, p. 9, emphasis added.

20. Leslie A. Flemming, ed., *Women's Work*; Leslie A. Flemming, "A New Humanity"; Kumari Jayawardena, *White Woman's Other Burden*; Barbara N. Ramusack, "Cultural Missionaries"; Antoinette Burton, *Burdens of History*.

21. In a review essay of feminist work dealing with European women in colonial Nigeria and Fiji (published several years before Burton's book), Jane Haggis similarly cautions against the blind spots in recent feminist work that focus on white women in the colonies: "by centering [on] *white* women, this approach actually serves to ungender the colonised people and contribute to silencing colonial women." See Haggis, "Gendering Colonialism," p. 105.

22. See "The Emergence of Women's Organizations" in Geraldine Forbes, *Women in Modern India*. See also "Women's Organisation" in Joana Liddle and Rama Joshi, *Daughters of Independence*.

23. Mary C. Holdsworth, "Woman Question," p. 165.

24. As cited in Mrinalini Sinha, "Reading Mother India," p. 23.

25. Partha Chatterjee, "Colonialism, Journalism, and Colonized Women"; Chatterjee, "Nationalist Resolution"; Chatterjee, *Nation and its Fragments*.

26. Partha Chatterjee, *Nation and its Fragments*; Malavika Karlekar, *Voices from Within*; Rosalind O'Hanlon, "Issues of Widowhood"; Veena Talwar Oldenburg, "Lifestyle as Resistance"; Vir Bharat Talwar, "Feminist Consciousness in Women's Journals in Hindi."

27. The Distinguished Indian Woman genre became so popular that in the controversies following Katherine Mayo's *Mother India*, one Charulata Devi wrote *The Fair Sex of India: A Reply to 'Mother India.'* However, as Mrinalini Sinha writes, "although the title of the book declared that it was a reply to Mayo's *Mother India*, the text itself made no direct reference to Mayo's book. Instead the book, which consisted entirely of short biographies of notable Indian women through the ages, responded to *Mother India* by offering Indian women's achievements as proof of the greatness of Indian culture." See Sinha, "Reading Mother India," p. 14.

28. Both this and the following review from the *Malabar and Travancore Spectator* appeared in 1894 and are cited in Krupa Satthianadhan, *Miscellaneous Writings*. Unless otherwise indicated in the text, the sources I cite come from Anglo-Indian newspapers, i.e., those intended predominantly for a British readership.

29. "Rev. of Satthianadhan's *Kamala*," *Madras Christian College Magazine* 12 (February 1895): 489–490.

6. THE EXILE AT HOME: AHMED ALI'S *Twilight in Delhi*

1. K. R. S. Iyengar, "Introduction," *Indian Writing in English*, p. 8. The introduction is the text of a lecture delivered at the University of Leeds on January 19, 1959.

2. See Horace Wilson, "Education of the Natives of India," *Asiatic Journal* (1836), 29:14, as quoted in Gauri Viswanathan, *Masks of Conquest*, 41–42.

3. Frantz Fanon, *Black Skin*, pp. 17–18.

4. Ahmed Ali, interview with the author October 26–30, 1992, in Karachi, Pakistan (archived at the Columbia University Oral History Collection, But-

ler Library, New York). In the same context, Ali continues: "[*Angarey*] was the first time that the short story was presented in Urdu as a short story. It was no longer a tale."

5. The British ban on *Angarey* is itself revealing: the colonial censor glosses the collection as "short stories, chiefly satires on Indian society and Muslim clergy," nowhere expressing a fear of its incendiary content. Yet, in an odd ploy of appeasement, it installed the ban, which is still on the books today. Graham Shaw and Mary Lloyd, *Publications Proscribed by the Government of India*, p. 163.

6. *The Leader* of Allahabad, 5 April 1933, as described by Ali in the afterword to Ahmed Ali, *Prison House*, p. 164.

7. Ahmed Ali, "Progressive Writers' Movement," p. 35.

8. The most prominent of these writers include Asrarul Haq "Majaz," Saadat Hasan Manto, Ali Sardar Jafri, and "Faiz" Ahmed Faiz in Urdu; Munshi Premchand and Krishen Chander in Hindi; Mulk Raj Anand in English; Prabhakar Machwe in Marathi; Jyotirama Ghosh and Suniti Kumar Chatterjee in Bengali. The movement's vast reach, notwithstanding, it was, in the words of Ahmed Ali, "essentially an Urdu movement" (interview with this author, Karachi, October 26–30, 1992), where its impact was felt most acutely in innovations of form, genre, and temperament, and from where it spread to other languages. While most critics concur with Ali's assessment of the AIPWA's influence on Urdu literature, they provide different chronologies for it, and there is no real consensus on when the movement really began or who articulated its intellectual program. Ralph Russell concedes that "in Urdu the ground for the success of the new movement had been prepared to some extent by the publication in 1932 of a collection of stories entitled *Angare*." However, he dates the movement's formal origins to a meeting among radical Indian students in a London restaurant in 1934–35, a meeting at which Ali was not present. See the chapter "The Progressive Writers' Movement," especially pp. 205–208 in Ralph Russell, *Pursuit of Urdu Literature*. Other critics such as Carlo Coppola and David Anderson provide a chronology that includes not just Ali's participation but also his formative influence on the AIPWA.

9. See Carlo Coppola, "All-India Progressive Writers' Association," for details of this meeting and the texts of speeches by selected speakers.

10. The full text of the manifesto was published in London in the *Left Review* of February 1935 and is quoted here from a reproduction in Carlo Coppola, "All-India Progressive Writers' Association," 6–9. The original manifesto was translated in India, where it appeared in a Hindi translation in *Hans*, the journal of the prominent Hindi writer, Premchand. Coppola compares the translation with the original and acutely identifies significant departures in language, tone, and content between the two ("All-India" 9–12): the London manifesto is neutralized of its Marxist terminology and its uncompromising outspokenness in the more moderate Hindi version. As Muhammad Sadiq argues, "the phenomenal success of the Progressive Writers' Association was also due to the adroit way in which its *Manifesto* had been drawn up. It said

nothing about Communism. . . . No right-thinking person could take exception to its programme." See Sadiq, *History of Urdu Literature*, p. 534.

11. Tom Nairn, *Break-Up of Britain*, p. 340.

12. Ahmed Ali, "Statement on Progressivism," paper read for the South Asia Conference at the University of Wisconsin at Madison, November 1978; ms. in possession of this author.

13. *Indian Writing* was placed under the editorship of Ahmed Ali and Iqbal Singh, who published four issues of the magazine in London between 1936 and 1938.

14. Ali's remarks come from his introduction, entitled "The *Raison d'être* of *Twilight in Delhi*," to a new edition of *Twilight in Delhi* (1994), p. xvi. All references to the novel come from this edition of the work.

15. David D. Anderson, "Ahmed Ali," p. 436. Other Indian writers in English were certainly around as well: see extensive studies by K. R. S. Iyengar, *Indian Writing*; Asha Kaushik, *Politics, Aesthetics, and Culture*; Meenakshi Mukherjee, *Twice-Born Fiction*; N. S. Pradhan, "Introduction," *Major Indian Novels: An Evaluation*. Each of these studies (and the many not mentioned), however, concur on the preeminence of these four Indian writers in English.

16. Carlo Coppola, "Short Stories of Ahmed Ali," p. 215.

17. Mulk Raj Anand, *Roots and Flowers*, p. 36.

18. The concept of "watchful revolutionary censorship" is part of Trotsky's program of revolutionary art with which Mulk Raj Anand was familiar. See Leon Trotsky, *Literature and Revolution* 1923 (rept. New York: Russell and Russell, 1957), p. 219. In his 1972 lecture (*Roots and Flowers*) Anand alludes to this obliquely when speaking about Indian writers of the 1930s (in which he includes only himself and Raja Rao, without mentioning Narayan or Ali, or, in fact, any other contemporary).

19. Ahmed Ali, "*Raison d'être*" pp. xiv–xv.

20. Ahmed Ali, "Statement on Progressivism," p. 2.

21. Ahmed Ali, "Introduction," *Twilight in Delhi* (1940; reprint, Karachi: Oxford UP, 1984) p. viiff.

22. Interview with Ahmed Ali, October 26–30, 1992.

23. In placing the city at the center of his narrative, Ali in many ways recalls a now familiar trajectory in British modernism, beginning with H. G. Wells (whose *Anticipations* [1901] focuses on "the probable diffusion of great cities") through Woolf, Eliot, and Joyce. This is a trajectory that, of course, has other celebrated axes, yet I mention the British faction first because Ali's representation of Delhi at the opening of *Twilight*, in which "the nymphs have all gone to sleep, and the lovers have departed" (4), is self-consciously Eliotic. The similarity with Britishness ends here.

24. Harish Trivedi, "Ahmed Ali," p. 70.

25. Premchand, "The Chess Players," (1924) in *Deliverance*, p. 182.

26. For an account of the transformation of Delhi under Lutyens, see Robert Grant Irving, *Indian Summer*. See also Veena Talwar Oldenburg's work

on Lucknow that graphically presents the British fear of crowded and poten-
tially insurgent sections of Indian cities, mapping them on surveys simply as
"Dense City." Oldenburg, *Making of Colonial Lucknow*, especially p. 22.

27. Max Weber, *City*, especially the chapter, "The Nature of the City." For
Simmel's most classic statement on the metropolis, see Georg Simmel,
"Metropolis," pp. 47–60.

28. V. G. Kiernan, *Lords of Human Kind*, p. 7.

29. Reinhart Koselleck, *Futures Past*, p. 17.

30. See Virgil (ca. 19 B.C.), *The Aeneid*, trans. Robert Fitzgerald (New York:
Vintage, 1981), 12.834–849, p. 398.

31. In Forster's *Passage to India*, for example, a modest Bengali family unwittingly responds to Mrs. Moore's impulse to visit them, a visit that in the end
never happens because the Bhattacharyas never send their carriage to fetch
Mrs. Moore and Adela, nor word that the tea has been canceled (36–37).
Despite the sincerity of the impulse and the elaborate expectations from it,
such intercourse is simply not to be between Indians and the British in colonial India after the Mutiny, and the only two surprised by this are the naïve
newcomers, Mrs. Moore and Adela.

32. See George Orwell's *Burmese Days* (1934), or any of the subsequent crop
of Indian novels in English: G. V. Desani's *All About H. Hatterr* (1948); Arun
Joshi's *The Foreigner* (1968); Salman Rushdie's *Midnight's Children* (1980), all
novels where the presence of Eurasian characters moves successively from the
peripheries of the plot (in Orwell) to the center (Saleem Sinai, Rushdie's hero
who is a metaphorical figure for modern India, is the illegitimate child of the
Englishman, Methwold, and a Hindu street magician's wife).

33. Muhammad Hasan Askari, "Novel by Ahmed Ali," np.

34. The phrase is from Benedict Anderson, *Imagined Communities*, p. 87.

35. Salman Rushdie, *Imaginary Homelands*, p. 12.

7. THE OTHER MODERNISM, OR THE FAMILY ROMANCE IN ENGLISH

1. Barada C. Mitra, "English Influence on Bengali Literature," p. 344–345.

2. Upamanyu Chatterjee, *English, August*, p. 1.

3. Rajeswari Sunder Rajan, "The Feminist Plot and the Nationalist Allegory," pp. 71–92.

4. In Europe and to some extent in the United States, the aesthetic practice most directed at critiquing this phase of what we now call modernity was
modernism, a variously motivated set of practices running the gamut of the
political spectrum that has simultaneously been hailed for its critical and
transnational motivations as well as condemned for being an empty signifier,
a portmanteau concept (Perry Anderson's term) without historical referent
or significance. Of the many claiming modernism's revolutionary potential,
consider the following: Fredric Jameson, "Postmodernism and Consumer

Society"; Jameson, *Postmodernism, or, the Cultural Logic of Late Capitalism*; Walter Benjamin, "The Work of Art in the Age of Mechanical Reproduction," in *Illuminations*, pp. 217–251; Marshall Berman, *All That is Solid*; and Ernst Bloch, *Principle of Hope*. See also the following essays in an extended debate between various members of the Frankfurt School collected in the volume edited by Rodney Livingstone, Perry Anderson, and Francis Mulhern, *Aesthetics and Politics*, especially Ernst Bloch, "Discussing Expressionism," and Bertolt Brecht, "Against Georg Lukács." Among those lamenting modernism's failed politics or its overstated ambitions are Perry Anderson, "Modernity and Revolution"; Georg Lukács, "Realism in the Balance." More recently, T. J. Clark, in *Farewell to an Idea*, poignantly laments and heroically attempts to revive modernism as a cultural and political category.

5. Bharati Mukherjee, "Immigrant Writing," p. 28.

6. Saree Makdisi has made a similar and passionate argument about reclaiming modernism as a conceptual category for reading modern Arab literature. See his "'Postcolonial' Literature in a Neocolonial World."

7. Jameson, "Postmodernism and Consumer Society," p. 114.

8. Timothy Brennan, *Salman Rushdie*, p. 139–142.

9. Brennan's work on Rushdie is admirable in many regards, although some critics remain baffled by his characterization of the novelist: it seems inspired by what he calls Rushdie's "cosmopolitanism" and the critical fantasy that "real" revolutionary aesthetics arise from a particular group that evidently does not include affluent, urban transnationals.

10. Anne McClintock, *Imperial Leather*, p. 11; the essay originally appeared as "The Angel of Progress: Pitfalls of the Term 'Post-Colonialism,'" *Social Text: Third World and Post-Colonial Issues* 31/32 (1992): 84–98.

11. Salman Rushdie, *Midnight's Children*, p. 125. Rushdie introduces this structural trope earlier in the novel, when, within a page of the opening, Saleem writes, "I have been a swallower of lives; and to know me, just the one of me, you'll have to swallow the lot as well" (4).

12. G. V. Desani, *All About H. Hatterr: A Novel*. The novel's publishing history is itself of some interest: shortly after publication in 1948, it was reissued by Saturn Press, in London in 1950; revised and published in New York by Farrar Straus and Young in 1951; further revised in 1970, subtitled "A Novel," and published with an introduction by Anthony Burgess by Farrar, Straus, and Giroux; revised with a new final chapter and published in 1972 in the United States by Lancer; by Penguin in England in 1972. A "final" edition was published in New York by McPherson in 1986 with a notation on the title page: "edition with final revisions." Citations to *Hatterr*, unless indicated otherwise in the text, will be from this 1986 edition.

13. Salman Rushdie, "Introduction," in *The Vintage Book of Indian Writing*, pp. ix–xxiii, xviii.

14. V. G. Kiernan, *Lords of Human Kind*, p. 319.

15. K. R. S. Iyengar, *Indian Writing*, p. 489.

16. The lines are self-consciously from Conrad's *Heart of Darkness* and refer of course to Marlow's modernist narratives (no longer yarns or seaman's stories) with their inconclusive endings. See Joseph Conrad, *Heart of Darkness* (1899 ed.) Norton Critical Edition, ed. Robert Kimbrough (New York: Norton, 1988), p. 9.

17. Salman Rushdie, interview with Vijaya Nagarajan, Berkeley Community Theatre and Pacifica Radio, May 6, 1999.

18. *The Mahabharata* (whose written composition is loosely dated ca. 400 B.C.E. to 400 A.D.) is the epic of dynastic succession in the warring clan of Pandu, and *The Ramayana* (ca. 200 B.C.E.. to 200 A.D.), the more popular work, is the epic of the voluntary exile of King Ram from his rightful throne. These are the earliest epics in the Indian literary tradition, which began with the written composition of the *Vedas* (ca. 1500 B.C.). Many consider *The Mahabharata* (sometimes called "the Fifth Veda") to be the culmination of Hindu religion and philosophy, reputedly dictated by the sage Vyasa to the elephant-headed, god-turned-scribe, Ganesh. Unlike epics in the European literary tradition, the two Indian epics—especially in oral mode—remain today an integral part of everyday life for many in India and are routinely recited, recounted, and performed in a number of venues—the most recent being the serialization of *The Ramayana* on primetime TV nationwide. Of the two, *The Mahabharata* is longer, at approximately one hundred thousand stanzas in verse. Numerous vernacular versions of both these epics have flourished throughout India, including (for the *Ramayana*) Kampan's eleventh-century Tamil *Irmavataram*, a thirteenth-century Telugu rendition by Buddharaj, a fourteenth-century version in Bengali by Krittibasa, and a seventeenth-century proto-Hindi version by Tulsidas called the *Ramacharitmanas*. Each textual version reinvents the Sanskrit one to suit the needs of its immediate audience much as each oral telling remakes the recorded text in order to suit the needs and temperament of its immediate listeners. See chapter 4 for more on these issues; see also Philip Lutgendorf, *Life of a Text*; Paula Richman, ed., *Many Ramayanas*; Edward Washburn Hopkins, *Great Epic*; J. A. B. van Buitenen, ed. and trans., *Mahabharata*.

19. J. A. B. van Buitenen, ed. and trans., *Mahabharata*, 1.1.25, p. 21.

20. J. A. B. van Buitenen, ed. and trans., *The Mahabharata*, vol. 1, p. xxii–xxiii. For the transformations and accretions specific to the oral tradition, see also the useful essays by Stuart Blackburn, "Patterns of Development for Indian Oral Epics," *Oral Epics in India*, pp. 15–32; Joyce B. Flueckiger, "Caste and Regional Variants in an Oral Epic Tradition," *Oral Epics in India*, pp. 33–52. Finally, on the genesis of the *Mahabharata* itself, see Edward Washburn Hopkins, *Great Epic*.

21. See Walter Benjamin, "The Storyteller," in *Illuminations*, esp. pp. 86–87. Among more recent critics, Fredric Jameson addresses this issue in his chapter, "Magical Narratives," in *Political Unconscious*, pp. 103–150, esp. p. 104. See also Franco Moretti, "The Long Goodbye. *Ulysses* and the End of Liberal Capitalism," in *Signs Taken for Wonders*, pp. 182–208.

22. Hayden White, *Content*, p. 3.

23. V. S. Naipaul, *Return*, p. 227.

24. This notion that an entire nation exists through an act of collective forgetting is, of course, Ernest Renan's: "L'essence d'une nation est que tous les individus aient beaucoup des choses en commun, et aussi que tous aient oublié bien des choses." (From "Qu'est ce qu'une nation?" in *Oeuvres Complètes*, 1:892; tr. Martin Thom, "What is a nation?" in Homi K. Bhabha, ed., *Nation and Narration*.

25. *Iliad*, 2.573, trans. Robert Fagles (New York: Penguin, 1990), p. 115. See *Iliad*, Loeb Classical Library Edition (Cambridge: Harvard UP, 1924), 2.482–4, pp. 85–86.

26. The reading I have been using is Lukács's, and it is worth remembering the care with which he restricts this sense-making capacity to Homer only. Later singers of the epic were chastised in Plato's *Ion* (see 541b–542) for knowing Homer's meter but not his *métier*, and Lukács, aware of this tension, concludes his reading of the forms of "integrated civilizations" by brilliantly remarking that Homer's unity with his audience could not have survived him into a later period in which tragedy and philosophy become the dominant forms. See Lukács, *Theory of the Novel*, especially p. 35. Having said this, I should also mention that the Homeric catalogue I cite is generally regarded to have come later than the *Iliad*, although most scholars concur that it was a fairly early addition to the epic. See also Thomas W. Allen, *The Homeric Catalogue of Ships*.

27. Furthering this confusion is the increasing collapse of Saleem's voice with the author's, which is not uncommon in Rushdie's oeuvre: a first-person narrator in *Shame* unabashedly integrates extensive biographical material from Rushdie's life into the novel. "I tell myself this will be a novel of leavetaking, my last words on the East from which, many years ago, I began to come loose. I do not always believe myself when I say this. It is a part of the world to which, whether I like it or not, I am still joined, if only by elastic bands." These authorial interjections saturate the work to the extent that *Shame*'s account of events is unmistakably *Rushdie's* account of Pakistani history.

28. Shortly after the novel appeared, Rushdie wrote (1982), "In the case of *Midnight's Children*, I certainly felt that if its Subcontinental readers had rejected the work, I should have thought it a failure, no matter what the reaction in the West. So I would say that I write 'for' people who feel part of the things I write 'about,' but also for everyone else I can reach." Salman Rushdie, *Imaginary Homelands*, p. 20. The gulf between those whom Rushdie writes "for" and those who "feel part of" the things he writes "about" is wide, as the calamitous reception of *The Satanic Verses* makes clear. But it is a useful distinction to highlight, and one I have heard echoed by a number of other writers. Speaking about his Bay Area verse-novel, *The Golden Gate* (1986), Vikram Seth told me that the response to it by readers in the United States was more significant to him than the response by readers in other parts of the world.

(Conversation with the author, June 1988, School of the Arts, Columbia University, New York).

29. Shashi Tharoor, *Great Indian Novel.* Tharoor acknowledges his literary forbears in his chapter headings, some serious some funny. Rushdie is acknowledged in "Midnight's Parents"; Forster in "Passages through India"; the Raj in "The Duel with the Crown"; and the ancient tradition in "The Rigged Veda."

30. *Dharma* is perhaps one of the hardest Hindu concepts to define, largely because it means so many things. It is colloquially used in Hindi to suggest "religion," but this usage is farthest from the word's meaning. *Dharma* means the code of conduct that no virtuous person reneges on, and it includes the sense of righteousness, custom, ritual, justice, and morality. It also means duty—and here is where the translation falters, for *dharma* implies duty to a number of orders: sacred, caste, guild, family, gender. If the *Mahabharata* is about one thing, it is about pursuing and preserving *dharma*, not as a blind abeyance to sacrosanct rules but in a daily *interpretation* and enactment of duties and responsibilities as *uniquely* appropriate to each individual, from king to serf. A number of pivotal scenes in the epic revolve around interpretations of who serves his/her *dharma* most faithfully, and in adjudicating these cases, the text invariably defers to tradition. As such, the concept of *dharma* is inseparably linked with a regard for tradition, making Yudhishtir's abnegation in Tharoor's novel deeply ironic.

31. Originally published in *New Left Review*, December 1982, pp. 87–95; reprinted as "Review of *Midnight's Children*," *Mainstream*, p. 23.

32. David Lipscomb, "Caught in a Strange Middle Ground," p. 170.

33. See Raja Rao, "Foreword," *Kanthapura*, p. v.

34. Partha Chatterjee, *Nationalist Thought*; Partha Chatterjee, *The Nation and its Fragments*; Veena Das, "Language and Body"; Sudipta Kaviraj, *Unhappy Consciousness.*

35. Ernst Bloch, "Nonsynchronism," p. 22.

36. The concept of "encyclopedic narratives" is Edward Mendelson's; see his, "Encyclopedic Narratives."

37. Chandrabhanu Pattanayak, "Interview with Salman Rushdie," p. 20.

38. Rani Dharkar, "An Interview," p. 355.

39. Among Indian critics who have written of Rushdie's use of English, see also the following: Feroza Jussawalla, "Beyond Indianness"; Uma Parameswaran, "Salman Rushdie"; Wimal Dissanayake, "Towards a Decolonized English"; Kumkum Sangari, "Politics of the Possible"; Maria Couto, "Midnight's Children and Parents," 61–77.

40. Rustom Bharucha, "Rushdie's Whale," p. 222. Bharucha's is one of the most thoughtful and detailed accounts of Rushdie's use of English with its larger argument that "there are more ambitious forms of rhetoric that are treasured within this gargantuan storehouse of words [*Midnight's Children*]" (225). "Salman Rushdie is, perhaps, the only writer in the world today who

could use the words, 'rutputty' and 'lassitudinous' within three lines, and make you accept the validity of both these words (from different cultures) in his own fictional context" (224).

41. Subhadra SenGupta, "Rev. of *Midnight's Children,*" p. 58.

42. Ranga Rao, "Chatterjee to Chatterjee," p. 110.

43. Shashi Tharoor, "Worlds of Magic," pp. 1, 11.

44. The claim here is of Indians *using* English, not being formally literate in it. See K. G. Jolly, *Literacy for All,* p. 9; O. P. Sharma, *Universal Literacy,* p. 18; O. P. Sharma, and Robert D. Retherford, *Literacy Trends,* p. 5.

45. Colonel Henry Yule and A. C. Burnell, *Hobson-Jobson.* The phrase "outlandish guests" appears in "Introductory Remarks," p. xv.

46. Johann Wolfgang von Goethe, "On World Literature," p. 229.

47. James Joyce, *Ulysses,* p. 709.

48. Moretti, *Modern Epic,* p. 249.

49. Sigmund Freud, "Family Romances."

50. For Vergès the fiction of the family romance is deployed by colonial France as a means to better control its island dependency in Réunion against which the Réunionais have to struggle for liberation. See her *Monsters and Revolutionaries.*

51. See Lynn A. Hunt, *The Family Romance of the French Revolution,* p. xiv and passim.

52. Gillian Beer, *Romance,* p. 79.

53. Dipesh Chakrabarty, "Postcoloniality and the Artifice of History: Who Speaks for 'Indian' Pasts?"in *Provincializing Europe,* pp. 27–46.

54. Salman Rushdie, "Empire Writes Back," p. 8.

BIBLIOGRAPHY

I. GOVERNMENT PUBLICATIONS

Auckland, Lord (Eden). *Minute on Native Education.* Cuttack: n.p., 1840.

Annual Report on the Administration of Public Affairs in the Bengal Presidency (var. years). Calcutta: Government Printing Press, 1856–1901.

Annual Report on the Administration of the Bombay Presidency (var. years). Bombay: Government Printing Press, 1856–1901.

Annual Report on the Administration of the Madras Presidency (var. years). Madras: Government Printing, 1856–1901.

Annual Statement of the Trade and Navigation of British India with Foreign Countries and of the Coasting Trade of the Several Presidencies and Provinces (var. years). Calcutta: Government Printing Press, 1850–1901.

Appendix to the Calcutta Gazette. Calcutta: n.p., 1883–1898.

A Catalogue of Books Printed in the Bengal Presidency (var. years). Calcutta: Government Printing Press, 1867-1901.

A Catalogue of Books Printed in the Bombay Presidency (var. years). Bombay: Government Central Press, 1867–1901.

A Catalogue of Books Printed in the Madras Presidency, Fort St. George Gazette Supplement (var. years). Madras: Fort St. George Gazette Press, 1867–1901.

Classified Catalogue of the Public Reference Library, Consisting of Books Registered from 1867 to 1889 at the Office of the Registrar of Books, Old College, Madras. Madras: Government Press, 1894.

General Report on the Administration of the Several Presidencies and Provinces of British India During the Year 1856–1857. Calcutta: John Gray, 1858.

Grant, Sir. A. *Catalogue of Native Publications in the Bombay Presidency up to 31st December 1864.* 2d. ed. Bombay: Education Society's Press, 1867.

Long, Rev. James. "Report on the Native Press in Bengal." *Selections from the Records of the Bengal Government, no. 32. Returns Relating to Publications in the Bengali Language, in 1857, to which is added a List of the Native Presses, with the Books Printed at Each, their Price, and Character, with a Notice of the Past Condition and Future Prospects of the Vernacular Press of Bengal and the Statistics of the Bombay and Madras Vernacular Presses.* Ed. Rev. J. Long. Calcutta: John Gray, 1859.

Peile, J. B. *Catalogue of the Native Publications in the Bombay Presidency from 1st January 1865 to 30th June 1867, and of some Works omitted in the previous Catalogue.* Bombay: Education Society's Press, 1869.

Thacker's India Directory (var. years). Calcutta: Thacker, Spink, 1867-1901.

II. CATALOGUES AND REPORTS FROM LIBRARIES AND READING ROOMS

Abstract of Proceedings of the Mahomedan Literary Society of Calcutta. Calcutta: Cambrian Press, 1871.

Alphabetical Catalogue of the Punjab Public Library. Rev. ed. Lahore: Victoria Press, 1897.

Anniversary Reports of the Family Literary Club [also the Borro Bazar Family Literary Club]. Calcutta: Sudaburson Press, 1859–1871.

Annual Report for the Imperial Library, Calcutta. Calcutta: Government Press, 1903–1923.

Annual Report of the Proceedings of the Bombay Native Education Society. Bombay: American Mission Press, 1827–1831.

Barnett, L. D. *A Catalogue of the Telugu Books in the Library of the British Museum.* London: British Museum, 1912.

——. *A Supplementary Catalogue of Tamil Books in the Library of the British Museum.* London: British Museum, 1931.

Barnett, L. D. and G. U. Pope. *A Catalogue of the Tamil Books in the Library of the British Museum.* London: British Museum, 1909.

The Bhuleshwar Library Catalogue of Books. Bombay: Ripon Printing Press, 1895.

Blumhardt, J. F. *Catalogue of Hindustani Printed Books in the Library of the British Museum.* London: British Museum, 1889.

——. *Catalogue of Marathi and Gujarati Printed Books in the Library of the British Museum.* London: Kegan Paul, Trench, Trübner, 1892.

——. *Catalogue of the Library of the India Office: Bengali, Oriya, and Assamese Books.* Vol. 2. London: Eyre and Spottiswoode, 1905.

——. *Catalogue of the Library of the India Office: Marathi and Gujarati Books.* Vol. 2. London: Eyre and Spottiswoode, 1908.

——. *A Supplementary Catalogue of Marathi and Gujarati Books in the British Museum*. London: British Museum, 1915.

The Bombay Native General Library Catalogue of Books. Bombay: Jehangier B. Marzban, 1898.

Buksh, Khuda. *The Islamic Libraries*. Calcutta: Thacker, Spink, 1902.

Calcutta Chaitanya Library Catalogue of English Books. Calcutta: n.p., 1903.

Catalogue and Index of the Allahabad Public Library. Allahabad: Indian Press, 1927.

Catalogue of Books in the Libraries of the Patna College, the Patna Collegiate School, and the Bihar School of Engineering. Calcutta: Bengal Secretariat Press, 1900.

Catalogue of Books in the Library of the Government Central Museum, Madras. Madras: Church of Scotland Mission Press, 1856.

Catalogue of Books in the Library of the Literary Society at Madras. Madras: J. B. Pharoah, 1839.

Catalogue of Books in the Presidency College Library. Calcutta: Bengal Secretariat Press, 1897.

Catalogue of Books in the Uttarpara Public Library. Calcutta: Gupta Press, 1903.

The Catalogue of Books of the Oriental and Mixed Library, Bangalore. Madras: Addison, 1899.

Catalogue of the Bengal Club Library. Calcutta: n.p., 1889.

A Catalogue of the Library of the East India College. Haileybury, England: East India College, 1821.

A Catalogue of the Library of the Hon. East India Company. London: J. and H. Cox, 1845.

Catalogue of the Library of the Madras Government Museum. Madras: Government Press, 1894.

Catalogue of the Library of the United Service Club, Calcutta. Calcutta: n.p., 1892.

Catalogue of the Madras Literary Society. Madras: Government Press, 1891.

Catalogue of the Printed Books of European Languages in Khuda Buksh Oriental Public Library, Patna. 1918 ed. Patna: Liberty Art Press, 1988.

Catalogue of the Delhi Public Library. Delhi: n.p., 1902.

Chatterjie, Mohitmohan, ed. *Golden Jubilee of the Patriotic Library [1902] and the Silver Jubilee of the Madan Mohan Library, 1920*. Calcutta: Bharati Printing Works, 1960.

Day, Sham Lall. *Annual Reports of the Calcutta Literary Society*. Vols. 1–41. Calcutta, 1875–1917.

——. *The Thirty-Third Annual Report of the Calcutta Literary Society*. Calcutta: n.p., 1921.

Duke Public Library, Howrah Classified Catalogue of Books. Calcutta: n.p., 1931.

Finances of the Calcutta Public Library. Report of the Subcommittee Appointed on the 10th February 1873. Calcutta: Government Printing, 1873.

Ghose, Mohendra Nath, ed. *The Annual Report of the Cottage Library and Young Men's Literary Association, Bhowanipore*. Bhowanipore: Urban Press, 1880.

The Jamsetjee Nesserwanjee Petit Fort Reading Room and Library, Bombay Classified Catalogue of Books. Bombay: Captain Printing Press, 1895.

The Journal of Bombay East Indian Literary Society. Bombay: B. E. I. Printing Press, 1895–1897.

Mandlik, Vishvanath Narayan and Ardaseer Framjee Moos. *Catalogue of Manuscripts and Books belonging to the Bhau Daji Memorial*. Bombay: Education Society's Press, 1882.

The Nineteenth Report of the Proceedings of the Calcutta School-Book Society, for 1856. Calcutta: Calcutta School-Book Society Press, 1857.

Perti, R. K. *Catalogue of Books of the Fort William College Collection in the National Archives of India Library*. New Delhi: National Archives of India, 1984.

Presidency College Literary Society Anniversary Addresses [Madras]. Madras: n.p., 1895.

Presidency College [Madras] Literary Society Lectures. Madras: Srinivasa Varadachari, 1895–1896.

Proceedings of the Vernacular Translation Society. Calcutta: P. S. D'Rozario, 1845.

Report of the Bagbazar Reading Library for the 19th Year Ending on June 1902. Calcutta: K. P. Mookerjee, 1903.

Report of the Calcutta Public Library for 1847–1893. Calcutta: Sanders, Cones, 1847–93.

Report of the Maju Public Library for Three Years from October 1902 to September 1905. Calcutta: K. Banerjee, 1905.

Report of the Maju Public Library for Two and a Half Years from October 1907 to March 1910. Calcutta: Harold Press, 1910.

Report of the Maju Public Library for Three Years from April 1910 to March 1913. Calcutta: Corinthian Press, 1913.

"Report on the Fort Improvement Library." *Times of India*, August 17, 1861, p. 2.

Report on the Administration of the Government Museum and the Connemara Public Library, 1890–1900. Madras: Government Printing, 1891–1900.

Roy, Girish Chunder, ed. *Catalogue of the Indian Library of His Excellency, Lord Lytton, Viceroy and Governor General of India*. Simla: Private Secretary's Office Press, 1877.

Ruheemooddeen, Mahomed. "A Quarter Century of the Mahomedan Literary Society of Calcutta." *The Mahomedan Literary Society of Calcutta*. Calcutta: Stanhope Press, 1889.

Rules of the Bara Bazar Library. Calcutta: n.p., 1901.

The Second Annual Report of the Bombay Native Benevolent Library. Bombay: L. M. DeSouza's Press, 1855.

Shahani, S., ed. *Wilson College Literary Society Lectures*. Bombay: Fort Printing Press, 1895.

Stewart, Charles. *Descriptive Catalogue of the Oriental Library of the Late Tippoo Sultan of Mysore to Which are Refixed Memoirs of Hyder Aly Khan, and his Son Tippoo Sultan*. Cambridge: University Press, 1809.

A Supplement to the Catalogue of the Library of the Hon. East India Company. London: J. and H. Cox, 1851.

Supplementary Catalogue of Books in the Public Library of the Government Central Museum, Madras, 1879–1881. Madras: Government Press, 1881.

Thoms, P. P., printer. *A Catalogue of the Library Belonging to the English Factory at Canton, in China.* Macao: Hon. East India Company's Press, 1819.

The Third Annual Report of the Madras Hindu Reading Room for 1855 with Appendices and a List of Members. Madras: Hindu Press, 1856.

Third Report of the Students' Literary & Scientific Society and of its Vernacular Branch Societies. Bombay: Bombay Gazette Press, 1852.

The Twenty-Eighth Report of the Proceedings of the Calcutta School-Book Society for 1872 & 1873. Calcutta: Baptist Mission Press, 1874.

III. CONTEMPORARY SERIALS

The Calcutta Review
The Friend of India
The Hindoo Patriot (Calcutta)
The Hindu (Madras)
The Madras Christian College Magazine
The Times of India (Bombay)

IV. PUBLISHERS' ARCHIVES

Richard Bentley
Cassells
Heinemann
Longman
Macmillan
John Murray
Routledge, Kegan Paul, Trench, Trübner

V. PRIMARY TEXTS AND SECONDARY SOURCES

Ahmad, Aijaz. *In Theory. Classes, Nations, Literatures.* New York: Verso, 1992.
——. "The Politics of Literary Postcoloniality." *Race & Class* 36, no. 3 (1995): 1–20.

Alexander, Meena. "Outcaste Power: Ritual Displacement and Virile Maternity in Indian Women Writers." *Journal of Commonwealth Literature* 24, no. 1 (1989): 12–29.

Ali, Ahmed. "Illusion and Reality: The Art and Philosophy of Raja Rao." *Journal of Commonwealth Literature* 5 (1968): 16–28.
——. *Mr. Eliot's Penny World of Dreams: An Essay on the Interpretation of T. S. Eliot's Poetry.* Bombay: New Book Company, 1936.
——. *The Prison House.* Karachi: Akrash Publishing, 1985.

——. "The Progressive Writers' Movement and Creative Writers in Urdu." In *Marxist Influences in South Asian Literature*, ed. Carlo Coppola, Vol. 1. East Lansing: Asian Studies Center, Michigan State University, 1974.

——. "The Progressive Writers' Movement in its Historical Perspective." *Journal of South Asian Literature* 13 (fall/summer 1977/78): 91–98.

——. "Recollections of E. M. Forster." In *E. M. Forster: A Tribute*, ed. K. Natwar-Singh. New York: Harcourt, Brace and World, 1964, 33–30.

——. "Some Reflections on the Novel." *Journal of Indian Writing in English* (January 1989): 1–11.

——. *Twilight in Delhi*. 1940. New York: New Directions, 1994.

Ali, Ahmed and Raja Rao, eds. *Tomorrow*. Bombay: Padma Publications, 1943.

Ali, Tariq. "Review of *Midnight's Children*." *Mainstream* 31, no. 18, (January 1,1983): 20–23.

Allen, Grant. *The Woman Who Did*. 1895. Ed. Sarah Wintle. Reprint, Oxford: Oxford UP, 1995.

Allen, James Smith. *Popular French Romanticism: Authors, Readers, and Books in the 19th Century*. Syracuse, N.Y.: Syracuse UP, 1981.

Allen, Thomas. *The Homeric Catalogue of Ships*. Oxford: The Clarendon Press, 1921.

Altbach, Philip. *Publishing in India: An Analysis*. Delhi: Oxford UP, 1975.

Altick, Richard D. "From Aldine to Everyman: Cheap Reprint Series of the English Classics, 1830–1906." *Studies in Bibliography* 11 (1958): 3–24.

——. *The English Common Reader: A Social History of the Mass Reading Public 1800–1900*. Chicago: U of Chicago P, 1957.

——. "Nineteenth-Century English Best-Sellers: A Further List." *Studies in Bibliography* 22 (1969): 197–206.

——. "Nineteenth-Century English Best-Sellers: A Third List." *Studies in Bibliography* 39 (1986): 235–241.

Amin, Samir. *Unequal Development*. Trans. Brian Pearce. New York: Monthly Review Press, 1976.

Anand, Mulk Raj. *Conversations in Bloomsbury*. 1981. Reprint, New Delhi: Oxford UP, 1995.

——. *Letters on India*. London: Labour Book Service, 1942.

——. "Recollections of E. M. Forster." In *E. M. Forster: A Tribute*, ed. K. Natwar-Singh. New York: Harcourt, Brace and World, 1964, 41–49.

——. *Roots and Flowers. Two Lectures on the Metamorphosis of Technique and Content in the Indian-English Novel*. Dharwar: Karnatak U, 1972.

——. "The Story of my Experiment with a White Lie." In *Critical Essays on Indian Writing in English*, ed. M. K. Naik, S. K. Desai and G. S. Amur. Rev. and enlarged ed. Madras: Macmillan, 1972.

——. "Variety of Ways: Is there a Shared Tradition in Commonwealth Literature?" In *Awakened Conscience: Studies in Commonwealth Literature*, ed. C. D. Narasimhaiah. New Delhi: Sterling, 1978.

Anderson, Benedict. *Imagined Communities: Reflections on the Origin and Spread of Nationalism*. 2d rev. ed. New York: Verso, 1991.

Anderson, David D. "Ahmed Ali and the Growth of a Pakistani Literary Tradition." *World Literature Written in English* 14, no. 2 (1977).

Anderson, Perry. "Components of the National Culture." *New Left Review* 50 (July/August 1968): 3–58.

——. "Modernity and Revolution." In *Marxism and the Interpretation of Culture*, ed. Cary Nelson and Lawrence Grossberg. Urbana: U of Illinois P, 1988, 317–338.

Anon. "Anglo-Indian Novels." *Calcutta Review* 50, no. 99 (1870): 182–205.

——. "Bankim Chandra." *Calcutta Review* 134, no. 167 (January 1887), pp. xxiv–xxv.

——. "Bengali Literature." *Calcutta Review* 52, no.104 (1871): 294–316.

——. "G. W. M. Reynolds, Obituary." *Bookseller* July 3, 1879, pp. 600–601.

——. "Genesis of *The Calcutta Review*." *Calcutta Review* 117, no. 233 (1903): 111–115.

——. *Mr. Jacobs. A Tale of the Drummer, the Reporter, and the Prestidigitateur.* Boston: W. B. Clarke and Carruth, 1883.

——. "Reynolds and Penny Fiction." *TLS* 24, January 1924, p. 56.

Appadurai, Arjun. ed. *The Social Life of Things*. Cambridge: Cambridge UP, 1986.

Apple, Michael W. *Ideology and Curriculum*. 2d. ed. New York: Routledge, 1990.

Armstrong, Nancy. *Desire and Domestic Fiction. A Political History of the Novel.* New York: Oxford UP, 1987.

Armstrong, Nancy and Leonard Tennenhouse. *The American Origins of the English Novel*. Berkeley: U of California P, 1994.

Arnold, W. D. "Indian Light Literature." *Calcutta Review* 26, no. 51 (1856): 1–23.

Asad, Talal, ed. *Anthropology and the Colonial Encounter*. London: Ithaca Press, 1973.

Asher, R. E. "The Tamil Renaissance and the Beginnings of the Tamil Novel." In *The Novel in India: Its Birth and Development*, ed. T. W. Clark. Berkeley: U of California P, 1970.

Askari, Muhammad Hasan. "A Novel by Ahmed Ali." Typescript of essay in *Maxzan* (Lahore) May 1949. Trans. Carlo Coppola, n.p.

Auerbach, Erich. *Mimesis. The Representation of Reality in Western Literature.* Trans. Willard R. Trask. Princeton: Princeton UP, 1953.

Bagal, Jogesh Chandra, ed. *Bankim Rachnavali*. Calcutta: Sahitya Samsad, 1969.

Bagchi, Jasodhara. "Positivism and Nationalism: Womanhood and Crisis in Nationalist Fiction: Bankimchandra's *Anandmath*." In *Narrative: Forms and Transformations*, ed. Sudhakar Marathe and Meenakshi Mukherjee. New Delhi: Chanakya Publications, 1986, 59–78.

——. "Shakespeare in Loin Cloths: English Literature and the Early Nationalist Consciousness in Bengal." In *Rethinking English: Essays in Literature, Langauge, History*, ed. Svati Joshi. New Delhi: Trianka, 1991, 146–159.

Bald, Suresht Renjen. *Novelists and Political Consciousness: Literary Expression of Indian Nationalism, 1919–1947*. New Delhi: Chanakya Publications, 1982.

Baldick, Chris. *The Social Mission of English Criticism, 1848–1932*. New York: Oxford UP, 1983.

Ballhatchet, Kenneth. *Race, Sex, and Class Under the Raj: Imperial Attitudes, Policies, and their Critics, 1793–1905*. London: Weidenfeld and Nicolson, 1980.

Bannerji, Himani. "Mothers and Teachers: Gender and Class in Educational Proposals for and by Women in Colonial Bengal." *Journal of Historical Sociology* 5, no. 1 (1992): 1–30.

Barbier, Frédéric. "The Publishing Industry and Printed Output in Nineteenth-Century France." In *Books and Society in History: Papers of the Association of College and Research Libraries, Rare Books and Manuscripts Preconference*, ed. Kenneth E. Carpenter. New York: R. R. Bowker, 1983.

Bardhan, Kalpana, ed. and trans. *Outcastes, Peasants, and Rebels. A Selection of Bengali Short Stories*. Berkeley: U of California P, 1990.

Barker, Francis, Peter Hulme, and Margaret Iversen, eds. *Colonial Discourse/Postcolonial Theory*. Manchester: Manchester UP, 1994.

——. "Introduction: Angelus Novus?" In *Post-Modernism and the Re-reading of Modernity*, ed. Francis Barker, Peter Hulme, and Margaret Iversen. Manchester: Manchester UP, 1992, 1–22.

Barker, Francis et al., eds. *Europe and its Others*. Colchester: U of Essex P, 1985.

Barnes, James J. *Authors, Publishers, and Politicians: The Quest for an Anglo-American Copyright Agreement,1815–1854*. Columbus: Ohio State UP, 1974.

Barns, Margarita. *The Indian Press. A History of the Growth of Public Opinion in India*. London: George Allen and Unwin, 1940.

Barrier, N. G. *Banned: Controversial Literature and Political Control in British India, 1907–1947*. Columbia: U of Missouri P, 1974.

——. "The British and Controversial Publications in Punjab." *Punjab Past and Present* 8 (1974): 32–60.

Barrow, Cecil Montefiore. *The Poetical Selections Prescribed for the Matriculation Examination of the University of Madras to be Held in December 1872*. Mangalore: C. Stolz, 1872.

Barrow, Cecil M. "Selections from English Literature from the Use of Schools in India (review)." *Calcutta Review* 117, no. 233 (1903): xiv–xv.

Basu, Aparna. *The Growth of Education and Political Development in India, 1898–1920*. Delhi: Oxford UP, 1974.

Bator, Paul G. "The Entrance of the Novel into the Scottish Universities." In *The Scottish Invention of English Literature*, ed. Robert Crawford. Cambridge: Cambridge UP, 1998.

Baudrillard, Jean. *The Mirror of Production*. Trans. Mark Poster. St. Louis: Telos Press, 1975.

Baxter, Ian. "The Establishment of the First Libraries for European Soldiers in India." *South Asia Library Group* 40 (January 1993): 25–30.

Bayly, C. A. *Empire and Information: Intelligence Gathering and Social Communication in India, 1780–1870*. Cambridge: Cambridge UP, 1996.

Baym, Nina. *Novels, Readers, and Reviewers: Responses to Fiction in Antebellum America*. Ithaca, N.Y.: Cornell UP, 1984.

——. *Women's Fiction: A Guide to Novels by and About Women in America, 1820–1870*. Ithaca, N.Y.: Cornell UP, 1978.

Beer, Gillian. *The Romance*. London: Methuen, 1970.

Behdad, Ali. *Belated Travelers: Orientalism in the Age of Colonial Dissolution*. Durham: Duke UP, 1994.

Bell, Michael Davitt. *The Problem of American Realism: Studies in the Cultural History of a Literary Idea*. Chicago: U of Chicago P, 1993.

Belliappa, N. Meena. "East-West Encounter: Indian Women Writers of Fiction in English." In *Fiction and the Reading Public in India*, ed. C. D. Narsimhaiah. Mysore: Wesley Press, 1967.

Benjamin, Walter. *The Origin of German Tragic Drama*. Trans. John Osborne. New York: Verso, 1977.

——. *Illuminations*. Ed. Hannah Arendt. Trans. Harry Zohn. New York: Schocken, 1968.

Bentley, Eric. *The Life of the Drama*. New York: Atheneum, 1964.

Berelson, Bernard. *The Library's Public*. New York: Columbia UP, 1949.

Berman, Marshall. *All that is Solid Melts into Air: The Experience of Modernity*. New York: Penguin, 1982.

Berman, Russell. "Writing for the Book Industry: The Writer Under Organized Capitalism." *New German Critique* 29 (spring/summer 1983): 39–56.

——. *Modern Culture and Critical Theory. Art, Politics, and the Legacy of the Frankfurt School*. Madison: U of Wisconsin P, 1989.

Bernal, Martin. *Black Athena: The Afroasiatic Roots of Classical Civilization*. New Brunswick: Rutgers UP, 1987.

Bhabha, Homi. "In a Spirit of Calm Violence." In *After Colonialism*, ed. Gyan Prakash. Princeton: Princeton UP, 1995, 326–344.

——. *The Location of Culture*. London: Routledge, 1994.

——, ed. *Nation and Narration*. New York: Routledge, 1990.

Bharucha, Rustom. "Rushdie's Whale." *Massachusetts Review* 27 (summer 1986): 221–237.

Bhatnagar, O. P. "The Search for Identity in Commonwealth Literature." In *Alien Voices: Perspectives on Commonwealth Literature*, ed. Avadhesh K. Srivastava. Lucknow: Print House, 1981.

Bhattacharya, Lokenath. *Books and Reading in India: Studies on Books and Reading*. Paris: UNESCO, 1987.

Bigland, Eileen. *Marie Corelli: The Woman and the Legend—A Biography*. London: Jarrolds, 1953.

Billington, Mary Frances. *Woman in India; by Mary Frances Billington. With an Introduction by the Marchioness of Dufferin and Ava*. London: Chapman and Hall, 1895.

Black, Alistair. *A New History of the English Public Library: Social and Intellectual Contexts, 1850–1914*. London: Leicester UP, 1996.

Blackburn, Stuart et al., eds. *Oral Epics in India*. Berkeley: U of California P, 1989.

Blake-Hill, Philip V. "The Macmillan Archive." *British Museum Quarterly* 36 (1971): 74–80.

Bloch, Ernst. "Discussing Expressionism." In *Aesthetics and Politics*, ed. Rodney Livingstone, Perry Anderson, and Francis Mulhern. London: New Left Books, 1977, 16–27.

——. "Nonsynchronism and the Obligation to its Dialectics." *New German Critique* 11, no. 4 (1977): 22–38.

——. *The Principle of Hope*. Trans. Neville Plaice, Stephen Plaice, and Paul Knight. Cambridge: MIT P, 1986.

Blunt, Alison and Gillian Rose, eds. *Writing Women and Space: Colonial and Postcolonial Geographies*. New York: Guilford, 1994.

Bocock, Robert. *Consumption*. London: Routledge, 1993.

Boehmer, Elleke. *Colonial and Postcolonial Literature. Migrant Metaphors*. Oxford: Oxford UP, 1995.

Boman-Behram, B. K. *Educational Controversies in India: The Cultural Conquest of India under British Imperialism*. Bombay: Taraporewala, 1942.

Borges, Jorge Luis. "The Argentine Writer and Tradition." Trans. James E. Irby. In *Labyrinths: Selected Stories and Other Writings*, ed. Donald A. Yates and James E. Irby. New York: New Directions, 1962, 177–185.

Bourdieu, Pierre. *Distinction: A Social Critique of the Judgement of Taste*. Trans. Richard Nice. Cambridge: Harvard UP, 1984.

——. *The Rules of Art: Genesis and Structure of the Literary Field*. Trans. Susan Emanuel. Stanford: Stanford UP, 1996.

Bradbury, Malcolm and James McFarlane, eds. *Modernism. 1890–1930*. London: Penguin, 1976.

Brander, Laurence. "Two Novels by Ahmed Ali." *Journal of Commonwealth Literature* 3 (1967): 76–86.

Brantlinger, Patrick. *The Rule of Darkness: British Literature and Imperialism, 1830–1914*. Ithaca, N.Y.: Cornell UP, 1988.

Bratton, Jacky. "The Contending Discourses of Melodrama." In *Melodrama: Stage Picture Screen*, ed. Jacky Bratton, Jim Cook, and Christine Gledhill. London: British Film Institute Publishing, 1994, 38–49.

Braudel, Fernand. *The Structures of Everyday Life: The Limits of the Possible*. Trans. Sian Reynolds. New York: Harper and Row, 1981.

Brecht, Bertolt. "Popularity and Realism." Trans. Stuart Hood. In *Aesthetics and Politics*, ed. Rodney Livingstone, Perry Anderson, and Francis Mulhern. London: New Left Books, 1977, 79–85.

Breckenridge, Carol A. and Peter van de Veer, eds. *Orientalism and the Postcolonial Predicament: Perspectives on South Asia*. Philadelphia: U of Pennsylvania P, 1993.

Breckenridge, Carol A., ed. *Consuming Modernity: Public Culture in a South Asian World*. Minneapolis: U of Minnesota P, 1995.

Brennan, Timothy. *At Home in the World: Cosmopolitanism Now*. Cambridge: Harvard UP, 1997.

——. *Salman Rushdie and the Third World: Myths of the Nation*. New York: St. Martin's Press, 1989.

Bretherton, Margaret. *Ten Noble Women*. Madras: Christian Literature Society for India, 1913.

Brewer, John. *The Pleasures of the Imagination: English Culture in the Eighteenth Century*. New York: Farrar, Straus, and Giroux, 1997.

Brewer, John and Roy Porter, eds. *Consumption and the World of Goods*. New York: Routledge, 1993.

Bridges, Robert. "F. Marion Crawford: A Conversation." *McClure's Magazine* 4, no. 4 (March 1895): 316–323.

——. *Suppressed Chapters and Other Bookishness*. New York: Charles Scribner's Sons, 1895.

Briggs, Asa, ed. *Essays in the History of Publishing in Celebration of the 250th Anniversary of the House of Longman, 1724–1974*. London: Longman, 1974.

Brittan, Harriet G. *Shoshie, the Hindoo Zenana teacher*. New York: T. Whittaker, 1873.

Brooke, Stopford A. *English Literature*. Toronto: Copp, Clark, 1901.

——. *A Primer of English Literature*. Ed. John Richard Green. London: Macmillan, 1876.

Brooks, Jeffrey. *When Russia Learned to Read: Literacy and Popular Literature, 1861–1917*. Princeton: Princeton UP, 1985.

Brooks, Peter. "Melodrama, Body, Revolution." In *Melodrama: Stage Picture Screen*, ed. Jacky Bratton, Jim Cook and Christine Gledhill. London: British Film Institute Publishing, 1994, 11–24.

——. *The Melodramatic Imagination. Balzac, Henry James, Melodrama, and the Mode of Excess*. New York: Columbia UP, 1985.

Brown, Philip A. H. *London Publishers and Printers, c. 1800–1870*. London: British Library, 1982.

Bullock, George. *Marie Corelli. The Life and Death of a Best-Seller*. London: Constable, 1940.

Bürger, Peter. *Theory of the Avant-Garde*. Trans. Michael Shaw. Minneapolis: U of Minnesota P, 1984.

Burke, Timothy. *Lifebuoy Men, Lux Women: Commodification, Consumption, and Cleanliness in Modern Zimbabwe*. Durham: Duke UP, 1996.

Burt, Daniel S. "A Victorian Gothic: G. W. M. Reynolds's *Mysteries of London*." *New York Literary Forum* 7, Special Issue on Melodrama (1980): 141–158.

Burton, Antoinette. *Burdens of History: British Feminists, Indian Women, and Imperial Culture, 1865–1915*. Chapel Hill: U of North Carolina P, 1994.

Butalia, Urvashi and Ritu Menon, eds. *In Other Words: New Writing by Indian Women*. New Delhi: Kali for Women, 1992.

Butler, Judith. *Gender Trouble: Feminism and the Subversion of Identity*. New York: Routledge, 1990.

——. *The Psychic Life of Power: Theories in Subjection*. Stanford: Stanford UP, 1997.

Carby, Hazel. *Reconstructing Womanhood: The Emergence of the Afro-American Woman Novelist*. New York: Oxford UP, 1987.

Carpenter, Kenneth E. and G. Thomas Tanselle, eds. *Books and Society in History*. New York: R. R. Bowker, 1983.

Carrier, Esther Jane. *Fiction in Public Libraries 1876–1900*. New York: Scarecrow Press, 1965.

Casey, Janet Galligani. "Marie Corelli & *Fin de Siècle* Feminism." *English Literature in Transition, 1880–1920* 35, no. 2 (1992): 163–178.

Cavalier, Anthony Ramsen, and Zenana Bible and Medical Mission. *In Northern India: A Story of Mission Work in Zenanas, Schools and Hospitals*. London: S. W. Partridge, 1899.

Césaire, Aimé. *Discourse on Colonialism*. Trans. Joan Pinkham. New York: Monthly Review, 1972.

Chakrabarty, Dipesh. *Provincializing Europe: Postcolonial Thought and Historical Difference*. Princeton: Princeton UP, 2000.

Chakravarti, K. *Sarala and Hingana: Tales Descriptive of Indian Life*. Calcutta, n.p., 1895.

Chakravarti, K. N. *The Liberation*. Calcutta: n.p., 1924.

Chandra, Sudhir. *The Oppressive Present: Literature and Social Consciousness in Colonial India*. Delhi: Oxford UP, 1994.

Chandra, Vikram. "The Cult of Authenticity." *Boston Review* (February/March 2000): 42–29.

Chapman, Mrs. E. F. *Sketches of Some Distinguished Indian Women*. London: W. H. Allen, 1891.

Chapman, Priscilla. *Hindoo Female Education*. London: Seeley and Burnside, 1839.

Chartier, Roger. *Cultural History: Between Practices and Representations*. Trans. Lydia Cochrane. Cambridge: Polity Press, 1988.

——. *The Cultural Origins of the French Revolution*. Trans. Lydia G. Cochrane. Durham: Duke UP, 1991.

——. *The Cultural Uses of Print in Early Modern France*. Trans. Lydia G. Cochrane. Princeton: Princeton UP, 1987.

––, ed. *The Culture of Print: Power and the Uses of Print in Early Modern Europe*. Trans. Lydia G. Cochrane. Princeton: Princeton UP, 1989.

——. *Frenchness in the History of the Book: From the History of Publishing to the History of Reading*. Worcester: American Antiquarian Society, 1988.

——. "Intellectual History or Sociocultural History? The French Trajectories." In *Modern European Intellectual History*, ed. Dominick La Capra and Steven L. Kaplan. Ithaca, N.Y.: Cornell UP, 1982.

——. "Laborers and Voyagers: From the Text to the Reader." *diacritics* 22, no. 2 (1992): 49–61.

——. *The Order of Books: Readers, Authors, and Libraries in Europe Between the Fourteenth and Eighteenth Century*. Trans. Lydia G. Cochrane. Stanford: Stanford UP, 1994.

Chase, Richard. *The American Novel and Its Tradition*. New York: Goridan Press, 1978.

Chatterjee, Bankim Chandra. See also "Chatterji." *Anandamath*. Trans. Aurobindo Ghose and Barindra Kumar Ghosh. Calcutta: Basumati Sahitya Mandir, 1909.

——. *Chandrashekhar*. Trans. Debendra Chandra Mullick. Calcutta: Thacker, Spink, 1905.

——. "Doctor Macurus." Trans. J. D. Anderson. In *Indira and Other Stories*, ed. J. D. Anderson. Calcutta: Modern Review Office, 1925.

——. *Durgesanandini; or, A Chieftain's Daughter*. Trans. Charu Chandra Mookerjee. Calcutta: H. M. Mookerjee, 1880.

——. "Indira." Trans. Marian Maddern. In *The Poison Tree: Three Novellas*, ed. Marian Maddern and S. N. Mukherjee. New Delhi: Penguin, 1996.

——. *Kamalakanta: A Collection of Satirical Essays & Reflections*. Trans. Monish Ranjan Chatterjee. Calcutta: Rupa, 1992.

——. *Kapalkundala*. Trans. Devendra Nath Ghose. Calcutta: K. M. Bagchi, 1919.

——. "Krishnakanta's Will." Trans. S. N. Mukherjee. In *The Poison Tree: Three Novellas*, ed. Marian Maddern and S. N. Mukherjee. New Delhi: Penguin, 1996.

——. "The Poison Tree [Bishabriksha]." Trans. Marian Maddern. In *The Poison Tree: Three Novellas*, ed. Marian Maddern and S. N. Mukherjee. New Delhi: Penguin, 1996.

——. "Radharani." Trans. J. D. Anderson. In *Indira and Other Stories*, ed. J. D. Anderson. Calcutta: Modern Review Office, 1925.

——. *Rajmohan's Wife. A Novel*. 1864; 1935 ed. Reprint, New Delhi: Ravi Dayal, 1996.

Chatterjee, Kalyan K. "The Indian Renaissance: European Text and Indian Context." *Indian Literature* 35, no. 4 (1992): 51–60.

Chatterjee, Partha. "Colonialism, Nationalism, and Colonized Women: The Contest in India." *American Ethnologist* 16, no. 4 (1989): 622–633.

——. *The Nation and its Fragments: Colonial and Postcolonial Histories*. Princeton: Princeton UP, 1993.

——. "The Nationalist Resolution of the Women's Question." In *Recasting*

Women: Essays in Colonial History, ed. Kumkum Sangari and Sudesh Vaid. New Delhi: Kali for Women, 1989, 233–253.

——. *Nationalist Thought and the Colonial World: A Derivative Discourse?* London: Zed, 1986.

——, ed. *Texts of Power: Emerging Disciplines in Colonial Bengal*. Minneapolis: U of Minnesota P, 1995.

Chatterjee, Upamanyu. *English, August: An Indian Story*. 1988. Reprint, London: Faber and Faber, 1989.

——. *The Last Burden*. London: Faber and Faber, 1993.

Chatterji, Bankim Chandra. See also "Chatterjee." *Anandamath*. Trans. Basanta Koomar Roy. New Delhi: Orient Paperbacks, 1992.

——. "Bengali Literature." In *Bankim Rachnavali*, ed. Jogesh Chandra Bagal. Calcutta: Sahitya Samsad, 1969, 103–124.

——. "A Popular Literature for Bengal." *Bankim Rachnavali*, ed. Jogesh Chandra Bagal. Calcutta: Sahitya Samsad, 1969.

——. *Sitaram*. Trans. Sib Chandra Mukerji. Calcutta: R. Cambray, 1903, 97–102.

——. "The Two Rings." Trans. Dakshina Charan Roy. In *The Two Rings and Radharani*. Calcutta: Students' Library, nd.

Chattopadhaya, R. C. *The Sorrows of a Subpostmaster*. Calcutta: n.p., 1927.

Chattopadhyay, Kamaladevi. *Indian Women's Battle for Freedom*. New Delhi: Abhinav Publications, 1983.

Chaudhuri, Nupur. "Shawls, Jewelry, Curry, and Rice in Victorian Britain." In *Western Women and Imperialism: Complicity and Resistance*, ed. Nupur Chaudhuri and Margaret Strobel. Bloomington: Indiana UP, 1992, 231–246.

Chaudhuri, Nirad C. *The Autobiography of an Unknown Indian*. 1951. Reprint, New York: Addison-Wesley, 1989.

Chester, Gail. "The Not so Gentle Reader: The Role of the Publisher's Reader as Gatekeeper, with Particular Reference to Macmillan and Co., 1895–1905." Master's thesis, Centre for English Studies, University of London, 1997.

Cheyfitz, Eric. *The Poetics of Imperialism: Translation and Colonization from The Tempest to Tarzan*. New York: Oxford UP, 1991.

Chow, Rey. *Woman and Chinese Modernity: The Politics of Reading Between East and West*. Minneapolis: U of Minnesota P, 1991.

Christian Literature Society. *Nautch Women: An Appeal to English Ladies on Behalf of their Indian Sisters*. Madras: SPCK Press, 1893.

Christian Vernacular Education Society. *The Women of India and What Can be Done for Them*. Papers on Indian Reform. Madras: Christian Vernacular Education Society, 1888.

Chugtai, Ismat. *The Quilt and Other Stories*. Trans. Tahira Naqvi and Syeda S. Hameed. New Delhi: Kali for Women, 1990.

Clark, Robert and Robert Maconachie. *The Missions of the Church Missionary Society and the Church of England Zenana Missionary Society in the Punjab and Sindh*. London: Church Missionary Society, 1904.

Clark, T. J. *Farewell to an Idea: Episodes from a History of Modernism.* New Haven: Yale UP, 1999.

Clark, T. W. "Bengali Prose Fiction up to Bankimchandra." In *The Novel in India: Its Birth and Development.* Ed. T. W. Clark. Berkeley: U of California P, 1970.

——. "The Role of Bankimchandra in the Development of Nationalism." In *Historians of India, Pakistan, and Ceylon,* ed. C. H. Philips. London: Oxford UP, 1961, 429–445.

Clifford, James. *The Predicament of Culture: Twentieth-century Ethnography, Literature, and Art.* Cambridge: Harvard UP, 1988.

Cohen, Margaret. *The Sentimental Education of the Novel.* Princeton: Princeton UP, 1999.

Cohn, Bernard. *An Anthropologist Among the Historians and Other Essays.* New York: Oxford UP, 1987.

——. *India: The Social Anthropology of a Civilization.* Englewood Cliffs, N.J.: Prentice Hall, 1971.

——. "Representing Authority in Victorian India." In *The Invention of Tradition,* ed. Eric Hobsbawm and Terence Ranger. Cambridge: Cambridge UP, 1983, 165–210.

Coleman, Deirdre. "Conspicuous Consumption: White Abolitionism and the English Women's Protest Writing in the 1790s." *ELH* 61 (1994): 341–362.

Collison, Robert. *Published Library Catalogues: An Introduction to their Contents.* London: Mansell Publishing, 1973.

Comaroff, John L. and Jean Comaroff. *Of Revelation and Revolution: Christianity, Colonialism, and Consciousness in South Africa.* Vol. 1. Chicago and London: U of Chicago P, 1991.

——. *Of Revelation and Revolution: The Dialectics of Modernity on a South African Frontier.* Vol. 2. Chicago and London: U of Chicago P, 1997.

Cooper, Frederick and Ann Laura Stoler, eds. *Tensions of Empire: Colonial Cultures in a Bourgeois World.* Berkeley: U of California P, 1997.

Coppola, Carlo. "The All-India Progressive Writers' Association: The European Phase." In *Marxist Influences and South Asian Literature,* ed. Carlo Coppola, 1:34. East Lansing: Asian Studies Center, Michigan State University, 1974.

——. "The *Angare* Group: The *Enfants Terribles* of Urdu Literature." *Annual of Urdu Studies* 1 (1981): 57–69.

——. "The Poetry of Ahmed Ali." *Journal of Indian Writing in English* 8, no. 1–2 (1980): 63–76.

——. "Politics and the Novel in India: A Perspective." *Contributions to Asian Studies* 6, Special Issue on Politics and the Novel in India (1975): 1–5.

——. "The Short Stories of Ahmed Ali." In *Studies in the Urdu Ghazal and Prose Fiction,* ed. Muhammad Umar Memon, 5:211–242. Madison: U of Wisconsin, 1979.

Corelli, Marie. *The Sorrows of Satan.* Philadelphia: J. P. Lippincott, 1896.

——. *The Soul of Lilith*. London: Methuen, 1897.

——. *Thelma: A Society Novel*. New York: William L. Allison, 1895.

——. *The Treasure of Heaven: A Romance of Riches*. New York: Dodd, Mead, 1906.

Court, Franklin E. *Institutionalizing English Literature: The Culture and Politics of Literary Study, 1750–1900*. Stanford: Stanford UP, 1992.

Couto, Maria. "Midnight's Children and Parents." *Encounter* 58, no. 2 (1982) 61–77.

——. "The Raj in Fiction and Film: Transformation as Distortion." In *Narrative. Forms and Transformations*, ed. Sudhakar Marathe and Meenakshi Mukherjee. New Delhi: Chanakya Publications, 1986, 119–138.

Cowasjee, Saros, ed. *Women Writers of the Raj: Short Fiction from Kipling to Independence*. London: Grafton Books, 1990.

Cox, Harold. *The House of Longman*. London: Longmans, 1925.

Crane, Ralph J. *Inventing India: A History of India in English-language Fiction*. New York: St. Martin's Press, 1992.

Crawford, F. Marion. "About Novels." *Boston Evening Transcript*, December 19, 1892, p. 4.

——. "British Rule in India." *New York Daily Tribune*, April 15, 1883, p. 3.

——. *Doctor Claudius: A True Story*. New York: Macmillan, 1883.

——. *Mr. Isaacs: A Tale of Modern India*. Reprint, New York: Grosset and Dunlap, 1882.

——. *The Novel: What it Is*. 1893. Reprint, New York: Macmillan, 1908.

——. "The Press in India." *New York Daily Tribune*, March 11, 1883, p. 3.

——. *Zoroaster*. New York: Macmillan, 1885.

——. *Saracinesca*. New York: Macmillan, 1887.

——. *Paul Patoff*. New York: Macmillan, 1887.

——. *Khaled: A Tale of Arabia*. New York: Macmillan, 1890.

——. *Katherine Lauderdale*. New York: Macmillan, 1894.

Crawford, Robert, ed. *The Scottish Invention of English Literature*. Cambridge: Cambridge UP, 1998.

Cruse, Amy. *After the Victorians*. London: George Allen and Unwin Limited, 1938.

——. *The Shaping of English Literature and the Readers' Share in the Development of Its Forms*. New York: Thomas Y. Crowell, 1927.

——. *The Victorians and their Books*. London: George Allen and Unwin, 1935.

Culler, Jonathan. "Prolegomena to a Theory of Reading." In *The Reader in the Text. Essays on Audience and Interpretation*, ed. Susan Suleiman and Inge Crosman. Princeton: Princeton UP, 1980, 46–66.

Cunningham, Gail. *The New Woman and the Victorian Novel*. London: Macmillan, 1978.

Dalmia, Vasudha. *The Nationalization of Hindu Traditions: Bharantendu Harischandra and Nineteenth-century Banaras*. New Delhi: Oxford UP, 1997.

——. "Sanskrit Scholars and Pandits of the Old School: The Benares Sanskrit College and the Constitution of Authority in the Late Nineteenth Century." *Journal of Indian Philosophy* 24, no. 4 (1996): 321–337.

Dalziel, Margaret. *Popular Fiction of Hundred Years Ago: An Unexplored Tract of Literary History*. London: Cohen and West, 1957.

Darnton, Robert."Literary Surveillance in the British Raj: The Contradictions of Liberal Imperialism." *Book History* 4 (2001): 133–176.

——. *The Business of the Enlightenment: A Publishing History of Diderot's Encyclopédie*. Cambridge: Harvard UP, 1968.

——. "First Steps Toward a History of Reading." *Australian Journal of French Studies* 23, no. 1 (1986): 5–30.

——. *The Forbidden Best-Sellers of Pre-Revolutionary France*. New York: Norton, 1995.

——. *The Great Cat Massacre and Other Episodes in French Cultural History*. New York: Basic Books, 1984.

——. "*Histoire du Livre, Geschichte des Buchwesens*: An Agenda for Comparative History." *Publishing History: The Social, Economic and Literary History of Book, Newspaper and Magazine Publishing* 22 (1987): 33–41.

——. *The Kiss of Lamourette: Reflections in Cultural History*. New York: Norton, 1990.

——. "Literary History and the Library." *Princeton University Library Chronicle* 48 (1987): 144–151.

——. "What Is the History of Books?" *Dædalus* 111 (1982): 65–83.

Darnton, Robert and Daniel Roche, eds. *Revolution in Print: The Press in France*. Berkeley: U of California P, 1989.

Das, Sisir Kumar. *The Artist in Chains: The Life of Bankimchandra Chatterji*. New Delhi: New Statesman Publishing, 1984.

——. *A History of Indian Literature: Western Impact, Indian Responses, 1800–1900*. Vol. 8. New Delhi: Sahitya Akademi, 1991.

——. *Sahibs and Munshis: An Account of the College of Fort William*. Calcutta: Orion Publications, 1978.

Das, Veena. "Language and Body: Transactions in the Construction of Pain." *Dædalus* 125, no. 1 (1996): 67–91.

DasGupta, Kalpana. "The National Library." In *National Library and Public Library Development: The 150th Anniversary of the Calcutta Public Library*, ed. Kalpana DasGupta. Calcutta: The National Library, 1989, 3–13.

Dasgupta, Subha Chakraborty. *A Bibliography of Reception: World Literature in Bengali Periodicals (1890–1900)*. Calcutta: Jadavpur University, 1992.

Davidson, Cathy, ed. *Reading in America: Literature and Social History*. Baltimore: Johns Hopkins UP, 1989.

——. *Revolution and the Word: The Rise of the Novel in America*. New York: Oxford UP, 1986.

——. "Toward a History of Books and Readers." *American Quarterly* 40, no. 1 (1988): 7–17.

Davis, Lennard. *Factual Fictions: The Origins of the English Novel.* New York: Columbia UP, 1983.

Day, Lal Behari. *Govinda Samanta; or, The History of a Bengal Raiyat.* London: n.p., 1874.

de Certeau, Michel. *Heterologies: Discourse on the Other.* Trans. Brian Massumi. Minneapolis: U of Minnesota P, 1986.

——. *The Practice of Everyday Life.* Vol. 1. Trans. Steven F. Rendall. Berkeley: U of California P, 1984.

de Vries, Jan. "Between Purchasing Power and the World of Goods: Understanding the Household Economy in Early Modern Europe." In *Consumption and the World of Goods,* ed. John Brewer and Roy Porter. New York: Routledge, 1993, 85–132.

Debord, Guy. *The Society of the Spectacle.* Trans. Donald Nicholson-Smith. New York: Zone Books, 1995.

Deleuze, Gilles and Félix Guattari. *Kafka: Toward a Minor Literature.* Trans. Dana Polan. Minneapolis: U of Minnesota P, 1986.

Denning, Michael. *Cover Stories: Narrative and Ideology in the British Spy Thriller.* London: Routledge and Kegan Paul, 1987.

——. *Mechanic Accents: Dime Novels and Working-Class Culture in America.* New York: Verso, 1987.

Denny, J. K. H. *Toward the Sunrising: A History of Work for the Women of India Done by Women from England, 1852–1901.* London: Marshall Brothers, 1901.

Desai, Anita. "Indian Fiction Today." *Dædalus* 118, no. 4 (1989): 207–232.

Desai, Thakorelal M. "Study of Fiction." *Calcutta Review* 7, no. 297 (1919): 331–339.

Desani, G. V. *All About H. Hatterr: A Novel.* New Paltz, N.Y.: McPherson, 1986.

Deshpande, Shashi. "The Dilemma of the Woman Writer." In *Women in Fiction, Fiction by Women,* ed. C. D. Narasimhaiah and C. N. Srinath. Mysore: Dhvanyaloka, 1987.

——. *Roots and Shadows.* 1983. Reprint, New Delhi: Disha Books, 1992.

——. *That Long Silence.* 1988. Reprint, New Delhi: Penguin, 1989.

Devi, Sunity. *Maharani of Cooch Behar: Bengal Dacoits and Tigers.* Calcutta: n.p., 1916.

Dharkar, Rani. "An Interview with Salman Rushdie." *New Quest* 42 (November/December 1983): 351–360.

Dickson, Lovat. *The House of Words.* London: Macmillan, 1963.

——. "Thomas Mark: Obituary." *Macmillan News* 1 and 2 (1963): 5.

Diehl, Katharine Smith. *Early Indian Imprints.* New York: Scarecrow Press, 1964.

Dirks, Nicholas B., ed. *Colonialism and Culture.* Ann Arbor: U of Michigan P, 1992.

Dissanayake, Wimal. "Toward a Decolonized English: South Asian Creativity in Fiction." *World Englishes* 4, no. 2 (1985): 233–242.

Donaldson, Laura E. *Decolonizing Feminisms: Race, Gender, and Empire Building.* Chapel Hill: U of North Carolina P, 1992.

Doody, Margaret Ann. *The True Story of the Novel.* New Brunswick, N.J.: Rutgers UP, 1996.

Dufferin and Ava, Hariot Georgina, Marchioness of. *Our Viceregal Life in India: Selections from my Journal, 1884–1888.* London: John Murray, 1890.

——. *A Record of Three Years' Work of the National Association for Supplying Female Medical Aid to the Women of India: August 1885 to August 1888.* Calcutta: Thacker, Spink, 1888.

Duncan, Ian. "Adam Smith, Samuel Johnson, and the Institutions of English." In *The Scottish Invention of English Literature*, ed. Robert Crawford. Cambridge: Cambridge UP, 1998, 37–56.

——. "Scott, Hogg, Orality, and the Limits of Culture." *Studies in Hogg and His World* 8 (1997): 56–74.

——. *Modern Romance and Transformations of the Novel: The Gothic, Scott, Dickens.* Cambridge: Cambridge UP, 1992.

Durai, J. Chinna. *Sugirtha: An Indian Novel.* London: Hulbert Publishing, 1929.

Dutt, Romesh Chunder. *The Literature of Bengal.* Rev. ed. Calcutta: Thacker, Spink, 1895.

Dutt, Shoshee Chandra. *Bengaliana: A Dish of Rice and Curry, and Other Indigestible Ingredients.* Calcutta: Thacker, Spink, 1880.

Dutta, Krishna and Andrew Robinson. *Rabindranath Tagore: The Myriad-Minded Man.* New York: St. Martin's Press, 1995.

Dyer, Helen S. *Pandita Ramabai: The Story of Her Life.* 9th ed. London: Morgan and Scott, 1913.

Eagleton, Terry. *Heathcliff and the Great Hunger: Studies in Irish Culture.* London: Verso, 1995.

Eco, Umberto. *The Role of the Reader: Explorations in the Semiotics of Texts.* Bloomington: Indiana UP, 1979.

Eden, Emily. *Portraits of the Princes and People of India.* London: J. Dickinson and Son, 1844.

——. *Up the Country: Letters Written to Her Sister from the Upper Provinces of India.* 1866. Reprint, London: Virago, 1983.

Eden, Fanny. *Tigers, Durbars, and Kings: Fanny Eden's Indian Journals, 1837–1838.* Ed. Janet Dunbar. London: Murray, 1988.

Eisenstein, Elizabeth L. *The Printing Press as an Agent of Change: Communications and Cultural Transformations in Early Modern Europe.* Cambridge: Cambridge UP, 1979.

Ekambaram, E. J. "Some Aspects of Indian Response to Fiction in English." In *Fiction and the Reading Public in India*, ed. C. D. Narsimhaiah. Mysore: Wesley Press, 1967, 8–17.

Eliot, Simon. *A Measure of Popularity: Public Library Holdings of Twenty-four Popular Authors, 1883–1912.* London: History of Book–On Demand Series 2, 1992.

———. *Some Patterns and Trends in British Publishing, 1800–1919*. Vol. 8. London: The Bibliographic Society, 1994.

Elliott, Maud Howe. *My Cousion F. Marion Crawford*. New York: Macmillan, 1934.

Elwood, Anne Katherine (Curteis). *Memoirs of the Literary Ladies of England*. Vol. 2. London: Henry Colburn, 1843.

Escarpit, Robert. *La Révolution du livre*. 2d rev. ed. Paris: UNESCO, 1969.

———. *Sociology of Literature*. Trans. Ernest Pick. London: Frank Cass, 1971.

Ezekiel, Nissim and Meenakshi Mukherjee, eds. *Another India: An Anthology of Contemporary Indian Fiction and Poetry*. New Delhi: Penguin, 1990.

Fanon, Frantz. *Black Skin, White Masks*. Trans. Charles Lam Markmann. New York: Grove Press, 1967.

———. *The Wretched of the Earth*. Trans. Constance Farrington. New York: Grove Press, 1963.

Farrukhi, Asif Aslam. " 'Human Beings Have Turned Human Beings Into Rats and Pigs': Interview with Ahmed Ali." *Herald* (March 1986): 116–119.

Fay, Eliza. *Original Letters from India, 1779–1815*. Ed. E. M. Forster. London: Hogarth Press, 1986.

Febvre, Lucien and Henri-Jean Martin. *The Coming of the Book: The Impact of Printing, 1450–1800*. Trans. David Gerard. London: Verso, 1990.

Fergus, Jan. "Eighteenth-Century Readers in Provincial England: The Customers of Samuel Clay's Circulating Library and Bookshop in Warwick, 1770–1772." *Papers of the Bibliographic Society of America* 78:2 (1984).

Fiedler, Leslie. *Love and Death in the American Novel*. 1960. Reprint, New York: Anchor Books, 1992.

Fieldhouse, D. K. *The Colonial Empires: A Comparative Survey from the Eighteenth Century*. 1965. Reprint, London: Macmillan, 1982.

Fielding, Penny. *Writing and Orality: Nationality, Culture, and Nineteenth-Century Scottish Fiction*. Oxford: Clarendon Press, 1996.

Finnegan, Ruth. *Literacy and Orality: Studies in the Technology of Communication*. Oxford: Basil Blackwell, 1988.

Flemming, Leslie A. "A New Humanity: American Missionaries' Ideals for Women in North India, 1870–1930." In *Western Women and Imperialism: Complicity and Resistance*, ed. Nupur Chaudhuri and Margaret Strobel. Bloomington: Indiana UP, 1992, 191–206.

———, ed. *Women's Work for Women: Missionaries and Social Change in Asia*. San Francisco: Westview Press, 1989.

Flint, Kate. *The Woman Reader, 1837–1914*. Oxford: Clarendon Press, 1993.

Flower, Newman. *Just as It Happened*. New York: William Morrow, 1950.

Forbes, Geraldine. *Women in Modern India*. Vol. 4, *The New Cambridge History of India*. Cambridge: Cambridge UP, 1996.

Forster, E. M. *Passage to India*. 1924. Reprint, New York: Harcourt, Brace, Jovanovich, 1984.

Foster, Hal, ed. *The Anti-Aesthetic: Essays in Postmodern Culture*. Port Townsend, Wash.: Bay Press, 1983.

Fraser, Angus. "John Murray's Colonial and Home Library." *Papers of the Bibliographical Society of America* 91, no. 3 (September 1997): 339–408.

——. "A Publishing House and Its Readers, 1841–1880: The Murrays and the Miltons." *Papers of the Bibliographic Society of America* 90, no. 1 (March 1996).

Fredeman, William E. "The Bibliographic Significance of a Publisher's Archve: The Macmillan Papers." *Studies in Bibliography* 23 (1970): 183–191.

Freud, Sigmund. "Family Romances." Trans. James Strachey. Vol. 9, *The Standard Edition of the Complete Psychological Works of Sigmund Freud*, ed. James Stratchey. 1909. London: Hogarth Press, 1959.

Frye, Northrop. *The Secular Scripture: A Study of the Structure of Romance*. Cambridge: Harvard UP, 1976.

Fullerton, Ronald. "Creating a Mass Book Market in Germany." *Journal of Social History* 10 (March 1977): 265–283.

Furet, François and Jacques Ozouf. *Reading and Writing: Literacy in France from Calvin to Jules Ferry*. Cambridge: Cambridge UP, 1977.

Gallagher, Catherine. *The Industrial Reformation of English Fiction: Social Discourse and Narrative Form, 1832–1867*. Chicago: U of Chicago P, 1985.

——. *Nobody's Story: The Vanishing Acts of Women Writers in the Marketplace, 1670–1820*. Berkeley: U of California P, 1994.

Gates, John M. *Schoolbooks and Krags: The United States Army in the Philippines, 1898–1902*. Contributions in Military History Number 3. Westport, Conn.: Greenwood Press, 1973.

Gaur, Albertine. *Women in India*. London: British Library, 1980.

Geller, Evelyn. *Forbidden Books in American Public Libraries, 1876–1939*. Westport, Conn.: Greenwood Press, 1984.

Gerson, Carole. *A Purer Taste: The Writing and Reading of Fiction in English in Nineteenth-Century Canada*. Toronto: U of Toronto P, 1989.

Gettman, Royal A. "The Author and the Publisher's Reader." *Modern Language Quarterly* 8, no. 4 (1947): 459–471.

——. *A Victorian Publisher: A Study of the Bentley Papers*. Cambridge: UP, 1960.

Ghose, Aurobindo. *Bankim Chandra Chatterji*. 1894. Reprint, Pondicherry: Sri Aurobindo Ashram Press, 1954.

——. *Bankim-Tilak-Dayananda*. 1907. Reprint, Calcutta: Arya Publishing, 1940.

Ghosh, Amitav. "Countdown." *The New Yorker*, October 26 and November 2, 1998, pp. 187–197.

——. *In an Antique Land*. New Delhi: Ravi Dayal, 1992.

——. "The March of the Novel Through History: The Testimony of My Grandfather's Bookcase." *Kenyon Review* 20, no. 2 (spring 1998): 13–24.

——. *The Shadow Lines*. New Delhi: Ravi Dayal, 1988.

Ghosh, J. C. *Bengali Literature*. Oxford: Oxford UP, 1948.

Ghosh, S. K. *One Thousand and One Nights: The Trials of Narayan Lal*. London: n.p., 1904.

——. *The Prince of Destiny: The New Krishna*. London: n.p., 1909.

Ginzburg, Carlo. *The Cheese and the Worms: The Cosmos of a Sixteenth-Century Miller*. Trans. John and Anne Tedeschi. Baltimore: Johns Hopkins UP, 1980.

Glover, Lady. *Famous Women Rulers of India and the East*, n.d.

Goethe, Johann Wolfgang von. "On World Literature." Trans. Ellen and Ernest von Nardroff. In *Goethe: Essays on Art and Literature*, ed. John Gearey. New York: Suhrkamp, 1986.

Goldmann, Lucien. *Toward a Sociology of the Novel*. Trans. Alan Sheridan. London: Tavistock Publications, 1975.

Gopal Pannikar, T. K. *Storm and Sunshine: A Novel Illustrative of Malayalee Domestic Life*. Calicut: n.p., 1916.

Gould, Warwick. "'Playing at Treason with Miss Maud Gonne': Yeats and His Publishers in 1900." In *Modernist Writers & the Marketplace*, ed. Ian Willison, Warwick Gould, and Warren Chernaik. Basingstoke: Macmillan, 1996, 36–80.

Gowda, H. H. Anniah. "Ahmed Ali's *Twilight in Delhi* and Chinua Achebe's *Things Fall Apart*." In *Alien Voices: Perspectives on Commonwealth Literature*, ed. Avadhesh K. Srivastava. Lucknow: Print House, 1981.

Graham, Ruth. "The Adaptation of pre-1850 British Library Models in Colonial New Zealand: The Early History of the Karori Library, 1844–1902." *New Zealand Libraries* 48, no. 7 (1996): 133–140.

Gramsci, Antonio. *Selections from Cultural Writings*. Trans. William Boelhower, ed. David Forgacs and Geoffrey Nowell-Smith. Cambridge: Harvard UP, 1985.

——. *Selections from the Prison Notebooks*. Trans. Quintin Hoare and Geoffrey Nowell-Smith. New York: International Publishers, 1971.

Grant, Charles. *Observation on the State of Society Among the Asiatic Subjects of Great Britain, Particularly with Respect to Their Morals; and on the Means of Improving It (Written Chiefly in the Year 1792)*. London: East India House, 1797.

——. "On the Restoration of Learning in the East." *Dissertations and Poems Which Gained the Rev. Dr. Buchanan's Prizes at Cambridge*. Cambridge: R. Watts at the University P, 1805.

Graves, Charles L. *Life and Letters of Alexander Macmillan*. London: Macmillan, 1910.

Gray, William S. and Ruth Munroe. *The Reading Interests and Habits of Adults*. New York: Macmillan, 1930.

Green, Martin. *Dreams of Adventure, Deeds of Empire*. New York: Basic Books, 1979.

Greenberger, Allen J. *The British Image of India: A Study in the Literature of Imperialism*. New York: Oxford UP, 1969.

Grigg, Mrs H. B. "Memoir of Krupabai Satthianadhan." In Krupa Satthianadhan, *Kamala: A Story of Hindu Life*. Madras: Srinivas Varadachari and Co., 1894.

Grimsted, David. *Melodrama Unveiled: American Theatre and Culture, 1800–1850*. Chicago: U of Chicago P, 1968.

Griswold, Wendy. *Bearing Witness: Readers, Writers, and the Novel in Nigeria*. Princeton: Princeton UP, 2000.

——. "The Fabrication of Meaning: Literary Interpretation in the United States, Great Britain, and the West Indies." *American Journal of Sociology* 92, no. 5 (March 1987): 1077–1117.

——. "The Writing on the Mud Wall: Nigerian Novels and the Imaginary Village." *American Sociological Review* 57, no. 6 (1992): 709–724.

Guha, Ranajit. *Dominance Without Hegemony. History and Power in Colonial India*. Cambridge: Harvard UP, 1997.

——. *A Rule of Property for Bengal: An Essay on the Idea of Permanent Settlement*. 1963. Reprint, New Delhi: Orient Longman, 1981.

——. *An Indian Historiography of India: A Nineteenth-Century Agenda and Its Implications*. Calcutta: K. P. Bagchi, 1988.

Guha, Ranajit and Gayatri Spivak, eds. *Selected Subaltern Studies*. New York: Oxford UP, 1988.

Gulvadi, Shiva Rao. *The Optimist and Other Stories*. Madras: n.p., 1925.

Gupta, Brijen K. *India in English Fiction, 1800–1970*. Metuchen, N.J.: Scarecrow Press, 1973.

Habegger, Alfred. *Gender, Fantasy, and Realism in American Literature*. New York: Columbia UP, 1982.

Habermas, Jürgen. "Modernity—An Incomplete Project." In *The Anti-Aesthetic: Essays on Postmodern Culture*, ed. Hal Foster. Port Townsend, Wash.: Bay Press, 1983, 3–15.

Haggis, Jane. "Gendering Colonialism or Colonising Gender? Recent Women's Studies Approaches to White Women and the History of British Colonialism." *Women's Studies Internatioanal Forum* 13, no. 1/2 (1990): 105–115.

Haldar, M. K. *Foundations of Nationalism in India: A Study of Bankimchandra Chatterjee*. New Delhi: Ajanta Publications, 1989.

Halperin, John, ed. *The Theory of the Novel: New Essays*. New York: Oxford UP, 1974.

Harlow, Barbara. *Resistance Literature*. New York: Methuen, 1987.

Harrison, Alexina Mackay. *A. Mackay Ruthquist: or, Singing the Gospel among Hindus and Gonds*. London: Hodder and Stoughton, 1893.

Hart, James D. *The Popular Book: A History of American Literary Taste*. Oxford: Oxford UP, 1950.

Hasan, Masoodul. *Nineteenth Century English Literary Works: A Bibliography of Rare Books Available in India*. New Delhi: B. R. Publishing, 1978.

Hashmi, Alamgir. "Ahmed Ali: The Transition into a Postcolonial Mode." *World Literature Written in English* 29, no. 2 (1989): 148–152.

Headrick, Daniel R. *The Tools of Empire: Technology and European Imperialism in the Nineteenth Century*. New York: Oxford UP, 1981.

Heaney, Seamus. *North*. London: Faber and Faber, 1975.

——. *Preoccupations: Selected Prose, 1968–1978*. New York: Farrar, Straus, and Giroux, 1980.

Heilman, Robert B. *Tragedy and Melodrama: Versions of Experience*. Seattle and London: U of Washington P, 1968.

Heiserman, Arthur. *The Novel Before the Novel*. Chicago: U of Chicago P, 1977.

Hobsbawm, Eric and Terence Ranger, eds. *The Invention of Tradition*. Cambridge: Cambridge UP, 1983.

Hoggan, Frances Elizabeth. *Medical Women for India*. Bristol: J. W. Arrowsmith, 1882.

Hoggart, Richard. *The Uses of Literacy: Aspects of Working-Class Life, with Special Reference to Publications and Entertainments*. London: Chatto and Windus, 1957.

Holdsworth, Mary C. "The Woman Question in India." *The Woman's Signal* September 13, 1894, p. 165.

Holmström, Lakshmi, ed. *The Inner Courtyard: Stories by Indian Women*. New Delhi: Rupa, 1991.

Hopkins, Edward Washburn. *The Great Epic of India: Its Character and Origin*. New York: Charles Scribner's Sons, 1902.

Hopkins, Saleni (Mrs. Armstrong). *Within the Purdah; Also, In the Zenana Homes of Indian Princes, and Heroes and Heroines of Zion; Being the Personal Observations of a Medical Missionary in India*. Cincinnati: Eaton and Mains, 1898.

Horder, Mervyn. "The Heinemann Hundred." *Bookseller*, March 30, 1990, pp. 1079–1082.

Houghton, Ross C. *Women of the Orient: An account of the Religious, Intellectual, Social Customs of the Women of Japan, China, India, and Turkey*. Cincinnati: Hitchcock and Walden, 1877.

Howsam, Leslie. *Kegan Paul: A Victorian Imprint*. Toronto: U of Toronto P, 1998.

Hughes, Thomas. *Memoir of Daniel Macmillan*. London: Macmillan, 1882.

Humpherys, Anne. "G. W. M. Reynolds: Popular Literature and Popular Politics." In *Innovators and Preachers: The Role of the Editor in Victorian England*, ed. Joel H. Wiener. Westport, Conn.: Greenwood Press, 1985.

——. "Generic Strands and Urban Twists: The Victorian Mysteries Novel." *Victorian Studies* 34, no. 4 (summer 1991): 463–472.

——. "The Geometry of the Modern City: G. W. M. Reynolds and *The Mysteries of London*." *Browning Institute Studies* 11 (1983): 69–80.

Humphrey, Mrs. E. J. *Gems of India; or, Sketches of Distinguished Hindoo and Mahomedan Women*. New York: Nelson and Phillips, 1875.

Hunt, Lynn A. *The Family Romance of the French Revolution*. Berkeley: U of California P, 1992.

Hunter, J. V. "Reynolds: Sensational Novelist and Agitator." *Book Handbook* 4 (1947): 225–236.

Hunter, W. W. *The Annals of Rural Bengal*. London: Smith Elder, 1868.

Hutchins, Francis G. *Illusion of Permanence: British Imperialism in India*. Princeton: Princeton UP, 1967.

Huxley, Leonard. *The House of Smith Elder*. London: Privately printed, 1923.

Inden, Ronald B. *Imagining India*. Cambridge: Basil Blackwell, 1990.

Irving, Robert Grant. *Indian Summer: Lutyens, Baker, and Imperial Delhi*. New Haven: Yale UP, 1981.

Iser, Wolfgang. *The Implied Reader: Patterns of Communication in Prose Fiction from Bunyan to Beckett*. Baltimore: Johns Hopkins UP, 1974.

——. "Interaction Between Text and Reader." In *The Reader in the Text. Essays on Audience and Interpretation*, ed. Susan Suleiman and Inge Crosman. Princeton: Princeton UP, 1980, 106–119.

Israel, Milton. *Communications and Power: Propaganda and the Press in the Indian Nationalist Struggle, 1920–1947*. Cambridge: Cambridge UP, 1994.

Israel, Samuel. "The Colonial Heritage in Indian Publishing." *Library Trends* 26, no. 4 (spring 1978): 539–552.

——. "English Language Book Publishing in India." *Indian Book Industry Journal* 18, no. 5/6 (1978): 59–75.

Iyengar, K. R. S. *Indian Writing in English*. 3d ed. New Delhi: Sterling Publishers, 1983.

James, Louis. *Fiction for the Working Man, 1830–1850*. New York: Oxford UP, 1963.

——. "The View from Brick Lane: Contrasting Perspectives in Working-Class and Middle-Class Fiction of the Early Victorian Period." *The Yearbook of English Studies* 2 (1981): 7–101.

James, Louis and John Saville. "George William MacArthur Reynolds." In *Dictionary of Labour Biography*, ed. Joyce M. Bellamy and John Saville, 3:146–151. London: Macmillan, 1972.

Jameson, Fredric. "Beyond the Cave: Demystifying the Ideology of Modernism." In *Contemporary Marxist Literary Criticism*, ed. Francis Mulhern. London: Longman, 1987, 168–187.

——. *The Political Unconscious: Narrative as a Socially Symbolic Act*. Ithaca, N.Y.: Cornell UP, 1981.

——. "Postmodernism and Consumer Society." In *The Anti-Aesthetic: Essays in Postmodern Culture*, ed. Hal Foster. Port Townsend, Wash.: Bay Press, 1983.

——. *Postmodernism, or, the Cultural Logic of Late Capitalism*. Durham: Duke UP, 1991.

JanMohamed, Abdul R. *Manichean Aesthetics: The Politics of Literature in Colonial Africa*. Amherst: U of Massachusetts P, 1983.

Jayawardena, Kumari. *The White Woman's Other Burden: Western Women and South Asia during British Colonial Rule*. New York: Routledge, 1995.

Johanson, Graeme. "A Study of Colonial Editions in Australia, 1843–1972." Ph.D. diss., Monash University, 1995.

Jolly, K. G. *Literacy for All by 2001: Strategies at the District Level.* Delhi: B. R. Publishing, 1992.

Jordan, John O. and Robert L. Patten, eds. *Literature in the Marketplace: Nineteenth-Century British Publishing and Reading Practices.* Cambridge: Cambridge UP, 1995.

Joshi, Priya. "Culture and Consumption: Fiction, the Reading Public, and the British Novel in Colonial India." *Book History* 1 (1998): 196–220.

Joshi, Svati, ed. *Rethinking English: Essays in Literature, Language, History.* New Delhi: Trianka, 1991.

Joyce, James. *A Portrait of the Artist as a Young Man.* 1916. Ed. Seamus Deane. Reprint, New York: Penguin, 1992.

——. *Ulysses.* 1922. Reprint, New York: Vintage, 1961.

Jusdanis, Gregory. *Belated Modernity and Aesthetic Culture: Inventing National Literature.* Minneapolis: U of Minnesota P, 1991.

Jussawalla, Feroza. "Beyond Indianness: The Stylistic Concerns of *Midnight's Children.*" *The Journal of Indian Writing in English* 12, no. 2 (1984): 26–47.

Kadir, Djelal. *The Other Writing: Postcolonial Essays in Latin America's Writing Culture.* West Lafayette, Ind.: Purdue UP, 1993.

Kali for Women, ed. *The Slate of Life: An Anthology of Stories by Indian Women.* New Delhi: Kali for Women, 1990.

——, ed. *Truth-Tales: Contemporary Writing by Indian Women.* New Delhi: Kali for Women, 1986.

Kanjilal, K. C. "Literary Societies in India: Their Objects and Methods of Work." *Calcutta Review* 134, no. 267 (1912): 46–54.

Karlekar, Hiranmay. "Popular Literature and the Reading Public." *Indian Horizons* 40, no. 3/4 (1991): 68–81.

Karlekar, Malavika. *Voices from Within: Early Personal Narratives of Bengali Women.* New Delhi: Oxford UP, 1991.

Kaufman, Paul. *Borrowings from the Bristol Library, 1773-1794: A Unique Record of Reading Vogues.* Charlottesville: U of Virginia P, 1960.

——. *Libraries and their Users: Collected Papers in Library History.* London: The Library Association, 1969.

Kaul, Suvir. "Separation Anxiety: Growing Up Inter/National in Amitav Ghosh's *The Shadow Lines.*" *Oxford Literary Review* 16, no. 1/2 (1994): 125–145.

Kaur, Manmohan. *Women in India's Freedom Struggle.* New Delhi: Sterling, 1985.

Kausch, Donald. "George W. M. Reynolds: A Bibliography." *The Library.* 5th Series. 28, no. 4 (December 1973): 319–326.

Kaushik, Asha. *Politics, Aesthetics, and Culture: A Study of the Indo-Anglian Political Novel.* New Delhi: Manohar Publications, 1988.

Kaviraj, Sudipta. *The Unhappy Consciousness: Bankimchandra Chattopadhyay and the Formation of Nationalist Discourse in India.* New Delhi: Oxford UP, 1995.

——. "Writing, Speaking, Being: Language and the Historical Formation of Identities in India." In *Nationalstaat und Sprachkonflikte in Süd-Und Südostasien*, ed. Dagmar Hellmann-Rajanayagam and Dietmar Rotthermund. Stuttgart: Franz Steiner Verlag, 1992, 25–65.

Kaye, John. "English Literature in India." *Calcutta Review* 5, no. 9 (1846): 202–220.

Keir, David. *The House of Collins: The Story of a Scottish Family of Publishers from 1789 to the Present Day*. London: Collins, 1952.

Kelly, Thomas. *A History of Public Libraries in Great Britain, 1845–1975*. London: The Library Association, 1977.

Kesavan, B. S. *History of Printing and Publishing in India: A Story of Cultural Awakening*. Vol. 1. New Delhi: National Book Trust, 1985.

Khurshid, Anis. "Growth of Libraries in India." *International Library Review* 4 (1972): 21–65.

Kiernan, V. G. *The Lords of Human Kind: Black Man, Yellow Man, and the White Man in an Age of Empire*. 1968. Reprint, New York: Columbia UP, 1986.

Kijinski, John L. "John Morley's 'English Men of Letters' Series and the Politics of Reading." *Victorian Studies* 34, no. 2 (winter 1991): 205–225.

King, Bruce. "From *Twilight* to Midnight: Muslim Novels of India and Pakistan." In *Worlds of Muslim Imagination*, ed. Alamgir Hashmi. Islamabad: Gulmohar, 1986.

——. *The New English Literatures: Cultural Nationalism in a Changing World*. London: Macmillan, 1980.

Kintgen, Eugene. "Reconstructing Elizabethan Reading." *Studies in English Literature, 1500–1900* 30, no. 1 (1990): 1–18.

Klancher, Jon P. *The Making of English Reading Audiences*. Madison: U of Wisconsin P, 1987.

Knox, Bernard M. W. "Silent Reading in Antiquity." *Greek, Roman, and Byzantine Studies* 9 (1968): 421–35.

Kojin, Karatani. *Origins of Modern Japanese Literature*. Trans. Brett deBary. Durham: Duke UP, 1991.

Koselleck, Reinhart. *Futures Past: On the Semantics of Historical Time*. Trans. Keith Tribe. Cambridge: MIT P, 1985.

Kothandarama Aiyar, K. S. *The Position of Women in India, in America, and Among Savages*. Madras: Gajapaty Press, 1897.

Krishnaswami, P. R. "Sir Walter Scott's Indian Novel, *The Surgeon's Daughter*." *Calcutta Review* 7, no. 297 (1919): 431–452.

Krishnaswami, T. B. *Selma*. Madras: n.p., 1910.

Kumar, Radha. *The History of Doing: An Illustrated Account of Movements for Women's Rights and Feminism in India, 1800–1990*. New Delhi: Kali for Women, 1993.

Larsen, Neil. *Modernism and Hegemony: A Materialist Critique of Aesthetic Agencies*. Minneapolis: U of Minnesota P, 1990.

Layoun, Mary N. *Travels of a Genre: The Modern Novel and Ideology*. Princeton: Princeton UP, 1990.

Leavis, Q. D. *Fiction and the Reading Public*. 1932. Reprint, London: Chatto and Windus, 1974.

Leenhardt, Jacques. "Toward a Sociology of Reading." In *The Reader in the Text: Essays on Audience and Interpretation*, ed. Susan Suleiman and Inge Crosman. Princeton: Princeton UP, 1980, 205–224.

Liddle, Joana and Rama Joshi. *Daughters of Independence: Gender, Caste, and Class in India*. New Delhi: Kali for Women, 1986.

Lipscomb, David. "Caught in a Strange Middle Ground: Contesting History in Salman Rushdie's *Midnight's Children*." *Diaspora* 1, no. 2 (1991): 163–189.

Livingstone, Rodney, Perry Anderson, and Francis Mulhern, eds. *Aesthetics and Politics*. London: New Left Books, 1977.

Lloyd, David. *Anomalous States: Irish Writing and the Post-Colonial Moment*. Durham: Duke UP, 1993.

Lloyd, Henrietta. *Hindu Women with Glimpses into their Lives and Zenanas*. London: n.p., 1882.

Long, Rev. James. "Early Bengali Literature and Newspapers." *Calcutta Review* 13, no. 25 (1850): 124–61.

Longman, Charles J. *The House of Longmans (1724–1800); A Bibliographical History*. London: Longmans, 1936.

Lovell, Terry. *Consuming Fiction*. London: Verso, 1987.

Lowe, Clara S. *Punrooty; or, The Gospel is Winning its Way among the Women of India*. London: Morgan and Scott, 1880.

Lowe, Lisa. *Critical Terrains: French and British Orientalisms*. Ithaca, N.Y.: Cornell UP, 1991.

Lucas, J. J., ed. *Pandita Ramabai: A Wonderful Life*. Madras: Christian Literature Society, 1919.

Lukács, Georg. *The Historical Novel*. Trans. Hannah and Stanley Mitchell. Lincoln: U of Nebraska P, 1983.

——. "Realism in the Balance." In *Aesthetics and Politics*, ed. Rodney Livingstone, Perry Anderson, and Francis Mulhern. London: New Left Books, 1977, 28–59.

——. *The Theory of the Novel*. Trans. Anya Bostock. Cambridge: MIT P, 1971.

Lunn, Eugene. *Marxism and Modernism: An Historical Study of Lukács, Brecht, Benjamin, and Adorno*. Berkeley: U of California P, 1982.

Lutgendorf, Philip. *The Life of a Text: Performing the Ramcaritmanas of Tulsidas*. Berkeley: U of California P, 1991.

Lyons, Martin. *Le Triomphe du livre: Une histoire sociologique de la lecture dans la France du XIXe siècle*. Paris: Promodis/Editions du Cercle de la Librarie, 1987.

Maadhaviah, A. *Lieutenant Panju: A Modern Indian*. Madras: n.p., 1924.

Macaulay, Thomas Babington. "The Literature of Britain (November 4, 1846)." In *The Works of Lord Macaulay: Speeches and Poems with the Report and Notes on the Indian Penal Code*, 2:31–41. New York: Riverside Press, 1867.

——. "Minute on Indian Education." In *Selected Writings: Thomas Babington Macaulay*, ed. John Clive and Thomas Pinney. Chicago: U of Chicago P, 1972, 237–251.

Macherey, Pierre. *A Theory of Literary Production*. Trans. Geoffrey Wall. London: Routledge and Kegan Paul, 1978.

Machwe, Prabhakar. "A Personal View of the Progressive Writers' Movement." In *Marxist Influences and South Asian Literature*, ed. Carlo Coppola. East Lansing: Asian Studies Center, Michigan State University, 1974, 45–53.

MacIvor, Anna Ross. *Indian Women Through Alien Eyes*. Calcutta: Information Research Academy, 1977.

Mackenzie, D. F. *The Book as an Expressive Form*. London: The British Library, 1986.

MacKenzie, John M. *Propaganda and Empire: The Manipulation of British Public Opinion, 1880–1960*. Manchester: Manchester UP, 1984.

Macmillan, Daniel. *A Bibliographic Catalogue of Macmillan and Co.'s Publications from 1843 to 1889*. London: Macmillan, 1891.

Macmillan, George A. *Brief Memoir of Alexander Macmillan*. Private ed. Glasgow: University P, 1908.

——. ed. *Letters of Alexander Macmillan*. Glasgow: University P, 1908.

Macmillan, Margaret. *Women of the Raj*. New York: Thames and Hudson, 1988.

Macmillan, Sir Frederick. *The Net Book Agreement 1899 and The Book War 1906–1908*. Glasgow: Privately printed by Robert Maclehouse, 1924.

MacMinn, Edwin. *Nemorama the Nautchnee: A Story of India*. Chicago: Missionary Campaign Library, 1890.

Madan, T. N. "The Hindu Woman at Home." In *Indian Women: From Purdah to Modernity*, ed. B. R. Nanda. New Delhi: Nehru Memorial Library and Radiant Pub., 1990, 67–86.

Madhaviah, A. *Clarinda: A Historical Novel*. Madras: n.p., 1915.

Mahmood, Syed. *A History of English Education in India: Its Rise, Development, Progress, Present Condition, and Prospects, 1781–1893*. 1895. Reprint, New Delhi: Idrah-i Adbiyat-i, 1981.

Mahood, M. *The Colonial Encounter: A Reading of Six Novels*. Totowa, N.J.: Rowman and Littlefield, 1977.

Majumdar, Bimanbehari. "The Ananda Math and Phadke." *Journal of Indian History* 44, no. 130 (1966): 93–107.

Majumdar, Bhagaban Prasad. *First Fruits of English Education, 1817–1857*. Calcutta: Bookland, 1973.

Makdisi, Saree. "'Postcolonial' Literature in a Neocolonial World: Modern Arabic Culture and the End of Modernity." *boundary 2* 22, no. 1 (1995): 85–115.

Malik, Yogendra K. *South Asian Intellectuals and Social Change: A Study of the Role of the Vernacular-Speaking Intelligentsia*. New Delhi: Heritage Publishers, 1982.

Mani, Lata. "Contentious Traditions: The Debate on Sati in Colonial India." In *Recasting Women: Essays in Colonial History*, ed. Kumkum Sangari and Sudesh Vaid. New Delhi: Kali for Women, 1989, 88–126.

Manners, Lady Janetta. *Some of the Advantages of Easily Accessible Reading and Recreation Rooms and Free Libraries, With Remarks on Starting and Maintaining Them and Suggestions for the Selection of Books*. London: William Blackwood and Sons, 1885.

Mannoni, Oscar. *Prospero and Caliban: The Psychology of Colonization*. 1950. Reprint, New York: Praeger, 1964.

Manto, Sadat Hasan. *Kingdom's End and Other Stories*. Trans. Khalid Hasan. New Delhi: Penguin, 1989.

Marathe, Sudhakar and Meenakshi Mukherjee, eds. *Narrative: Forms and Transformations*. Delhi: Chanakya Publications, 1986.

Marston, Edward. *After Work: Fragments from the Workshop of an Old Publisher*. London: William Heinemann, 1904.

Martin, Henri-Jean. *Livre, pouvoirs, et société à Paris au XVIIe siècle (1598–1701)*. Vol. 2. Geneva: Droz, 1969.

——. *The Power of History and the Power of Writing*. Trans. Lydia G. Cochrane. Chicago: U of Chicago P, 1994.

Marx, Karl. "Introduction to a Critique of Political Economy." Trans. Lawrence and Wishart. In *The German Ideology*, ed. C. J. Arthur. New York: International Publishers, 1970, 124–152.

Mason, Mary G. "The Other Voice: Autobiographies of Women Writers." In *Autobiography: Essays Theoretical and Critical*, ed. James Olney. Princeton: Princeton UP, 1980.

Matthews, Brander. *The Home Library*. New York: D. Appleton, 1883.

Maxwell, Herbert. "The Craving for Fiction." *The Nineteenth Century* CXCVI.196 (January/June 1893): 1046–1061.

Maxwell, Richard C. *The Mysteries of Paris and London*. Charlottsville: UP of Virginia, 1992.

Mazumdar, Shudha. *Memoirs of an Indian Woman*. Foremother Legacies, ed. Geraldine Forbes. Armonk, N.Y.: M. E. Sharpe, 1989.

Mazumdar, Vina. *Education and Social Science: Three Studies on Nineteenth Century India*. Simla: Indian Institute of Advanced Study, 1972.

——. "The Social Reform Movement in India: From Ranade to Nehru." In *Indian Women: From Purdah to Modernity*, ed. B. R. Nanda. 1976. Reprint, New Delhi: Nehru Memorial Library and Radiant Pub., 1990, 41–66.

McClintock, Anne. *Imperial Leather: Race, Gender, and Sexuality in the Colonial Contest*. New York and London: Routledge, 1995.

McClure, John and Aamir Mufti, eds. *Social Text: Third World and Post-Colonial Issues*. Vol. 31/32 (1992).

McCutchion, David. "The Novel as Shastra." In *Considerations*, ed. Meenakshi Mukherjee. New Delhi: Allied Publishers, 1977, 111–121.

McGregor, Ronald Stuart. *Hindi Literature from Its Beginnings to the Nineteenth*

Century. A History of Indian Literature, ed. Jan Gonda. Wiesbaden: Otto Harrassowitz, 1984.

McKeon, Michael. "Generic Transformation and Social Change: Rethinking the Rise of the Novel." In *Modern Essays in Eighteenth-Century Literature*, ed. Leopold Damrosch, Jr. New York: Oxford UP, 1988, 159–180.

——. *The Origins of the English Novel, 1600–1740*. Baltimore: Johns Hopkins UP, 1987.

Mee, Jon. "After Midnight: The Indian Novel in English of the 80s and 90s." *Postcolonial Studies* 1, no. 1 (1998): 127–141.

Mehta, Jaya. "English Romance; Indian Violence." *The Centennial Review* 39:3 (1995): 611–657.

Mendelson, Edward. "Encyclopedic Narratives: From Dante to Pynchon." *Modern Language Notes* 91 (1976).

Menkes, William. "William Heinemann: A Continuing Instinct for What the Reading Public Wants." *British Book News* October (1989): 688–692.

Mill, James. *The History of British India: Abridged with an Introduction by William Thomas*. Chicago: U of Chicago P, 1975.

Miller, Barbara Stoler. "Contending Narratives: The Political Life of the Indian Epics." *Journal of Asian Studies* 50, no. 4 (November 1991): 783–792.

Miller, Daniel. *Material Culture and Mass Consumption*. Oxford: Basil Blackwell, 1987.

Miller, D. A. *The Novel and the Police*. Berkeley: U of California P, 1988.

Miller, Mrs. Fenwick. "A Book of the Hour. Review of *Kamala* and *Saguna* by Krupabai Satthianadhan." *Woman's Signal* June 13, 1895, pp. 379–380.

Misra, Jogesh. *History of Library and Librarianship in Modern India Since 1850*. New Delhi: Atma Ram and Sons, 1979.

Mitra, Barada C. "English Influence on Bengali Literature." *Calcutta Review* 81, no. 162 (1885): 330–345.

Mitra, S. M. *Hindupore: A Peep Behind the Indian Unrest*. London: n.p., 1909.

Miyoshi, Masao. *Accomplices of Silence: The Modern Japanese Novel*. Berkeley: U of California P, 1974.

Modleski, Tania. "My Life as a Romance Reader." *Paradoxa* 3, nos. 1–2 (1997): 15–28.

Mohanty, Chandra Talpade, Ann Russo, and Lourdes Torres. *Third World Women and the Politics of Feminism*. Bloomington: Indiana UP, 1991.

Mookerjee, Subodh Kumar. *Development of Libraries and Library Science in India*. Calcutta: World Press, 1969.

Moorhouse, Geoffrey. *India Britannica*. London: Harvill Press, 1983.

Moran, John C. *An F. Marion Crawford Companion*. Westport, Conn.: Greenwood Press, 1981.

——. *Seeking Refuge in Torre San Nicola: An Introduction to F. Marion Crawford*. The Worthies Library. Nashville, Tenn.: F. Marion Crawford Memorial Society, 1980.

Moretti, Franco. *The Atlas of the European Novel, 1800–1900*. London: Verso, 1998.

——. *Modern Epic: The World System from Goethe to García Márquez*. Trans. Quentin Hoare. New York and London: Verso, 1996.

——. *Signs Taken for Wonders: Essays in the Sociology of Literary Forms*. Trans. Susan Fischer, David Forgacs, and David Miller. London: Verso, 1988.

——. *The Way of the World: The Bildungsroman in European Culture*. New York and London: Verso, 1987.

Morgan, Charles. *The House of Macmillan, 1843–1943*. London: Macmillan, 1943.

Morrison, Elizabeth. "Serial Fiction in Australian Newspapers." In *Literature in the Marketplace: Nineteenth-Century British Publishing and Reading Practices*, ed. John O. Jordan and Robert L. Patten. Cambridge: Cambridge UP, 1995.

Mott, Frank Luther. *Golden Multitudes: The Story of Best Sellers in the United States*. New York: Macmillan, 1947.

Mukherjee, Bharati. "Immigrant Writing: Give us Your Maximalists!" *New York Times Book Review*, August 28, 1988, pp. 1, 28–29.

Mukherjee, Jaykrishna (Joy Kissen Mookerjee). "Autobiography." *Calcutta Review* 118, no. 1/2 (January/February 1951).

Mukherjee, Meenakshi. "The Anxiety of Englishness: Our Novels in English." *Economic and Political Weekly*. 28, no. 48 (November 27, 1993): 2607–2611.

——. "Interrogating Post-colonialism." In *Interrogating Post-colonialism: Theory, Text, and Context*, ed. Harish Trivedi and Meenakshi Mukherjee. Shimla: Indian Institute of Advanced Study, 1996, 3–11.

——. "Macaulay's Imperishable Empire." *The Literary Criterion (Mysore)* 17, no. 1 (1982): 30–39.

——. "Mapping a Territory: Notes on Framing a Course." In *The Lie of the Land: English Literary Studies in India*, ed. Rajeshwari Sunder Rajan. New Delhi: Oxford UP, 1992, 229–245.

——. "Narrating a Nation." *Indian Literature* 35, no. 4 (1992): 138–151.

——. *Realism and Reality: The Novel and Society in India*. Delhi: Oxford UP, 1985.

——. *The Twice-Born Fiction: Themes and Techniques of the Indian Novel in English*. New Delhi: Heinemann, 1971.

Mukherjee, Nilmani. "A Bengal Zamindar." *Bengal Past and Present* 90 (January/June 1972).

Mumby, Frank. *The House of Routledge, 1834–1934*. London: George Routledge and Sons, 1934.

Mumby, F. A. and Ian Norrie. *Publishing and Bookselling, Part 1: From the Earliest Times to 1870 and Part 2: 1870–1970*. London: Jonathan Cape, 1974.

Murshid, Ghulam. *Reluctant Debutante: Response of Bengali Women to Modernization, 1849–1905*. Rajshahi: Sahitya Samsad, 1983.

Naipaul, V. S. *A Bend in the River*. 1979. Reprint, New York: Vintage, 1989.

——. *In a Free State*. 1971. Reprint, New York: Vintage, 1984.

——. *The Return of Eva Perón with the Killings in Trinidad*. New York: Alfred Knopf, 1980.

Nairn, Tom. *The Break-Up of Britain: Crisis and Neonationalism*. London: New Left Books, 1981.

Nandy, Ashis. *The Intimate Enemy: Loss and Recovery of Self Under Colonialism*. New Delhi: Oxford UP, 1983.

Narasimhaiah, C. D. "Why Commonwealth Literature?" In *Alien Voices: Perspectives on Commonwealth Literature*, ed. Avadhesh K. Srivastava. Lucknow: Print House, 1981.

Narasimhaiah, C. D. and C. N. Srinath, eds. *The Rise of the Indian Novel*. Mysore: Dhvanyaloka, 1986.

——, eds. *Women in Fiction, Fiction by Women*. Mysore: Dhvanyaloka, 1987.

Narayana Rao, Velcheru. "A *Ramayana* of their Own: Women's Oral Tradition in Telugu." In *Many Ramayanas: The Diversity of a Narrative Tradition in South Asia*, ed. Paula Richman. 1991. Reprint, New Delhi: Oxford UP, 1992, 114–136.

Natarajan, D., ed. *Extracts from the All India Census Reports on Literacy*. New Delhi: Ministry of Home Affairs, 1971.

Natarajan, S. *A History of the Press in India*. New Delhi: Asia Publishing House, 1962.

Natesa Sastri, S. M. *Harshacharita: A Historical Romance*. Madras: Srinivasa, Varadachari, 1901.

National Archives of India. *Patriotic Poetry Banned by the Raj*. New Delhi: National Archives of India, 1982.

Ngugi, wa Thiong'o. *Decolonising the Mind: The Politics of Language in African Literature*. London: Heinemann, 1986.

Niven, Alistair. "Historical Imagination in the Novels of Ahmed Ali." *Journal of Indian Writing in English* 8, no. 1/2 (1980): 3–13.

Nowell-Smith, Simon. *The House of Cassell, 1848–1958*. London: Cassell, 1958.

——. *International Copyright Law and the Publisher in the Reign of Queen Victoria*. Oxford: Oxford UP, 1968.

——, ed. *Letters to Macmillan*. London: Macmillan, 1967.

Obiechina, Emmanuel. *Culture, Tradition, and Society in the West African Novel*. Cambridge: Cambridge UP, 1975.

O'Hanlon, Rosalind. *Caste, Conflict, and Ideology: Mahatma Jyotirao Phule and Low-Caste Protest in Nineteenth-Century Western India*. Cambridge: Cambridge UP, 1985.

——. "Issues of Widowhood: Gender and Resistance in Colonial Western India." In *Contesting Power: Resistance and Everyday Social Relations in South Asia*, ed. Douglas Haynes and Gyan Prakash. New York: Oxford UP, 1991, 62–108.

Ohdedar, A. K. *The Growth of the Library in Modern India, 1498–1836*. Calcutta: World Press, 1966.

Oldenburg, Veena Talwar. "Lifestyle as Resistance: The Case of the Courtesans of Lucknow." In *Contesting Power: Resistance and Everyday Social Relations in South Asia*, ed. Douglas Haynes and Gyan Prakash. New York: Oxford UP, 1991, 23–61.

——. *The Making of Colonial Lucknow, 1856–1877*. 1984. Reprint, New Delhi: Oxford UP, 1989.

Olney, James, ed. *Autobiography: Essays Theoretical and Critical*. Princeton: Princeton UP, 1980.

Olson, David R. et al., eds. *Literacy, Language, and Learning: The Nature and Consequence of Reading and Writing*. Cambridge: Cambrige UP, 1985.

Orwell, George. *Burmese Days*. 1934. Reprint, New York: Harcourt Brace Jovanovich, 1962.

Ouida (Marie-Louise de la Ramée). *Critical Studies*. London: T. Fisher Unwin, 1900.

Owen, Roger and Bob Sutcliffe, eds. *Studies in the Theory of Imperialism*. London: Longman, 1972.

Pal, R. B. *A Glimpse of Zenana Life in Bengal*. Calcutta: n.p., 1904.

Palgrave, F. T. "On Readers in 1760 and 1860." *Macmillan's Magazine* 1 (April 1860): 487–489.

Palmer, Jerry. *Potboilers: Methods, Concepts, and Case Studies in Popular Fiction*. London: Routledge, 1991.

Parameswaran, Uma. "Salman Rushdie in Indo-English Literature." *The Journal of Indian Writing in English* 12, no. 2 (1984): 15–25.

Parker, George L. "Another Look at Haliburton and His Publishers Joseph Howe and Richard Bentley: The Colonial Author and his Milieu." In *The Thomas Chandler Haliburton Symposium*, ed. Frank M. Tierney. Ottawa: U of Ottawa P, 1985, 83–92.

Parry, Benita. *Delusions and Discoveries: Studies on India in the British Imagination*. Los Angeles: U of California P, 1972.

Pattanayak, Chandrabhanu. "Interview with Salman Rushdie." *The Literary Criterion* 18, no. 3 (1983): 17–22.

Paul, Dhirendra Nath. *The Mysteries of Calcutta*. 3 vols. Calcutta: Datta, Bose, 1923.

Perera, Suvendrini. *Reaches of Empire: The English Novel from Edgeworth to Dickens*. New York: Columbia UP, 1991.

Peterson, Kirsten Holst and Anna Rutherford, eds. *A Double Colonization: Colonial and Post-colonial Women's Writing*. Mundelstrup: Dangaroo Press, 1986.

Petherick, Edward Augustus. *The Colonial Book Circular and Bibliographic Record*. Vol. 1. London: Colonial Bookseller's Agency, 1887.

——. *E. A. Petherick & Co.'s Monthly Catalogue: Literary, Artistic, Scientific*. Melbourne, Sydney, Adelaide, 1890–1894.

——. *Petherick's General Catalogue of Books*. London: Colonial Bookseller's Agency, 1890–1892.

Pilkington, Jr., John. "F. Marion Crawford." In *Dictionary of Literary Biography: American Literary Critics and Scholars, 1880–1900*, ed. John W. Rathbun and Monica M. Grecu. 71:58–65. Detroit: Gale, 1988.

——. *Francis Marion Crawford*. New York: Twayne Publishers, 1964.

——. "The Genesis of *Mr. Isaacs*." *The University of Missippi Studies in English* 2 (1961): 29–39.

Pinch, William R. *Peasants and Monks in British India*. Berkeley: U of California P, 1996.

Plomer, Henry Robert, et. al. *Dictionary of the Printers and Booksellers Who Were at Work in England, Scotland, and Ireland, 1557–1775*. London: The Bibliographic Society, 1977.

Pollock, Sheldon. "The Cosmopolitan Vernacular." *Journal of Asian Studies* 57, no. 1 (February 1998): 6–37.

——. "India in the Vernacular Millenium: Literary Culture and Polity, 1000–1500." *Dædalus* 127, no. 3 (summer 1998): 41–74.

Pool, John J. *Woman's Influence in the East: As Shown in the Noble Lives of Past Queens and Princesses of India*. London: E. F. Stock, 1892.

Poovey, Mary. *Making a Social Body: British Cultural Formation, 1830–1864*. Chicago: U of Chicago P, 1995.

——. *Uneven Developments: The Ideological Work of Gender in Mid-Victorian England*. Chicago: U of Chicago P, 1988.

Poster, Mark. "The Question of Agency: Michel de Certeau and the History of Consumerism." *diacritics* 22, no. 2 (1992): 94–107.

Pottinger, David T. *The French Book Trade in the Ancien Regime, 1500–1791*. Cambridge: Harvard UP, 1958.

Pradhan, N. S., ed. *Major Indian Novels: An Evaluation*. Atlantic Highlands, N.J.: Humanities Press, 1986.

Prakash, Gyan, ed. *After Colonialism*. Princeton: Princeton UP, 1995.

Premchand. *Deliverance and Other Stories*. Trans. David Rubin. New Delhi: Penguin, 1988.

Quayson, Ato. *Strategic Transformations in Nigerian Writing: Orality and History in the Work of Rev. Samuel Johnson, Amos Tutuola, Wole Soyinka, and Ben Okri*. Bloomington: Indiana UP, 1997.

Queiroz, Jean Manuel de. "The Sociology of Everyday Life as a Perspective." *Current Sociology* 37, no. 1 (1989): 31–40.

R. C. *Notices of Some Indian Women, to Accompany the Second Report of the Punjab Branch of the Indian Female Normal School and Instruction Society*. Lahore: Victoria Press, 1875.

Radway, Janice. *A Feeling for Books: The Book-of-the-Month Club, Literary Taste, and Middle-class Desire*. Chapel Hill: U of North Carolina P, 1997.

——. *Reading the Romance: Women, Patriarchy, and Popular Literature*. Chapel Hill: U of North Carolina P, 1984.

Raeside, Ian. "Early Prose Fiction in Marathi." In *The Novel in India: Its Birth and Development*, ed. T. W. Clark. Berkeley: U of California P, 1970, 75–101.

Rafael, Vicente. *Contracting Colonialism: Translation and Christian Conversion in Tagalog Society under Early Spanish Rule*. 1988. Reprint, Durham: Duke UP, 1993.

Rahill, Frank. *The World of Melodrama*. University Park: Pennsylvania State UP, 1967.

Rai, Amrit. *Premchand: His Life and Times*. Trans. Harish Trivedi. New Delhi: Oxford UP, 1991.

Rajan, Balachandra. "Identity and Nationality." In *Considerations*, ed. Meenakshi Mukherjee. New Delhi: Allied Publishers, 1977, 1–4.

Ramabai, Pandita. "Introduction." In *The Wrongs of Indian Womanhood*, ed. Mrs. Marcus B. Fuller. Edinburgh and London: Oliphant Anderson and Ferrier, 1900.

Ramamurti, K. S. *Rise of the Indian Novel in English*. Vol. 26. New Delhi: Sterling Publishers, 1987.

Ramanujan, A. K. "Three Hundred Ramayanas: Five Examples and Three Thoughts on Translation. In *Many Ramayanas: The Diversity of a Narrative Tradition in South Asia*, ed. Paula Richman. New Delhi: Oxford UP, 1992.

Ramusack, Barbara N. "Cultural Missionaries, Maternal Imperialists, Feminist Allies: British Women Activists in India, 1865–1945." In *Western Women and Imperialism: Complicity and Resistance*, ed. Nupur Chaudhuri and Margaret Strobel. Bloomington: Indiana UP, 1992, 119–136.

Ranade, Ramabai. *Himself: The Autobiography of a Hindu Lady*. Trans. and ed., Katherine van Akin Gates. New York: Longmans, Green, 1938.

Rangarajan, V. *Vande Mataram*. Madras: Sister Nivedita Academy, 1977.

Rao, Raja. "The Caste of English." In *Awakened Conscience. Studies in Commonwealth Literature*, ed. C. D. Narasimhaiah. New Delhi: Sterling Publishers, 1978.

——. *Kanthapura*. 1938. Reprint, New Delhi: Oxford UP, 1989.

——. "The Writer and the Word." In *Critical Essays on Indian Writing in English*, ed. M. K. Naik, S. K. Desai, and G. S. Amur. Rev. and enlarged ed. Madras: Macmillan, 1972.

Rao, Ranga. "From Chatterjee to Chatterjee." *Indian Literature* 144 (July/August 1991): 103–111.

Ray, Gordon N. "The Bentley Papers." *The Library* 7, no. 3 (1952): 178–200.

Raychaudhuri, Tapan. *Europe Reconsidered: Perceptions of the West in Nineteenth Century Bengal*. New Delhi: Oxford UP, 1988.

Rege, Josna. "Victim into Protagonist? *Midnight's Children* and the Post-Rushdie National Narrative of the Eighties." *Studies in the Novel* 29, no. 3 (1997): 342–375.

Renan, Ernest. "What is a Nation?" 1882. Reprinted in *Nation and Narration*, ed. Homi K. Bhabha, trans. Martin Thom. New York: Routledge, 1990.

Reynolds, George W. M. *Alfred; or, The Adventures of a French Gentleman*. London: Henry Lea, 1840.

——. *Caroline of Brunswick; or, The "Third Series" of the Mysteries of the Court of London*. Philadelphia: T. B. Peterson and Brothers, 1860.

——. *The Loves of the Harem*. London: John Dicks, 1855.

——. *Mary Price; or, The Memoirs of a Servant-Maid*. 2 vols. London: John Dicks, 1852.

——. *The Modern Literature of France*. 2 vols. London: George Henderson, 1839.

——. *The Mysteries of London, 1846–1855*. Ed. Trefor Thomas. Keele, U.K.: Keele UP, 1996.

——. *The Mysteries of London: Containing Stories of Life in the Modern Babylon*. Reprint, London: Milner, 1890.

——. *The Parricide; or, The Youth's Career in Crime*. London: John Dicks, 1847.

Reynolds, Quentin. *Fiction Factory; or, From Pulp Row to Quality Street*. New York: Random House, 1955.

Richetti, John J. *Popular Fiction Before Richardson: Narrative Patterns, 1700–1739*. Oxford: Clarendon Press, 1969.

Richman, Paula, ed. *Many Ramayanas: The Diversity of a Narrative Tradition in South Asia*. 1991. Reprint, New Delhi: Oxford UP, 1992.

Robert, Marthe. *Origins of the Novel*. Trans. Sacha Rabinovitch. Bloomington: Indiana UP, 1980.

Roberts, Emma. *The East India Voyager; or, Ten Minutes Advice to the Outward Bound*. London: J. Madden, 1839.

——. *Scenes and Characteristics of Hindostan with Sketches of Anglo-Indian Society*. 3 vols. London: W. H. Allen, 1835.

Robins, Elizabeth. *Ibsen and the Actress*. London: Hogarth Press, 1928.

Robinson, Andrew. *Satyajit Ray: The Inner Eye*. London: André Deutsch, 1989.

Robinson, F. J. G. and P. J. Wallis. *Book Subscription Lists: A Revised Guide*. Newcastle-upon-Tyne: Harold Hill and Son, 1975.

Rogers, Mary F. *Novels, Novelists, and Readers: Toward a Phenomenological Sociology of Literature*. Albany: State University of New York P, 1991.

Rose, Gillian. "The Dispute over Modernism." *The Sociology of Literature*. Vol. 1, *The Politics of Modernism*, ed. Francis Barker, et al. Essex: U of Essex P, 1979.

Routledge, James. *English Rule and Native Opinion in India from Notes Taken 1870–1874*. London: Trubner, 1878.

Roy, Modhumita. "'Englishing' India: Reconstituting Class and Social Privilege." *Social Text* 39 (summer 1994): 83–108.

Rudolph, Lloyd I. and Susanne Hoeber Rudolph. *The Modernity of Tradition: Political Development in India*. Chicago: U of Chicago P, 1967.

Rushdie, Salman. "The Empire Writes Back with a Vengeance." *Times* (London), July 3, 1982, p. 8.

——. *The Ground Beneath Her Feet: A Novel*. New York: Henry Holt, 1999.

——. *Imaginary Homelands: Essays and Criticism, 1981–1991*. New York: Granta/Viking, 1991.

——. "In Defense of the Novel, Yet Again." *The New Yorker*. June 24 and July 1, 1996, pp. 48–55.

——. "Introduction." In *The Vintage Book of Indian Writing, 1947–1997*, ed. Salman Rushdie and Elizabeth West. London: Vintage, 1997, ix–xxiii.

——. *Midnight's Children*. New York: Avon, 1980.

——. *The Satanic Verses*. London: Viking, 1988.

——. *Shame*. New Delhi: Picador/Rupa, 1983.

Russell, Ralph. "The Development of the Modern Novel in Urdu." In *The Novel in India. Its Birth and Development*, ed. T. W. Clark. Berkeley: U of California P, 1970.

——. *The Pursuit of Urdu Literature: A Select History*. New Delhi: Oxford UP, 1992.

Ruswa, Mirza Mohammad Hadi. *Umraon Jan Ada*. Trans. Khushwant Singh and M. A. Husaini. Delhi: Disha/Orient Longman, 1982.

S. D. R. "Joy Kissen Mokherjee: A Few Facts Connected with His Life." *National Magazine* New Series 6, June 1899.

Sadiq, Muhammad. *A History of Urdu Literature*. New Delhi: Oxford UP, 1984.

Sadleir, Michael. *Authors and Publishers: A Study in Mutual Esteem*. London: J. M. Dent, 1932.

Saenger, Paul. "Silent Reading: Its Impact on Late Medieval Script and Society." *Viator, Medieval, and Renaissance Studies* 13 (1982): 367–414.

Sahgal, Manmohini Zutshi. *An Indian Freedom Fighter Recalls her Life*. Foremother Legacies. Ed. Geraldine Forbes. Armonk, N.Y.: M. E. Sharpe, 1994.

Said, Edward W. *Beginnings: Intention and Method*. New York: Columbia UP, 1975.

——. *Culture and Imperialism*. New York: Alfred A. Knopf, 1993.

——. *Orientalism*. New York: Vintage, 1978.

Sangari, Kumkum. "The Politics of the Possible." *Cultural Critique* 7 (1987): 157–186.

Sangari, Kumkum and Sudesh Vaid, eds. *Recasting Women: Essays in Colonial History*. New Delhi: Kali for Women, 1989.

Sarasvati, Pandita Ramabai. *The High-Caste Hindu Woman*. Philadelphia: Privately printed by Jas. B. Rodgers Printing, 1887.

Sarkar, Sumit. *A Critique of Colonial India*. Calcutta: Papyrus, 1985.

——. *Modern India, 1885–1947*. Basingstoke: Macmillan, 1983.

Sarkar, Tanika. "Bankimchandra and the Impossibility of a Political Agenda." *Oxford Literary Review* 16, no. 1–2 (1994): 177–204.

——. "Imagining Hindurashtra: The Hindu and the Muslim in Bankim Chandra's Writings." In *Contesting the Nation: Religion, Community, and the Politics of Democracy in India*, ed. David Ludden. Philadelphia: U of Pennsylvania P, 1996, 162–184.

Satthianadhan, Anna. *A Brief Account of Zenana Work in Madras*. London: Seeley, 1878.

Satthianadhan, Krupa. *Kamala: A Story of Hindu Life*. Madras: Srinivas Varadachari and Co., 1894.

——. *Miscellaneous Writings*. Madras: Srinivasa, Varadachari, 1896.

——. *Saguna: A Story of Native Christian Life*. 1892. Reprint, Madras: Srinivas Varadachari and Co., 1895.

Satthianadhan, Samuel. *History of Education in the Madras Presidency*. Madras: Srinivasa, Varadachari, 1894.

——. *Missionary Work in India (From a Native Christian Point of View)*. Madras: Methodist Episcopal Mission Press, 1889.

Satthianadhan, Samuel and Kamala Satthianadhan. *Stories of Indian Christian Life*. Madras: Srinivasa, Varadachari, 1899.

Schama, Simon. "Perishable Commodities: Dutch Still-Life Painting and the 'Empire of Things.' " In *Consumption and the World of Goods*, ed. John Brewer and Roy Porter. New York: Routledge, 1993, 478–488.

Schick, Frank L. *The Paperbound Book in America*. New York: R. R. Bowker, 1958.

Schwarz, Roberto. *Misplaced Ideas: Essays on Brazilian Culture*. Ed. John Gledson. New York: Verso, 1992.

Scott, James C. *Weapons of the Weak: Everyday Forms of Peasant Resistance*. New Haven: Yale UP, 1985.

Scott, Joan Wallach. *Gender and the Politics of History*. New York: Columbia UP, 1988.

Scott, Sir Walter. *Waverley*. 1814. Ed. Andrew Hook. Reprint, Harmonsdsworth, U.K.: Penguin, 1985.

Scott, William Stuart. *Marie Corelli: The Story of a Friendship*. London: Hutchinson, 1955.

Seal, Anil. *The Emergence of Indian Nationalism: Competition and Collaboration in the Later Nineteenth Century*. Cambridge: Cambridge UP, 1971.

Sealy, I. Allan. *The Trotter-Nama: A Chronicle*. 1988. Reprint, New Delhi: Penguin, 1990.

Sen, Bireswar. *The Influence of English Education: Bengal and the N. W. Provinces*. Benares: New Medical Hall Press, 1876.

Sen, Nabaneta Dev. "Man, Woman, and Fiction." In *Women in Fiction, Fiction by Women*, ed. C. D. Narasimhaiah and C. N. Srinath. Mysore: Dhvanyaloka, 1987.

Sen, Sukumar. *History of Bengali Literature*. New Delhi: Sahitya Akademi, 1960.

Seth, Vikram. *A Suitable Boy*. New York: Knopf, 1993.

Shah, A. B., ed. *The Letters and Correspondence of Pandita Ramabai: Compiled by Sister Geraldine*. Bombay: Maharashtra State Board for Literature and Culture, 1977.

Shankar, D. A. "Ahmed Ali's *Twilight in Delhi*." *Literary Criterion* 15 (1980): 73–80.

Sharma, O. P. *Universal Literacy: A Distant Dream*. New Delhi: Kar Kripa, 1993.

Sharma, O. P. and Robert D. Retherford. *Literacy Trends of the 1980s in India: Occassional Paper No. 4*. New Delhi: Census Commissioner, 1993.

Sharma, Shobha. *Reading Habit and Reader's Interest*. New Delhi: Shree Publishing, 1989.

Sharpe, Jenny. *Allegories of Empire: The Figure of the Woman in the Colonial Text*. Minneapolis: U of Minnesota P, 1993.

Shaw, Graham. *South Asia and Burma Retrospective Bibliography: Stage I, 1556–1800*. London: The British Library, 1987.

Shaw, Graham and Mary Lloyd. *Publications Proscribed by the Government of India*. London: The British Library, 1985.

Shome, Mohendronath. *The Spirit of the Anglo-Bengali Magazines in a Series of Reviews*. Calcutta: Thacker, Spink, 1873.

Simmel, Georg. *The Conflict in Modern Culture and Other Essays*. Trans. K. Peter Etzkorn. New York: Teachers College Press, 1968.

——. "The Metropolis and Mental Life." Trans. H. H. Gerth and C. Wright Mills. In *Classic Essays on the Culture of Cities*, ed. Richard Sennett. New York: Appleton-Century-Crofts, 1969, 47–60.

Singh, Namwar. "Decolonising the Indian Mind." *Indian Literature* 35, no. 5 (1992): 145–156.

Singh, Ram Dular. *National Union Catalogue of Incunabula and Early Printed Books in India*. Vol. 1: 1481–1600. Calcutta: Bibliograhical Society of India, 1981.

Sinha, Mrinalini. *Colonial Masculinity: The "Manly Englishman" and the "Effeminate Bengali" in the Late Nineteenth Century*. Manchester: Manchester UP, 1995.

——. "Reading Mother India: Empire, Nation, and the Female Voice." *Journal of Women's History* 6, no. 2 (1994): 6–44.

Skrine, F. H. *An Indian Journalist: Being the Life and Letters of Dr. S. C. Mookerjea*. Calcutta: Thacker, Spink, n.d.

Small, Annie H. *Light and Shade in Zenana Missionary Life*. Paisley, Scotland: J. and R. Parlane, 1890.

Smiles, Samuel. *A Publisher & His Friends. Memoir & Correspondence of the Late John Murray, with an Account of the Origin and Progress of the House, 1768–1843*. 2 vols. London: John Murray, 1891.

Smith, George. "First Twenty Years of *The Calcutta Review*." *Calcutta Review* 19, no. 117 (1874): 215–233.

Smith, James L. *Melodrama*. London: Methuen, 1973.

Sommer, Doris. *Foundational Fictions: The National Romances of Latin America*. Berkeley: U. of California P, 1991.

Sorabji, Cornelia. *Love and Life Behind the Purdah*. London: Freemantle, 1901.

Spear, Percival. *A History of India*. Vol. 2. Harmondsworth: Penguin, 1970.

Spencer, Dorothy M. *Indian Fiction in English: An Annotated Bibliography*. Philadelphia: U of Pennsylvania P, 1960.

Spencer, Jane. *The Rise of the Woman Novelist: From Aphra Behn to Jane Austen*. Oxford: Oxford UP, 1986.

Spivak, Gayatri. "The Burden of English." In *Orientalism and the Postcolonial Predicament: Perspectives on South Asia*, ed. Carol A. Breckenridge and Peter van der Veer. Philadelphia: U of Pennsylvania P, 1993, 134–157.

Sprinker, Michael. "Fictions of the Self: The End of Autobiography." In *Autobiography: Essays Theoretical and Critical*, ed. James Olney. Princeton: Princeton UP, 1980.

St John, John. *William Heinemann: A Century of Publishing, 1890–1990*. London: Heinemann, 1990.

Stam, Robert and Louise Spence. "Colonialism, Racism, and Representation." *Screen* 24, no. 1983 (1983): 2–20.

Stetz, Margaret Diane. "*New Grub Street* and the Woman Writer of the 1890s." In *Transforming Genres: New Approaches to British Fiction of the 1890s*, ed. Nikki Lee Manos and Meri-Jane Rochelson. New York: St. Martin's Press, 1994, 21–45.

Stokes, Eric. *English Utilitarians and India*. London: Oxford UP, 1959.

Storrow, Edward. *Our Indian Sisters*. London: Religious Tract Society, 1898.

Story of the House of Cassell. London: Cassell, 1922.

Suleiman, Susan R. and Inge Crossman, eds. *The Reader in the Text: Essays on Audience and Interpretation*. Princeton: Princeton UP, 1980.

Suleri, Sara. *The Rhetoric of English India*. Chicago: U of Chicago P, 1992.

——. "Woman Skin Deep: Feminism and the Postcolonial Condition." *Critical Inquiry* 18 (1992): 756–769.

Summers, Montague. *A Gothic Bibliography*. New York: Russell and Russell, 1964.

Sunder Rajan, Rajeswari. "The Feminist Plot and the Nationalist Allegory: Home and World in Two Indian Women's Novels in English." *Modern Fiction Studies* 39, no. 1 (1993): 71–92.

——, ed. *The Lie of the Land: English Literary Studies in India*. New Delhi: Oxford UP, 1992.

——. *Real and Imagined Women: Gender, Culture, and Post-colonialism*. London: Routledge, 1993.

Sutherland, John. "Publishing History: A Hole at the Center of Literary Sociology." *Critical Inquiry* 14, no. 3, Special Issue on the Sociology of Literature (1988): 574–589.

——. *The Stanford Companion to Victorian Fiction*. Stanford: Stanford UP, 1989.

——. *Victorian Fiction: Writers, Publishers, Readers*. Basingstoke: Macmillan, 1995.

Tagore, Rabindranath. *The Broken Nest [Nashtanir]*. Trans. Mary M. Lago and Supriya Sen. 1901. Reprint, Columbia: U of Missouri P, 1971.

——. *Home and the World*. 1916. Trans. Surendranath Tagore. Reprint, London: Penguin, 1985.

——. *My Reminiscences*. Trans. Surendranath Tagore. 1917. Reprint, London: Macmillan, 1991.

Talwar, Vir Bharat. "Feminist Consciousness in Women's Journals in Hindi, 1910–1920." In *Recasting Women: Essays in Colonial History*, ed. Kumkum Sangari and Sudesh Vaid. New Delhi: Kali for Women, 1989, 201–232.

Thackeray, W. M. *Vanity Fair: A Novel Without a Hero*. 1848. Reprint, New York: Norton, 1994.

Tharoor, Shashi. *The Great Indian Novel*. New Delhi: Penguin, 1989.

——. "Worlds of Magic and Yearning. Review of *East, West* by Salman Rushdie." *Washington Post Book World*, January 8, 1995, pp. 1, 11.

Tharu, Susie. "The Arrangement of an Alliance: English and the Making of Indian Literatures." In *Rethinking English: Essays in Literature, Language, History*, ed. Svati Joshi. New Delhi: Trianka, 1991, 160–180.

——. "Is There a Tradition of Women's Literature?" In *The Rise of the Indian Novel*, ed. C. D. Narasimhaiah and C. N. Srinath. Mysore: Dhvanyaloka, 1986.

——. "Oral History, Narrative Strategy, and the Figure of Autobiography." In *Narrative: Forms and Transformations*, ed. Sudhakar Marathe and Meenakshi Mukherjee. New Delhi: Chanakya Publications, 1986, 181–200.

——. "Rendering Account of the Nation: Partition Narratives and Other Genres of the Passive Revolution." *Oxford Literary Review* 16, no. 1/2 (1994): 69–91.

——. "Tracing Savitri's Pedigree: Victorian Racism and the Image of Women in Indo-Anglian Literature." In *Recasting Women: Essays in Colonial History*, ed. Kumkum Sangari and Sudesh Vaid. New Delhi: Kali for Women, 1989, 254–268.

Tharu, Susie and K. Lalita, eds. *Women's Writing in India, 600 BC to the Present*. 2 vols. New York: Feminist Press, 1992.

Thomas, Nicholas J. *Colonialism's Culture: Anthropology, Travel, and Government*. Cambridge: Polity Press, 1994.

Thurston, Carol. *The Romance Revolution: Erotic Novels for Women and the Quest for a New Sexual Identity*. Urbana and Chicago: U of Illinois P, 1987.

Todd, Richard. *Consuming Fictions: The Booker Prize and Fiction in Britain Today*. London: Bloomsbury, 1996.

Todd, William B. and Ann Bowden. *Tauchnitz International Editions in English, 1841–1955: A Bibliographical History*. New York: Bibliographical Society of America, 1988.

Todorov, Tzvetan. "Reading as Construction." In *The Reader in the Text. Essays on Audience and Interpretation*, ed. Susan Suleiman and Inge Crosman. Princeton: Princeton UP, 1980, 67–82.

Tompkins, Jane P. "Sentimental Power: *Uncle Tom's Cabin* and the Politics of Literary History." In *Feminisms: An Anthology of Literary Theory and Criticism*, ed. Robyn R. Warhol and Diane Price Herndl. New Brunswick: Rutgers UP, 1991, 20–39.

——. ed. *Reader-Response Criticism: From Formalism to Post-Structuralism*. Baltimore: Johns Hopkins UP, 1990.

Trevelyan, Charles E. *On the Education of the People of India*. London: Longman, 1838.

Trevelyan, George Otto. *The Competition-Wallah*. 1864. Reprint, New Delhi: Indus/HarperCollins, 1992.

Trevor-Roper, Hugh. "Introduction." In *Critical and Historical Essays, Thomas Babington, Lord Macaulay*, ed. Hugh Trevor-Roper. New York: McGraw-Hill, 1965.

Trivedi, Harish. "Ahmed Ali: *Twilight in Delhi*." In *Major Indian Novels: An Evaluation*, ed. N. S. Pradhan. Atlantic Highlands: Humanities Press, 1986, 41–73.

——. *Colonial Transactions: English Literature and India*. Calcutta: Papyrus, 1993.

——. "India and Post-colonial Discourse." *Interrogating Post-colonialism: Theory, Text, and Context*, ed. Harish Trivedi and Meenakshi Mukherjee. Shimla: Indian Institute of Advanced Study, 1996, 231–247.

——. "Reading English, Writing Hindi: English Literature and Indian Creative Writing." In *Rethinking English. Essays in Literature, Language, History*, ed. Svati Joshi. New Delhi: Trianka, 1991, 181–205.

——. "The St. Stephen's Factor." *Indian Literature* 145 (September/October 1991): 183–187.

Trumpener, Katie. *Bardic Nationalism: The Romantic Novel and the British Empire*. Princeton: Princeton UP, 1997.

Tuchman, Gaye with Nina E. Fortin. *Edging Women Out: Victorian Novelists, Publishers, and Social Change*. London: Routledge, 1989.

Turner, Michael L. *Index and Guide to the Lists of the Publications of Richard Bentley & Son, 1829–1898*. Teaneck: Chadwyck-Healey, 1975.

Twain, Mark. "Following the Equator: A Journey Around the World." In *The Complete Travel Books of Mark Twain*, ed. Charles Neider. 1897. Vol. 2. Reprint, Garden City: Doubleday, 1967.

van Buitenen, J. A. B., ed. *The Mahabharata: The Book of the Beginning*. Vol. 1. Chicago: U of Chicago P, 1973.

Varma, Balgopal. "Some Thoughts on English Fiction and the Reading Public." *Fiction and the Reading Public in India*, ed. C. D. Narsimhaiah. Mysore: Wesley Press, 1967, 1–7.

Veblen, Thorstein. *The Theory of the Leisure Class*. 1899. Reprint, London: Penguin, 1994.

Vedalankar, Shardadevi. *The Development of Hindi Prose Literature in the Early Nineteenth Century, 1800–1856*. Allahabad: Lokbharti Publications, 1977.

Venkatesaiya Naidu, M. *The Princess Kamala; or, The Model Wife*. Madras: A. L. V. P, 1904.

Vergès, Françoise. *Monsters and Revolutionaries: Colonial Family Romance and Métissage*. Durham and London: Duke UP, 1999.

Verma, H. N. *Eminent Indian Women*. New Delhi: Great Indian Publishers, 1978.

Vicinus, Martha. *The Industrial Muse: A Study of Nineteenth-Century British Working-Class Literature*. London: Croom Helm, 1974.

Viswanathan, Gauri. "Beyond Orientalism: Syncretism and the Politics of Knowledge." *Stanford Humanities Review* 5, no. 1 (1995): 19–34.

——. *Masks of Conquest: Literary Study and British Rule in India*. New York: Columbia UP, 1989.

——. *Outside the Fold: Conversion, Modernity, and Belief*. Princeton: Princeton UP, 1998.

Wagenknecht, Edward. *Cavalcade of the American Novel from the Birth of the Nation to the Middle of the Twentieth Century*. New York: Henry Holt, 1952.

Wallerstein, Immanuel. *The Modern World System*. 3 vols. New York: Academic Press, 1974.

Wallis, Philip. *At the Sign of the Ship: Notes on the House of Longman, 1724–1974*. London: Longman, 1974.

Wallis, P. J. *An Eighteenth-Century Book Trade Index Based on "Newtoniana" and Book Subscription Lists*. Newcastle-upon-Tyne: U of Newcastle-upon-Tyne, 1977.

Walsh, Judith E. *Growing Up in British India: Indian Autobiographers on Childhood and Education under the Raj*. New York: Holmes and Meier, 1983.

Wang, David Derwei. *Fin-de-Siècle Splendor: Repressed Modernities of Late Qing Fiction, 1849–1911*. Stanford: Stanford UP, 1997.

Waples, Douglas, Bernard Berelson, and Franklyn R. Bradshaw. *What Reading does to People: A Summary of Evidence on the Social Effects of Reading and a Statement of Problems for Research*. Chicago: U of Chicago P, 1940.

Watt, Ian. *The Rise of the Novel: Studies in Defoe, Richardson, and Fielding*. Berkeley: U of California P, 1957.

Waugh, Arthur. *A Hundred Years of Publishing: Being the Story of Chapman & Hall, Ltd.* London: Chapman and Hall, 1930.

Webb, R. K. *The British Working-Class Reader, 1790–1848: Literacy and Social Tension*. London: George Allen and Unwin, 1955.

Weber, Max. *The City*. Trans. Don Martindale and Gertrud Neuwirth. New York: The Free Press, 1958.

White, Hayden. *The Content of the Form: Narrative Discourse and Historical Representation*. Baltimore: Johns Hopkins UP, 1987.

——. *Metahistory: The Historical Imagination in Nineteenth-Century Europe*. Baltimore: Johns Hopkins UP, 1975.

Whyte, Frederic. *William Heinemann: A Memoir*. London: Jonathan Cape, 1928.

Williams, Raymond. *The English Novel from Dickens to Lawrence*. 1970. London: Reprint, Hogarth Press, 1984.

——. *The Long Revolution*. New York: Columbia UP, 1961.

——. *Problems in Materialism and Culture: Selected Essays*. London: Verso, 1980.

Wilson, Chris. "The Rhetoric of Consumption: Mass Market Magazines and the Demise of the Gentle Reader, 1880–1920." In *The Culture of Consumption*, ed. Richard Wightman Fox and T. J. Jackson Lears. New York: Pantheon Books, 1983.

Yule, Colonel Henry, and A. C. Burnell. *Hobson-Jobson: A Glossary of Colloquial Anglo-Indian Words and Phrases, and of Kindred Terms, Etymological, Historical, Geographic and Discursive*. 1886. Reprint, New Delhi: Rupa, 1986.

Zbavitel, Dusan. *Bengali Literature: A History of Indian Literature*. A History of
 Indian Literature, ed. Jan Gonda. Wiesbaden: Otto Harrassowitz, 1976.
Zeno. "A Writer Committed to Progressivism." *Dawn* June 13, 1986: IV.
Zhao, Henry Y. H. *The Uneasy Narrator: Chinese Fiction from the Traditional to
 the Modern*. Oxford: Oxford UP, 1995.
Ziff, Larzer. *The American 1890s: Life and Times of a Lost Generation*. New York:
 Viking, 1966.

INDEX